Agile Development with ICONIX Process

People, Process, and Pragmatism

DOUG ROSENBERG, MATT STEPHENS, AND MARK COLLINS-COPE

Apress®

Agile Development with ICONIX Process: People, Process, and Pragmatism

Lead Editor: Jim Sumser
Technical Reviewer: Dr. Charles Suscheck

Assistant Publisher: Grace Wong
Project Manager: Tracy Brown Collins
Copy Manager: Nicole LeClerc
Production Manager: Kari Brooks-Copony
Production Editor: Beth Christmas
Compositor: Diana Van Winkle, Van Winkle Design Group
Proofreader: Elizabeth Berry
Indexer: Michael Brinkman
Artist: Kinetic Publishing Services, LLC
Interior Designer: Diana Van Winkle, Van Winkle Design Group
Cover Designer: Kurt Krames
Manufacturing Manager: Tom Debolski

Library of Congress Cataloging-in-Publication Data

Rosenberg, Doug.
Agile development with ICONIX process : people, process, and pragmatism / Doug Rosenberg, Matt Stephens, Mark Collins-Cope.
p. cm.
Includes index.
ISBN 1-59059-464-9
1. Computer software--Development. I. Stephens, Matt. II. Collins-Cope, Mark. III. Title.

QA76.76.D47R666 2005
005.1--dc22
2005000163

Printed and bound in the United States of America 9 8 7 6 5 4 3 2 1

Distributed to the book trade in the United States by Springer-Verlag New York, Inc., 233 Spring Street, 6th Floor, New York, NY 10013, and outside the United States by Springer-Verlag GmbH & Co. KG, Tiergartenstr. 17, 69112 Heidelberg, Germany.

In the United States: phone 1-800-SPRINGER, fax 201-348-4505, e-mail orders@springer-ny.com, or visit http://www.springer-ny.com. Outside the United States: fax +49 6221 345229, e-mail orders@springer.de, or visit http://www.springer.de.

For information on translations, please contact Apress directly at 2560 Ninth Street, Suite 219, Berkeley, CA 94710. Phone 510-549-5930, fax 510-549-5939, e-mail info@apress.com, or visit http://www.apress.com.

The latest information on this book can be found at www.softwarereality.com/design/agileiconix.jsp.

To Irv, and in loving memory of Vivian
—Doug Rosenberg

For Michelle and Alanah
—Matt Stephens

To Oliver, Nathan, and Lewis
—Mark Collins-Cope

Contents at a Glance

Contents

About the Authors

DOUG ROSENBERG is the founder and president of ICONIX Software Engineering, Inc. (`www.iconixsw.com`). Doug spent the first 15 years of his career writing code for a living before moving on to managing programmers, developing software design tools, and teaching object-oriented analysis and design.

Doug has been providing system development tools and training for nearly two decades, with particular emphasis on object-oriented methods. He developed a unified Booch/Rumbaugh/Jacobson design method in 1993 that preceded Rational's UML by several years. He has produced more than a dozen multimedia tutorials on object technology, including "COMPREHENSIVE COM" and "Enterprise Architect for Power Users," and is the co-author of *Use Case Driven Object Modeling with UML* (Addison-Wesley, 1999) and *Applying Use Case Driven Object Modeling with UML* (Addison-Wesley, 2001), both with Kendall Scott, and *Extreme Programming Refactored: The Case Against XP* (Apress, 2003), with Matt Stephens.

A few years ago, Doug started a second business, an online travel website (`www.VResorts.com`) that features his virtual reality photography and some innovative mapping software, which you can read about in this book.

MATT STEPHENS is a senior architect, programmer, and project leader based in Central London. He has led a number of agile projects through successive customer releases. He's also spoken at several software conferences, and he regularly writes on software development, having written for magazines including *Dr. Dobb's Journal*, *Software Development* magazine, *Application Development Advisor*, and *Application Development Trends*. His key interests include software agility, architecture, and interaction design. Check out his latest thoughts at `www.softwarereality.com`.

Matt co-authored *Extreme Programming Refactored: The Case Against XP* (Apress, 2003) with Doug Rosenberg. In fact, Matt and Doug are collaborating on yet another book, *Use Case Driven Object Modeling: Theory and Practice* (Addison-Wesley, 2005).

MARK COLLINS-COPE is technical director of Ratio Group Ltd., a UK-based company undertaking development, training, consultancy, and recruitment in the object and component technology arena (see `www.ratio.co.uk`). Collins-Cope has undertaken many roles in his 20 years in the software development industry, including analysis, design, architecture definition/technical lead; project manager; lecturer; and writer. His key interests include use-case analysis, software architecture, and component-based development and software process.

About the Technical Reviewer

DR. CHARLES SUSCHECK is an assistant professor of computer information systems at Colorado State University, Pueblo campus. He specializes in software development methodologies and project management, and has over 20 years of professional experience in information technology. Dr. Suscheck has held positions of process architect, director of research, principal consultant, and professional trainer at some of the most recognized companies in America. He has spoken at national and international conferences on topics related to project management.

Acknowledgments

Our thanks go to:

All the folks from ESRI, including Dave Lewis, Amir Soheili, and Jim McKinney for getting the mapplet built; Jack Dangermond for approving the project; and the ESRI marketing team (Debra Van Gorden, Paige Spee, and friends) for providing us with technical information on ArcGIS Server.

The fabulous Apress production team, including the "PM," Tracy Brown Collins; "the world's greatest copy editor," Nicole LeClerc; our production editor, Beth Christmas; our editor, Jim Sumser; and, of course, "Mr. Apress," Gary Cornell.

Our technical reviewer, Chuck Suscheck.

Our "unofficial" reviewer, David Putman of `www.exoftware.com`, for his extensive feedback on all the chapters (in particular the "agile core subset" and TDD chapters).

Geoff Sparks and Dermot O'Bryan from Sparx Systems.

Andy Carmichael for the material on three-point estimation.

Dino Fancellu and Robin Sharp from `www.javelinsoft.com`.

Introduction

Rigor Without the Mortis

Many people (especially agilists) associate a high-ceremony software development process with a dead project (i.e., rigor mortis), and this association is not entirely incorrect. Our approach aims to put back the rigor while leaving out the mortis—that is, we can do rigorous analysis and design without killing the project with an excessively high-ceremony approach. The goal of this book is to describe that process in full detail.

Agility *in theory* is about moving ahead at speed, making lots of tiny course corrections as you go. The theory (and it's a good one) is that if you spend months or years producing dry specifications at the start of the project and then "set them in concrete," this doesn't necessarily (and in practice, doesn't) lead to a product that meets the customer's requirements, delivered on time and with an acceptably low defect count.

It's likely that the requirements will change over time, so we need to be prepared for that, and it's likely that a lot of the original requirements will turn out to be wrong or new requirements will be discovered after the requirements "concrete" has set. Agile methods answer this problem in a number of different ways, but the overriding principle is to break things down into smaller chunks and not to go setting anything in concrete (least of all your requirements specs).

That's great in theory, but it might leave you wondering how to go about doing it in practice. There are plenty of agile books out there that set out to tell you how to "be agile" at a management or process level, but this book is different for a number of reasons. First, we look at each level of agility and show how it can be applied to a real-life project, from issues with team adoption of agile practices down to a specific logical design process.

We also believe that *being agile doesn't mean you should have to abandon up-front analysis and design* (although we do agree with agilists that *too much* up-front analysis and design can be a bad thing). So, in this book we define a core subset of UML diagrams and techniques, and show how to apply them to your own project using a core subset of established agile practices. Our goal is to show how to make your own process *minimal yet sufficient.*[1]

Another reason this book is different is because we're essentially "outsiders" in the agile world. We've been in the industry for a long time and have taken part in a number of agile projects, but we're approaching agility from the standpoint of more traditional software engineering. We examine how agility can be applied in organizations that may approach "all-out, party-on extreme agility" with a heavy dose of caution and distrust. As a result, the process we describe in this book could well be more applicable to traditional or more disciplined organizations than other agile processes.

In our attempt to find the "sweet spot" between agility and discipline, the spot we've landed on is probably far removed from where some agilists (most notably the creators of Extreme Programming [XP]) would expect it to be. For example, we place a higher emphasis on UML modeling than XP does. However, if you're an XP practitioner, you may well find that the object modeling process this book demonstrates works very well in collaborative modeling workshops (in fact, we place a high emphasis on the value of collaborative modeling).

1. This isn't dissimilar to Agile Modeling's principle of making documentation "just barely good enough," though we distinguish it because there are some important differences in our guidance, as we describe in this book.

Plan Driven and Feedback Driven

Agile ICONIX Process is plan-driven and feedback-driven, small-increment, short-iteration development, using the following artifacts:

- Use case model (including personas)
- Domain model
- Release plan

Then for each release, we aim to produce the following:

- Robustness and sequence diagrams for each use case
- An updated class diagram
- Source code
- Unit and acceptance tests as appropriate

Using this process, we tie the persona modeling[2] into the iteration plan and drive the feature set, via the iteration plan, from the usage requirements. (This is similar in some ways to Feature-Driven Development [FDD], which we discuss in Chapter 4.)

Recurring Themes

Throughout this book, you'll encounter the themes described in the sections that follow.

People, Process, and Pragmatism

The ICONIX approach to software agility starts with a subtle but significant refactoring of the Agile Manifesto's value of "individuals and interactions over processes and tools."

We have redefined this as "people *and* processes *and* pragmatism." We believe that neither people nor processes are second-class citizens, and that both (in conjunction with a pragmatic approach) are equally important factors in a project's eventual success.

Real Agility vs. Illusory Agility

A software-engineering maxim that has fallen out of fashion lately is "There is no such thing as a shortcut." (Another one that seems to have been abandoned recently is "Get it right the first time.") In high-velocity projects that must be produced in "Internet time," there is always pressure to cut corners, by skimping on testing, designing, reviews, and so on. This is not the same as agility (at least not in theory, although in practice it often gets justified in the name of agility).

In fact, this approach almost invariably delays the project. We will explain how to distinguish between the elimination of practices that are weighing down the project ("excess fat") and practices that are actually there to save time. Cutting out these latter practices might appear to save some time early on, but in reality doing so stores up trouble for later.

2. See Chapter 10.

Cookbook Development

A common view held in the agile world is that cookbook approaches to software development don't work. We agree with this to an extent, because analysis and programming are massive, highly complex fields, and the number of different types of software project is roughly equal to the number of software projects. However, we firmly believe that the core "logical" analysis and design process can (and in fact should) be a specific sequence of repeatable steps. These steps aren't set in stone (i.e., they can be tailored), but it helps to have them there. In a world of doubt and uncertainty, it's nice to have a clearly defined, definitive sequence of "how-to" steps to refer back to.

Way back in the pre-UML days when Doug first started teaching a unified Booch/Rumbaugh/Jacobson modeling approach (around 1992/93), one of his early training clients encouraged him to "write a cookbook, because my people like following cookbook approaches." While many have claimed that it's impossible to codify object-oriented analysis and design (OOAD) practices into a simple, repeatable set of steps (and it probably isn't possible in its entirety), ICONIX Process probably comes as close as anything out there to a cookbook approach to OOAD.

While there's still room for significant flexibility within the approach (e.g., adding in more state or activity diagrams), ICONIX Process lays down a simple, minimal set of steps that generally lead to pretty good results that have proven to be consistent and repeatable over the last 12 years.

So, Let's Get Started

There are three major parts in this book. In Part 1, we examine what agility is and isn't, explore the characteristics of a good software process, introduce ICONIX Process and its core UML subset and, in Chapter 4, introduce a core subset of agile practices.

In Part 2, we illustrate our core subset in action by exploring the design and code of an example project, a C#/.NET mapping application for the travel industry, which we call "the mapplet." The mapplet example represents "the authors practicing what they preach," as this is the real-life story of a commercial application for a website that's owned by one of them. So, if you've ever wondered what one of those #%$%& methodologists would really do if they needed to get something built, and if they'd follow the methodology they preach, you'll find this example interesting.

Part 3 presents some extensions to ICONIX Process related to persona-driven analysis and test-driven development. This part complements the material presented in the first two parts, and it also contains some last-minute innovations in the area of use case–driven testing that we hope you find as interesting as we do.

PART 1

ICONIX and Agility

The first part of this book lays the groundwork for the discussions and examples that follow. We begin in Chapter 1 by trying to define what *agility* is and what it isn't. In Chapter 2 we take a generic look at software processes in general, with some specific focus on finding the "sweet spot" between agility and discipline, and on the human-centric and communication issues that are strongly stressed in agile processes. In Chapter 3 we summarize ICONIX Process (as defined in Doug's first two books), and in Chapter 4 we attempt to define a minimalist core-subset of agile practices, which we illustrate by example in Part 2.

CHAPTER 1

What Is Agility? (And Why Does It Matter?)

"What is agility?" is a simple question with a complex answer. The answer is complex because there is no central authority to dictate the "agile standard" and define in legally binding terms what agility is or isn't.[1] While many (including us) would argue that this is a good thing, the result is that not everyone will ever agree on a single definition. To some, agility is all about the people: emphasizing people over tools. To others, agility is all about the ability to change requirements late in a project (in fact, this is what most people mean when they talk about "being agile"). To the industry thought-leaders, agility is a combination of these things. But in true agile spirit, the very definition of agility evolves and warps over time.

To be honest, we're glad that there isn't a central standards authority for software agility, handing down the "agile spec" from on high and stipulating that all agile processes must conform to its ideals to be allowed to call themselves AGILE™, because that would stifle the exciting air of innovation and exploration of new development techniques that have ignited the industry over the past few years.

Of course, with the excitement of new ideas and new frontiers, there's always the danger that we will disappear down a blind alley or two in our search for better ways of doing things. There's also a danger that previously learned lessons will be forgotten in the rush to discover new improvements. These lessons include the benefits of doing an up-front design and exploring requirements in sufficient detail before coding. We discussed the dangers of forgetting these important lessons in our previous book, *Extreme Programming Refactored: The Case Against XP* (Apress, 2003).

The pendulum has swung from one extreme to the other. It's gone from the inflexible, inefficient, old-guard, waterfall, high-ceremony methodologies to the highly fluid, trendy agile processes that we're seeing today.[2] As you might expect, the pendulum has already begun to swing back the other way, and it will hopefully come to rest somewhere between the two extremes.

We're hoping that this book will contribute toward finding the ideal middle ground. This book tells you how to create software using a small increment, short iteration, feedback-driven strategy while still modeling up-front and using that up-front thinking to avoid lots of rework (i.e., it has the benefits of agility but not the penalties of skipping up-front design).

ICONIX Process is a use case–driven analysis and design methodology. Its main focus is on how to get reliably from use cases to code in as few steps as possible. In this book, we describe ICONIX Process and show how it was applied to a real-life project. We also describe in detail how to apply ICONIX Process to a broader agile project environment. This combination of process and practices is shown in Figure 1-1. Informally, we refer to this combined process as *Agile ICONIX*.

---

1. Of course, there is the Agile Alliance (see `www.agilealliance.org`), although this isn't quite the same sort of thing. We discuss the Agile Alliance later in this chapter and in Chapter 4.

2. If we think of a big, high-ceremony process as elephantine, and an extremely minimal/agile one as mouselike, it's amusing to note that some folks try to equate the mouse to the elephant because both are gray mammals with tails. In reality, however, there are significant differences between a mouse and an elephant, and neither of those animals does the work of a horse very well.

Figure 1-1. *Agile ICONIX in a nutshell*

This book is all about how to be agile and accommodate the real-world situations of changing requirements, new technology baselines, and so on, without skipping analysis and design, using a small increment, short iteration, model-driven *and feedback-driven* approach. This book also teaches how to drive the development from UML models, and then shows how to adjust both the models and the code using an interleaved approach in a way that the model and code become more tightly linked over time.

Although much of ICONIX Process can be considered agile, some parts of it stand in stark contrast to recent agile thinking. In particular, agile methods often tell us not to bother keeping design documentation and source code synchronized. The theory is that once code has been written, we don't need the diagrams anymore.[3] ICONIX Process, on the other hand, suggests exactly the opposite: the more tightly synchronized the design documentation is with the code, the faster, more maintainable, and more accurate (i.e., closer to the customer's requirements) your project will be over successive releases.

Luckily, ICONIX Process also aims to make this process easier (again in contrast to other agile processes). To achieve this tight synchronization between diagrams and code, we need to cut down on the number of diagrams that we have to draw (and therefore maintain). It's also important to know which diagrams are going to be important to ongoing iterations and which can safely be discarded. "Minimal but sufficient" analysis and design is right at the core of ICONIX Process.

Of course, there's an ever-increasing number of development processes claiming to be agile. Project leaders may decide that the project they're embarking on will be agile, or their existing project may not be working out too well, so they decide to introduce some agile practices. But what exactly does "agile" mean? What's the yardstick by which agility is measured? Where's the magic point of latitude when a project flips from being nonagile to being agile?

In this chapter, we examine the somewhat nebulous term "agility" and attempt to disambiguate it. In doing so, we aim to answer the questions in the previous paragraph.

3. This mind-set comes from thinking of diagrams as documentation rather than as tools that enable the design process and efficient communication about the design across the team. In our estimation, this is 100% backward. Modeling should be about doing design and communicating the design to the rest of the team, *not* about documentation.

What Software Agility Isn't

To better explain what software agility is, it's worth beginning with a description of what it isn't. Software agility isn't about

- Big up-front requirements gathering and design
- Hacking
- High ceremony (i.e., lots of paperwork and bureaucratic hoops to jump through)
- Low levels of communication
- "Carrying" mediocre developers
- Politics and secrets

Let's take a quick look at each of these topics in turn.

Big Up-front Requirements Gathering and Design

Up-front requirements gathering and design are, of course, vital parts of any software process, and they have their place in an agile project. What agile practitioners are generally opposed to is the "pure waterfall" concept of eliciting all requirements and modeling the architecture in detail for the entire project before starting on individual sections. Instead, you gather together everything you think you'll need just for the next iteration, and proceed with that. This approach is similar to the iterative and incremental process that has been developed in the Rational Unified Process (RUP).

Hacking

Adopting an agile process isn't (or shouldn't be) a license to hack. Agile processes are typically high-discipline, and it often takes hard work and patience for developers to get the full benefit.

High Ceremony

Sometimes the organization requires a high level of paperwork (e.g., change requests to be signed off on by three levels of management). If your organization doesn't, then why bury yourself out of choice?

Low Levels of Communication

As with any process, agile processes benefit from teams that tell each other what's going on, and that both talk and listen to the customer. Agile processes are very much opposed to "low-communication" environments—for example, environments that separate programmers into isolated cubicles.

"Carrying" Mediocre Developers

Agile processes typically require high-caliber staff if they are to work at all. There is no place for slouchers and "bug jockeys" on such projects!

Politics and Secrets

Agility places a big emphasis on increased transparency—that is, allowing the customer to see exactly what's going on in the project at any time. If a project is behind schedule, the agile planning methods generally make it difficult to hide this from the customer. Although this might seem alarming at first, it has the very important benefit that you don't find yourself storing up nasty surprises for later—in particular, on the day before the delivery deadline, having to tell the customer that it's going to be at least another 6 months before any working software can be delivered.

Increased transparency also extends to individuals and teamwork. Because agile teams tend to work more closely together, it's difficult for one team member to operate deviously (e.g., hanging on the coattails of more talented programmers and taking the credit for their work).

The Goals of Agility

When deciding whether to adopt agile practices for your project, it's important to take a step back from the hype and ask what's in it for you (or, more accurately, for your project). So, what does your project stand to gain from adopting agile practices? What are the benefits, the goals, the problems that agility sets out to solve? And do these problems exist on your project?

The Agile Manifesto website (see `www.agilemanifesto.org`) describes the principles and values that agile teams need to follow to describe themselves as "agile." But oddly, it doesn't describe the actual goals of software agility—that is, why you would want to make your project agile in the first place (although some goals are described by the group's 12 principles, listed at `www.agilemanifesto.org/principles.html`).

We've interpreted the goals of agility as the ability to

- Respond to changing requirements in a robust and timely manner.
- Improve the design and architecture of a project without massively impacting its schedule.
- Give customers exactly what they want from a project for the dollars they have to invest.
- Do all this without burning out your staff to get the job done.

These goals are sometimes overlooked in the rush to address the values. The agile values are important but, we feel, are really there to fulfill these goals.

The overriding agile goal is responsiveness to changing requirements. This was the main problem out of which agile processes grew. Offset against responsiveness is the need for the project to be robust. Usually, *robustness* means contingency—that is, having safety nets in place to mitigate risk and provide a backup plan if (when) things do go wrong. Robustness implies more effort; more practices to put in place that, while reducing risk, can slow down the project's overall pace (see Figure 1-2). (Sometimes, though, robustness can also mean simply using smarter practices to reduce risk).

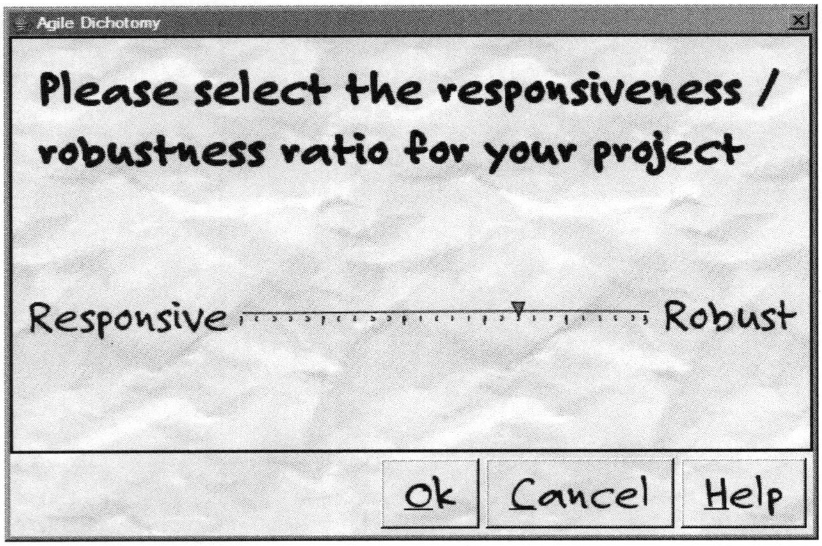

Figure 1-2. *The agile software dichotomy: responsiveness versus robustness*

Responsiveness in this context means the ability to react quickly (without regard for keeping all your safety nets in place, which is where robustness comes in). If you react to a change quickly but immediately introduce lots of defects as a result, that's very responsive but not particularly robust! Safety nets include things like unit tests, customer acceptance tests, design documents, defect tracking software, requirements traceability matrices, and so on.

So, ironically perhaps, to be really responsive (and to not introduce lots of defects every time the code changes), you need to push the slider further toward robustness. But then, the more safety nets you have in place, the more difficult it becomes to react quickly (i.e., the project becomes less agile).

Agility, then, is the ability to adapt to change in a timely and economic manner, or the ability to change direction while moving at speed. So a leopard is agile; an elephant isn't. But an elephant can carry a lot more than a leopard. But a horse is a lot more agile than an elephant and can carry a lot more than a leopard. ICONIX Process, without the agile extensions we present in this book, can be thought of as a "workhorse" process. By adding in a core subset of agile practices, we're aiming to create a "thoroughbred racehorse" process.

In other words, agile techniques work best for small projects but don't always scale very well. The techniques we describe in this book scale better than those in some agile processes because they place a greater emphasis on up-front design and documentation.

SCRIBBLED ON THE BACK OF A NAPKIN

The screenshot in Figure 1-2 looks like it was drawn on a crumpled-up piece of paper, although it is actually from a "real" program. It uses a readily available Swing look and feel called Napkin Look & Feel (see `http://napkinlaf.sourceforge.net`; this page also includes a link to a Java WebStart demo).

The idea behind this look and feel is that sometimes, when a developer shows a prototype GUI to a manager or customer, the customer assumes that what he's seeing is working software. (Appearances *are* everything, after all. . .)

On the other hand, if the working prototype was presented looking like a user interface mockup that had been scrawled on the back of a napkin, then the customer would be more likely to see it for what it actually is: a slightly working but mostly nonfunctional prototype that was cobbled together quickly so as to give the customer a rough idea of what the finished product will look like.

Seems like a great idea to us!

Why Is Agility Important?

Agile development has virtually exploded onto the software development world, bringing with it a shift in the way that software is developed. Agility makes a lot of sense because it addresses some of the common reasons why projects have failed over the years.

Back in 1995, the Standish Group's CHAOS Report[4] (a commonly cited report focusing on reasons for project successes and failures) showed that the primary reason for project failure was "lack of user input." The same study also found that the top element that dramatically increases the chance of success is "user involvement." So it isn't surprising that user involvement (and, in particular, user feedback, as early in the process as possible) is a hugely important driver behind agility.

Another commonly recognized contributor toward project failure is the "big monolithic project" syndrome, where a project doesn't get to see the light of day for a year or two. Finally, when this monstrosity rolls out of the programmers' workshop, the customer grows purple-faced and demands to know what this has to do with his original specification. It's quite likely that what the customer thought he was specifying was completely different from the way in which the programmers interpreted the spec, or the requirements might simply have changed beyond recognition in those 2 years, and somebody forgot to tell the programmers. It sounds absurd, but it happens—a lot.

Agile development addresses these issues: it cuts down the amount of time before the customer sees working software, and it encourages increased communication among everyone involved in the project (the programmers, the analysts, the customer, the users, the managers, the tea lady, and so on). If business customers are concerned

4. See `www.standishgroup.com/press/article.php?id=2`.

about trusting their millions of dollars to your IT consultancy, you need a pretty good story to convince them that you will deliver what they need, when they need it.

In an ailing software industry in which it is still unacceptably common for projects to fail, the most visible (and probably the most often cited) reason for failure is unstable requirements. In other words, requirements that were thought to be "set in stone" are liable to change midproject, causing code to be hacked and the most insidious and time-consuming bugs to creep into the product. Often the requirements change so much, and the code becomes so hacked about as a result, that many of the bugs are not discovered until the software is released. Projects that follow heavyweight (or *high-ceremony*) methodologies may also suffer as a result, due to the amount of documentation that must be kept up to date (doubling the amount of work to be done), sent back and forth, reviewed, and signed off on to cover each and every change. Such projects face the danger of collapsing beneath their own weight.

Another problem faced by many different project teams is that the design will warp and evolve over the course of a single project. In other words, the design that you began with will likely not be the same as the finished design; rather, it will change as the team's understanding of the problem improves. The extent of this problem varies from project to project, depending on a number of factors such as how well understood the problem is, whether a similar project has been written before by anyone on the team, the skill level of the people involved, the quality of the design process and supporting environment and, sometimes, simply whether or not there is a prevailing wind to send the project on its way.

Given this situation, it was inevitable that the industry would begin looking for ways to accommodate changing requirements and evolving designs more easily. A number of agile processes have grown out of this need, each taking a slightly different approach. We describe some of these agile processes in the next section.

What Makes a Project Agile?

A variety of practices, principles, values, and other factors go into making a project agile. In this section, we describe the more important ones (we also sum up these practices as a "top 10" list at the end of this chapter).

Tuning the Process As You Go Along

A doomed project is one that fails to adapt its development process as it goes along. If a particular practice obviously isn't working, it should be replaced with a practice that does work for your team.

Keeping It Low Ceremony

Keeping a process *low ceremony* is the art of producing just enough documentation to proceed, and having just enough process hoops to jump through to provide some structure and coordination, without slowing down the team. For example, if a team is unable to start programming because another 100 pages of design documentation need to be written (using the extensive company template with 12 pages of "front matter," of course), then that would classify as a high-ceremony project.

ICONIX Process aims to keep the project low ceremony, by identifying a minimum set of UML diagrams that can be produced to get reliably from use cases to code with as few hoops to jump through as possible.

Enhancing Agility Through Good Design

If sufficient time is spent on getting the architecture and design right near the start of the project, then it becomes a lot easier to extend and modify the design later on (when changes are traditionally more expensive).

As we describe later in this chapter, Robert C. Martin identifies the need for *continuous care*—that is, constant attention to the design and the state of the source code. If the design begins to fray at the edges (e.g., because some functionality is being added that the design wasn't originally intended to cope with), then time needs to be spent readjusting the design and tidying up the code through refactoring. The alternative—just shoehorning the new functionality in (also known as hacking)—means that the problem never goes away, and over time it just gets worse.

However, a vital extra component can also help to keep the design extensible: time spent on up-front design. Contrary to popular belief, designing for change doesn't mean adding layers of indirection to your code. Unless there's a really good reason for it, this sort of design ultimately just produces more code, making it more difficult to modify later.

Instead, designing for change (also known as *defensive programming*) means following sound, object-oriented (OO) design principles, the following in particular:

- *Keep the code in a highly modular state.* Make sure each class has just one responsibility, and that it handles that responsibility well. Also, make sure each method performs just one task (e.g., by delegating to other methods).
- *Keep your classes highly cohesive and loosely coupled.* Make sure everything in each class fits well and is there to fulfill the reason for the class's existence. Try to reduce the number of dependencies between classes.
- *Don't overcomment your code.* Any code that you have control over should be made self-explanatory (see the next point), reducing the need for comments. The exception is with calls to library code that you have no control over; often, some deftly placed comments can help a lot here.
- *Use method names that describe the method's purpose, not how the method achieves that purpose.* For example, instead of calling a method `addToList(String str)`, call it `addToCatalog(String productID)`.
- *Use class names that are closer to the problem domain than the implementation details.* We'll explore this in more detail when we talk about domain models in Chapter 3.
- *Don't overcommit.* That is, don't use a concrete type where a more abstract type would suffice. For example, if you've declared a return type as a `java.util.ArrayList`, you might find it's better to declare the return type as a `Collection` interface instead. And speaking of interfaces . . .
- *Use interfaces as return types and parameter types wherever possible.*

Improving Communication and Teamwork

One of the most important factors separating agile development methods from traditional development methods is the focus on people. For example, Agile Modeling promotes communication and teamwork through the following practices:

- Active stakeholder participation
- Modeling with others
- Displaying models publicly
- Collective ownership

You build systems for your stakeholders. It is their requirements that you need to fulfill, they are the source of critical information, and they need to make important decisions such as the setting of priorities. For iterative and incremental development to succeed, your stakeholders must be available to provide information, to work with you to explore their requirements, and to make decisions in a timely manner. In other words, your stakeholders must be actively involved with your project.

Software development is a lot like swimming: it is very dangerous to do it alone. Whenever you work on something by yourself, you risk going in an inappropriate direction and not realizing you're doing so. Furthermore, you risk making a common mistake due to lack of experience with or knowledge of a technique or technology. This is why it's so important for design work to be collaborative: by modeling with one or more people, the quality of your work is likely to be much greater, you're likely to get the job done faster, and the information gained during the modeling effort is communicated to everyone involved.

BUT WHAT ABOUT RESPECTING YOUR CO-WORKERS?

Agile processes do place a greater emphasis on the people factor, but it's debatable whether this is intrinsically what makes a project agile. Respecting your co-workers is equally important on nonagile projects, for example. If people feel valued, they'll be more productive, and more willing to participate and contribute actively to the project.

Reducing Exposure to the Forces of Change

The premise behind this idea is simple: making changes halfway through an iteration is expensive and can cause bugs as the new requirements get shoehorned into an unsuspecting design. So to reduce the likelihood of requirements being introduced halfway through an iteration, keep the iterations short. This is like a boxer creating a smaller target by turning side-on to his opponent.

We can also reduce the likelihood of requirements changing at the most inopportune moment by getting from use cases to code in as short a time frame as possible. We do this by spending a little extra time focusing on the requirements and the design modeling (when a change in the requirements is welcomed), so that we cut a straight line to the source code, developing short iterations in short spaces of time.

Measuring Progress with Working Software

If working software has been delivered to the customer, then we know we've made at least some progress (even delivering a small amount of working functionality to the customer is a lot further than some projects get). Working software can also be used to measure (in precise terms) how near to completion the project is (see Chapter 9 for more on agile planning).

But how do we know that the software is working? "Working" doesn't just mean "doesn't crash"; it means that the software matches up with the customer's requirements—that is, it does what it's meant to do. Testing the software against the requirements (often referred to as *customer acceptance testing* or *functional testing*) is generally how we verify that the software works.

During analysis and design, you should constantly ask yourself, "How am I going to test this?" If you can't test something, then you should seriously consider whether you should be building it. Considering testability while modeling is important because it keeps the team focused on realistic designs. Furthermore, it gives the team a head start on writing the test cases, as some thought has already been put into them. Model reviews, described in Chapter 3, are also a good option for validating both the requirements and the design.

Agile Project Management

As with improving communication and teamwork, the people factor plays a large part in agile project management. In many ways, this is no different from the "traditional" project management role: it's about managing groups of people and keeping them at their optimum efficiency without burning them out.

In practical terms, this might simply involve seating people near appropriate colleagues so that they're more inclined to communicate well, moving individuals across teams so that the correct skill sets are applied to individual problems, and so on.

Agile Planning

The very term "agile planning" might strike some people as oxymoronic. How can you create a plan for something that by its very nature keeps changing? In fact, the more volatile a project's requirements, the more agile planning is needed.

Agile planning operates at two levels:

- *Adaptive planning*: This involves planning ahead, tracking changes, and adapting the plan as the project progresses. *Predictive planning*, on the other hand, involves making predictions such as "On June 14, we'll start doing module A, and it will take 4 days for Eric to write it." Adaptive planning stands in stark contrast to predictive planning, because adaptive planning involves synchronizing the plan with reality as we go along.[5]

- *Planning* for *agility*: This entails preparing for the unknown so that when changes take place, their impact is kept to a minimum. Agile planning is a way of anticipating and controlling change.

Typically, agile planning consists of various practices, including performing short, fixed-length iterations (usually of 1 to 2 weeks); regularly reviewing the project plan; time boxing (i.e., specifying a fixed amount of time

5. See Martin Fowler's paper "The New Methodology" at `www.thoughtworks.com/us/library/newMethodology.pdf`.

in which to deliver a variable amount of functionality); and tracking velocity (i.e., the rate at which new working software is being delivered).

Managing Change

While some agile methodologies tell us to "embrace change," we prefer to see change as something that should be actively managed—controlled, even. This doesn't mean *discouraging* change (that wouldn't be very agile, after all), but instead keeping a pragmatic focus on the costs involved in making a change to the requirements at a late stage in the project.

If the customer is made aware that change isn't free, and that the cost to fix a requirements defect increases exponentially the longer it's left, she might prefer to take the hit and leave a requirement as is, at least until the next release. For the customer to make an objective decision, she needs accurate planning data, including cost estimates. So a big part of managing change is tracking *project velocity* (see Chapter 9).

Delivering the System That the Customer Wants at the End of the Project, Not What He Thought He Wanted at the Start

This goal is probably the most intrinsically *agile* of the agile factors listed here. The customer might, in all good faith, specify a set of requirements at the start of the project, believing them to be correct. During the project, however, things change. The business changes, causing the goalposts to shift; our understanding (and the customer's understanding) of the problem domain grows; our understanding of the required solution increases; and the design evolves, meaning a better solution is sometimes found.

Agility is all about recognizing that these things happen in just about every software project and, rather than trying to suppress them (e.g., by "freezing" requirements with another 8 months to go before the deadline), we use change to our advantage to drive the project toward the working system that is the most optimal for the user's needs.

We can use a variety of practices to achieve this goal. In fact, pretty much all of the agile practices contribute to this goal in some way.

Challenges of Being Agile

Often, introducing agility into your project can involve a trade-off. For example, certain levels of documentation and modeling may be scrapped so that the team can "travel light." Striking the right balance can be difficult.

Here, in our view, are the top 10 challenges of being agile.

10. Sticking to the Path

Many agile processes, though low ceremony, are high discipline and require consistent effort from the whole team to keep the project on track. You may well find that you start to do certain practices less (e.g., if you're using pair programming, team members might start to pair up less). Agile processes put various safety nets in place to lessen the impact when you fall. (Of course, some processes have more safety nets than others, as we discuss in *Extreme Programming Refactored: The Case Against XP*.)

If you're finding it increasingly difficult to maintain certain practices, it's time to review the process. Perhaps a particular practice is too difficult because it simply doesn't fit your project. There may be an equivalent practice (or group of practices)—something easier—that you could do instead and that your team is more likely to stick to.

9. Keeping Releases Short

Short releases (i.e., releasing working code to the customer on a rapid turnaround) can be difficult to keep on doing, for a number of reasons. Examples include interface changes, database changes, user retraining, and help file rewriting.

Similarly, it's tempting to stop doing short releases simply because they're so difficult. Funnily enough, the answer in many cases is to release more often (a similar solution to difficulties associated with continuous integration; see the section titled "Continuous Integration" later in this chapter for more information).

8. Keeping Entropy at Bay

Even in nonagile projects, software designs degrade over time because new requirements emerge, and the software needs to be made to do things it wasn't originally supposed to. In agile projects the risk is higher, because requirements are analyzed in smaller groups; releases and iterations are smaller, so the team isn't looking ahead quite as far.

While this approach solves many problems, it does mean that agile practitioners must keep a closer eye on the design, regularly refactoring to keep it in trim. In short, unit test your code and have a realistic strategy to manage change, or watch your project "decompose" in all the wrong ways!

7. Doing Less Without Increasing Risk

Cutting down on the wrong things increases risk (e.g., design, testing, and drawing certain types of diagrams). So it's important to know which practices you can safely do less of (see Figure 1-2). These practices can also vary from project to project.

Reducing contingency (i.e., removing safety-net practices such as testing and code inspections) can save time in the short term, but it also increases risk. Make sure your agile process gives you more options for when things go wrong, not fewer.

6. Discovering Your True Master

Always remember that the "customer" is not one person—not even one role—but is usually several people covering the roles of end user, domain expert, decision maker, and project sponsor. Similarly for product development, different groups of people will try to pull the project in different directions: the marketing department, customers, the QA department, the company directors, and so on.

Losing track of this important fact increases the risk of project failure, because requirements can be flung at you from unexpected quarters, or a key project stakeholder might become disgruntled because her interests aren't being upheld in the project.

5. Keeping the Customer Involved

Increasing the customer's involvement may not seem like a challenge, but it certainly can be. Active stakeholder participation is a key principle in agile development, and it can greatly increase the chances of your project succeeding. However, not all customers want the additional responsibility that certain agile processes give them. They might prefer to "rule from afar," signing off on requirements and waiting for the finished project to be delivered. Your team might interpret this as aloofness, but it's more likely that the customer, like most people, is just incredibly busy. Even agile projects (or should that be *especially* agile projects) need to tailor their process to suit the customer.

While there's no silver bullet solution to this difficult situation, ICONIX Process can help because of its emphasis on requirements exploration and disambiguation.

4. Managing Change

While some agile processes positively encourage change (rightly seeing a change in requirements as an increased business opportunity for the customer), it's easy to lose sight of the risks and expense that change can cause. Without controlling change, we forget to do our utmost to get the requirements right early in the project, and the result may be requirements churn.

3. Training

Introduction of a new way of developing software can potentially cause misunderstandings (e.g., programmers who wrongly see agility as an invitation to hack: "Woo hoo—no design!"). In some sense, the way that some agile approaches have been marketed makes this problem worse than it should be. (For example, telling programmers that they can skip documentation is a bit like selling catnip to cats.)

2. Avoiding the Other Extreme

Agility brings with it many promises and possibilities. There may be a temptation to throw the whole organization onto the agile bandwagon. Transitioning to an entirely agile process just can't be done overnight—it must be taken in stages (depending on how deeply ingrained the "big monolithic high-ceremony development" culture is in the company).

1. Facing Resistance to Change

Speaking of development culture, you may find that your organization is stuck in high-ceremony gear: every "i" must be dotted and every "t" crossed. This deeply ingrained attitude is possibly the single biggest challenge to running an agile project.

In organizations that are traditionally high-ceremony, ICONIX Process should be a more acceptable agile process than others because of its core emphasis on requirements gathering, UML, and up-front design. Enterprising developers or managers may see ICONIX Process as a "way in" for agile processes in such organizations.

Agile Methodologies

To give you a flavor of the variety and amount of activity going on in the agile world, in this section we briefly describe some of the most popular (or certainly the most talked about) of the agile methodologies:

- Extreme Programming (XP)
- Test-Driven Development (TDD)
- Agile Modeling (AM)
- Agile Database Techniques (AD)
- Adaptive Software Development (ASD)
- Crystal methodologies
- Feature-Driven Development (FDD)
- Dynamic Systems Development Method (DSDM)
- Scrum

Some processes are designed to complement other methodologies (such as RUP or XP) with additional practices, for example:

- AM adds high-level, people-oriented practices, plus guidance for the amount of up-front modeling that should take place, which models to maintain, and so on.
- Scrum adds agile project management and planning in an effort to control the chaos of conflicting interests and needs from which many projects suffer.
- ICONIX Process can be applied to agile projects, to help disambiguate the requirements and the design before coding begins. This can add a vital element of up-front analysis and design to processes that might otherwise be lacking in such areas.

Whatever such practices add, their primary goal is to reduce the level of risk involved in driving the project forward while the requirements take shape.

Let's look at each of these agile processes in turn. You won't need to know all (or indeed any) of these processes to be agile, but it helps to know what's out there and the various directions that agile methods are taking.

Note To be agile, you also don't have to follow all of the practices that we describe in this chapter. You should always tailor a process to suit your project and do just the practices that fit. In Chapter 4, after analyzing what it really means to be agile, we'll present a core subset of agile practices. Of course, you should tailor even this core subset to suit your project.

Extreme Programming

Extreme Programming (XP) is the most popular (certainly the loudest) of the agile methodologies. For more information, see `www.extremeprogramming.org` or the book *Extreme Programming Explained: Embrace Change* by Kent Beck (Addison-Wesley, 2000). For a detailed analysis of how XP can be high risk without extensive tailoring, see our book, *Extreme Programming Refactored: The Case Against XP*.

In this section, we briefly describe the agile practices in XP and some of the thinking behind them.

Test-Driven Development

This practice involves designing the code by writing unit tests. Each test proves that a particular feature of the design either works or doesn't work. You sometimes hear test-driven programmers shouting "Green bar!" or "Red bar!" when running the tests. This is because the popular xUnit family of test frameworks[6] shows either a green or a red bar to indicate whether the tests passed or failed.

In XP, the TDD practice also covers writing customer acceptance tests (often using an acceptance testing framework such as FitNesse) to define the requirements.

We cover TDD in more detail in Chapters 11 and 12.

The Planning Game

XP has two planning games: the *release* planning game and the *iteration* planning game. Planning in XP involves breaking the project into very short, 1- to 3-week iterations and taking the project one iteration at a time. For each iteration, the customer needs to decide which user stories to include and which to leave until a future iteration.

Any piece of work that takes time is written up as a user story and written on a story card. User stories must be testable and estimable. To aid this goal, stories are often broken down into estimable tasks. Each task is assigned an arbitrary value to indicate how long the programmers think it will take. Over time, these values (and the number of tasks completed) are measured to give an indication of the *project velocity*.

Whole Team

This practice involves trying to squeeze as many people as possible (including the customer or business analysts) into one room. That may sound like a recipe for a noisy, stinky room on a hot summer's day, but the thinking behind it is quite pragmatic: the more barriers (e.g., walls) there are between team members, the more expensive it becomes to share information, and the less likely it is that team members will actually communicate. So putting all these people into one room increases not only the amount but also the quality of communication—at least that's the theory.[7]

Small Releases

The aim here is to get feedback from the user as quickly as possible, primarily by releasing working software often. In XP, this may mean releasing as often as once every couple of weeks, though you would, of course, modify this time frame depending how feasible it would be to achieve on your project.

The thinking behind small releases is that valuable functionality is placed into the user's hands as soon as possible and that the system never gets too far removed from what the customer really wants.

6. jUnit, nUnit, cppUnit, and so on.

7. For a different perspective, see Matt and Doug's other collaboration, *Extreme Programming Refactored: The Case Against XP* (Apress, 2003).

System Metaphor

The *system metaphor* is a simple shared story of how the system works. All naming and design theories stem from that one story. Lately, XPers have begun to adopt *domain-driven design* (i.e., driving the design from a domain model) as an important method of keeping the design consistent and sharing a common vocabulary. Domain-driven design is also a fundamental part of ICONIX Process (as we'll see in Chapter 3).

Simple Design

An important lesson in all aspects of software design (including designing the user interface) is to keep it simple. This doesn't mean removing all software layers so that your JSP pages are littered with SQL code, for example. In fact, sometimes adding a slightly more complex design can ultimately make the software much simpler to write. It's a judgment call—but when in doubt, keep it simple.

Refactor Mercilessly

In any project, as time marches on, the design inevitably starts to fall apart. New requirements (which were never thought of when the software was first designed) need to be hacked in, so the design starts to become *crufty* (i.e., more fragile and increasingly difficult to extend). In XP, this common effect is countered by constant attention to the design: so-called merciless refactoring.

Refactoring is the practice of improving the design of existing code while still passing all of the unit tests. Improving the design generally means simplifying it—making your classes more cohesive and less tightly coupled. It's a constant process, something that XP author Robert C. Martin describes as "continuous care."[8]

Collective Ownership

With *collective ownership*, everyone is responsible for the entire code base. If a programmer sees something in the code that she doesn't like, she (and her pair-programming buddy) can go in and change it, regardless of who originally wrote it. (XP's safety nets here are comprehensive unit and acceptance test harnesses, and constant mandatory pair programming.)

Pair Programming

In XP you can code on your own for "nonproduction" code such as prototypes. However, for all production code (i.e., code that will be used on a live system by "real" end users), XP recommends that everyone on the team program in pairs. Pairing up is an effective way of catching errors and helping each other identify methods to further improve the design.

Continuous Integration

By *integration*, we mean putting your latest changes to the source code into a central source control system (e.g., PVCS, Visual SourceSafe, and CVS). *Continuous* integration means doing this as often as possible (at the very least once per day). This practice is often also supplemented by a dedicated "build" PC that regularly gets all the latest source code, builds it (in the Java world, typically using an Ant build script), and runs all the unit tests. If this is done often (e.g., once per hour), then build or test errors are caught very quickly, almost as soon as they are introduced.

In the nonagile world, many teams either forget to integrate their code for weeks at a time or hold back on doing it because they know that it's a major headache. And it's no surprise, really: if several programmers are working on different parts of the same system in parallel, they're bound to diverge over time and will produce incompatible code. So, though it may seem counterintuitive, the answer to the integration issue is not to do it less, but to integrate your code *more often*.

8. See `www.objectmentor.com/resources/articles/Continuous_Care.pdf`.

Sustainable Pace

The more tired a programmer is, the more mistakes he'll make. Many of us have experienced the horrors of late-night coding, up against some perilously important deadline or other. XP makes the point that on projects where this is the norm, programmers simply burn out and end up as near-catatonic dropouts propping up street corners and smelling heavily of stale beer. (Perhaps this is why XP talks about "coder smells"?[9])

Sustainable pace (which used to be called "40-hour week") will result in higher productivity levels in the long run than making frequent mad dashes that quickly burn out your programmers.

Coding Standards

Coding standards are important in any programming project, and more so in an XP project because there's no specialization: any programmer pair can dive in and work on any part of the code base. The thinking is that we spend five to ten times as much time reading code as we do writing code, so if we all write it to the same conventions, it should improve our productivity.

Test-Driven Development

Test-Driven Development (TDD) is an integral part of XP, but it can also be extracted in its entirety and applied to non-XP projects. For example, in Chapter 12 we show how TDD can be used in conjunction with ICONIX Process to good effect.

Using TDD, you design code by writing code. While this sounds circular, it means that you write client test code that serves as both an example and a definition of what you want the object code to do. For example, if you were writing a hotel booking system, you would write tests for placing a booking, adding customer details, retrieving the details, and so on, and then assert that the correct results are returned.

Agile Modeling

The Agile Modeling (AM) methodology[10] is a "chaordic"[11] collection of practices, guided by principles and values, that should be applied by software professionals on a day-to-day basis. AM is not a prescriptive process—in other words, it does not define detailed procedures for how to create a given type of model. Instead, it provides advice for how to be effective as a modeler. Think of AM as an art, not a science.

Overview of Agile Modeling

An agile modeler is anyone who models following the AM methodology, applying AM's practices in accordance with its principles and values. An agile developer is someone who follows an agile approach to software development. An agile modeler is an agile developer. Not all agile developers are agile modelers.

AM has three goals:

- *To define and show how to put into practice a collection of values, principles, and practices pertaining to effective, lightweight modeling.* What makes AM a catalyst for improvement isn't the modeling techniques themselves—such as use case models, robustness diagrams, sequence diagrams, or class diagrams—but how to apply them productively.
- *To address the issue of how to apply modeling techniques on projects following agile software development methodologies.* Sometimes it is significantly more productive for a developer to draw a sketch while thinking through an idea, or to compare several different approaches to solving a problem, than it is to simply start writing code. There is a danger in being too code-centric; a quick sketch can often avoid significant churn when you are coding.

---

9. Okay, we know, it's really "code smells". . . .
10. Scott W. Ambler, *Agile Modeling: Effective Practices for eXtreme Programming and the Unified Process* (Hoboken, NJ: John Wiley & Sons, 2002).
11. The term *chaordic* describes a self-organizing, adaptive system, the behavior of which exhibits characteristics of both order and chaos.

- *To address how you can improve your modeling activities following a "near-agile" approach to software development.* In particular, this applies to project teams that have adopted an instantiation of the Unified Process such as the Rational Unified Process (RUP) or the Enterprise Unified Process (EUP). Sometimes it is more productive for developers to spend less time writing documentation and creating complex models, and more time creating models that are just barely good enough.

In short, AM strives to find the "sweet spot" between too little and too much modeling. Because this sweet spot changes from project to project, you will need to tailor your application of AM each time.

Agile Modeling Practices

AM consists of a variety of core principles, secondary principles, core practices, and secondary practices, not to mention values. You can find full descriptions of these at the AM website (`www.agilemodeling.com`). However, to give you an idea of what AM is about, here are the core practices:

- Active Stakeholder Participation
- Apply the Right Artifact(s)
- Collective Ownership
- Consider Testability
- Create Several Models in Parallel
- Create Simple Content
- Depict Models Simply
- Display Models Publicly
- Iterate to Another Artifact
- Model in Small Increments
- Model with Others
- Prove It with Code
- Use the Simplest Tools

The top 10 points to remember for AM are as follows:

10. You should create several models in parallel, iterating back and forth as required.
9. Models aren't necessarily documents, and documents aren't necessarily models.
8. Modeling is a lot like swimming: it's very dangerous to do alone.
7. Sometimes the simplest modeling tool is a whiteboard; sometimes it's a complex CASE tool.
6. Keep your models as simple as possible.
5. Travel light and update documentation only when it hurts.
4. Models don't need to be perfect—they just need to be barely good enough.
3. Create the right models for the job, even if they're not defined by the UML (e.g., data models).
2. Your project stakeholders must be actively involved in modeling.
1. The three secrets to successful modeling are feedback, feedback, feedback.

Agile Database Techniques

Agile Database Techniques (AD) applies refactoring and emergent design principles to database models. It correctly recognizes that as a project develops, it isn't just the design of the code that changes—the database model also evolves. AD provides a number of techniques for evolving databases while keeping a close eye on the integrity of your data. It's a difficult subject because we're dealing with live customer data, but it's an important one to keep in mind.

This methodology is described in the book *Agile Database Techniques: Effective Strategies for the Agile Software Developer* (John Wiley & Sons, 2003) by Scott W. Ambler (creator of AM). Also see `www.agiledata.org`.

Adaptive Software Development

Adaptive Software Development (ASD) consists of the following:

- *Adaptive Conceptual Model*: The theoretical foundation
- *Adaptive Development Model*: A software development life cycle for complex projects
- *Adaptive Management Model*: Principles for managing complex projects

ASD places an emphasis on adaptive development cycles (basically iterations). Adaptive cycles are mission driven, component based, iterative, time boxed, risk driven, and change tolerant. A project is also divided concentrically into versions, cycles, and builds.

This approach to software development is described in the book *Adaptive Software Development: A Collaborative Approach to Managing Complex Systems* by James A. Highsmith III (Dorset House Publishing Company, 2000).

Crystal Methodologies

According to Alistair Cockburn's Crystal Methodologies site at `http://alistair.cockburn.us/crystal/crystal.html`

> *Crystal collects together a self-adapting family of "shrink-to-fit," human-powered software development methodologies based on these understandings:*
>
> 1. *Every project needs a slightly different set of policies and conventions, or methodology.*
> 2. *The workings of the project are sensitive to people issues, and improve as the people issues improve, individuals get better, and their teamwork gets better.*
> 3. *Better communications and frequent deliveries reduce the need for intermediate work products.*

We'll look at the Crystal methodologies and practices in more detail in the sections that follow.

Overview of the Crystal Methodologies

The Crystal methodologies are delineated according to factors such as project size, proximity of team members, and project risk. For example, Crystal Clear[12] is targeted at small projects, whereas Crystal Orange is targeted at projects with up to 40 people sitting in one building, working on a system that might cause loss of discretionary monies.

The Crystal methodologies were created by Alistair Cockburn, and are described in his books *Agile Software Development* (Addison-Wesley, 2001) and *Surviving Object-Oriented Projects* (Addison-Wesley, 1997). A key point about the methodologies in the Crystal family is that they are self-adapting—that is, you need to keep reviewing and tailoring the methodologies throughout the project.

12. See Alistair Cockburn's *Crystal Clear: A Human-Powered Methodology for Small Teams* (New York: Addison-Wesley, 2004).

You should find that there are many similarities (not least in the philosophy behind software development) between Cockburn's work and James Highsmith's ASD work. In fact, Highsmith and Cockburn have begun combining their efforts. See `http://alistair.cockburn.us/crystal/crystal.html` for the latest developments.

Crystal Practices

Crystal Clear is targeted at similar projects to XP (small projects with up to 12 people located in the same room), so we'll describe it briefly here.

The key person in a Crystal Clear project is the senior designer-programmer. Other roles (which require separate people) are the sponsor, designer-programmer, and user (part-time at least).

The policy standards are that[13]

- Software is delivered incrementally and regularly, every 2 to 3 months.
- Progress is tracked by milestones consisting of software deliveries or major decisions, as opposed to written documents.
- There is some amount of automated regression testing of application functionality.
- There is direct user involvement.
- There are two user viewings per release.
- Downstream activities start as soon as upstream is stable enough to review.
- Product and methodology-tuning workshops are held at the start and middle of each increment.

Crystal Clear includes some mandatory work products, including a release sequence, a schedule of user viewings and deliveries, use cases or feature descriptions, design sketches and notes as needed, screen drafts, a common object model, running code, migration code, test cases, and a user manual. By contrast, Crystal Orange scales up to meet the challenge of larger projects. For example, it includes 14 roles over Crystal Clear's 4, and more formal work products (such as a requirements document, a user interface (UI) design document, interteam specs, and status reports).

DSDM

Dynamic Systems Development Method (DSDM) has been around for at least a decade. It predated the agile movement and was originally marketed as a Rapid Application Development (RAD) methodology. However, DSDM is continuously evolving, so its definition today is still up to date with current software knowledge. DSDM differs from the other agile processes described here in that it is commercially driven. Companies that use DSDM pay a membership fee. The DSDM Consortium also offers training and certification.

The DSDM "spec" is released as a specific version (much like software). At the time of this writing, the Consortium is on version 4.2. For more information, see `www.dsdm.com`.

Scrum

Scrum is an agile development process aimed primarily at managers. Its focus is on helping project leaders to manage teams of highly skilled developers, and get the best from them without treading on their toes. As such, Scrum can be "wrapped" around more technical development processes such as XP or ICONIX Process.

Scrum divides projects into monthly "sprints," with an incremental amount of new functionality delivered at the end of each sprint. Uniquely in an agile process, the customer is not allowed to change the requirements during the monthly sprint. If the requirements are discovered to be off base once the sprint is under way, the customer must wait until the 30-day sprint has ended before instigating a change. While this can help to stabilize development (and to make project stakeholders very focused on getting the requirements right), most other agile processes

13. Alistair Cockburn, *Agile Software Development* (New York: Addison-Wesley, 2001), p. 202.

(including ICONIX Process) make the point that if a requirement is discovered to be wrong, you should take steps to correct it as soon as possible.

The book *Agile Software Development with Scrum* by Ken Schwaber and Mike Beedle (Prentice-Hall, 2001) contains useful advice on how to introduce agile methodologies into large organizations. Also see `www.controlchaos.com`.

Feature-Driven Development

Of the agile methodologies described here, Feature-Driven Development (FDD) is in many ways closest at heart to ICONIX Process.

FDD places an emphasis on up-front design techniques and driving the design from "features" described using a domain object model. FDD is closely linked with the Together CASE tool/development environment (originally from Peter Coad's company TogetherSoft, which was bought by Borland). FDD can, of course, also be used with other software tools if needed.

FDD was originated by Peter Coad, and later the methodology was described in much more detail by Stephen R. Palmer and John M. Felsing. Also see `www.featuredrivendevelopment.com`.

Feature-Driven Development Practices

As previously mentioned, FDD places a strong emphasis on up-front design modeling, driving the development effort from self-contained functional requirements, or *features*.

FDD consists of five processes, each one providing the input into the next:

1. Develop an overall model.
2. Build a features list.
3. Plan by feature.
4. Design by feature.
5. Build by feature.

Let's look at each process in turn.

Develop an Overall Model

The domain and development team members work together to create a high-level walk-through of the system. Then the domain members present more detailed walk-throughs of each area of the problem domain.

Build a Features List

Building on the knowledge gathered during the initial modeling activity, the team next constructs as complete a list of features as it can. A *feature* is defined as a small, client-valued function expressed in the form: <action> <result> <object> (e.g., "*calculate* the *total* of a *sale*"). Existing requirements documents (use cases or functional specs) are also used as input.

Within each domain area (also called a *major feature set*), the features are grouped into feature sets, where a feature set reflects a particular business activity. Then the users and customer review the feature list for validity and completeness.

Plan by Feature

The feature sets are sequenced into a high-level plan and assigned to chief programmers (aka team leaders). The classes identified in the modeling activity are assigned to individual developers; the owner of a class is responsible for its development.

In large projects, DSDM-style time boxing may be used (e.g., a time box of 3 months might be set to complete the first few feature sets and demonstrate the working software to the customer).

Design by Feature and Build by Feature

These two processes are highly iterative and are where the serious development work goes on. The team leader selects a small group of features to develop over the next iteration (ranging from a few days to 2 weeks). He identifies the classes likely to be involved and matches these up with the class owners. In this way, he selects his feature team for this iteration.

The feature team creates detailed sequence diagrams for the features, and writes class and method skeletons. The team then conducts a design inspection. After a successful inspection, the class owners add the actual code for their classes, unit test, integrate, and hold a code inspection. Once the team leader is satisfied, the completed features are promoted to the main build, and the designing and building processes repeat for the next group of features.

As you might gather from reading this description (and especially after reading Chapter 3), FDD and the ICONIX object modeling process are a very suitable match for each other. As ICONIX Process places an emphasis on sequence diagrams, it can fit into FDD's design-by-feature process, and it can also complement FDD's review stages with its own critical design review techniques. Similarly, FDD's concepts of organizing use cases into features and planning by feature can be applied to an ICONIX Process project.

FDD is described in lots more detail in the book *A Practical Guide to Feature-Driven Development* by Stephen R. Palmer and John M. Felsing (Prentice-Hall, 2002).

Agile ICONIX

To provide a fair comparison with the agile methodologies described here, we finish up with a brief description of Agile ICONIX, described in a similar style to the previous methodologies.

Overview of Agile ICONIX

Agile ICONIX takes ICONIX Process (a minimal object-modeling process) and describes how to use it in an agile project. Agile ICONIX retains the core philosophy of ICONIX Process, which is that less is more. The less we have to do to *safely* achieve our goal, the quicker and more effectively we'll do it. The agile practices that Agile ICONIX uses are a combination of current agile thinking and some practices of its own, which create a core subset of agile practices—the bare minimum that you'd need to do in order to achieve the goals of agility.

How Do ICONIX Process's Agile Practices Differ?

In Chapter 4, we describe ICONIX Process's agile practices, and then in the rest of the book we show how they're applied by example. For now, here's an overview of how ICONIX Process differs from the agile methods described here.

The key differences are as follows:

- With ICONIX Process, an emphasis is placed on getting the requirements right up front. This is done through a variety of practices that root out ambiguity in the requirements and uncover gaps in the use cases and domain model.
- With ICONIX Process, design is not something that you "quickly do a bit of" before coding (where the real design work happens). Instead, design modeling and coding are tightly interleaved, each providing feedback to the other. Essentially, in ICONIX Process, we "model like we mean it"—that is, we intend to drive the coding of the system from the model. This in turn means that . . .
- With ICONIX Process, the design and the code don't diverge over time. Instead, they converge, with the design model and the code becoming more in sync.

For more about Agile ICONIX, see . . . well, the book you're reading at the moment.

■ **Modeling Question** *Does this mean that you do all of your use cases, then go back and reanalyze the use cases, and then write all the code?* Although we place a big emphasis on getting the requirements right up front, ICONIX Process isn't by any means a "waterfall" process. It's actually highly iterative (as we describe in Chapter 4). One way to describe it is with an example of iteratively painting your house. You can primer the whole house, then sand the whole house, then primer it again, then sand it again, then primer it again, then sand it again, then primer it again. That's one type of iterative process: doing the whole thing over and over. The other way is to primer the front of the house, sand the front, primer the front, paint the front, and then move to the right side of the house and repeat. The first way is more of a repetitive waterfall; the second way is repetitive, but in small chunks. ICONIX Process (and most other agile methods) take the "repetitive small chunks" approach.

Agile Fact or Fiction: What Does "Being Agile" Mean?

We've gone some way toward answering this question throughout this chapter, but we thought it would be kind of fun to get our three coauthors' separate opinions on the subject. So in this section (which also continues in Chapters 2 and 4), we discuss some of the myths and misconceptions that have grown up around agile software development.

Mark: A dictionary definition of agility would be something like "the ability to change direction while moving at speed," and this motivation is at the heart of software agility.

I see agility as a logical extension of moving away from waterfall-style software development (i.e., do all analysis, then all design, then all coding, then all unit testing, then integrate the software, then system test it, etc.) to iterative and incremental development, whereby systems are delivered in a number of stages. Functionality is prioritized, and a self-contained useful subset of functionality is delivered on a regular basis.

Agility takes this idea further and puts additional emphasis on the ability to be able to change direction—and by "direction" I mean the direction in which business requirements are pulling us—while still moving at some speed toward our number one goal of a working software system. In order to move at speed, agile development approaches downplay the importance of nonsoftware deliverables to varying degrees, certainly when compared to very heavyweight, documentation-oriented processes like RUP or those used in many conventional software houses.

Matt: Hey, Mark, a quick search on Dictionary.com defines agility as "being nimble." But somehow I don't think "software nimbleness" would have caught on in quite the same way as "software agility"! Seriously, though, what defines software agility is really the goals of agility—that is, why you'd choose to apply agile practices to your project—and the agile practices themselves. Short iterations, test-driven development, interleaved modeling/testing—these are all practices that help us to achieve agility, but they aren't themselves agility.

Agility, in my mind, is an increased ability to change direction without causing excessive expense, with the end result being a system that closely matches the customer's needs (which might not have been fully understood at the start of the project).

However, changing direction without excessive expense is something of a Holy Grail, because changing the requirements (or the design) midproject is never going to be free. But it's an ideal that we strive toward on each project, by applying various agile practices. Knowing which practices to apply—tailoring the process for each project—is, of course, the difficult part. So it's best to start with a core subset (hey, like the one we define in this book!) and build on top of that.

Doug: Well, the nebulous use of the term "agility" is one of our main motivations for writing this book. In general, there's probably a consensus that agility is about being able to respond to changing requirements, and there probably aren't too many people that would argue that avoiding long, drawn-out periods of specification and design without doing any coding is agile. Going a step further, we probably wouldn't be controversial if we claimed that small increments, short iterations, and frequent releases are near the core of agility, and that getting early and frequent feedback from customers is agile.

Beyond that, there's a plethora of advice, practices, and guidance that purport to be agile—some of it's good, some of it's bad, some of it's interesting but not particularly relevant to achieving "agile goals," and some of it's just plain awful. What we're trying to do in this book is define a core subset of agile concepts and practices, and then illustrate it by example. My earlier books define a core subset of UML modeling techniques to support use case–driven development, and I'm hoping that between that subset and the subset we define in this book, we'll be able to give people a really useful set of techniques to apply on their projects.

Summary

Taking an agile approach to your project does not have to mean abandoning up-front requirements gathering or up-front architecture and design. Often, spending the time to get the design right, based on what the customer really wants, can actually increase a project's agility.

We aren't suggesting that, taking this approach, requirements won't change later on: they will. However, the level of "requirements churn" should be much lower, and what changes there are will have a lower probability of forcing a big, costly, high-risk change to the architecture.

The most visible (and probably the most often cited) reason for project failure is lack of effective user involvement, which often results in unstable requirements. One approach to fix this problem is to make the project as malleable (or agile) to the forces of change as possible. Another approach is to improve the requirements elicitation process (in other words, talk to the customer; find out what the customer really needs; use effective requirements elicitation techniques [as we describe in this book]; ask the customer hard, detailed questions; and hit the brakes if the customer doesn't have the answers) and to model these requirements in the form of use cases.

Contrary to popular opinion, these two approaches are not mutually exclusive. In fact, combining the two approaches (traditionally seen as diametrically opposite—agile versus nonagile) should drastically reduce the risk that requirements churn places on your project.

Top 10 Practices and Values That Make a Project Agile

Here are the top 10 practices and values:

10. Tune the process as you go along.
9. Make the process low ceremony (i.e., produce just enough documentation to proceed).
8. Enhance agility through good design (with tried and trusted techniques).
7. Improve teamwork and communication.
6. Reduce exposure to the forces of change (e.g., by getting from use cases to code in the shortest time possible, and by short iterations).
5. Measure progress with working software.
4. Implement agile project management (identifying and delivering customer value).
3. Implement agile planning (use short iterations and review the plan regularly).
2. Manage change (a more controlled form of adapting to change, which is an important agile principle).
1. Aim to deliver the system that the customer wants at the end of the project, not what he thought he wanted at the start.

CHAPTER 2

Characteristics of a Good Software Process

How much process is enough, and how much is too much? That question has been the subject of intense debate for several years now, and the debate has been carried out most vociferously by the agile community—especially by the extreme elements within that community.

Barry Boehm described the problem graphically in his 2002 article titled "Get Ready for Agile Methods, with Care."[1] In that article, he shows the increasing costs due to both excessive planning and inadequate planning on either side of the "sweet spot" (see Figure 2-1).

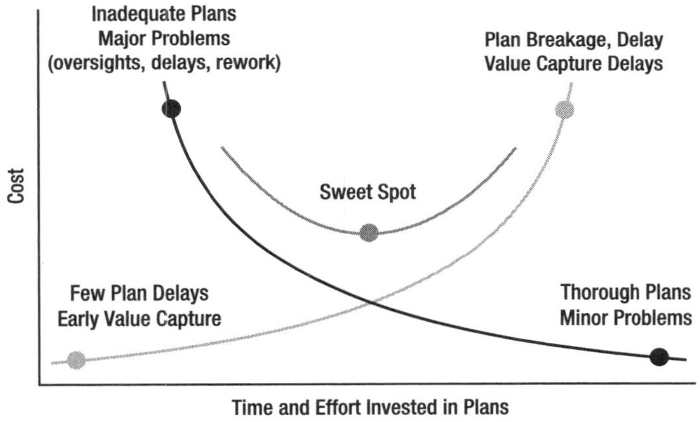

Figure 2-1. *Searching for the sweet spot between agility and discipline*

In a more lighthearted vein, two of the authors (Doug and Mark) were thinking about this problem a couple of years prior to the publication of Boehm's article when Mark published Doug's "Goldilocks and the Three Software Processes"[2] article in Ratio Group's *ObjectiveView* magazine back in 2000. Specifically referring to RUP, XP, and ICONIX Process, "Goldilocks" makes the case that "one's too big, the other's too small, and the third one is just right." We'll let you guess for yourself which process was which (or you can download the article).

The authors of this book believe that the Agile ICONIX approach is certainly in the near vicinity of the sweet spot between plan-driven and feedback-driven processes, if not dead-center in the bull's-eye. In the remaining chapters of this book, we describe that sweet spot both in theory and in practice (by example), although the exact sweet spot will vary among organizations and projects. But as a basis for that discussion, we'd like to first examine exactly what the components of a software process are, and then we'll discuss trade-offs that can be made within each of these process components to help you find the appropriate level of process for your project.

---

1. Barry Boehm, "Get Ready for Agile Methods, with Care," *IEEE Computer*, January 2002, pp. 64–69.
2. Doug Rosenberg and Kendall Scott, "Goldilocks and the Three Software Processes," *ObjectiveView*, Issue 5, p. 35. (This article is available for download from `www.iconixsw.com/Articles/Articles.html` and also from `www.ratio.co.uk/objectiveview.html`.)

What's in a Software Development Process?

There are many different aspects to running a software development process. We could choose to adopt a rigorous, highly defined process in a pure waterfall fashion, with a hierarchically organized team distributed over three sites. We could choose a minimalist logical process like ICONIX, and phase it in highly iterative and incremental fashion (i.e., locating our team in a single room with lots of whiteboards to assist in discussion of issues, having daily stand-up meetings, etc.). And so on.

If we examine the decisions made when running a collaborative (multiperson) software development project, looking back over the last 30 years in particular, it is possible to discern a number of categories of the decisions to be made. These consist of the logical process, if any, adopted; the planning and phasing strategy adopted; the approach to human-centric and communication-related issues; and the regular working practices adopted. We discuss these categories in more detail in the sections that follow (also see Figure 2-2).

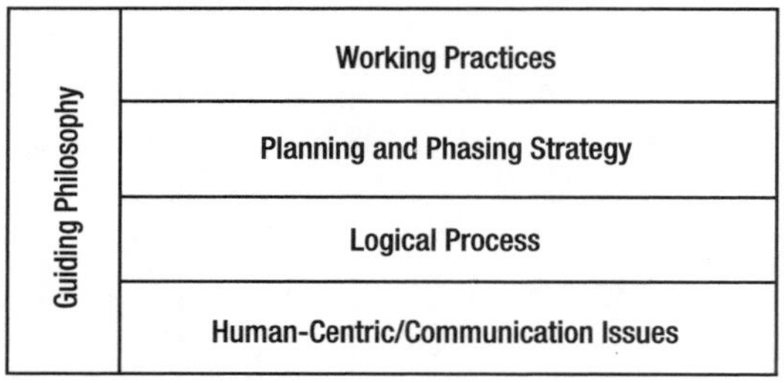

Figure 2-2. *Like a good sandwich: layers of a development process*

Logical Process

A *logical process* defines what sequence of substeps, if any, we can follow to assist us in getting from our starting point (i.e., some vague idea of the requirements our development is trying to satisfy) to our end point of a working software system that meets a much fuller (and we hope more correct) understanding of the same requirements. Candidates for logical processes include SSADM, ICONIX Process, and the Unified Process (UP), to name just a few.

It is important to note here that we can follow the same logical process using many different planning and phasing approaches. We could adopt a fully waterfall approach (analyze every use case, then design a solution for every use case, etc.) using the steps of UP, or we could adopt (as recommended in this book) a highly incremental approach (analyze the use cases for a prioritized subset of the overall requirements, then do some design for them, etc.) using the steps outlined by ICONIX Process. Put another way, the logical process and planning and phasing are orthogonal concerns.

This book focuses on ICONIX Process, a minimal UML-based logical process that promotes the use of an easy-to-digest subset of UML techniques as signposts to delivering working software. We discuss the qualities of ICONIX Process that make it a good candidate for agile software development later in this chapter.

Planning and Phasing Strategy

At its most fundamental, a project's *planning and phasing strategy* dictates how often working software is delivered to the client.

Waterfall approaches to software development attempt to deliver software in one large drop at the end of the project, sometimes years, but generally many months, after the start of the project. Often, but not necessarily, waterfall approaches to development are tied to heavyweight, highly formalized logical processes such as SSADM (to give one example). Planning therefore tends to focus on the timing of the analysis phase, the design phase, and so on.

Iterative and incremental development approaches put the focus on delivering software at shorter intervals and gradually building up a full set of functionality over a period of time. Different approaches mandate different delivery timescales, but these are in general between a couple of weeks to 3 or 4 months. At the core of planning an iterative and incremental project is the decision of what functionality or features are to be delivered in what iteration of the project. The risk-reducing benefits of incremental development are (thankfully) generally accepted in the software development industry nowadays. However, few approaches explicitly deal with the downside of this approach—that the requirements of later increments may mandate a redesign (and subsequent code refactoring) of existing code if the system is not to be put into a state of terminal decline (as often happened in waterfall projects once the much-ignored maintenance phase was reached).

We discuss planning and phasing further in Chapter 9.

Human-Centric and Communication Issues

Do we situate the team in one or multiple locations (assuming we have the choice)? Do we encourage communication through the use of whiteboards and well-positioned "information radiators" (or via e-mail of electronic models)? Are team members assigned specific roles, or do we let roles emerge naturally? Is the development team actually a team? Do the team members pull together and help each other, or are they sniping at each other all the time? Are the team members' aspirations, desires, and motivations being harnessed correctly by the project?

These concerns are, of course, mostly orthogonal to the logical process and planning/phasing strategy adopted by the project, although it can be argued that incremental development assists in team motivation as team members actually get to see the results of their labor in use at regular intervals.

We further discuss human-centric and communications issues later in this chapter.

Working Practices

Related to communication issues are the regular *working practices* employed by a project:

- Adopting daily stand-up or weekly sit-down team meetings
- Having (or not having) a formal review of prospective designs
- Ensuring a full set of automated functional tests is kept running at all times
- Putting time aside to refactor bad code when the need arises
- Adopting a code-based test-first design approach
- And so on

We also discuss working practices in the context of various agile processes in Chapter 4.

Guiding Philosophy

Our approach to the aspects of software development just mentioned may be guided by an overall "philosophy," different flavors of which have been popular at various points in time. The following list presents some examples that we've attacked with our sense-of-humor hats on (also see Figure 2-3):

Hacking: More a non-philosophy, this approach to development is, unfortunately, still present in the software industry. Most often the home of the "unconsciously unconscious," hacking's primary prerequisite is to ignore any consideration of the issues we've just discussed—or any other issues important to good software development, come to that.

Agile: This philosophy is currently very much in vogue (hey, we're writing this book, aren't we?). The overriding objective is to deliver working software that does what your customer wants. All other aspects of the way you run your project are customized to this end and may change dynamically if they aren't working. This is the first philosophy to really focus on human-centric issues. Momentarily confused with hacking by some, it has enough flavors to meet most needs.

Formalism: Still with its (generally university-based) advocates, this philosophy involves proving (or at least knowing that you could prove) in a mathematic fashion that your software does what it's supposed to do—and then not bothering to implement it as you've done the really interesting bit already. Generally, it has nothing to say about the human-centric or working-practices aspects of running a project, and very often little about logical process.

High ceremony: Often seen on government projects or driven with the needs of the quality assurance (QA) department's ISO8811-77c.44 certification in mind, this approach involves following and documenting every step of whatever logical process you've adopted (regardless of its relevance to your particular circumstances) to the *n*th degree. Sometimes characteristic of organizations that tend to ignore human-centric concerns, this philosophy's most common working practice is ensuring all the right boxes are ticked, even if you have to pretend you've done the activity (one of the authors was really involved in doing this once). It's often associated with waterfall development. Also, it's generally inflexible, in that you can't adjust things to meet your actual needs. One underlying assumption is that monitoring software development is akin to monitoring a well-defined industrial process, such as silicon-chip manufacturing or photographic-film production.

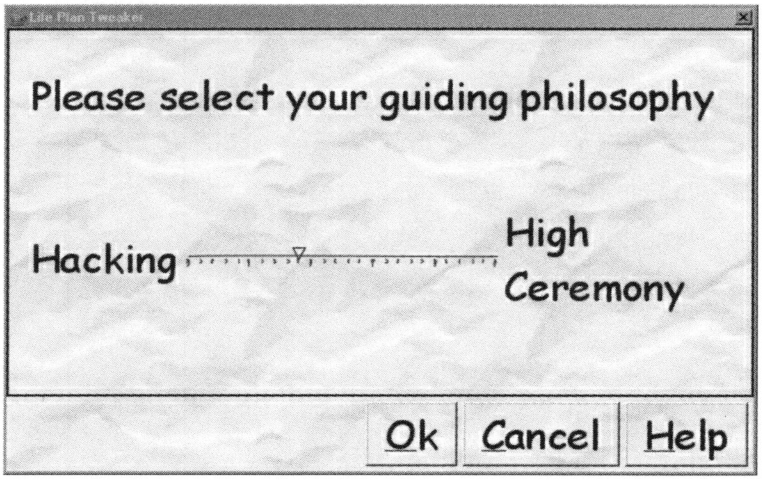

Figure 2-3. *Sliding from Hacking to High Ceremony*

What Makes a Good Agile Logical Process?

Having discussed the elements that make up a software development approach, we're now going to examine in a bit more detail the qualities we should look for in a logical process.

We Need an Obvious Logical Flow

While in an agile context, we're unlikely to formally record traceability between deliverables, but it should at least be conceptually possible to trace from the earlier to the later deliverables. We must be able to see how the whole process hangs together, otherwise we'll start making the wrong decisions as we model. In this sense, many earlier deliverables can be seen as abstractions (high-level views with detailed information missing) of later deliverables. For example, the classes in a first-cut domain model with no attributes or methods are likely to still be present in the final code of the system.

ICONIX Process meets this criterion by giving us four major stopover points on our way to working software:

- *Requirements analysis*, consisting of UI prototyping, use case identification, and domain modeling
- *Analysis and preliminary design*, consisting of detailed descriptions of use cases, robustness analysis, and a more fleshed-out domain model
- *Detailed design*, consisting of sequence diagramming and class modeling
- *Implementation*, consisting of code development and unit, integration, and system testing

We Don't Want Unnecessary Dependencies Slowing Us Down

Instead, we want closely related deliverables to be grouped together. Our motivation in using a development process is to speed up and decrease the risk of the overall development, not to slow it down. Processes with unnecessary dependencies and/or poor grouping of deliverables are likely to slow us down if we adhere too strictly to them. A process that, for example, dictates that we develop a full set of use cases before we start a domain model will suffer from this problem.

Agile ICONIX avoids this problem by grouping heavily interrelated deliverables into the same basic step, assisting us in following Scott Ambler's agile modeling principle of iterating to another model.[3] Domain modeling and use case analysis, for example, are clearly interrelated activities. Use case descriptions cross-reference the entities in the domain model, and by iterating between the two models, the process builds an inherent consistency into its approach, while enabling each technique to reinforce the other.

We Want Each Step to Clearly Move Us Toward Our True Goal of Working Software

A development process can be viewed as a sequence of steps to turn a fairly vague initial requirement into a solid software deliverable. Each step within the process must first and foremost add value, taking us nearer to our true goal of working software. To achieve this, the work we produce in each step must be structured to make the next steps easier. We'll need to iterate to the next step, whether formally or informally, to ensure we're making true progress.

For example, take the approach used within older-style processes such as SSADM. Analysis in SSADM was performed using, among other things, data flow diagrams (DFDs), which, while they undoubtedly assisted the analysts in clarifying their ideas, offered little or no assistance to the design and development team in structuring the software. Much of the work undertaken during analysis had to be redone, with the designers having to completely restructure analysis results. OO methods and notation avoid this pitfall to some degree, but some are still prone to this problem in some areas.

Again, each of the four basic steps in the Agile ICONIX process meets this requirement:

- *Requirements analysis* takes us from a vague list of requirements to a detailed description of the use cases that will make up the functional design of our system.
- *Analysis and preliminary design* gives us an accurate domain model of the system—an important step if we are to truly deliver the right system to our users.
- *Detailed design* gives us the fundamental class structure we are going to implement.
- *Implementation* gives us our working system.

Note that Agile ICONIX is an inherently incremental process, so each of these four steps typically addresses a subset of the overall system, with each increment building on the previous one.

We Want Guidance That Will Reduce Unnecessary Work Later On

We're faced with many decisions when writing software. It's important that we understand that some decisions are more important than others—there are *high-impact* decisions and there are *low-impact* decisions. High-impact decisions are those that will have a pervasive effect across our software and models. These decisions tend to be "architectural" in nature. Take, for example, the effect of changing a single-user system to be a concurrent multiuser system. This is a very high-impact change, and it will most likely affect a large percentage of our software. Low-impact decisions, on the other hand, are those that will have only a localized impact. Changing the implementation of a many-to-one relationship from a vector to a linked list is such a decision—its impact is clearly very limited.

---

3. This is the Agile Modeling core practice "Iterate to Another Artifact" (Scott W. Ambler, *Agile Modeling: Effective Practices for eXtreme Programming and the Unified Process* [Hoboken, NJ: John Wiley & Sons, 2002], p. 44). The premise is that each modeling artifact (use case, business process diagram, robustness diagram, etc.) provides insight into a particular area, so if you find yourself getting stuck on one artifact, try switching iteratively to a different artifact to get unstuck.

From a logical process perspective, therefore, we'd like assistance in ensuring that we focus on high-impact decisions at an appropriate stage. Effectively, agility is about knowing which decisions have high impact and which decisions can be changed easily on the fly. By focusing our effort on the right decisions, we increase our agility.

ICONIX Process assists in this by putting a clear focus on understanding requirements, enabling us to get as much as possible of the "right system" developed in the first place, and also by recognizing that not all requirements are functional (i.e., can be expressed in use case terms) and that we must pay appropriate attention to these as well. Domain modeling enables us to get a grip on the fundamental way in which users perceive the "real world" and to build a system that meets this perception. Detailed class modeling helps us get more of our code right first time, reducing the need for unnecessary refactoring.

Being inherently incremental, Agile ICONIX does this without throwing away the benefits of empirical feedback. *You get more right the first time, but if you (or your customer) do get it wrong, you can improve the system in the next increment.* Agile ICONIX takes the best of both process-driven and feedback-driven approaches to software development, providing a truly agile and cost-effective approach to satisfying customer needs.

We Want Help Prioritizing, Scoping, Planning and Estimating, and Monitoring Work

We need a logical process that will help us scope and prioritize the work we're going to undertake. We'll usually achieve this by using deliverable structure (e.g., use cases) as the basis for discussion of what is important and what isn't. Similarly, we'd like help in estimating how long work will take to complete, and we'd like a way to monitor our actual progress against our estimates to improve later estimating. A good logical process like Agile ICONIX will help us here by providing a structure upon which we can base and monitor our estimates.

We Want Broad Steps That Provide General Guidance

Given the rate of technology change in our business, many elements of software development are empirical in nature. We can't attempt to provide a foolproof "algorithmic" sequence of micro-instructions describing how to go about writing software. An agile process like ICONIX doesn't do this. It provides a broad-stroke sequence of granular steps—signposts, if you like—that help point us in the direction of our ultimate goal of a working software system.

We Don't Have to Do Every Step (to the *N*th Degree)

When we use an agile logical process, we are in charge, not the process. We have to always "model with a purpose," to borrow a phrase from Scott Ambler, and make intelligent decisions about which deliverables to work on and when to stop working on them. The process is there to provide broad guidance, not to dictate our every action. Take care, however, not to skip a step just because you want to get to coding as soon as possible. Intelligent decision-making requires an evaluation of the pros and cons of the situation, and each step in the Agile ICONIX process has a clearly defined objective.

We Can Undertake Additional Activities (Coding, in Particular) at Any Point

As we discussed previously, some decisions are more important than others. We want to minimize the chance of getting high-impact decisions wrong, and to do this we need to follow Scott Ambler's principle of "prove it with code." We want to round-trip the development process to produce some working software that proves our decisions are correct. Agile logical processes like ICONIX don't preclude us from undertaking other activities, in particular coding, that we deem appropriate at any point.

To summarize, our primary objective is to deliver reliable working software. If we adopt a development process, we do so because we believe it will help us meet that objective. An agile development process in particular is a development process that assists us in applying our overall agile philosophy and doesn't constrain us in ways that violate the principles we are following.

Human Factors

That it is people who write software is terribly obvious . . . and ignored.[4]

So quotes Alistair Cockburn (himself quoting Gerald Weinberg) in his book *Agile Software Development*. While it is beyond the scope of this book to give the full coverage to the teamwork, communication, and interpersonal aspects of software development, we would be doing a disservice to our readers if we didn't touch on these topics to some degree. That is the purpose of this section.

Choosing the Right Team

Probably the most important decisions you will make—if charged with running a project—relate to selecting the people to work on the project. Getting this right requires matching the people to the technology and skill roles, while also making sure you get the right team dynamics.

From a technology point of view, getting skills in the right technology (Java, C#, etc.) is important, but it's perhaps overstated (in job advertisements, at least). A good software developer will be able to learn a lot on the job given the opportunity. Noncore skills may also be important. Do some team members need to be able to write well? Do they need a good understanding of testing? Do they need to be able to present ideas clearly? Do they need good questioning skills? A good understanding of the broader skill needs of your project is important in selecting the right team.

On the team dynamics front, it's important to get a mixture of personality types and behavioral styles. A good team is like a good diet: well balanced (with apologies to Atkins devotees). In particular, having too many people who want to occupy the same "space" can cause conflicts.

One particular system of team-player classification that we've found useful was developed by Dr. R. Meredith Belbin. It identifies various roles and highlights their strengths and weaknesses (see `www.belbin.com/belbin-team-roles.htm`).

Team Buy-in

If you select a group of intelligent and able people, and then you try to dictate every decision to them, you may as well have not bothered in the first place. For a team to work effectively, it must feel a sense of ownership of the work it undertakes, be that with respect to the development process or any other aspects of the project. This applies equally to the development approach.

Having said that, most people are prepared to give things a try if they believe their feedback is going to be taken into account. By holding well-chaired (increment-based) regular reviews of major working practices, you can maintain a sense of ownership and self-determination. This approach will also have the not insubstantial side effect of actually improving the practices themselves!

One area of particular importance in software development is getting team buy-in on project timescales. We discuss the trade-off between scope and timescales in Chapter 9, but getting developers to estimate and monitor the time spent on their own work is particularly important if you want them to actually try to meet the estimates.

Motivation

Understanding what motivates people is a difficult topic; every person has different motivations.

Remuneration is obviously important, but as Alistair Cockburn discusses as some length in his book *Agile Software Development*, developers are also motivated by contributing something of value and having that contribution recognized. This illustrates that software developers are, perhaps counter to some perceptions, human beings with feelings after all! Failure to give feedback that clearly demonstrates the developers' value can often lead to an unmotivated team.

---

4. Alistair Cockburn, *Agile Software Development* (New York: Addison-Wesley, 2001).

On a more individual level, if you take the time to understand how each team member sees himself progressing in his career, it will be possible to harness his desires to the benefit of the project as a whole. By understanding the skills the team members will need to fulfill their envisaged future roles, and matching these against the needs of the current project, you can create a win-win situation that benefits all. Most people want to learn and progress, and doing the thing they already know best can sometimes be tedious. So giving people the opportunity to learn something new can be the right move (bearing in mind, of course, the risk associated with the activity in question).

Levels of Ability

In *Agile Software Development*, Cockburn discusses three distinct "levels" at which people may work:[5]

- Following (early stages of learning, often accompanied by step-by-step guidance)
- Detaching (trying out new ways of doing things)
- Transcending (fluency)

A not dissimilar classification has four stages of learning:

- Unconsciously unconscious stage (you don't know it, and you don't know you don't know it)
- Consciously unconscious stage (you've at least worked out what you don't know)
- Consciously conscious stage (you're learning and doing, but you're actively having to think about it)
- Unconsciously conscious stage (you know it, and you don't really even have to think about it)

Both approaches are useful in determining who is best suited to undertake a particular role and the level of support, guidance, and mentoring she'll need to do so.

Feedback

A simple rule to follow is to *always give as much positive feedback as you do negative*. It is all too easy to give a misleading impression of your opinion of someone by only pointing out mistakes.

Communication

A couple of years ago, one of the authors chaired a conference panel session made up of the great and the good from both industry and academia. The session was entitled "What Is Software Architecture?" Surely, there could be no disagreement over the meaning of "software architecture," a fundamental term in our industry. Wrong! Definitions varied between "the components and their interrelationships that make up a system" to "the runtime deployment structure of a system" to "the patterns and styles of development that are used in the development of a system." We passed a happy hour discussing the pros and cons of these various alternative definitions—without, of course, coming to any concrete conclusion at the end.

The fact is that miscommunication is rife in the software development industry. Given the invisible and abstract nature of the things we have to communicate about (e.g., threads, processes, classes, control flows, etc.), and that we often have to delve into domains of which we have no previous experience (e.g., finance, healthcare), this is perhaps not so difficult to understand. Almost every term we use is loaded with multiple meanings, and if you ever have to visit different companies on a consultancy basis, one of the first challenges you'll face is reconciling your understanding of a term with your client's (potentially multiple) uses of the same term.

Misunderstandings and miscommunication can occur on a daily basis within teams if team members are not on their guard. On many occasions, we've seen people discuss an issue and apparently agree on a resolution, only to come back to each other later saying, "But we agreed to do this . . ."—the only problem being that the "this" in question was misinterpreted by the parties involved.

5. Ibid.

We all carry our own baggage with us (this is often called "experience") and our perceptions of what we think is important. Our understanding of terminology or what someone else is saying is inevitably clouded by this "baggage." Unfortunately (or perhaps fortunately), we all have different experiences, so faced with the inevitable holes in what we actually "say" to each other (be that verbally—face to face—or in writing), it is our differing experiences that may well fill the gaps.

The only thing we can do to rectify these types of misunderstandings is establish a culture of communication in our project teams and encourage everyone to accept responsibility for avoiding miscommunication. The sections that follow present some techniques that can help in establishing this type of culture.

Establish a Common Vocabulary

Developing the domain model and use cases in Agile ICONIX gives us an opportunity to establish a common and well-understood set of problem domain terms. During the development of these artifacts, working hard to be as concise and consistent as possible will reduce miscommunication down the line.

Display Major Artifacts Visibly

To encourage a common understanding of what you're doing, you should display major ICONIX artifacts visibly in your development area (on a bulletin board on the wall, if possible). In particular, these are all ideal candidates for public display:

- Domain model diagrams
- Use case summary diagrams
- Subsystem/package decompositions and dependencies (not, per se, ICONIX, but . . .)
- Key interaction diagrams/class model fragments (e.g., a typical persistence subsystem interaction)

Drive Your Development Based on Feedback

Being feedback driven is at the heart of Agile ICONIX, and for good reason: nothing reveals misunderstandings as dramatically as having to round-trip the whole development process at regular intervals. Doing this will bring any communication issues—be they within the team (analyst to developer, developer to developer) or between the customer and the team—sharply into focus. Identifying and actively reducing miscommunication will help you deliver the right working software to your clients.

Get Test-Driven Requirements Feedback

Another useful technique is to have one developer generate tests for a particular part of a system and another developer implement that part of the system. The chances of two developers both misunderstanding requirements in the same way are fairly remote, so miscommunication is likely to manifest itself as a divergence between expected and actual test results. We discuss Test-Driven Development (TDD) further in Chapters 11 and 12. We also describe a process for automatically creating test cases from control objects on UML diagrams (see the last few pages of Chapter 12).

Review Misunderstandings

ICONIX Process encourages reviews at regular intervals, and particular attention should be paid to potential miscommunication during these.

Ask and Answer

Be willing to both ask questions of others and answer their questions. It's very easy when developing software to get into "head-down" mode; sometimes the silence of development teams can be quite overwhelming! But remember, software development is most often a team-based activity, and that means members must be willing to ask questions of others when necessary and answer questions when asked. RTFM isn't the desired response in a high-communication environment.

The following are some further tips for communicating effectively in a team environment:
When you're listening

- Be careful when making assumptions about what a person is saying to you.
- Restate what has been said to you in your own words.
- Demonstrate your understanding by stating the logical consequences of what has been said, and request confirmation that these consequences are correct.
- Ask questions that probe the point(s) being raised in such a manner as to confirm your understanding (and to keep you interested in what is being said).
- Most of all, don't be afraid to say you don't understand!

When you're speaking

- Check understanding by weaving questions into your dialogue that require thought and comprehension to answer correctly.
- Be interactive to keep your listeners interested.
- Look for visual cues that your listeners have (or haven't) understood correctly.
- Use diagrams, analogies, and so forth to clarify your points.

When you're writing

- Say it in as few words as possible (but not too few). Avoid obfuscatory scrivenery.
- Directly address any misunderstandings you've encountered before (say, during increment reviews).
- Use terms consistently, to an agreed standard (e.g., domain model). Writing prose and writing technical specs are different things—don't use another word just for the sake of doing so when talking about technical items.
- Do try and keep your readers' interest (the odd enticing forward reference or bit of humor can sometimes help here).

When you're reading

- Expect to read it twice—the first time to raise questions, and the second time to look for answers to those questions.
- Build a list of questions that come to mind as you read during the first pass.
- Look for answers to unanswered questions during the second pass.
- If it is a very long, dry text, take regular coffee breaks!

Agile Fact or Fiction: Team Structure and Human Factors

Agility is a subjective thing. For example, if you design your software before coding it, does that mean you're not agile? You'll find that everyone has a slightly different interpretation of agility, so for fun, we've provided a set of agile statements—some common viewpoints of what agility is or isn't—and asked each of our co-authors to provide his viewpoint on whether each statement is fact or fiction.

There are two schools of management thought:

- *Theory X*: The average human being dislikes all work and will avoid it if possible. People must be coerced, offered inducements, and threatened with punishment to do work, and they need to be directed in all their activities.
- *Theory Y*: Work is as natural and as much fun as play. People have the capacity for self-management, and true motivation arises from intrinsic needs such as self-esteem, achievement, and learning. People, if allowed, will accept responsibility, and can be creative and team spirited.

Agility, in theory at least, promotes theory Y. But naturally, there's more to it than that . . .

Being Agile Means Placing a Strong Emphasis on Human Factors

Mark: Human factors are vitally important in any multiperson, team-oriented endeavor. And anyone who says otherwise should immediately be shot, or at least sent on a management training course. Team communication is vital—no doubt about that—and all those things that Alistair Cockburn emphasizes in *Agile Software Development* are definitely worthy of serious note. I do think, however, that Alistair's book could just as easily be targeted at, say, civil engineers instead of software engineers. And by this I mean that I don't think there is anything particularly unique about the human-factors issues in software development as opposed to many other disciplines. The only potential caveat here is that software development often attracts more introverted personalities—and I'm not sure how much this is the case in other scientific or engineering disciplines.

Matt: Human factors such as placement of office furniture and being nice to your fellow programmer are important, but I don't believe that they are a direct contributor to the core goal of agility, which is to reliably give the customer what he wants as quickly as possible. So, this idea is important but isn't really to do with agility (even though human factors are central to much of the agile discussion that goes on "out there").

Doug: Certainly a strong emphasis on human factors is a good thing. So if you define agility as "whatever is good," then it would be a fact. But if you define agility as the ability to respond to changing requirements, then a strong emphasis on human factors is really somewhat orthogonal. So, I'll say fiction.

Being Agile Means There Are No Role Divisions (Architect, Senior Developer) Within the Development Team—Everyone Is Equal

Doug: Fiction. Even if you take the titles away, people will still adopt roles. On the other hand, the divisions don't need to be strict, and it's certainly possible for one person to take on multiple roles.

Mark: This is a difficult one. I don't think people should be obsessed with job titles (garbage collection executives notwithstanding), but I do think different people have different skills. In most cases, there would be little point in assigning a recent college graduate to the role of system architect, for instance, during an early design phase. But I don't like overly hierarchical structures and am attracted to the idea of emergent roles. I'm a bit on the fence on this one.

Matt: Agile methods discourage specialization to an extent, but this tends to be specialization in terms of different areas of the product: Bob will work on module A; Sally will work on module B. So it's a good thing that this is discouraged, and everyone gets greater exposure to different areas of the product. But specialization in terms of roles is a different matter. Even on agile projects, you'll still find that one person is an architect, another person is a sysadmin, someone else specializes in SQL and DBA activities, and so on.

Being Agile Means the Team Must "Collectively Own" the Code Base (with No Room for Specialization)

Mark: Fiction—on balance. Having one person be the only one who can work on a particular area of code is never really a good idea; it makes the project vulnerable to that person leaving. On the other hand, there is a cost (in terms of lost development time) associated with everyone knowing everything—and different levels of skill and knowledge may make this impractical. The only advice I can give here is that you should distribute knowledge as much as possible across the team, given the constraints facing the project. Always try to have at least two people involved in any area of specialization, rotating these people in and out when possible.

Doug: Fiction. Different people have different experiences and expertise. It's silly not to take advantage of this. The "everybody knows everything about everything" philosophy doesn't work. A friend of mine once poetically expressed this in an e-mail: "So, it's okay if a proctologist does brain surgery, then?"[6]

Matt: Fiction. A general "atmosphere" of collective ownership isn't such a bad thing. Specialization, where one person "owns" and is responsible for a single part of the system, has some major drawbacks, not least of which is what happens when that person gets run over by a bus. A slightly less dramatic drawback is where one person ends up on the critical path because she's the only one who knows how her part of the system works. In other words, specialization can (and frequently does) create bottlenecks in the project plan.

But specialization also has its advantages. The main one (from what I've seen in almost every project I've worked on) is that people who are given responsibility for a subsystem take greater pride in their work. Specialization also prevents the annoying situation where a junior coder leaps in and "fixes" some code for you and forgets to tell you, resulting in a system that gets released with surprise bugs in it. So, fostering a general atmosphere of collective ownership, where it's mostly okay to make careful changes in other people's code (as long as you tell them), but where individuals retain responsibility for specific subsystems, is the way to go. So rather than collective ownership, let's call it "responsible ownership" and "collective responsibility."

Being Agile Means Your Entire Team Must Program in Pairs for All Production Code

Matt: Fiction. If your team members all enjoy pair programming, then why not? But not all programmers do enjoy it. I was called by an employment agency recently, and (before I could tell her I'm happy in my job, naturally!) the agent described an "agile" role available, but she complained that she was having great difficulty finding programmers who are prepared to pair program. It just isn't popular (at least not in the UK, it seems). So you need to keep in mind that mandating constant pair programming could seriously limit the field of software developers available to you. Any process that requires constant pair programming should be regarded with great caution.

Doug: Fiction. Constant mandatory pair programming is problematic for reasons we explored at length in *Extreme Programming Refactored: The Case Against XP*, although voluntary pair programming as appropriate is certainly fine. However, pair programming makes a poor substitute for doing a good job at design.

Mark: Fiction. Some pairing up during both design and development is a good idea, but it is not mandatory by any means for a project to be agile.

Being Agile Means There Is No Need for Testers—the Developers Can Test the System Themselves

Doug: Fiction. It's a great thing to have programmers unit testing and regression testing their code, but this is an entirely different activity and involves a different mind-set from having independent QA folks who are actively trying to break the code.

---

6. Chuck Suscheck, private e-mail to Doug Rosenberg, January 2004.

Matt: Programmers are paid to create, whereas QA testers are paid to destroy. If a programmer finds a bug, that's a minus point, but if a tester finds a bug, she gets a gold star. So if programmers are doing their own QA, there's a serious conflict of interest.

Mark: Fiction, on any sizeable project at least. While it's important that all developers take responsibility for testing their own software to some degree, my experience is that they won't find all the bugs. The last thing I want when running a project is to leave it to the customer to find all the bugs, so on any sizeable project I'd recommend some degree of nondeveloper testing.

Being Agile Means You Can Get Top Results with Mediocre Developers

Doug: Fiction. Of course most teams will contain some developers of average or mediocre skill. So your odds of success will generally be in proportion to the average skill level across your team. I don't think "agile or not" really changes this equation very much.

Matt: A common maxim among managers in the know is, "The best methodology is simply to hire top developers and let them get on with it." This is absolutely true. Why wouldn't you want to hire the top people in any field? Ranging from top-notch prospect down to the basement, most clueless developer, would you want a developer who is, say, 10% clueless? 50%? Someone who doesn't know what he's doing inevitably creates more work: bad designs that need to be refactored, bugs, misleading code, and so on. Or he may take several weeks to do something that a real programmer could do in a day. Applying any methodology, agile or otherwise, doesn't change this basic fact.

Mark: Fiction. If you're responsible for a project, probably the single most important decision you will make is selecting the right people for the project, in terms of raw ability, knowledge of the relevant technologies, general project experience and, most important, willingness to work effectively as part of a team.

Being Agile Means You Can Work Only with Top Developers

Doug: Fiction. Although the higher your percentage of top developers, agile or not, the greater your chances of success.

Mark: Fiction, in that you can adopt agile practices regardless of the ability of your team, the only caveat being that the team members must be willing to adopt the practices. But you can't get away from the fact that the better the people on the team—in terms of the criteria mentioned in the last question—the better the results you will get.

Matt: Fiction. You could probably get away with not hiring clued-up developers; the economics might just work out in your favor. But by definition, the top developers will do a better job.

Being Agile Means There Is Never a Role for Analysts

Mark: Fiction, as I've already said, although with the caveat that I prefer developer analysts.

Doug: Fiction. I'll refer the reader to the discussions in our example project for details.

Matt: Fiction. Pretty much any project will benefit from having someone skilled in the art of extracting the correct requirements from the customer and end users. Programmers (me included, I suspect) will code something that we think is cool, believing that we're giving the customer what he wants, but an analyst will make sure that what we're creating exactly addresses the customer's business requirements.

Being Agile Means You Must Work in a Single Office with a Good Seating Arrangement and Lots of Whiteboards

Mark: Fact, in the sense that working across multiple sites will definitely decrease your agility, and that a good seating arrangement (so the team members can talk to each other without leaving their desks) and lots of whiteboards for discussions or for important information will significantly improve your agility.

Doug: Fiction—not to say that these are necessarily bad things. Personally, I still think there's a place for private offices where you can get quiet time to sit and think. But to build seating arrangements into your software process is pretty risky business. Many projects get done with distributed teams in multiple locations (again, see the example in this book). This practice, in conjunction with an overreliance on oral communication and a full-time on-site customer, to the exclusion of written requirements and UML models that can be e-mailed around (for example), can contribute to a process that's fragile rather than agile. If it works out that you can set up your project in a single location and all of your team members like working in a shared space, that's great. But it's a risky thing to bet your project's success on how the furniture is arranged.

Matt: Fiction. Working within a single office is good if your team is small enough. But your process shouldn't stipulate this. Some people like to work from home, and there's no reason they shouldn't. Many programmers simply prefer peace and solitude in which to program. If they're forced to work in a noisy cattle-pen environment, they'll likely disappear behind headphones so they can get some work done. Personally, I think that the office arrangement has no bearing on the goals of agility; it just helps or hinders productivity, an important but separate issue.

Having lots of whiteboard space is a good thing, but I have found that if one group leaps up and starts discussing a design issue, sketching away wildly at the whiteboard like it's a Rolf Harris convention, that can be quite disruptive to other programmers in the same room. So it pays to have a separate room for team design workshops and to encourage the habit of darting out there often to draw on the whiteboard and talk away.

Of course, this raises the question, when are the decisions communicated back to the rest of the team? The answer is partly in the question: the *decisions* are communicated back to the team (e.g., at the following morning's team update meeting), not the hour of discussion and/or unproductive argument that led up to each decision.

Summary

In this chapter, we set a primary goal for this book of identifying the sweet spot between agile, feedback-driven software processes and disciplined, plan-driven software processes. We then dissected a software process into its subcomponents and analyzed each subcomponent individually, discussing the trade-offs that you can make within each layer. We followed that with a "fact or fiction" discussion that focused on the human-centric communication issues related to software process.

The next chapter presents a brief introduction to ICONIX Process, a use case–driven approach that uses a minimalist core subset of UML. In Chapter 4, we'll next attempt to define a minimalist core subset of agile practices. Then we'll see how close we came to the sweet spot by exploring the design and code for our example project.

CHAPTER 3

ICONIX Process: A Core UML Subset

In this chapter, we provide an overview of ICONIX Process, a minimal object modeling process that is well suited to agile development. This overview should give you enough information to get started using the modeling techniques in your own project. For an in-depth description of ICONIX Process, see Doug's previous two books, *Use Case Driven Object Modeling with UML: A Practical Approach*[1] and *Applying Use Case Driven Object Modeling with UML*.[2]

Note Doug and Matt are currently under contract with Addison-Wesley to replace the two previously mentioned titles with a combined title: *Use Case Driven Object Modeling: Theory and Practice*.[3]

You'll find that we don't cover software agility much in this chapter. We're presenting ICONIX Process as a core object modeling process, then in Chapter 4 we'll add a "layer" of agile practices on top, and in Part 2 of this book we'll show an example of how to apply Agile ICONIX to a real-life project.

Note In later chapters we provide lots of practical examples to show exactly how ICONIX Process is applied. So in reading this chapter, you might find it useful to skip ahead and look at some of the later examples. Similarly, when reading the later chapters in detail, you might find it useful to refer back to this chapter frequently to get a reminder of the underlying theory.

---

1. Doug Rosenberg and Kendall Scott, *Use Case Driven Object Modeling with UML: A Practical Approach* (New York: Addison-Wesley, 1999).
2. Doug Rosenberg and Kendall Scott, *Applying Use Case Driven Object Modeling with UML* (New York: Addison-Wesley, 2001).
3. Doug Rosenberg, Matt Stephens, and Kendall Scott, *Use Case Driven Object Modeling: Theory and Practice* (New York: Addison-Wesley, 2005).

Figure 3-1 shows how ICONIX Process defines a practical core subset of the Unified Modeling Language (UML). This diagram ties in with Figure 4-1, which shows how Agile ICONIX defines a core subset of agile practices.

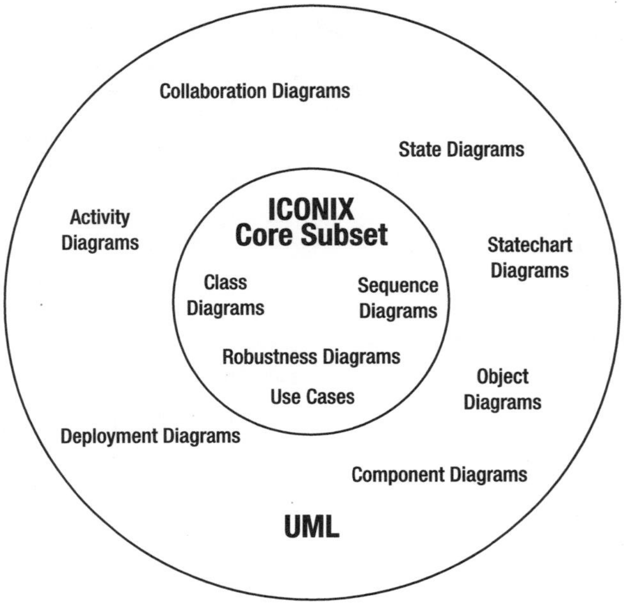

Figure 3-1. *ICONIX Process core UML subset*

A Brief History of ICONIX Process

In this section, Doug explains the history and background of ICONIX Process.

ICONIX Process originated several years before the UML and the Unified Process as a synthesis and distillation of the best techniques from the original methodologies that formed the UML: Jim Rumbaugh's Object Modeling Technique (OMT), Ivar Jacobson's Objectory method, and Grady Booch's Booch method.

We attempted a synthesis of these three very different schools of object-oriented (OO) thought because the strengths and weaknesses of these methodologies seemed to complement each another. OMT was useful for *problem domain* (analysis-level) modeling, but it was not as strong for *solution space* (detailed design) class modeling, while the Booch method was strong at the detailed level but unintuitive at the analysis level. The Objectory method took Booch's concept of a dynamic model and extended it with a step-by-step approach that leads cleanly from a use case view to a detailed design (sequence diagram) view of the runtime behavior. Both OMT and the Booch method were stronger for static (class) modeling, while the Objectory method is mostly focused on dynamic runtime behavior. Booch also introduced component and deployment views of the system.

Rather than taking the complete contents of three 400-page methodology books and encompassing everything about everything (see *The Unified Modeling Language User Guide*[4]), we preferred to focus on a core subset of these techniques that removed the redundancy and overlap from the notations. For example, both sequence and collaboration diagrams show essentially the same thing: a runtime view of object collaboration. These views are so redundant that you can draw a sequence diagram in Rational Rose, press F5, and automatically generate a collaboration diagram.

4. Grady Booch, James Rumbaugh, and Ivar Jacobson, *The Unified Modeling Language User Guide* (New York: Addison-Wesley, 1998).

Over the decade or so that we've been teaching this material, we discovered that most people generally prefer learning (and using) a smaller set of diagrams over a larger set, and we were able to consistently get good results by focusing our students more intensively on a smaller set of diagrams.[5] Ultimately, we wound up with a *UML core subset* consisting of the following:

- *Class diagrams*, at both an analysis (problem domain) and design (Booch) level of abstraction.
- *Use cases* (diagrams and text).
- *Sequence diagrams*. We skipped collaboration diagrams because they were redundant, and we deemphasized state diagrams because we discovered that many projects needed fewer of them than we anticipated if project teams rigorously created sequence diagrams.
- *Robustness diagrams*. We "rescued" these from Jacobson's Objectory work because we discovered that use case–driven development simply worked better with these diagrams than without them.

What Can ICONIX Process Do for My Project?

ICONIX Process is a cookbook-style guide that describes how to get from use cases to code. As such, its main concern is with the analysis and design modeling aspects of software production.

If ICONIX Process had a mission statement, it would be this:

Root out ambiguity from the requirements, and then do a clean design.

There's a good reason for taking this approach. Inconsistently written use cases immediately give you ambiguity to resolve. If the ambiguity isn't addressed, then it wends its way into the full set of use cases, the design, and (worst of all) the source code. This in turn leads to all sorts of costly, insidious bugs. That's why it's important to root out the ambiguity as early as possible—right back at the requirements analysis stage.

ICONIX Process provides the low-level logical process: how to get from use cases to code in a specific, repeatable manner. What it doesn't specifically address is the high-level organization of a project, which agile methodologies tend to address. As we discussed in Chapter 1, it's these high-level organizational areas that usually vary the most from project to project, so these parts of any process need to be the most flexible.

Working code that meets the requirements and is developed in a timely manner is what it's all about. ICONIX Process' *safety nets* of written requirements and written use cases make it easy to verify that the code meets the requirements.

ICONIX Process is also about avoiding *analysis paralysis*. We are very much opposed to high-ceremony methodologies that demand that you produce X, Y, and Z layers of documentation, and dot every "i" and cross every "t" before proceeding to the next stage. ICONIX Process, by contrast, is lightweight and highly iterative, and it's focused on getting you to the source code as quickly as possible (but without throwing away the benefits of an up-front analysis and design process).

ICONIX Process in Theory (aka Disambiguation and Prefactoring)

ICONIX Process is about driving a software design from behavior requirements, one step at a time. In other words, it's about writing the user manual first (or at least a couple of paragraphs of it at a time, in the form of use cases); double checking the use cases to ensure that we've accounted for both sunny-day and rainy-day scenarios, and that the behavior description we've written down is really the behavior that the users want; making sure we've defined a set of objects (classes, really) that can collaborate to implement the required behavior; and then checking that we have the right set of attributes and operations on those classes.

5. We're happy to note that some enlightened visual modeling tool vendors have recognized that the UML is just too big for many folks and that a core subset is much easier to work with. For example, the Enterprise Architect tool from Sparx Systems, which fully supports UML2, and which we used for the example project in this book, offers an "ICONIX Process visual layout" that hides about 70% of the UML from users who prefer a minimalist, streamlined approach to modeling.

When working through the various steps of ICONIX Process, what we're really doing is distilling the behavior requirements to a more complete, more precise, and less ambiguous form. In other words, we're disambiguating the behavior requirements and then driving the software design from these disambiguated requirements. So we make sure that we're building the right system (i.e., we understand the required behavior) and then that we're building the system right (i.e., we define a well-factored set of classes with appropriate attributes and methods that will implement the required behavior). In short, disambiguation of requirements is about *building the right system*, and prefactoring of the design is about *building the system right*.

In ICONIX Process, everything has a primary purpose:

- *Use case text*: Define the behavior requirements.
- *Domain model*: Describe the real-world objects and relationships.
- *Robustness diagram*: Disambiguate the behavior requirements (and tie them to the object model).
- *Sequence diagram*: Allocate behavior (i.e., assign functions to classes).

So you repeat the following for every scenario you're going to build:

1. Define the behavior requirements.
2. Disambiguate the behavior requirements and tie them to the object model.
3. Assign functions to classes.

This is the essence of use case–driven development.

Three key principles underlie the approach, which, as you can see, is inside out, outside in, and top down, all at the same time:

- Work inward from the requirements.
- Work outward from the domain objects.
- Drill down from high-level models to detailed design.

What Is a Use Case?

A *use case* is a sequence of actions that an actor (usually a person, but perhaps an external entity, such as another system) performs within a system to achieve a particular goal.

A use case is most effectively stated from the perspective of the user as a present-tense verb phrase in active voice. For example, one use case within a travel website might be called "Find Hotel," while a portfolio system is likely to contain use cases named "Do Trade Entry," "Update Portfolio Information," and "Generate Reports."

A complete and unambiguous use case describes one aspect of the system without presuming any specific design or implementation. The result of use case modeling should be that all required system functionality is described in the use cases. If you don't adhere to this basic principle, you run the risk of having your bright engineers build a cool system that isn't what your customers want.

Tip Don't waste time with long and involved use case templates. Templates that include sections for preconditions, postconditions, and so forth tend to be a real energy drain and don't give much in return. A use case should be a short, succinct statement of a user's interaction with the system to achieve a specific goal—nothing more.

THE TWO-PARAGRAPH RULE

A useful rule of thumb when writing use cases is to limit them to a maximum of two paragraphs. If the use case text goes beyond this, it probably wants to be more than one use case.

This two-paragraph rule (or guideline) is intended to make it easier to create a sequence diagram for every use case in the model. We intend to bring each of our use case scenarios to code, and we aim to prefactor our design and make sure we've done a good, clean allocation of behavior (assigning operations to classes) using sequence diagrams. Two paragraphs is not an absolute, but two sentences is too small to bother with, and two pages is too long. The happy medium lies somewhere around two paragraphs.

If you've ever tried to read a sequence diagram for a three-page use case, the reason for the two-paragraph rule is obvious. You won't be able to print the sequence diagram on an 8×10 sheet of paper in any font that a human can read. Therefore, your diagram won't be able to be reviewed, either by yourself or by your peers. It will also contain more errors than a diagram that is comprehensible and reviewable.

MODELING QUESTION: IS A USE CASE A REQUIREMENT?

The relationship between requirements and use cases is the subject of much heated debate in the OO community. Here's a handy mantra to sum up the answer:

> *Requirements are requirements, use cases are use cases; requirements are not use cases, use cases are not requirements.*

However (it just wasn't going to be that easy, was it?), use cases *are* really behavior requirements. Here's a slightly more elaborate way of distinguishing use cases from requirements:

- A use case describes a unit of behavior.
- A requirement describes a law that governs behavior.
- A use case can satisfy one or more functional requirements.
- A functional requirement may be satisfied by one or more use cases.

Note our use of the words "may" and "functional." A system will have its share of functional requirements, but it will also have other types of requirements, such as those involving performance and maintainability, that won't map well to use cases.

One of the really common use case modeling errors is to try to do everything in use cases. However, by remembering to keep nonfunctional requirements out of the use cases, the whole thing becomes a lot easier: just keep a separate list of requirements (which may include some behavior requirements at a high level), and fill in the functional details via use cases.

What Is an Actor?

An *actor* represents a role a user can play with regard to a system or an entity, such as another system or a database, that will reside outside the system being modeled. The total set of actors within a use case model reflects everything that needs to exchange information with the system. Within a hotel booking system (see the example project in Part 2), actors may include Travel Agent Staff, Administrative Staff, and end users (people going on the web to book hotels). A portfolio system would have actors called Risk Manager and Trader.

A user can serve as more than one type of actor. For instance, a Travel Agent might also perform administrative duties. Similarly, more than one user can appear as a particular actor (e.g., multiple Trading Assistants interacting with a portfolio system).

We show use cases and actors on a use case diagram. Within a use case diagram, use cases appear as ovals, generally in the middle of the diagram, and actors appear as stick figures, usually to the left and right of the ovals. (These layout conventions are optional, of course. If you like your actors on the top and the ovals on the bottom, feel free.)

Figure 3-2 shows a use case diagram from the example project we cover in Part 2 of this book.

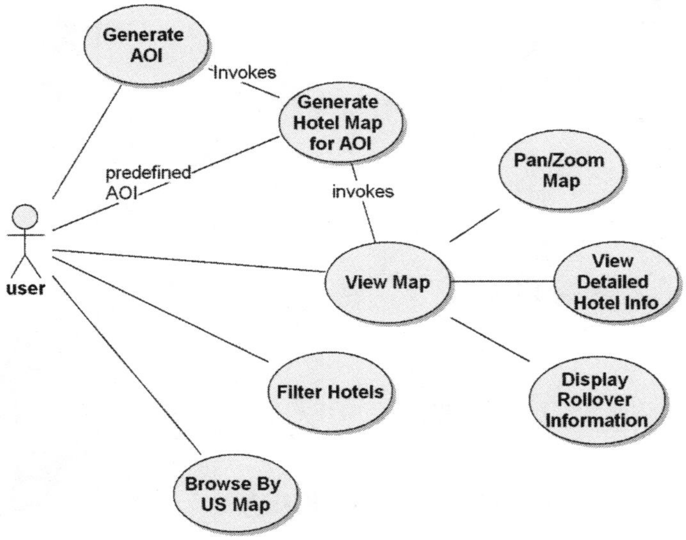

Figure 3-2. *Example use case diagram*

As we'll explore in Chapter 10 (and in the example in Chapter 9), an actor can also be used to represent a specific target user or *persona* when exploring the user goals that the system needs to implement. Applying the use cases to specific personas instead of generic actors can help to make the product more focused on the user's goals.

ICONIX Process in a Nutshell

In this section, we describe the process itself. In a nutshell, ICONIX Process describes how to get from use cases to code reliably, in as few steps as possible.

Figure 3-3 shows how the different activities in ICONIX Process fit together.

ICONIX Process can be broken down into the following steps (the items in **bold** are the concrete modeling activities that you perform at each step):

Step 1: Identify your real-world domain objects (**domain modeling**).

Step 2: Define the behavioral requirements (**use cases**).

Step 3: Perform **robustness analysis** to disambiguate the use cases and identify gaps in the domain model.

Step 4: Allocate behavior to your objects (**sequence diagrams**).

Step 5: Finish the static model (**class diagram**).

Step 6: Write/generate the code (**source code**).

Step 7: Perform system and user-acceptance testing.

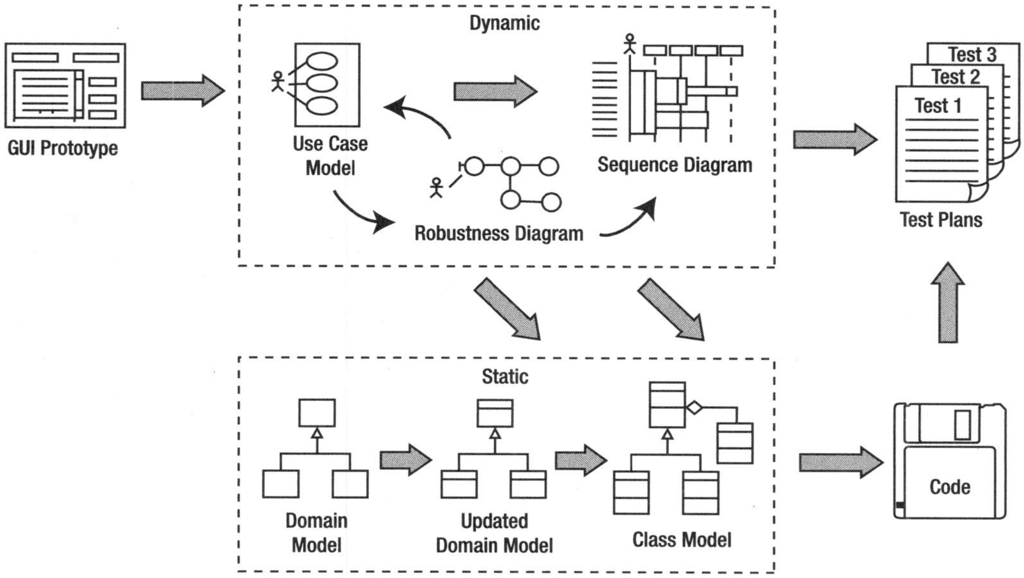

Figure 3-3. *ICONIX Process*

If you follow this process to the letter for your analysis and design modeling activities, then your project will stand a good chance of meeting the customer's requirements—and doing so within a reasonable time frame.

As we walk through each of these steps in detail in the sections that follow, we'll note four key milestones that tend to look good on a project plan (they're also useful planning checkpoints, as they provide key stages where you can both say and demonstrate that "this XYZ work is done, so now we're moving on to the next stage").

Milestone 1: Requirements Review

Milestone 2: Preliminary Design Review

Milestone 3: Detailed/Critical Design Review

Milestone 4: Delivery

Step 1: Identify Your Real-World Domain Objects

Getting this step right is possibly the most important part of the whole project, because it establishes a solid foundation upon which absolutely everything else in the project (requirements, design, code, and so forth) is built.

Tip As important as it is to spend time getting the domain model right, it shouldn't stall the rest of the project. Throughout the analysis and design activities, we'll keep coming back to the domain model to add to it and correct it. The domain model evolves over time along with our understanding of the problem domain.

This step can be further subdivided into the following steps:

1. Identify your real-world domain objects and the generalization and aggregation relationships among those objects. Start drawing a high-level class diagram.
2. If it's feasible, do some rapid prototyping of the proposed system, or gather whatever substantive information you have about the legacy system you're reengineering.

When this step is finished, you should have a reasonably correct domain model, which everyone on the project (the customer, the programmers, the analysts, the testers, and even the end users) can share and use as a common vocabulary. The domain model will continue to evolve and grow (and hopefully be whittled down to something simpler that still captures the business domain) as the project progresses.

Note It's worth emphasizing that in ICONIX Process, we *begin with a domain model and then write the use cases in the context of the domain model* (further evolving the domain model as we go). Other processes advise starting with the use cases and then creating the domain model, but there are good reasons to do it the ICONIX way, notably that the domain model provides a common vocabulary for the use cases to be written against, thus avoiding ambiguous naming (using different names for the same thing) in the use case text.

The domain model is a preliminary guess at the static model (class diagrams) based strictly on problem-domain entity classes—no solution-space stuff. No attributes or operations are shown on the classes.

The domain model contains real-world things and concepts related to the problem that the system is being designed to solve. When we create a domain model, we're creating a representation of the objects and actions that form the business and are focused on the problem that the project is attempting to solve. The initial domain model that you create for any project will never be perfect. It will evolve throughout the project as your understanding of the problem domain evolves.

Tip As you identify patterns and similarities in the domain model (and resolve ambiguities), you might suddenly discover ways of representing the same information from the business domain in a simpler, less ambiguous form. When this happens, don't hold back: go ahead and update the domain model, because the discovery of a simpler model could well lead to further improvements.

How do you actually identify objects to go in the domain model? There are a number of techniques, the most important of which is simply to use your own experience and judgment. A good starting point if you're really stuck, however, is to use the *grammatical inspection* technique:[6] quickly pass through the available relevant material (requirements, business glossaries, and so forth), highlighting nouns and verbs as you go. Note that the relevant material should also include your own interviews with the customer and end users of the system. Often these discussions help more than anything else to resolve ambiguities and identify further domain objects.

After refining the lists as work progresses, you should find that

- Nouns and noun phrases become classes and attributes.
- Verbs and verb phrases become operations and associations.
- Possessive phrases indicate that nouns should be attributes rather than classes.

These items represent only a general rule, of course (though a darned useful one). You might well find, for example, that some verbs eventually become objects rather than operations (particularly if you're modeling a business process, or if you've identified a manager, or controller, class).

6. Kurt Derr, *Applying OMT: A Practical Step-By-Step Guide to Using the Object Modeling Technique,* (New York: Cambridge University Press, 1995).

You should continue to iterate and refine the domain model, but this doesn't mean that you should keep grinding nouns and verbs indefinitely. The goal is to *build a glossary of object names that will serve as the nouns, as appropriate, within your use case text.*

It's worth establishing a time budget for building your initial domain model (e.g., restrict it to a collaborative workshop taking no more than a morning, or even just a couple of hours). The domain model is important, but you don't want it to prevent the remainder of the project from ever getting started! You can generally find the most important 80% of your domain classes within a couple of hours—and that's good enough to get going. You don't have to get it perfect, because you'll discover the remaining classes as you work through the use cases.

Step 2: Define the Behavioral Requirements

As you've probably gathered by now, the behavioral requirements in an ICONIX project are defined by use cases. The use cases expand on the high-level requirements (discussed in the previous step) and define how the system will behave in terms of user interactions. As we'll discuss later in this book, this step benefits from being augmented with detailed interaction design (especially persona analysis; see Chapter 12).

This step can be further subdivided into the following steps:

1. Identify your use cases using use case diagrams.
2. Organize the use cases into groups. Capture this organization in a package diagram.
3. Allocate functional requirements to the use cases and domain objects. (This step is optional depending on the formality of the project.)
4. Write descriptions of the use cases (i.e., basic courses of action that represent the mainstream and alternative courses for less frequently traveled paths and error conditions).

Tip Most projects will begin with a list of high-level requirements. These requirements define what the customer wants from the project, and they should in turn be based on a definition of the problem. If all this can be based on the domain model, then so much the better. Often, however, the requirements will be handed down to your team from upon high, and it's left to you to make sense of them and produce a set of use cases. In such cases where there's ambiguity, your only recourse is to ask questions, and lots of them—and keep asking them until you get answers that resolve the ambiguity.

How do you know when you've finished use case modeling? You're ready to move to the next phases of the development process when you've achieved the following:

- You've built use cases that together account for *all* of the system's desired functionality.
- You've produced clear and concise written descriptions of the basic course of action, along with appropriate alternative courses of action, for each use case.
- You've factored out scenarios common to more than one use case, using the precedes and invokes constructs (or whichever constructs you generally prefer using).

Milestone 1: Requirements Review

Step 3: Perform Robustness Analysis to Disambiguate the Use Cases and Identify Gaps in the Domain Model

This is the final analysis step in the project. As you'll see later in this chapter, robustness analysis plays a key role in ICONIX Process. At its core is the *robustness diagram* (see Figure 3-4).

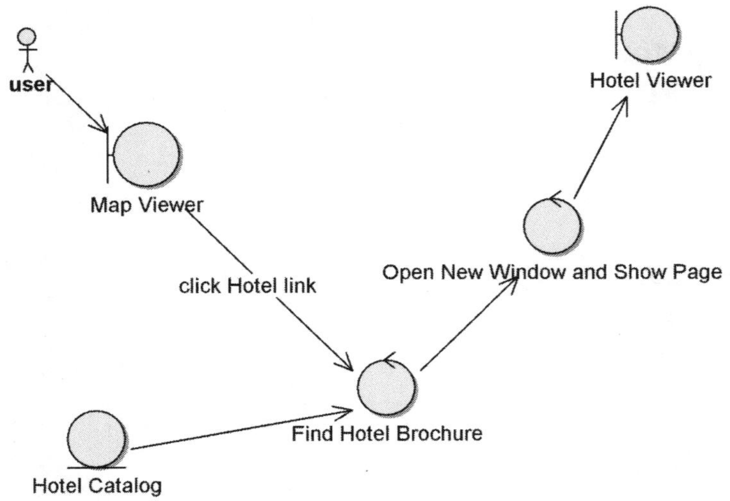

Figure 3-4. *Example robustness diagram*

Robustness analysis involves working through the text of a use case and taking a preliminary peek at how you might design some software to implement a given use case, using the objects you've discovered up to this point. One of the main purposes of this activity is to discover when you don't have all the objects you need, and then add them to your class diagram.

The robustness analysis step is further subdivided into the following steps:

1. Draw robustness diagrams. For each use case
   a. Identify a first cut of objects that accomplish the stated scenario. Use the UML Objectory stereotypes (see Figure 3-5).
   b. Update your domain model class diagram with new objects and attributes as you discover them.
   c. Update (disambiguate) the use case text so that it matches the robustness diagram.
2. Finish updating the class diagram so that it reflects the completion of the analysis phase of the project.

Milestone 2: Preliminary Design Review

■ Tip Though not essential, a useful trick is to highlight alternative scenario stuff on the robustness diagram in a different color. This makes it easier to read through and follow along with the basic scenario, and it helps you ensure you've covered all the alternatives.

Figure 3-5. *Robustness analysis stereotypes*

Ivar Jacobson introduced the concept of *robustness analysis* to the world of OO in 1991. Robustness analysis involves analyzing the narrative text of each of your use cases and identifying a first-guess set of objects that will participate in the use case, and then classifying these objects into the following three object types:

- *Boundary objects*, which actors use in communicating with the system.
- *Entity objects* (also referred to as *entities*), which are usually objects from the domain model.
- *Control objects* (also referred to as *controllers*), which serve as the "glue" between Boundary objects and Entity objects. Sometimes these are real Control objects, but most of the time they simply represent verb placeholders for functions.

This simple but highly useful technique serves as a crucial link between analysis (the *what*) and design (the *how*). We'll walk through several examples of robustness analysis later in this book.

These three object types translate well into the Model-View-Controller (MVC) design pattern,[7] which is used heavily in both client-server and GUI development. Entity objects are delivered by the *Model*, Boundary objects form the *View*, and Control objects form the *Controller*. For example, in a three-tier web application, a Boundary (or View) object could be a JSP page (sometimes also referred to as the *presentation layer*); the entities (i.e., the data) would be served up by a database, usually via a business object layer; and the Control object that binds the whole enchilada together would be provided by a business logic layer housed in an application server.

In a rich-client GUI application, a Boundary (or View) object could be a table or combo box component (e.g., in Java Swing, a JTable or JComboBox), the Model object would be the data model (e.g., DefaultTableModel) that serves up the entities to be displayed by the component, and the Control code would handle the UI events (e.g., scrolling up and down through the table) to determine which data from the model the view needs to display.

As projects grow in functionality (or in other ways, such as the number of users accessing the deployed system concurrently), the architecture must scale up to meet the challenge. This often leads to a more complex architecture, typically with functionality divided into separate layers (e.g., different areas of application logic might be separated out into different layers). This can be viewed as an extension of the Boundary-Control-Entity (BCE) architecture (or the MVC architecture), so ICONIX Process can still readily be applied to more complex architectures (i.e., the process can scale up to meet the demands of your project).

---

7. See `http://java.sun.com/blueprints/patterns/MVC.html`.

Step 4: Allocate Behavior to Your Objects

This step is where the design phase of the project begins. Our main diagram of choice for this step is the sequence diagram (see Figure 3-6), although you might also use additional diagrams and activities (such as state diagrams, activity diagrams, or unit tests following a strict test-driven methodology; see Chapters 11 and 12) as you see fit.

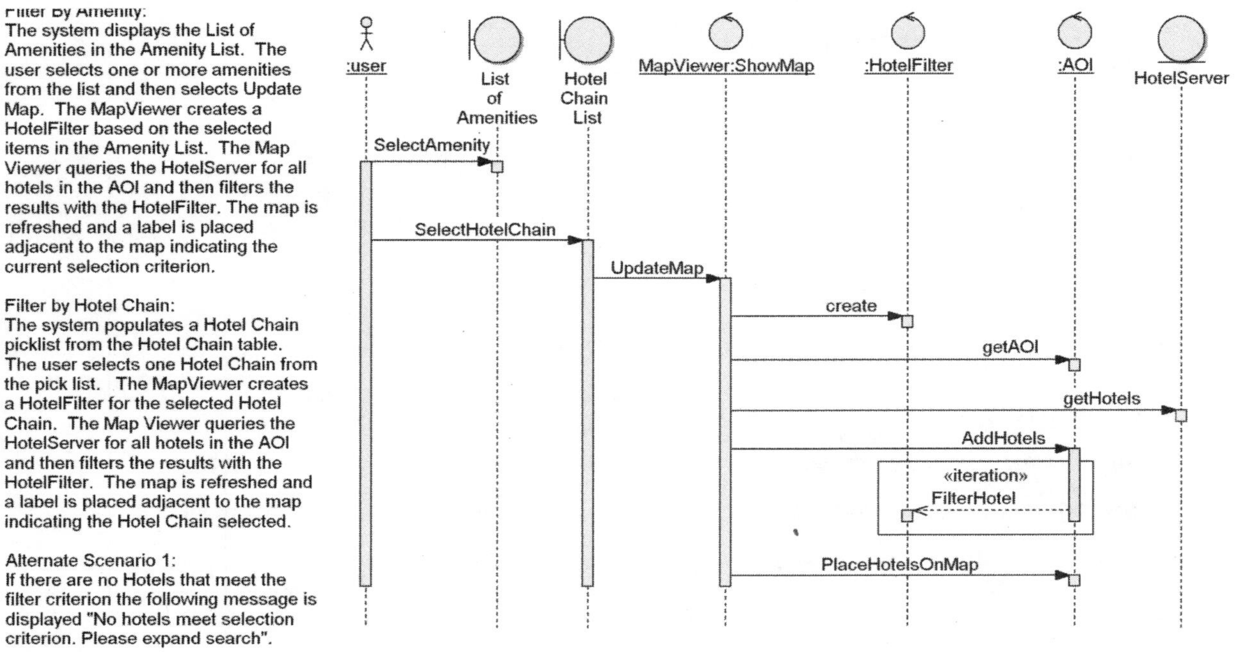
Filter by Amenity:
The system displays the List of Amenities in the Amenity List. The user selects one or more amenities from the list and then selects Update Map. The MapViewer creates a HotelFilter based on the selected items in the Amenity List. The Map Viewer queries the HotelServer for all hotels in the AOI and then filters the results with the HotelFilter. The map is refreshed and a label is placed adjacent to the map indicating the current selection criterion.
Filter by Hotel Chain:
The system populates a Hotel Chain picklist from the Hotel Chain table. The user selects one Hotel Chain from the pick list. The MapViewer creates a HotelFilter for the selected Hotel Chain. The Map Viewer queries the HotelServer for all hotels in the AOI and then filters the results with the HotelFilter. The map is refreshed and a label is placed adjacent to the map indicating the Hotel Chain selected.
Alternate Scenario 1:
If there are no Hotels that meet the filter criterion the following message is displayed "No hotels meet selection criterion. Please expand search".
:user
List of Amenities
Hotel Chain List
MapViewer:ShowMap
:HotelFilter
:AOI
HotelServer
SelectAmenity
SelectHotelChain
UpdateMap
create
getAOI
getHotels
AddHotels
«iteration»
FilterHotel
PlaceHotelsOnMap

Figure 3-6. *Example sequence diagram*

This step is further subdivided into the following steps for each use case:

1. Identify the messages that need to be passed between objects and the associated methods to be invoked.
2. Draw a sequence diagram with use case text running down the left side and design information on the right.
3. Continue to update the class diagram(s) with attributes and operations as you find them.

If you're not allocating operations to classes on the sequence diagram, you're ignoring its primary mission in life.

For each use case, you create one sequence diagram. This is an important point to remember, because you don't want to end up getting bogged down with many diagrams just to map out the interaction in a single use case. Doing so would give you a nasty case of analysis paralysis so, even if you have multiple alternative scenarios on your use cases, put everything on the one sequence diagram.

This is the reason for the two-paragraph rule on use case text: you can fit the whole thing on one sequence diagram. The net result of this approach is that it prevents the diagrams from becoming too fragmented. It means you can validate that you've addressed the whole use case by reading a single diagram. Too many fragments make it hard to be sure you got all of the use case.

■ **Modeling Question** The basic path and all the alternative paths are shown on one sequence diagram. *But what happens if you have 20 alternative paths?* You're almost definitely looking at more than one use case if it has 20 alternative courses of action. You should split up the use case. If your alternatives start having their own alternatives, for example, it's time to split 'em off.

Step 5: Finish the Static Model

As the title of this step suggests, the key design artifact here is the static model, which is made up of one or more class diagrams (see Figure 3-7).

This step is further subdivided into the following steps:

1. Add detailed design information (e.g., visibility values and patterns).

2. Verify with your team that your design satisfies all the requirements you've identified.

Milestone 3: Detailed/Critical Design Review

The static model is the grittier, more detailed version of the domain model, and it contains more implementation details. The static model has detailed class diagrams (perhaps even reverse engineered from the source code, but not necessarily) that are at a very detailed abstraction level and match the sequence diagrams.

Tip In an ideal world, the operations on the classes on the static model should have gotten there by message arrows drawn on sequence diagrams, and the source code headers should have been generated from these class diagrams. Over successive iterations, the UML and as-built models would start moving closer together (converging) so that the use case ➤ robustness ➤ sequence ➤ classes ➤ code progression is really being followed. Realistically, this doesn't always happen, but if the team can demonstrate that the code meets the written requirements and the use cases, then that may be "good enough" even if it isn't always optimal.

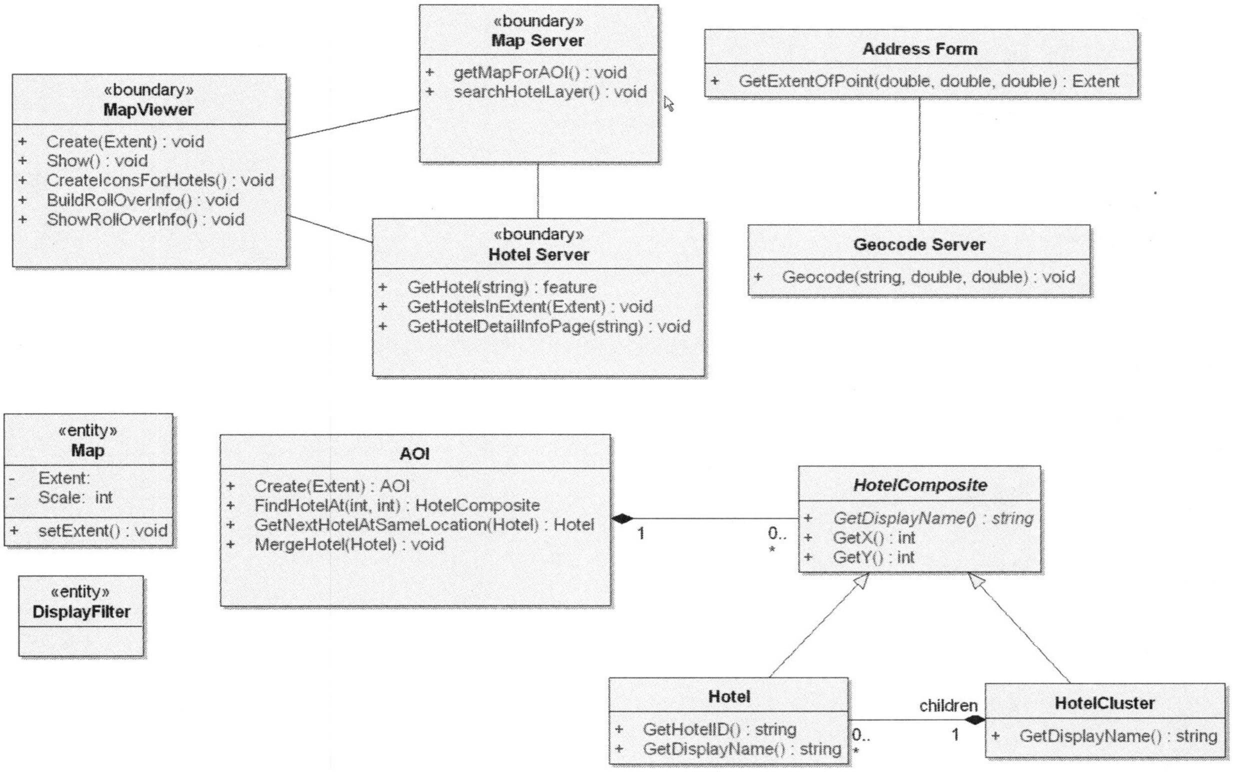

Figure 3-7. *Example class diagram for the mapplet project presented in Part 2*

MODELING QUESTION: SHOULD WE REUSE THE DOMAIN MODEL DIAGRAM AND SIMPLY KEEP ADDING TO IT UNTIL WE HAVE OUR STATIC MODEL?

If you know that your project is going to go through only one release (or a couple of releases at most), this approach serves nicely. However, in an agile project with lots of short releases and with domain modeling activities at the start of each release, it pays to keep separate diagrams for the domain model and class diagrams. The class diagram still grows and evolves from the original domain model (this approach is fundamental to ICONIX Process), but the diagrams are kept separate.

The domain model reflects our current understanding of the business domain (i.e., it's an analysis-level artifact), whereas the fleshed-out class diagrams (there may be several) are collectively a detailed design artifact. As our understanding of the business domain evolves, we need to be able to quickly update and maybe also refactor the domain model, without getting slowed down by having to consider design details from previous iterations (at least not yet—that comes when we get to the design stage).

Of course, this means that you have an extra diagram to update, but it's a trade-off. The benefit is that it's much easier to keep the domain model up to date, and it's easier to read (because it's uncluttered by design details and records of design decisions).

If the domain model and the class diagram are the same diagram, it's also more difficult to update the domain model in light of new business understanding, because you're in effect modifying the detailed design without going through all the intermediate steps to get there (robustness analysis, sequence diagrams, and so forth).

Step 6: Write/Generate the Code

This step is, of course, where the programmers take the design and start to code from it. The programmers should have been involved in all the design steps (ideally the designers are also the programmers), so that the design has some grounding in the reality of the technologies in which the system will be implemented.

This step is subdivided into the following steps:

1. Write/generate the code.
2. Perform unit and integration testing.

If you are combining ICONIX Process with a test-driven approach (see Chapter 12), then the unit tests will be written before the code. An important point here is that the programmers are doing their own testing, including integration testing.

■ **Tip** It pays to have integration testing performed by a different programmer from the one who coded the module being tested, in addition to the testing performed by the original programmer. This often catches more defects, and it has the added benefit that each programmer gains more exposure to the rest of the project.

Step 7: Perform System and User-Acceptance Testing

For this stage, a different group from the programming team (ideally a separate QA team) performs system and user-acceptance testing, using the use cases as black-box test cases for the latter.

Milestone 4: Delivery

More About Disambiguation

Here again (because it's worth repeating over and over) is the primary mission statement of ICONIX Process:

Root out ambiguity from the requirements, and then do a clean design.

We refer to this "rooting out ambiguity" as *disambiguation*, partly because that's what it is, but also because we like the word itself (but we'd never knowingly admit to that!).

In this section, we'll look at how ICONIX Process helps to disambiguate the requirements (which in turn greatly increases your chances of creating a clean design).

Do the Domain Model First to Avoid Ambiguity in the Use Cases

The domain model is done before use cases are written to provide a first level of disambiguation (i.e., removing namespace ambiguity from the use cases by making the team use the major nouns consistently in the use cases when they're first drafted).

■ **Modeling Question** *How much time should be spent on domain modeling?* Generally a couple of hours. This activity should really be given an upper limit of half a day. You're trying to pick the low-hanging fruit, and see if you can get maybe 80% or so of the most important objects from the problem domain and give them distinct and unambiguous names. Those few hours are generally some of the most productive modeling hours you'll ever spend, because that way you don't have some users going off and writing a number of use cases that use "shopping cart," others that use "shopping basket," and (if you have some British developers on your team) some that use "trolley."

■ **Modeling Question** *A couple of hours for domain modeling? But what if you're writing a safety-critical system?* That's the funny thing. Even if you're writing a safety-critical system, you really don't need to spend more than a couple of hours (or a morning at most) on the initial domain modeling (really!). The reason is that the process assumes that the domain model is incomplete and that the first-draft use cases will be ambiguous. This is where the robustness diagrams come into play. They help fill in the gaps in the domain model while disambiguating the use cases. Since the process has this built-in disambiguation and object discovery mechanism, you can spend just a few hours domain modeling nearly any kind of system, because you don't rely on the domain model being correct (or complete, for that matter)—instead, you assume it's *not* complete, and you complete it incrementally, one scenario at a time.

Once the use cases get drafted with everyone using ad-hoc vocabulary for the domain entities, then you already have a mess to unravel. It's far more efficient to get everybody to agree to one set of terms first (before the team invests time in writing use cases that use ambiguous terminology).

The reason this is so important is that namespace ambiguity is an insidious drain on your productivity in modeling. ICONIX Process is really a "seek-and-destroy" mission to take the ambiguity out of the requirements—the basic theory being that programming is easy (or at least much easier) when you're coding against unambiguous requirements. So, the first step in disambiguation is to do the domain model.

Here's a typical example (we see this sort of thing all the time) of disambiguation via domain modeling. In a recent JumpStart class, Doug was dealing with procurement of hospital supplies. The terms "PR," "Purchase Requisition," "Requisition," "Purchase Requirement," and "Requirement" were all being used interchangeably in the functional requirements descriptions. In fact, further exploration revealed that "Requirement" (e.g., "We need 300 syringes") was something that existed before a "Purchase Requisition" was created. So the team needed to have both "Requirement" and "Purchase Requisition" on the domain model, and the use cases were written with consistent usage of the vocabulary.

Using Robustness Analysis to Disambiguate the Use Cases

After the domain model is used to disambiguate the requirements and conversations with business users (before writing the use cases), you'll use robustness analysis to further disambiguate the use cases (after they're written, of course). How's that for a double safety net!

The robustness diagrams perform a more in-depth disambiguation than the domain model, because they enforce the linkage between the use cases and the object model. They also help with *object discovery* (i.e., discovering objects that were left off the initial domain model).

Robustness diagrams span the space that includes detailed requirements analysis and exploratory, conceptual design, thus bridging the gap between analysis and design (which we discuss in the next section). However, it's important to not use robustness diagrams for detailed design. It's better to leave the detailed design until the sequence diagrams (and possibly also the unit tests if you're combining ICONIX Process with TDD; see Chapter 12).

Robustness diagrams are quick to draw (if you have a well-formed use case), and you can discard them when you're finished with them. They're a *transitory artifact*—a means of getting from one state to another.

Bridging the Gap Between Analysis and Design

As mentioned earlier, robustness analysis provides a highly useful technique to bridge the gap between analysis (the *what*) and design (the *how*). The Three Amigos (Booch, Rumbaugh, and Jacobson) point out the rather large gap between analysis and design in *The Unified Modeling Language User Guide* (our emphasis added):

> *In software, the Achilles heel of structured analysis techniques is the fact that there is a basic disconnect between its analysis model and the system's design model.* ***Failing to bridge this chasm causes the system as conceived and the system as built to diverge over time.*** *In object-oriented systems, it is possible to connect all the nearly independent views of a system into one semantic whole.*[8]

Robustness analysis plays several essential roles within ICONIX Process:

- *Sanity check*: Robustness analysis helps you make sure that your use case text is correct and that you haven't specified system behavior that's unreasonable—or impossible—given the set of objects you have to work with.
- *Completeness check*: Robustness analysis helps you make sure those use cases address all the necessary alternative courses of action.
- *Ongoing discovery of objects*: You may have missed some objects during domain modeling.
- *Preliminary design*: Robustness analysis helps bridge the gap between analysis and design.

8. Booch et al., op. cit., p. 9.

Is Robustness Diagramming an Art or a Science?

Creating robustness diagrams is half art and half science. Once you see the final robustness diagram you'll say, "Hey, how come I didn't think of that? This is pretty easy." Robustness diagramming can be likened to riding a bicycle: once you figure it out, it's really easy, but it can be a bit confounding until you get the hang of it.

Programmers in particular can find it tricky to learn because they tend to think literally, whereas the robustness diagram operates at the conceptual design abstraction level. Refactoring is the result of code that has been written to the wrong conceptual design (we give a concrete example of this in Chapter 7). *Constant Refactoring After Programming* is the result of consistently skipping the conceptual design step and jumping directly from behavior requirements ("stories" or use case text) to detailed design.

As Figure 3-8 shows, when programmers become more skilled at manipulating designs at the conceptual level of abstraction (i.e., on robustness diagrams), their leverage to build better software is increased, as is communication with analysts. When analysts only speak requirements, and programmers only speak code, major communication problems can occur.

The point of following ICONIX Process is to learn how to manipulate software designs at that conceptual design abstraction level, because that is a very powerful abstraction level to be able to control. "Jedi Master" software designers inherently know how to manipulate the conceptual design abstraction level. Robustness analysis allows this skill to be learned by others.

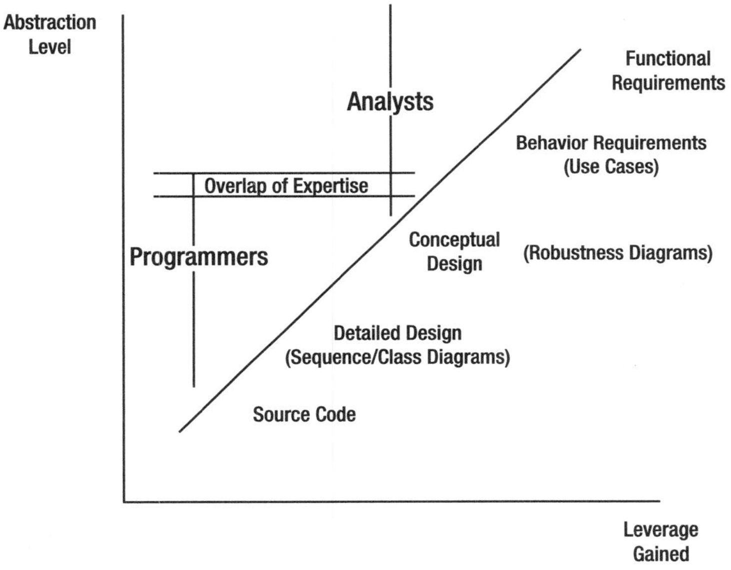

Figure 3-8. *Leverage gained by thinking at a more abstract level*

An example of where robustness diagrams sometimes confound literal-minded programmers is with the message arrows between objects. A literal-minded programmer will naturally interpret these as software messages—for example (leaping ahead to Chapter 8 for a moment), in Figure 8-3 the arrow from Get Hotel Name(s) to Create the Tip Text might be interpreted as a method call. Surely, a literal-minded person would naturally assume, there must be a sequence of method calls going Get Hotel Name(s) . . . Create the Tip Text . . . Show the Tip Window . . . and so on. However, the arrows on robustness diagrams simply indicate logical associations.

Tip Because you won't code from robustness diagrams, focus on the logical flow of the use case and worry about the direction of arrows later, in the sequence diagrams.

More About Prefactoring and Model Refactoring

Refactoring means improving the design without changing the functionality. It generally refers to changes made to the source code; unit tests are used to ensure that the functionality hasn't changed while the code is being refactored.

Model refactoring means changing the design at the object modeling stage, prior to coding, without changing the functionality. Unit tests aren't really applicable at this level because we're not dealing with code yet. (Of course, we should still write unit tests when we do get to coding. See Chapters 11 and 12 for some examples of how to drive unit testing from the object model.)

Model refactoring affects the class diagrams (i.e., the structure of the code) and is driven by both the robustness diagram and the sequence diagram. Robustness diagrams serve a dual purpose: disambiguation of requirements and object discovery. Sequence diagrams focus on making a clean allocation of functions to classes (aka behavior allocation or prefactoring, which we can define as getting the factoring of methods to classes right the first time instead of relying on refactoring to get it right). We try to discover all the classes we need first (using robustness diagrams) and then decide how the behavior is accomplished by the participating objects during detailed design (using sequence diagrams). So we have two distinct diagrams for two distinct thought processes.

Object discovery (on robustness diagrams) can be thought of as conceptual design. It involves manipulation of the (still fluid) object model at the conceptual level of abstraction, without worrying too much about implementation details. We're basically analyzing the behavior of a use case, trying to determine whether our current set of classes is sufficient to handle the required behavior, and adding new classes if they're needed.

Prefactoring, or behavior allocation, really gets at the essence of detailed OO design.[9] Prefactoring involves identifying which class should be responsible for each software function by drawing messages between objects on sequence diagrams and assigning operations to classes as we diagram out the message passing. *Doing a good job of prefactoring the design minimizes the need for Constant Refactoring After Programming.*

Key Points to Remember

This chapter is a (very) condensed summation of Doug's other books on ICONIX Process, and those books are in turn a compact distillation of the UML and Jacobson's Objectory method. So you could view this chapter as one big "key point to remember." However, it's still worth closing with the most important take-away concepts, which are presented in the sections that follow.

Key Terms

When applying ICONIX Process to an agile project, keep these terms and their definitions in mind:

- *Elicitation*: Writing the requirements and use cases down. For use cases, this includes basic and alternative courses (sunny-day/rainy-day scenarios).
- *Disambiguation*: Removing the ambiguity from the requirements that have just been elicited.
- *Object discovery*: Deciding what classes and objects you'll need to support the disambiguated requirements (this happens concurrently with disambiguation during robustness analysis).
- *Prefactoring/model refactoring*: Mapping the set of software functions you've identified to implement the (disambiguated) requirements onto the set of classes you've discovered. Making sure this mapping is clean and that each class is responsible for a cohesive set of methods, following the principles of responsibility-driven development. Prefactoring is best accomplished on sequence diagrams, which are used to allocate operations to classes on class diagrams. (We revisit prefactoring in more detail in Chapter 4.)

---

9. An excellent reference on this thought process is the book on Responsibility-Driven Design by Rebecca Wirfs-Brock, Brian Wilkerson, and Laura Wiener titled *Designing Object-Oriented Software* (Upper Saddle River, NJ: Prentice-Hall, 1990). A good "capsule summary" way to think about the responsibility-driven thought process (taught to Doug many years ago by Dan Rawsthorne) is this: think of each object as having a personality, and try to avoid schizophrenic objects. Another useful thought is to put the functions where the data lives.

Core Analysis Modeling Practices

ICONIX Process' analysis phase centers on these three essential activities:

- Functional requirements definition (write 'em down)
- Behavioral requirements capture (use cases)
- Requirements disambiguation (robustness analysis)

If you perform all three of these activities (in one form or another), then you greatly increase the chances of your project succeeding.

Core Design Modeling Practices

ICONIX Process' design phase centers on these essential activities:

- Cleaning up, adding infrastructure/scaffolding to, and applying design patterns on (if appropriate) the class diagrams. (That is, moving the class model from a pure problem domain model into a solution space model that reflects the detailed technical architecture of the system. This includes nailing down "plumbing" issues on both the GUI and the database ends.)
- Prefactoring operations to classes (behavior allocation by drawing message arrows on sequence diagrams).
- Reviewing and cleaning up the detailed class diagrams, adding in details like parameter-passing on the operations, and doing any other preparation needed to finalize the class diagrams before coding. This is done in parallel with the sequence diagrams.
- Writing unit tests (see Chapter 12).
- Generating code skeletons.

As with the core analysis modeling practices, performing these activities will greatly increase your project's chances of success.

Putting It All Together

So, what does all this stuff about "elicitation, disambiguation, and prefactoring" mean in practice?

ICONIX Process attempts to provide the most efficient path to building high-quality OO code. This doesn't mean "just start coding immediately," because, while jumping in prematurely might be the quickest path to code, it isn't usually the quickest path to *high-quality* code. Rather, it's more often the quickest path to code that "smells funny."[10] Before we can get high-quality code, a few things need to happen:

1. A shared understanding of the problem domain and accompanying vocabulary for describing it must exist.
2. Requirements need to be defined by the customer.
3. Requirements need to be unambiguously communicated from the customer to the developer.
4. Both sunny- and rainy-day scenarios need to be explored as a detailed understanding of required system behavior is gained.
5. Classes need to be defined that can encapsulate the required behavior of the system.
6. A clean allocation of functions to classes must be performed.

10. As we explored in *Extreme Programming Refactored: The Case Against XP*, XPers often like to talk about "code smells," meaning crufty code (i.e., badly written code that's trying to tell you it needs rewriting).

While there are differences of opinion on how these steps should be accomplished, nearly every approach to software development—including agile approaches—at least acknowledges the existence of the steps. In XP, for example, the list looks like this:

1. Create a system metaphor.[11]

2 and 3. Co-locate the on-site customer with the programmers. Rely on error-free verbal communication.[12]

4. YAGNI[13] the rainy-day scenarios—just code what you need today.

5. Code the simplest thing that can possibly work (DTSTTCPW).

6. Perform Constant Refactoring After Programming.

So, the steps are the same, but the approach is very different. Here's how the steps look in ICONIX Process:

1. Perform domain modeling. Draw a simplified class diagram that identifies the major nouns (objects) from the problem domain. Use generalization and aggregation relationships as appropriate to relate these classes to one another. Don't spend more than half a day on your domain model.

2 and 3. Elicit requirements. Write the requirements down. You'll be amazed how this exercise helps to focus your view of the system.

Obviously, this is a customer-driven activity. You'll be amazed at how much less you'll need to rely on a full-time on-site customer if the customer just writes a (brief, minimalist) statement of what the system has to do. A two- or three-page list of requirements can go a long way. See the mapplet requirements in Chapter 6 for an example of how to do this.

4a. Write first-draft use cases. Keep them to about two paragraphs apiece, and make sure they have both sunny- and rainy-day sections. Expect them to be vague, ambiguous, incomplete, and (in some cases) incorrect. Also expect them to be a heck of a lot better than what you'd have if you didn't write them.

Review the use cases with your customer, and try to clean them up the best you can. Try especially hard to make sure you haven't forgotten any of the rainy-day scenarios.

4b. Disambiguate the use cases (remove the ambiguity from them) using a robustness diagram. Drawing an "object picture" of the use case works incredibly well as a disambiguation technique. Once you learn the technique, these diagrams take about 10 minutes apiece to draw.

5. Discover classes/objects. This is also accomplished on robustness diagrams concurrently with disambiguation. When you draw an "object picture" of a use case, you may discover that you've forgotten some objects. So you add them and produce an updated domain model. Time spent to do this is included in the preceding 10 minutes per robustness diagram estimate.

6. Perform prefactoring. Allocate methods to classes. Do this using a sequence diagram, and with modern tools the operations automatically get assigned to the classes. Spending half an hour drawing a sequence diagram is a lot more efficient than refactoring it and rewriting your unit tests, rerunning your unit tests, and so on.

---

11. A *system metaphor* is an overview of the architecture. It's a simple, shared story of how the system works. See `http://c2.com/cgi/wiki?SystemMetaphor`.

12. Riiiight . . .

13. YAGNI is an acronym for *You Aren't Gonna Need It*. That is, don't code what you think you need, just code what the tests need to make them pass. To put it another way, "Don't worry, be happy."

Summary

In this chapter, we summarized ICONIX Process, a minimal object-modeling analysis and design process that gets you from use cases to source code in very few steps.

In Part 2 of this book, we'll build on the theory described in this chapter with a real-world example project, tied in of course with some agile practices. And in Part 3, we'll show you how to extend ICONIX Process with additional software development techniques.

But first, let's see if we can apply the same kind of "noise filter" to agility that ICONIX Process does for UML, and define a core subset of agile practices.

CHAPTER 4

A Core Subset of Agile Practices

We begin this chapter with a minimal subset of agile practices that should be applied to any software project. This core subset should enable you to hit the ground running when tailoring agile practices for your own project.

Following that, we look at the agile principles that underpin the practices. We follow this with a description (and refactoring) of the Agile Manifesto, from which we derived the main goals of agility. And finally, to put it all in perspective, we continue our "fact or fiction" analysis of what software agility really means.

So if you're in a hurry and want just the executive summary, the first part of this chapter should suffice. If you later want to come back and read the justification for the individual practices, the remainder of this chapter provides the detail.

Why Define a Core Subset of Agile Practices?

There's a huge number of agile processes available: Scrum, FDD, ASD, Crystal, DSDM, and XBreed, to name but a few. Typically, each process is defined in books and on many different websites, newsgroups, and so forth. The most prodigious of these agile processes must be XP, with in excess of 20 books published on the topic and some very active online discussion forums.

While this amount of activity and discussion about how to improve the way we develop software must be a good thing, the downside is that the definition and application of software agility has become decidedly nebulous. In Chapter 1, we attempted to define software agility and concluded that (aside from some accord on the basics) agility can mean different things to different gurus. The rest of us may be left wondering where to begin if we want to get our projects agile and start to benefit from the *goals* of agility (which we also defined in Chapter 1).

It seems prudent to begin with a core subset: the bare minimum set of practices that you can apply in order to achieve the agile goals. We've left out a multitude of practices from this core set. This doesn't necessarily mean those other practices aren't as good or are in some way invalid; what we've done is simply put together a collection of practices that work well with each other (and, in particular, work well with ICONIX Process, which we defined in Chapter 3).

Agile ICONIX: The Core Subset of Agile Practices

In this section, we define the core subset of agile practices that is Agile ICONIX. The intention is to be able to apply this minimal set of practices to a project to safely achieve the agile goals that we defined in Chapter 1.

As we showed in Chapter 3, ICONIX Process represents a core subset of UML diagrams (see Figure 3-1). In a similar vein, Agile ICONIX represents a core subset of agile practices (see Figure 4-1). For a more detailed diagram of how the agile practices work together, see Figure 4-2.

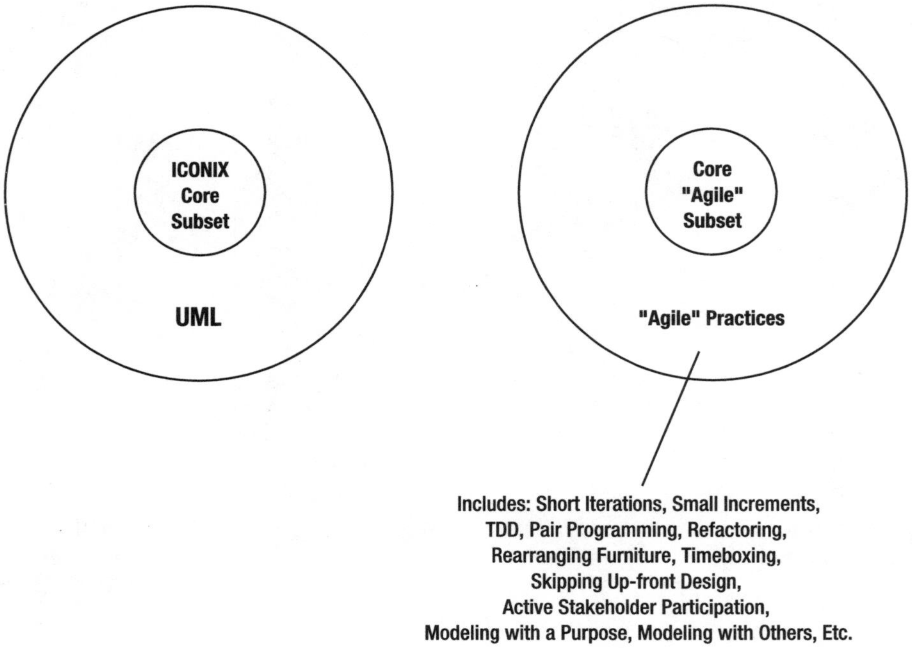

Figure 4-1. *ICONIX core UML subset and core agile subset*

As we'll explore in the next section, our core subset is based on the premise that the Agile Manifesto (which states "people OVER processes and tools"), while close, is off by just a little bit. Our refactored manifesto makes the (somewhat heretical) claim that people *and* processes *and* tools are *all* intrinsically important to success on a project. To us, it doesn't make sense to say that one is more important than the others, because they're all mandatory. The core subset we present here is based on that premise.

To recap Chapter 1, here are the goals of agility derived from the Agile Manifesto and various books and discussions on agility, reduced to four bullet points in the interest of information boil-down:

- Respond to changing requirements in a robust and timely manner.
- Improve the design and architecture without massively impacting the schedule.
- Give the customer(s) exactly what they want from this project for the dollars they have to invest.
- Do all this without burning out your staff to get the job done.

Any practices that don't contribute toward fulfilling these agile goals are extraneous to our cause, so we leave them out.

The agile goals could be further summed up as

Give the customer(s) what they want within a reasonable time frame without botching it up.

■ **Note** Why might the task be botched up? Possibly because, in trying to deliver working software in record time, we cut too many corners (requirements exploration, up-front design, unit testing, QA testing, and so forth). It's an all too common story, and one that we can learn from.

To support the agile goals, we also need to be able to accurately predict when each requirement will be finished. To do this, we need a way of breaking down requirements into *deliverables*—estimable fine-grained chunks of work.

We also need to be able to quickly estimate the impact of making a change in the requirements and present this information in such a way that the customer can see exactly how his change requests are affecting the project's timescale.

WHY CAN'T WE JUST SET THE REQUIREMENTS IN STONE?

In an ideal world, our customers would be omnipotent; have infinite, logical, forward-thinking ability; be able to foresee changes in their business way before they happen; and never make mistakes. Similarly, the development team would never make mistakes, always completely understand all requirements, have a full understanding of the latest technology changes that have hit the industry, and always work perfectly as a team.

Unfortunately, this isn't the case in most circumstances. As well as the customer, team members learn as they go along, and they figure out better technical and business solutions. So we have to be prepared to accept that changes to software may be required for a variety of reasons. What we want to do is to minimize the impact of this change when it does happen. It's important to educate customers that there is a cost to change, though.

The practices and principles we describe here are definitely not new; they're derived (or borrowed directly) from a variety of agile methodologies. *What's new in this book is that we've attempted to decide which practices are essential and which we might be able to leave out.* Often, what you leave out is more important than what you leave in. Certainly, the core subset approach has worked well with the ICONIX approach to UML. The intention is to gather up all these different interpretations of how to be agile and present a single, boiled-down, working set of practices and principles.

To work really well, the agile practices and principles listed here must be used in conjunction with an up-front analysis and design modeling process, and we can't think of a better one than ICONIX Process, a minimal set of object modeling practices that we define in Chapter 3.

Agile/ICONIX Practices

These practices, used together, are the bare minimum set that can be used to achieve the agile goal of *safely* giving the customer what he wants in a short time frame. We've divided the practices into two parts: the ICONIX Process practices and the "true" agile practices.

ICONIX Process Practices

These practices cover ICONIX Process as described in Chapter 3, plus interaction design, which is a useful way of controlling change by reducing requirements churn (see Chapter 10).

1. Requirements analysis and disambiguation
2. Domain analysis (capturing a common language that can be shared by everyone involved in the project, including the customer and users)
3. Interaction design (insert your favorite interaction design technique here) to reduce requirements churn and therefore also reduce the need to respond to changing requirements
4. Prefactoring/model-driven refactoring (applying the right practices, as described in this book, to get the design as good as possible up front)

Agile Practices

The remaining practices can be thought of as "traditional" agile practices.

5. Aggressive testing
6. Frequent small releases[1]
7. Frequent integration (aka very-nearly-continuous integration; integrating all production code at frequent intervals)
8. Synchronizing model and code after each release
9. Agile planning
10. Responsible ownership/collective responsibility
11. Optimizing team communication
12. Short iterations (for planning purposes; dividing a release into fixed-size iterations)

Figure 4-2 shows the way these practices relate to each other. (You can also download the latest version of this diagram from here: `www.softwarereality.com/design/agileiconix.jsp`.)

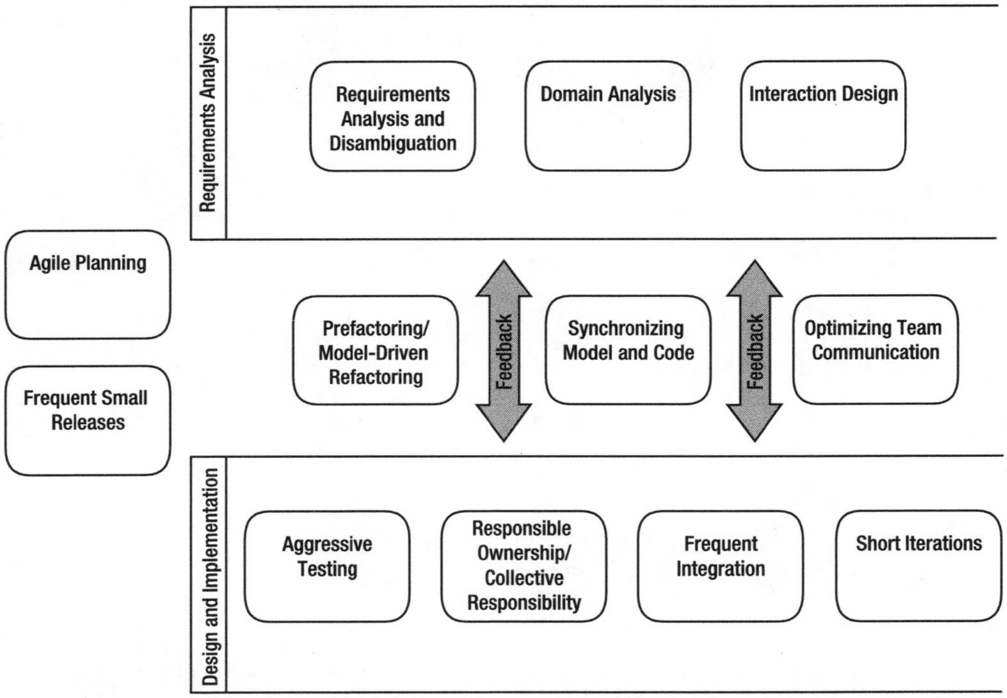

Figure 4-2. *Core agile practices*

1. As we describe in Chapter 9, there are three types of release: an internal, investigative release seen only by the development team; a customer-visible investigative release; and a customer-visible production release. There are also different stages of release (release to testing, beta release, full customer ship, and so on). Frequent small releases are typically used to refer to the "customer-visible, full-on, customer-ship, bring-it-on production release," but they can actually be any of these types.

Practices 1 to 3 in the list might not, on the surface, seem like "true" agile practices. However, practice 1 manifests in XP as the so-called on-site customer,[2] and even practice 2 gets some exposure in XP in the form of the "metaphor." Practice 3, while not mentioned as a practice in other agile processes, is certainly good advice that most agile adherents would give. *We include these practices up front because we view them as linchpins in the success of your project.*

In fact, the practices as listed here are ordered from the indispensable to the most flexible. You can use this list as an "adoption roadmap" when applying these practices in your own project.

As this is a core subset, we suggest that you do all these practices in your project as a bare minimum. However, we also have to be realistic—it would be a bit much to introduce all these practices at once and expect everyone on the team to instantly adapt, to shift their minds wholesale to this new way of working. So adopting the practices a few at a time makes more sense. So, to do this, start with the first six practices (these are the core, essential practices) and once you have those down, consider adopting the remaining practices one by one.

The arrows in Figure 4-2 show the feedback that takes place between the analysis and design stages, facilitated by the three practices in the middle (prefactoring, synchronizing model and code, and optimizing team communication). Agile ICONIX is intensely feedback driven. Each stage of the process is validated with some form of feedback, whether it's a model review (e.g., via robustness diagrams), unit tests helping to validate the design (and, of course, whether the code works), or customer feedback on an early prototype.

The two practices on the left of the figure, agile planning and frequent small releases, govern (and are governed by) all the other practices, again through a process of intensive feedback.

Let's look at the practices in a little more detail.

1. Requirements Analysis and Disambiguation

This practice involves talking to the customer and end users, getting a properly trained business analyst to extract the correct requirements up front, and using robustness analysis (see Chapter 3) to disambiguate the functional requirements.

"Talking to the customer and end users" may seem obvious, but the point is really that it takes considerable skill to extract the correct requirements from them. It's a skill that is separate from design and programming skills, so it wouldn't be entirely reasonable to expect designers and programmers to perform this task.

Our goal with this practice is to reduce *requirements churn* (i.e., rapidly changing requirements). Sometimes, the requirements will change because the business changes, but more often, requirements change because they were suddenly discovered to be incorrect. The correct requirements are there, buried beneath the veneer of the customer and users' confusion. A variety of techniques, including domain analysis (see the next practice), can help to clarify what the project needs to do, both for you and for the customer.

2. Domain Analysis

Domain analysis involves analyzing the business domain and creating a domain model (see Chapter 3). The domain model helps to properly capture and elucidate the requirements by providing a common vocabulary. This common vocabulary can be shared by everyone involved in the project, including the customer and users. The domain model is central to ICONIX Process. It's also described in Eric Evans' book *Domain-Driven Design: Tackling Complexity in the Heart of Software* as "ubiquitous language."[3]

After the domain model is created, it will continue to evolve throughout the project, and it should always be kept up to date. This is vital, because its key purpose is to eliminate ambiguity.

The domain model also provides the basis for the system design, so we end up designing the system using the exact same model that the businesspeople used to define the requirements.

---

2. *On-site customer* is an innocent-sounding name for something that actually turns out to be a team of customer analysts equal in size to or larger in size than the team of programmers, who must all squeeze into the same room. Picture a roomful of programmers being squeezed out by a whoop of sharp-suited, clipboard-wielding businesspeople . . .

3. Eric Evans, *Domain-Driven Design: Tackling Complexity in the Heart of Software* (New York: Addison-Wesley, 2003), p. 24.

3. Interaction Design

Note that "design" in this case means designing the UI and the way that users interact with it. Interaction design means

Designing interactive products to support people in their everyday and working lives.[4]

Interaction design, performed as early in the project life cycle as possible, can have a profound effect on the team's understanding of the problem domain. Interaction design is both an art and a science in its own right; you could spend years studying how to make software usable and how to make it fulfill the real goals of the end users. However, to get you started, in Chapter 10 we describe how persona analysis (a staple ingredient of interaction design) can be combined with the ICONIX Process in an agile project.

4. Prefactoring/Model-Driven Refactoring

We introduced the term "prefactoring" in Chapter 3. It means

Using up-front design modeling to refactor and improve the design before writing the code.

More specifically, it means mapping the set of software functions you've identified to implement the (disambiguated) requirements onto the set of classes you've discovered.

Doing just enough prefactoring can help to reduce the amount of refactoring you'll need to do later.[5] Prefactoring also helps to provide feedback into the analysis stage, by providing a review of the analysis model (the Requirements Review and Preliminary Design Review milestones; see Chapter 3).

Model-driven refactoring can be broken down into the following steps (as applied to iteration n+1). The intent is to synchronize the class diagrams with the existing code (as per iteration n):

1. Write the new use cases and perform robustness analysis.
2. Draw new sequence diagrams over class diagrams, noting any changes to existing class structure/relationships, and so on (refactoring the model for the new requirements, effectively).
3. Refactor the existing code to the new class structure as modeled without adding the new functionality (yet), and rerun the tests to show we haven't broken the system.
4. Add the new functionality and the unit tests (we write the unit tests first if we're following a TDD approach; see Chapter 12).

This sequence of steps assumes that we have a good set of functional unit tests that cover existing functionality. Which leads us neatly to the next practice . . .

5. Aggressive Testing

After you've begun writing code, the design will inevitably change somewhat (though hopefully to a much lesser extent than if you'd simply begun writing the tests and code without any preliminary design work). This means refactoring, which in turn means having a healthy number of unit tests at your disposal to help catch errors while making the changes.

TDD, which involves designing at the class and method levels using tests, can be used in conjunction with ICONIX Process to create a more rigorous design and a set of highly focused unit tests. Unit tests of this kind are sometimes referred to as *micro tests* because of their fine-grained nature; there may be several tests for each method on a class.

We discuss the combination of ICONIX and TDD processes in Chapters 11 and 12.

---

4. Jennifer Preece, Yvonne Rogers, and Helen Sharp, *Interaction Design: Beyond Human-Computer Interaction* (Hoboken, NJ: John Wiley & Sons, 2002), p. 6.
5. See Chapters 6, 7, and 8 of this book for a hands-on example of model-driven refactoring in action.

6. Frequent Small Releases

It pays to release the product to the customer often, so that you can get feedback as early as possible on whether the product's heading in the right direction. If you leave a release for more than 3 months, that's taking a risk. Conversely, if you release more often than once a month, then the process can become clumsy, with too many releases for the customer, the users, and your own QA team to handle effectively.

It's common for the first release to take longer than the rest, because the first release often creates a technical foundation for the whole system.

7. Frequent Integration

Each individual (or pair) should integrate all his latest production code into the source control system at least once per day[6] and have an automated build that checks the code out of source control, builds it, and runs all the unit tests at least once per day (though once per hour is better—if the automated build is doing it once per day, then why not once per hour? It doesn't take any extra effort, but it does provide earlier feedback when things go wrong—for example, if someone checked in some code that doesn't compile).

This practice is a slight step back from the common notion of continuous integration[7] (which implies that throughout the day you continually integrate code into the source control system, almost as soon as you've typed it in and it's been shown to pass the unit tests). The longer you leave integration, the more problematic it eventually becomes. However, continuous integration can also be problematic, because sometimes it's just easier to get something finished before checking it in and sharing it with the rest of the team.

So while frequent integration is a useful and fundamentally important guideline, it is just that: a guideline. There are occasions when a programmer may need to "drop out" of the core development trunk to work separately for a couple of days. However, in the meantime, the rest of the team is continuing the practice—that's essential. We cover some of the reasons for this in the "Agile Fact or Fiction (Continued)" section later in this chapter.

As described in Martin Fowler's article on the subject,[8] *continuous integration* can involve just daily integration, so the main difference here is primarily a name change. *Frequent integration* emphasizes the importance of making sure your code is working (and doesn't break anything else) before checking it in.

8. Synchronizing Model and Code

With this practice, we're essentially enabling the next bout of work ("enabling the next effort" to describe it in Agile Modeling terms). After each release, pause briefly to bring the code and the design back in sync. This might mean updating the code, or (more likely) it means updating the model. But only update what you need to—if a diagram is no longer needed, discard it.

This practice also allows the design to feed back into the analysis model. In other words, having implemented part of the system and released it to the customer, you may find that part of the original use cases or domain model just didn't map correctly to the implementation. This is a good opportunity to correct the analysis work, resetting the foundations ready for work to begin apace on the next release.

This practice gets its own chapter and is tied in with our example C# project (see Chapter 8).

9. Agile Planning

An agile project is one that is *planning driven* rather than *plan driven*. In traditional plan-driven projects, the plan (created up front) becomes the gospel by which the project will be driven and ultimately judged. Conversely, in an agile planning–driven project, a lot more planning goes on, in smaller increments and finer detail, throughout the project. This practice is also sometimes referred to as *adaptive planning*, because the plan is adapted to the changes in the project.

We cover agile planning in more detail in Chapter 9.

---

6. The obvious exception (at least we hope it's obvious!) being if the code isn't compiling or if it's causing unit tests to fail.

7. See `http://c2.com/cgi/wiki?ContinuousIntegration`. As noted on this web page, continuous integration should really be called "continual integration . . . a discrete action/event repeated endlessly, such as the sound made by a playing card stuck in bicycle spokes."

8. See `www.martinfowler.com/articles/continuousIntegration.html`.

10. Responsible Ownership/Collective Responsibility

This is a reworking of *collective ownership* (a common agile practice in which everyone on the team "owns" the entire code base; there's no specialization as such). Because we're not mandating pair programming, we don't specifically need collective ownership. So instead we can do something a bit healthier: allow people to "own" specific areas of the system, but make everyone collectively responsible for the overall code base. This is a much more natural way of working, and it means that while programmers aren't limited to one particular niche in the project, they do get a sense of ownership and therefore take more pride in their work.

The corollary to this advice is that making someone responsible for something she has no control over is a perfect recipe for stress. For example, letting Fred own a piece of the code base but making Alice responsible for it could lead to arguments of the most vicious order—it depends on the people. How well this practice works (or doesn't) is entirely dependent on the personalities involved. Similarly, "true" collective ownership doesn't work for everyone. Probably more than any other practice listed here, this one needs to be tailored and closely monitored.

As a result, this practice has been deliberately left so that, as a project leader, you can take from it what you want to. If you want to go with XP's "extreme" collective ownership, it still fits in with the other practices here. Or you might prefer to scale it back (the other extreme being individual code ownership, where each person specializes in specific areas of the code base). The practice as described here is somewhere between the two extremes, allowing programmers to take individual pride and ownership in their work but avoiding the problems typically associated with specialization.

11. Optimizing Team Communication

This practice primarily means looking at the way your team is currently organized and moving team members around (both physically and in terms of their responsibilities) to improve the level and quality of communication.

While intrateam communication is an important part of this practice, communication between the programmers and the business analysts is also important. If the analysts are too far removed from the technical realities of a project, they may produce a set of behavior requirements that is far from being the optimum solution that it could be. Early feedback from the programmers can save time and expense in describing what is and isn't technically feasible within the customer's time constraints.

Similarly (and perhaps more important), the programmers need a solid grasp of exactly what they're supposed to be creating. Getting feedback from the analysts on the new software *as the software is being created* helps to identify mistakes early. In other words, try to organize the team members so that they're near the analysts. Then the programmers are more likely to call the analysts over to show them an early working version of the system and get their feedback on whether it meets the real requirements.

For many people, human factors are what software agility is all about: moving away from the cold, logical, dispassionate process definitions of old and addressing the fact that people are the main ingredient in any software project. Observing human factors means keeping an eye on the way teams interact and arranging the team members so that they're working at their optimum level. For example, it's good to try and seat people working on the same part of the project in the same room so that they're more inclined to communicate.

Team size also plays a large part in the level (and quality) of communication that goes on. The smaller the team, the better quality the communication tends to be, and also the less costly it is. It's also been demonstrated that smaller teams are generally more productive. As the number of people on your team increases, so does the amount of effort involved in communicating and coordinating activities. Large teams are generally less efficient, so it's always best to start small and add new team members only if you really have to.

■ Tip On large-scale projects, effectively dividing the project into smaller, self-contained subprojects can help, but this is only really "agile" if each team also maintains its own self-contained domain model and code base. If it's difficult to refactor (both the domain model and the code design), then people won't.

Human factors and communication issues are very important, but a detailed analysis of these topics is beyond the scope of this book. We recommend you take a look at Alistair Cockburn's book *Agile Software Development* for more on the subject.[9] (We also touch on the subject in Chapter 2.)

12. Short Iterations

A project often finds a natural rhythm. For example, each week on Monday morning, we have a team progress meeting where we discuss issues from last week and sort out what each person will do this week. It pays to make the planning process follow the same rhythm, by dividing the project into fixed-size planning iterations of 1 week each.

Note What happens if the iteration isn't done by Friday? Do you work the weekend or slip the schedule? The purpose of the planning iteration *isn't* to set a deadline by which all scheduled work must be wrapped up "or else." Instead, it's a way of monitoring progress—the amount of work getting done by the team during each week. So if the work scheduled for this week isn't finished by Friday, then of course the work carries over into the following week, but the planning iteration provides an early indication that the team is underestimating its work.

The iteration size can be tailored to suit your organization and project. Matt has found 1 week to be the ideal iteration size, as the weekend provides a natural break between iterations and, of course, it helps to get everyone focused on their work on a Monday morning when they might otherwise be blurry-eyed and wishing they were still on their weekend fishing trip. Doug, on the other hand, prefers the Zen-like simplicity of keeping the releases short and not subdividing them into weekly iterations. You should tailor the iteration size to suit your project.

We've put this practice last on the list (suggesting that it's the one you might add to your project last of all). This is because you could get by without this practice but, having said that, it's also one of the most natural of these practices for your team to adopt. Getting everyone in sync at the start of the week, allocating work, checking up on progress from the previous week, updating the plan, and just getting people talking to each other about their areas of the system—once you get into the habit of doing this each week, it's a difficult habit to break!

Tracking progress each week can also help to track *project velocity* over time (see the earlier agile planning practice).

Agile Values That Drive the Agile Practices

The first three values we describe in this section are borrowed directly from XP and can be traced back to the agile goals. As a set of values by which to drive your project, they can't be faulted (although we have adapted them slightly to present the "digest" version here).[10] We've also added a value of our own: *judgment and balance*.

- Communication
- Early feedback
- Simplicity
- Judgment and balance

You can think of these values as the glue between the goals and the practices. The goals are to maximize the values; the practices are how we go about doing that.

---

9. Alistair Cockburn, *Agile Software Development* (New York: Addison-Wesley, 2001).

10. As our regular readers will know, it's XP's combination of practices (driven by the values) that let it down. See our other book, *Extreme Programming Refactored: The Case Against XP* (Apress, 2003) for an in-depth analysis of why we believe this to be the case.

Communication

We see communication as an integral part of early feedback, but we've included communication separately because it's such a vital and fundamental aspect of developing software. If the various members of your team don't talk to each other regularly about the system they're building together, then the project is probably doomed.

As with early feedback, communication is also about talking to the customer and end users and finding out what they want, either through traditional (but effective) interview techniques or by regularly showing them incremental releases of the product and getting their feedback as early in the product life cycle as possible.

■ **Note** The primary purpose of a model (besides designing, of course) is to communicate the design (and/or requirements) to others. Modeling is a communication tool. Always *model for readability*, because if nobody else can read it, it isn't worth much.

Early Feedback

Early feedback means finding out as soon as possible if you're "straying from the path of rightness." It includes such things as getting the customer to review an early release of the system, finding out as soon as possible if a change you made to the code has broken anything, and getting peer feedback on a design decision before it gets coded up.

It also means monitoring and adjusting the development process as you go along, based on whether current practices appear to be working or not. To rework the old saying, "If it *is* broke, fix it immediately!"

■ **Note** The saying just mentioned is especially true when it's the build that's broken, and it's one of the reasons an automated hourly build is preferable to a daily build. The most important time in any defect's life cycle is the first 24 hours after it has been injected into the system. If you can catch the defect in that time, it will be much, much easier to repair than if you catch it at a later date.

Simplicity

Simplicity means, simply, to keep it simple. Okay, we should probably elaborate on that a little bit . . . Simplicity, when it comes to software development, means not doing more than you really need to.

■ **Note** It's worth stressing that "keep it simple" doesn't mean "don't do the alternative courses." We'll try to drive the following point home throughout this book: the alternative courses are a vital part of development and need to be taken into account during design.

In terms of what the software does, simplicity means that the software should do what the customer has asked for and nothing more. In determining what the customer is really asking for, the software can often be made simpler by identifying patterns in the requirements—combining elements of the product's UI to fulfill the same requirements, for example. One way to do this is to define the problem that we're setting out to solve in terms of a domain model and to use domain analysis to further break down the problem, and in this way produce a simpler solution.

In terms of how the software works, simplicity means keeping the design simple and not overdoing the design with layers of abstraction and indirection. Complex code is generally written that way because the programmers thought that putting all those layers in there would make it easier to change. Ironically, the opposite happens: a simple change involves modifying some aspect of the code in each and every layer. Simplicity can be taken to an undesirable extreme, however—for example, abandoning business objects and putting SQL code or application logic directly in your presentation tier (e.g., JSP pages). While this might suffice for very small projects, mostly this is something to be avoided.

Judgment and Balance

We were tempted to call this principle "moderation in all things," but even moderation, per se, can't always be called a good thing. There are trade-offs to be made at all points in the development process. Trade-offs require understanding both the pros and cons of doing things, evaluating your current circumstances, and making a decision. Here are a couple of examples:

- The company will go out of business unless we release in the next 2 weeks. This requires extreme action! There are obvious downsides, but they have to be lived with.
- The persistence mechanism doesn't perform very well. But this isn't causing a problem at the moment, and there are other issues causing problems. So we choose to ignore this issue for the time being (while also trying to judge when it will become a real problem).

However, judgment and balance may well mean taking a moderate approach, and moderation in turn means finding a balance somewhere between adopting a practice completely and unconditionally ("pushing the dial all the way up to 10") and not doing it at all. For example, in *Extreme Programming Refactored: The Case Against XP*, the refactored process that we describe is mostly about finding ways to tone down XP's "extreme" approach and let things simmer gently rather than boil over.

Refactoring the Agile Manifesto

For the rest of this chapter, we'll explain our thinking behind the core agile subset and why it shaped up to be the list of practices that it is.

In this section, we examine whether the values put forward by the Agile Manifesto are a suitable basis for defining an agile process. At the risk of giving away the ending on page 1, the answer is that the agile values are basically sound but could do with a little tweaking to state the message less ambiguously. While that doesn't sound like a very exciting conclusion, it does provide a useful basis for tailoring a development process to your own projects.

The Agile Values

The Agile Manifesto website has this to say about agile values:

> *We are uncovering better ways of developing software by doing it and helping others do it. Through this work we have come to value:*
>
> ***Individuals and interactions*** *over processes and tools*
>
> ***Working software*** *over comprehensive documentation*
>
> ***Customer collaboration*** *over contract negotiation*
>
> ***Responding to change*** *over following a plan*
>
> *That is, while there is value in the items on the right, we value the items on the left more.*[11]

The agile goals (described in Chapter 1) are sometimes overlooked in the rush to address these values. The agile values are important, but they're really there to fulfill the goals.

---

11. See www.agilemanifesto.org.

Taken at face value, the agile values suggest that processes and tools are second-class citizens—that as long as you have high-quality people working on your project, the order in which they do things doesn't matter as much. For example, it wouldn't matter as much if the team were to launch straight into coding without first eliciting some requirements from the customer. (This would, of course, be a recipe for disaster, quality staff or not!)

Bearing this in mind, we would like to "refactor" the agile values as follows:

- To get individuals interacting effectively, you need flexible processes and tools.
- To communicate unambiguously, you need minimal but sufficient documentation.
- To gain customer collaboration, you need to negotiate a contract first.
- To know when to change and to recognize that you are changing, you need a plan.

Of course, the preceding list goes beyond refactoring because we're also changing the meaning—placing a different emphasis on and creating a caveat for each value. We understand that all agile processes take these additional caveats into account. However, we believe that for any agile process to be effective, it is as important to recognize these caveats up front as it is the original set of values.

Let's look at each of these values in turn.

To Get Individuals Interacting Effectively, You Need Flexible Processes and Tools

While it is important to use quality staff in your project, the process itself remains a first-class citizen. Or, to put it more accurately, *the need for a process* remains paramount. What does need to be avoided is the canonization of a particular process as being "THE way we shall all adhere to rigidly" (as in, "These steps shall be followed precisely without exception," "These documentation templates shall be used," etc.). The process needs to be flexible; if the process isn't optimal, then the people need to be able to fix it.

Equally, the tools you use to analyze and create new software need to be flexible enough to let you do the job without getting in your way. This doesn't detract from their importance, however: without tools (including compilers, text editors—hey, even computers!), the project could take a very long time to finish.

The flip side to this is when a team insists on using a particular tool (e.g., the manager's favorite programming language), even when it's obviously not well suited to the task at hand. Recognizing the importance of tools in development doesn't mean latching onto the "official corporate toolkit" or "company-standard super-expensive CASE tool" and stipulating its use—quite the opposite. *If we recognize the importance of tools, then it's obvious that the team must be given the flexibility to choose the right tools, every time.*

To Communicate Unambiguously, You Need Minimal but Sufficient Documentation

Documentation is a communication tool to help keep everyone on the team on the same page. Object models (a type of documentation) are an important method of getting from analysis to design. "Just go read the code" really isn't the best we can do.

As we discuss elsewhere in this book, effective documentation needs to be minimal yet sufficient, and we need to recognize which documents should be kept up to date and which ones have served their purpose and can therefore be discarded. Sometimes, a picture is worth 1,000 lines of code (and usually the picture is easier to read than 1,000 lines of code).

To Gain Customer Collaboration, You Need to Negotiate a Contract First

A contract (even one in the form of a verbal agreement or understanding) is important, because without one there is no project. The contract is the sealed negotiation between you and the customer—the agreement that states what will be delivered, by when, and how much it will cost, and it even can specify quality issues such as how many defects are acceptable. Depending on the type of contract, each of these items may be flexible, but the contract will (or should) state this.

Without thrashing out the issues just mentioned with the customer first (even if the contract just says, to sum up, "We agree to be flexible"), the project risks starting out on a shaky foundation.

To Know When to Change and to Recognize That You Are Changing, You Need a Plan

The project plan (whatever form it takes) is important because without it, no one knows how much progress has been made or what they're supposed to do next, and the management (or customer) may get the jitters, so again, no project!

Most important, we need to be able to change the plan if it doesn't reflect the current reality. This doesn't lessen its importance in the slightest, however; it simply means that the plan has a different purpose from what some people might think. (We discuss plan-driven versus planning-driven projects in Chapter 9.)

The plan should also be visible to everybody and revisited frequently, although the original baseline should also be kept visible, so that by frequently adjusting the plan, we're not fooling anyone (including ourselves) that we're still "on track" if the schedule keeps getting pushed out every month.

Boiling Down the Values to Their Essence

As *refactoring* is the practice of simplifying things (granted, it's usually applied to source code), we could further refactor the agile values until we are left with the following distilled version:

> *Neither people over process nor process over people, but people* ***and*** *process* ***and*** *pragmatism.*

It might seem as though we're nitpicking an obviously generic manifesto, but these issues have broad ramifications for the process that you choose for your own projects and the level to which you tailor it. For example, launching into designing and coding without doing in-depth requirements exploration up front might seem like a good idea because your programmers are highly skilled and can drive the design, as they code, to whatever the requirements turn out to be. This is an incredibly inefficient way of doing things, though. There has to be a better way . . .

Giving the Customers What They Want

To explore the requirements in depth and have a better chance of giving the customer something he can use (and getting the requirements right early in the project), you'll need a process that does the following. The techniques for eliciting the in-depth requirements might vary, but the basis is simply the following:[12]

- Run away from any technology; assume no solution. Focus on the problem domain. Describe everything in terms of user experience—for example, "A day in the life of . . ." (In other words, do some storyboarding and write as many valid use cases as you and the project stakeholders can think of.)
- Make sure the proposed solution is a good fit with both the user needs and the business needs (ROI). They may well be different. You have many masters.
- Describe everything you can imagine (within reason, of course—don't take this wording too literally) in detail. Do not attempt to produce production code yet. This takes discipline. (Prototypes are different, of course. Effective prototyping helps to elicit further, better, and more accurate requirements from the customer and users.)
- Once you have wrung the towel dry (i.e., you can get no more information from the customer and users, and the described scenarios are widely accepted as being a realistic and accurate portrayal of what needs to be done and what is desired to be done), then you can start designing and coding.

The basic principle is to take aim—very good aim—and then fire in a straight line, like firing an arrow straight to a target.

Note But will the target still be in the same place by the time the arrow gets there? The essence of agility is to account for the possibility that the target might move. A good way to account for this is to release in smaller increments (1–3 months, as we discuss in Chapter 9). In other words, fire the arrow over short distances. Standing close to your target increases your chances of a bull's-eye every time.

---

12. Thanks to Dino Fancellu of `www.javelinsoft.com` for this list.

This is the best way to be agile: develop your software quickly and reliably. Reducing development time is like a boxer presenting a smaller target to his opponent: it reduces your project's exposure to the forces of change.

Is it really possible to take such an approach and still fulfill your agile goals? It is, because spending sufficient time up front is an investment. It reduces the amount of time you will need to rewrite code later on.

As previously suggested, the behavior requirements can be defined using use cases (and there are detailed guidelines for doing so that work reliably). Since we *can* do this, we'd be dumb not to. We can still use short iterations, small increments, aggressive unit testing, automated acceptance testing, and so on (i.e., we can leverage many agile techniques).

It's worth emphasizing this point:

Well-defined and reliable guidelines exist for doing use case–driven development.

(Originally Jacobson's Object-Oriented Software Engineering [OOSE],[13] this is now refined as ICONIX Process.)

The existence of these well-defined guidelines means that jumping prematurely to code isn't a very good idea, because you lose the benefits associated with following them.

Refactored Manifesto Summary

To recap our "refactored" agile values

- *The process is as important as the individuals.* The individuals create the product, but the process helps the individuals to keep themselves out of mischief along the way.
- *Having just enough documentation is as important as having working software.* The software is the finished product, but documentation enables communication within your team and thus helps to get you there. In addition, it lets you check whether you reached the place you really meant to. The documentation also enables the next stage of the project, the all-important maintenance phase (i.e., the next round of functionality).
- *Contract negotiation is as important as customer collaboration.* The customer is king, but without the contract you won't have a customer.
- *Following a plan is as important as responding to change.* Effective planning manages change and keeps chaos under control.

CHANGE IS GOOD, BUT IT'S ALSO EXPENSIVE

Imagine that you're painting a house white and, after a week of intensive brushing, you've reached the final wall. Nearly there . . . but then the customer suddenly changes her mind and wants the house to be a nice shade of blue. It would, of course, be pointless to continue and finish painting the current wall white—it's best to switch to blue as soon as possible. The longer you wait, the more costly and pointless it is for the customer.

But however quickly you switch to the new requirement, it's going to be expensive for the customer, because pretty much the entire house will need to be redone. So the overall project will end up costing nearly twice as much as originally anticipated. (Note that not all requirements changes are created equal; the problem is worse if you start with dark blue and decide to switch to white, as you'll need an extra coat of primer.)

Software agility can help to reduce the costs of switching, but it can't recoup the costs that have already been spent on developing to the old requirements. This is why, even in an agile world, it's as essential as ever to do our utmost to get the requirements right, as early as possible. This means asking the customer hard questions (which she probably won't like), interviewing users, and so on.

13. Ivar Jacobson, *Object-Oriented Software Engineering: A Use Case Driven Approach* (New York: Addison-Wesley, 1992).

Agile Fact or Fiction (Continued)

In this section, we conclude the fact or fiction discussion we began in Chapters 1 and 2, extending the discussion beyond team structure and human factors. We'll cover the following categories:

- Modeling and documentation
- Change and change management
- Customer- and contract-related issues
- Working practices
- Planning and design

This discussion should help to highlight some of the thinking behind the core agile subset we presented earlier in this chapter. Plus it should provide a bit of light relief!

Modeling and Documentation

One of the more controversial areas of agile development is its apparent disdain for modeling and documentation. Of course, "not doing documentation" is not what agile development is about—it's about being realistic about the amount of documentation that should be done. In this section, we tackle this and other similar agile misconceptions.

Being Agile Means You Don't Need to Write Down Requirements

Doug: There's the notion espoused by the XP community that requirements are properly handled by jotting down a few notes on index cards. In my opinion, this is a poor way to go about developing software. So while this may be widely perceived as an "agile practice," it is fiction in my opinion. Our example for this book starts with a brief statement of written requirements, and as the development proceeds, we refer back to the requirements and show how the design and the code satisfy them.

Matt: Fiction. I don't think any agile methodology in existence says that you shouldn't write down requirements (at least in some lightweight form or other). XP gets there with user stories, though over the last couple of years these have tended toward the even more lightweight (a single sentence per story). The rest is left to acceptance tests (defining requirements through a set of executable rules) and conversations with the team of on-site analysts. But, human nature being what it is, not having a permanent record of agreements between you and the customer can come back to bite you. So, fewer detailed written requirements means being able to defer decisions until later, but at an increased risk of a disillusioned, confused, and angry customer (and disillusioned, confused, and angry developers!) if change management isn't handled incredibly well.

Mark: Fiction, on a project of any size at least. The objectives of writing down requirements are to a) make sure you understand the requirements yourself; b) give your customer the maximum opportunity to correct any misunderstandings you may have about the software (and this is important because it's a lot more cost-effective to change a few words in a document than to rewrite the software); c) give your customer the chance to spot any omissions; d) communicate the requirements to a wider team audience; and e) assist in prioritizing requirements. There are, however, many ways in which you can write down the requirements. On my current project, we use a customized version of an open source software tool called Gnats. It's particularly useful in planning and prioritizing in what is a very incremental project. I do think it's a good idea to have requirements stored in some electronic form, however.

Being Agile Means You Should Never Write Documentation

Matt: Definitely fiction, but then, I don't think any agile gurus are really saying this. A lot of them are saying that you can get away with writing less documentation, and some even say that you can write almost no documentation, with the caveat that the source code itself is written clearly enough to be self-documenting and everyone on the team (including the customer) works very closely together.

But source code doesn't provide complete insight into a design. Sure, you could use a tool to reverse engineer the code into some form of documentation, but the tool has only the information available in the code to do this. Also, you could look at the code for module A to analyze why it needs to communicate with module B, but it would be much easier to simply look at a high-level design document that tells you the End-Of-Week payroll module uses the Tax Calculation module after allocating wages but before deductions have been calculated, for example. Effective documentation is an essential part of agility, because it allows you to find answers quickly and move on to the next problem. But it becomes less agile when you have too much documentation, or a design document is simply paraphrasing the source code, or you have documentation just for the sake of having some documentation.

Does having less permanent documentation allow us to be more agile? Probably, because there's less stuff to change, but possibly at the cost of higher risk—a lower "bus number" and so on. There's an agile sweet spot to be found, where you write down just enough documentation (and write down the *right* documentation) to keep the project afloat without overloading it.

Doug: Fiction. Do the agile gurus say this? Maybe not precisely in those words, but it certainly gets implied from their remarks, and if you read between the lines it is quite often the message that comes across. One quote that immediately comes to mind is Bob Martin's "Extreme Programmers are not afraid of oral documentation."[14]

Of course, sending this message to programmers is like selling catnip to cats. Most programmers prefer writing code to documenting their work, but this doesn't make it a good practice. It's kind of like cooking and washing dishes. It's more fun to cook than to clean up afterward, but you have to clean up just the same.

The other fundamental point here is that documentation is first and foremost a communication tool. So it makes no sense to "optimize communication" by eliminating documentation.

Mark: Fiction, but it's a matter of emphasis. The overall goal is to deliver a software system that meets our user's needs, not to produce a documentation set per se. However, documentation—and perhaps more important the models it may well contain—can be of benefit if it helps us in meeting our key objectives. And we certainly believe that in some circumstances it can do that. That's what this book is about.

Being Agile Means You Should Never Use Development Tools

Mark: Fiction. If a tool helps you deliver software more quickly, use it. However, tools can be very expensive, and they can often cause more problems than they solve. Do be careful you aren't just being sucked into using something because of marketing hype or corporate policy (which is usually the result of marketing hype aimed at higher levels of management). If it is a new tool, try it out on a subset of the project before committing the whole team to it!

Matt: Quite the reverse, if we're talking about programming or code-level design tools. However, the agile misconception tends to be more around the use of analysis tools, CASE tools in particular. Sometimes, a CASE tool slows you down and can be overkill for the task at hand. At other times, a CASE tool can be a lifesaver, providing a data dictionary of interconnected domain objects; a binding, cohesive overview of the design; and a way of identifying good designs that we might not have spotted if we were immersed deep down in the code. It can save a lot of "baby-step" refactorings that might have eventually arrived at the same good design but with a lot

14. Mark Collins-Cope, "Interview with Robert C. Martin," *ObjectiveView*, `www.iconixsw.com/ObjectiveView/ObjectiveView4.pdf`, Issue 4, p. 36.

more time and effort. Also, code-generator tools (not just the MDA variety) are increasingly generating large parts of applications from analysis-level descriptions of the problem. It doesn't get much more agile than that.

Doug: Fiction. Most of the excuses for not using tools don't really hold up anymore. Enterprise Architect, the tool we use for the example in this book, costs about $150, is extremely intuitive and easy to use, and supports both forward and reverse engineering. We used the reverse engineering capability extensively in making sure the model and code synced up over successive iterations and releases.

Being Agile Means You Don't Use UML or Other Modeling Techniques

Mark: Fiction. If you choose the right techniques from UML or other places, ensure you understand why you are using them and what value they add, and know when to stop using them, then modeling can speed up your development efforts. It's a lot quicker to update a model on a whiteboard than it is to endlessly refactor functioning code as you uncover *yet another* thing you hadn't thought about.

Doug: Fiction, as I hope we demonstrate with the example project in this book. Any and all techniques that help get the job done efficiently and correctly should be used. If you know how to make use of it, this certainly includes UML.

I'd go so far to say this is not only fiction, but also utter rubbish.

Matt: Pretty much every agile process including XP advocates using at least some form of modeling technique in addition to programming, so definitely fiction.

Being Agile Means You Should Always Prove Concepts in Code As Working Software

Mark: Fact. Architectural spikes, screen prototypes, and so on are examples of this principle in action. It's all about risk minimization: communication risks, technology integration risks, and so forth. Models, despite their usefulness, don't actually have to work ("No one ever got fired for producing the wrong model," as John Daniels once said to me).

Doug: Fact. Modeling is useful for about 300 different reasons, but at the end of the day, if you can't build it, it's not a good model.

Matt: This is still true and probably always will be. But the distinction between a specification or model and source code/working software is becoming blurred, as more and more code gets generated directly from the spec.

Being Agile Means Oral Communication Is Always the Best Method

Mark: Fiction. To say that oral communication is always the best form of communication doesn't make a lot of sense to me. There are many forms of communication we can use—oral, SMS (much used in the UK and Europe), e-mail, written document, whiteboards, to name a few—and each has its place. If I want a list of IP addresses for 20 machines, I'll ask someone to e-mail them to me, and then I'll have a reference. If I want to know what the person sitting next to me is working on, I'll ask him directly. If I want to discuss a design issue, I might well go and discuss it in front of a whiteboard while drawing some models to clarify details. In some circumstances, I'll go and put those informal models into a CASE tool, as I know there are some details that need to be fleshed out and thought through a bit more. And if it's an important model, I'll print out the end result and put it on the wall where everyone on the team can see it. Some things do need to be documented for later reference.

However, having said all that, I think that the motivation behind this type of statement is to stress the importance of oral communication in many circumstances. I've worked in environments where two people sitting next to each other will use e-mail to communicate rather than talk to each other—and this is equally stupid!

The overriding rule has to be to engage your brain and communicate in the most effective manner.

Matt: Fiction. There's a common attitude in the agile world that talking to each other is more precise and less prone to ambiguity than writing something down. Part of the reasoning behind this is that when people talk, they communicate not just with their words, but also with their body: raised eyebrows, rolling eyes, sweaty palms, tone and inflection of voice, hesitation, that sort of thing. This is great for transient information ("What are you working on right now?" or "How do I do this?" or "Do you really know the answer or are you just guessing?"), but it's not so good for things like agreed-upon customer requirements, records of design decisions, and so on.

Doug: Fiction. Our project for this book, for example, was developed entirely with a remote, off-site customer, with written requirements and e-mailed use cases and UML diagrams. I don't think it kept us from being agile in the slightest. It certainly didn't keep us from being successful on the project, whether you regard our efforts as "agile" or not. In the real world, it's often just not practical to have a full-time on-site customer (or customer team) co-located with a programming team for months at a time.

Change and Change Management

Agility is about change. More specifically, it's about managing change: allowing the customer to change her mind about what she wants the finished product to contain. But of course, agility isn't a silver bullet. Although it puts practices in place to ease the difficulties commonly associated with change, it doesn't (for example) make change free.

Being Agile Means You Should Encourage Your Customer to Think That Change Is Free and Won't Affect Your Overall Development Timescales/Costs/Deliverables

Matt: A customer can always change his mind; it's his prerogative. But he may not be able to do anything about it, of course! The problems that arise often have less to do with the process and more to do with the contract (which in many ways drives the process). If the customer is locked into a particularly nasty contract that states the requirements up front in iron-clad, unchangeable legalese, then the project will probably fail, or what is eventually delivered won't be very close to what the customer really needs, which is pretty close to failure anyway. So I'd say that this statement is fiction, because the customer can change his mind anyway, and it isn't really agility that prevents or allows him from effecting a change in the requirements. Where agile practices do help is in reducing the pain of making a change midway through the project.

Mark: Change is always possible, even when using a waterfall approach to software development. The problem with the waterfall approach was that the analysis and design periods were often so long—quite often months—that changes put them into a continual process of flux, and they consequently never actually got finished before the customer decided to pull the plug because nothing concrete had been delivered. This was especially true on internal software development projects.

More-traditional software houses had some success with a waterfall approach because they could lock the customer (often at the customer's own request) into a fixed-price development (based on a fixed set of requirements, of course) and then change-control the customer (getting more money, of course) for every subsequent requirements change. The customer couldn't pull out—he'd committed to the project, so he'd have no choice but to pay up. While this worked in some way at a commercial level, I don't think it delivered real value for the money, and I think it often left a lot of people on both sides feeling frustrated.

Anyway, coming back to the question, change is always possible—the question is at what cost and in what timescale. It's important to understand that anyone who says you can get change for free is being either dishonest or naive. Agile, iterative, and incremental approaches to software development attempt to mitigate the cost of change using a variety of techniques, from incremental delivery to using cost-of-change-minimizing design techniques. But remember, once pen has been put to paper or fingers have been put to the keyboard, there is an additional cost involved. After all, if the change wasn't necessary, it wouldn't be necessary to change models or code, would it?

Doug: Fiction that you should do this, but in some cases fact that it happens. And, in my opinion, this is one of the great myths of agile development. Many of the popular agile approaches involve rewriting code over and over again. Developers are encouraged to repeatedly toss out and rewrite code. But nobody bothers to tell the poor customer, who has been sold on the virtues of agility, that this approach actually costs time and money.

Customer- and Contract-Related Issues

Increased customer involvement is one of the areas on which agile methods place a particularly high emphasis. Of course, customer involvement isn't just about getting the requirements right (which is pretty fundamental); it's also about negotiating a suitable contract to suit the type of development being undertaken.

Being Agile Means You Can't Undertake Fixed-Price Contracts

Matt: Fiction . . . but only just! Agile methods tend to be geared at making changes as the project fishtails toward a fixed deadline. If the deadline is fixed but the requirements are changing, then the overall price is something that you probably wouldn't want to fix (except in the sense that the price per iteration, or per release, may be fixed). But that doesn't mean you can't do agile development to a fixed price. As I mention elsewhere, the contract drives the process to an extent; you have to tailor the process to suit the contract.

Doug: Fiction for "any agile approach" but fact with some agile approaches. The whole notion of an "optional scope contract" as defined in XP is the example that jumps to mind.

Mark: Fact and fiction. Fact in that, as I've already mentioned, the whole concept of large fixed-price developments relies on the customer knowing every requirement in detail at the start of the project (an unlikely scenario), and this type of project is the antithesis of agile software development. Fiction in that it is, however, possible to fix the cost of a number of small-ish increments (1–3 months in duration, depending on the project) by incrementally phasing requirements gathering and costing (for the next increment) on top of the software delivery of the current one. This approach enables the customer to bite off well-costed chunks of the development, while also having the opportunity to request change in what would be "midproject" in a traditional-style fixed-price development.

Being Agile Means You Must Have a Full-Time On-Site Customer and All the Developers Should Talk to Him

Mark: Fiction. Of course, on any project it is important that your customer understand his commitments and responsibilities, but a dedicated full-time on-site customer is an unrealistic expectation in most circumstances. No project I have ever worked on has had such a beast. I also wonder whether this is actually necessary in many circumstances, and this relates to the second part of this question: should all developers interact with the customer?

While I'm not in favor of stopping anyone from talking to the customer if a question needs answering, I do believe that some people are better at getting information in a concise, effective, and timely manner than others. I also believe there is a particular skill to taking a somewhat ill-defined requirement and turning it into a set of commands that can be issued to a computer—not just in the UI design sense, but also in terms of coming up with a minimal set of operations that meet the needs of the customer. Getting human-computer interaction right is difficult, and not everyone can do it.

Doug: Fiction. And once again, I'm hoping that our example project demonstrates this successfully. I was the customer for this project, and I don't think I spent more than 8 hours in the same area-code as the developers while the code was being written, although I did spend 3 days on-site when we did the initial modeling workshop, when we defined the use cases. But I brought a written set of requirements with me to that workshop.

As I recall, I made three trips to the location where the developers were working, and virtually all of the remaining communication was by e-mail. I met with the developers for a couple of hours each time I visited.

Matt: If you can get a permanent on-site customer, that's great—it really can make a big difference. But it's probably a bit much to ask of the customer, and generally speaking, it isn't likely that you'll find a customer who is prepared to do this for a whole project. Even the proponents of XP, which propagated the idea of an on-site customer, have changed their minds and gone instead for a team of business analysts who act as a proxy between the customer and the programmers. But the problem with the on-site customer practice (whether it's an analyst or the real customer) is that it goes hand in hand with the concept of not defining the requirements in detail up front, so it runs the risk of not discovering entire systems that need to be developed (which might take several months, a year, or whatever) until late in the project. Or insufficient time spent exploring the problem domain might result in an immature domain model, which results in software that is more complex than it needs to be and therefore more expensive to change later on when the real requirements emerge.

Working Practices

Agility changes the way team members work together at a fundamental level. However, if members of a "nonagile" team are creating unit tests and integrating their code frequently into PVCS (or their source control system of choice), chances are they're already more agile than they thought they were.

Being Agile Means You Must Use Automated Tests

Matt: Fact, especially if the tests are written up-front, as fine-grained unit tests (i.e., micro tests). Unit/acceptance tests have become a vital element of developing software, and not just in the agile world. But when making design changes (or factoring in new or changed requirements), a comprehensive suite of tests can save a lot of debugging time. There's a cautionary note, though, which is that teams can become overconfident that their test suite will save them. It will save them from the defects that they're expecting to occur, but it's the unexpected ones that always catch people out.

Doug: This is a tough one, I guess because of the word "must." I think that in most cases this would be a fact, but there are some kinds of systems in which these techniques are not as useful as others. In our book example, which is a map-based system, it turned out that visual inspection of a comprehensive set of maps was the most efficient way to proceed. So we still had a strong emphasis on testing, but it wasn't the classic regression-test environment for a number of reasons. Which means that, I guess (with some reluctance), I'll have to say fiction, because of the "must."

Mark: Automated tests mean you can have confidence that your code is working correctly at any point in time and also that when necessary you can "refactor with confidence."

Being Agile Means You Must Continuously Integrate (That Is, Check Your Code Back into the Source Control System After Every Change and Make Sure It All Still Works)

Mark: Fact. Continuous integration means you are reducing the risks of technology or code incompatibilities. You know where you stand at any point in time.

Doug: Fiction. You should be able to keep a chunk of code checked out for a couple of weeks while you work on it, without being deemed nonagile. On any project of any decent size and complexity, there are times you want to "own" some stuff for awhile and make it work right before trying to integrate it with everybody else's stuff.

I once had a manager who required me to check uncompiled/untested code into source code control, so if I wanted to add a semicolon I had to explain why I was doing it. And I was the only programmer on the project. It was asinine.

Matt: Fact . . . ish. Continuous integration, where you check in code almost at the point where you changed it and got a green bar, reeks of idealism. At a lesser extreme, though, it does pay to integrate your code at least once a day and have an automated build running, also at least once a day.[15]

It's common nowadays to have a dedicated build PC that does an automated hourly build. It gets the latest source out of the source control system, builds it, and runs all the unit tests. If there's any failure along the way (particularly for the compiling part), an e-mail gets sent to the whole team, alarms go off, and so forth.

A side effect I've noticed is that individual team members prefer to keep code out of source control (or label it so it's hidden from the automated build) for longer periods of time while they're getting it working, so as to

15. See `www.martinfowler.com/articles/continuousIntegration.html`.

avoid that dreaded "build failed" or "tests failed" e-mail being sent to the whole team. As long as the code they're working on is sufficiently insular, this generally doesn't cause a problem, but there's a lot to be said for working in smaller increments and verifying that what you've written works so far.

So I'd say that if individual team members are integrating code less often than once a day, then your team is not being as agile as it could be, and if you don't have an automated build running at least once a day, that definitely isn't agile!

Being Agile Means You Must Release a (Production) Version of the System Every Few Weeks (the Fewer, the Better)

Mark: Strictly speaking, I'd say fiction, but there is a dilemma here. On the one hand, you want to release a production version of the system to your customer as often as possible, as this gives her access to new features as soon as possible and enables you to get feedback from her. On the other hand, there is always an overhead of making a full production release of the system—and the larger your code base, the bigger this overhead becomes—even if you're undertaking automated tests and continuously integrating. The reason for this is that some activities or deliverables (e.g., migrating live data, training users, creating release notes, updating the user manual, performing acceptance testing, etc.) are inherently related to production releases (as opposed to internal releases). The more production releases you undertake, the less time there is for raw development. Ultimately, I think you have to discuss this trade-off with your customer. She may not be happy if 40% of potential development time is spent on production release–related activities.

Doug: Fiction. Not only is this not necessarily true, but also there are some real serious drawbacks to mandating this practice.

Matt: It definitely pays to never be far away from a working version of the software you're creating. Being able to run tests end to end helps to identify issues early. But this is a far cry from actually releasing working software to the customer every few weeks. QA won't be a happy bunch, for starters. Having said that, it is essential that the customer gets to see progress on the product *at least* every few weeks, and that the customer gives feedback on whether the product is doing what he was expecting.

Being Agile Means the Project Should Make Frequent Short Releases (Once Every 2–3 Months, for Example)

Matt: Yep, definitely fact—with a few caveats, the most obvious one being that the product should only release when it's ready, when QA gives it the "all clear" (or at least the "mostly clear"). Another caveat is that an unrealistic release cycle shouldn't be forced on a project. If it's going to ruffle feathers, exhaust the testers, result in rushed code, or whatever, then the organization probably isn't ready yet. In the meantime, the project can still adopt other agile practices and get its "agile badge."

Mark: On balance, fact. While releasing every 2–3 weeks can mean the overhead of doing production releases may be excessive, there are significant risks involved in not releasing something at least once every 3 months, in terms of both visibly demonstrating progress made to your customer and also getting feedback from the customer, although the latter can be mitigated by doing interim "investigative" releases for your customer to play with.

Doug: Fact. Avoiding lengthy intervals (i.e., those lasting several months) without the customer seeing any new functionality is one of the keys to being agile.

Being Agile Means Prototypes Should Always Be Evolved into Production Systems

Matt: There are really two different kinds of prototype. There's the "big" kind, the proof-of-concept type, which has been developed using some up-front design and for which some requirements analysis was done, and which could feasibly stand as a product in its own right (albeit a slightly wobbly one). And then there's the kind of small, ad-hoc prototype that is a tiny subset of the overall system (a "spike" in XP terms) and that is used to investigate a particular part of the design (usually for estimating purposes).

Whichever type of prototype you start with, turning it into a real production system will always involve some risk. You need to do some work to make it production-worthy (e.g., refactoring the design, bringing the code in line with the design documentation and vice versa, and so on). We show some of this in Chapter 8. But another (probably easier) alternative is to scrap the prototype and start over with a new system, using what you learned from the prototype to accelerate development. Funnily enough, our example project in this book (the ESRI mapplet) starts with a prototype that then gets developed further into a production system. But the initial version of the mapplet was solid enough that the team was able to do this. Also, the requirements didn't change for the next release, but the initial set of requirements was added to. If the prototype had revealed that the first set of requirements was plain wrong (or that the design wasn't appropriate), we would have scrapped it and started over.

Doug: I suppose it's a fact that this *can* happen. Whether or not it's the best way to develop software is another question entirely, because there are significant issues associated with doing it, although I'm certainly in favor of doing a healthy amount of prototyping. Should it always happen, in the name of agility? I'd say fiction.

One of the big differences between prototype code and code that has been designed following a use case–driven approach is that prototypes tend to deal mainly with sunny-day scenarios, while use cases (should) consider both sunny- and rainy-day cases (basic and alternate courses of action) for each scenario. In many cases, the structures put in place to support sunny-day scenarios don't hold up properly when you start throwing all the special cases, exceptions, and error conditions into the mix. So evolving a prototype into production code isn't always the best idea. In our example project, there was indeed a prototype release, but a substantial amount of engineering was done to it before it became the production system.

Mark: If you're going to develop something called a "prototype" (rather than, say, the first release of the system), I'd say fiction. The main reason being that the moment something has the prototype label associated with it, developers tend to drop any consideration of quality. Personally, I'd avoid calling something a prototype if I had any interest whatsoever in using the source code in a later production release.

Being Agile Means Refactoring Is Still Useful After Doing Use Case–Driven Modeling

Doug: Refactoring can still be useful, but the scope of the improvements that will be made to code as a result of refactoring will be dramatically reduced when compared to an approach in which refactoring is a primary design technique and insufficient attention is paid to up-front design. There might still be (relatively minor) code-level improvements that can be made, but these will generally not be make-or-break architecture/design issues. So, refactoring isn't rendered completely useless by use case–driven design, but its importance is greatly diminished.

Matt: Fact. No matter how good your up-front design skills, the design will change (even a little bit) once you begin coding. Effective up-front design reduces the extent that this happens, but when it does happen, you'll want to be able to make changes to the code safely. This means refactoring, which means having a set of unit tests in place.

Mark: Fact, with the caveat that refactoring shouldn't be considered an alternative to doing some analysis and design. However, one reason you might want to refactor the code (after doing your modeling and so forth to make sure you get it right) is if you have a rule that says, "Thou shalt not screw up the existing system by checking in crap code to CVS." It means that developers can't check stuff into CVS unless they are 99% sure it works. If they're working on a big change that takes days, this leaves them vulnerable to other changes and merge conflicts, so if they don't want this, they have to structure their changes into stages—each of which demonstrably won't screw up the existing system. Refactoring the existing design to *accommodate* the new functionality (but not yet to implement the new stuff) and validating it with unit tests helps here.

Planning and Design

On the surface, agile methods seem to have thrown away the rulebook when it comes to planning and design. But look beneath the surface, and you'll see some marked similarities with traditional development methods.

Being Agile Means You Don't Have to Worry About Design Because You Can Refactor Later

Matt: Definitely fiction. On a very small project (like a few classes), you might just get away with it, but that's about it.

Doug: Fiction, fiction, fiction. (This is a pet peeve of mine.)

Mark: I've heard of some "gurus" saying things like "You shouldn't even worry about this afternoon—just focus on the tests you're currently trying to satisfy, and refactoring will sort out any issues later on." To me this is, to borrow a phrase from Doug, "plain moronic." Let's get one thing straight: it's cheaper to change a class model on a whiteboard, for example, than it is to change the corresponding implementation code. So to say "Don't think ahead to this afternoon" is pretty darn stupid, not to mention an incredible waste of customer's money.

If you know you have ten requirements to implement over the next few weeks, then getting the design right (or at least as right as you can) up front has got to be the right thing to do. And modeling techniques like class diagrams have been specifically developed to assist you in thinking through design issues in a cost-effective manner.

Of course, if you don't actually know what the ten requirements are (because you haven't done any analysis), then getting the design right is going to be somewhat problematic. But the answer to this problem is to do the analysis and write down your requirements, not to bury your head in the sand and say, "Okay, let's find out what we're doing this morning and let this afternoon worry about itself later."

Having said this, you may come up against unknowns (e.g., technology issues) that make it difficult to make the right design decision. This is when you should do some investigative coding—a *spike*, to borrow an XP term—to tie down the unknowns. This, however, has to be done in a directed manner, and it must be targeted at finding the answers to specific questions. In the early days of my current project, the team went off in a frenzy of coding and investigation for a week or so. At the end of this, we all sat down and tried to review what we'd found out. Surprisingly, the answer was "little of any use"!

As we discussed earlier on, old-style waterfall development processes often had very large analysis and design stages up front. The problem is that while a core set of requirements were often stable, others weren't—or at least they hadn't been thought through properly or were likely to become obsolete before the system actually got implemented.

Another possibility is that your customers don't actually understand your requirements documentation; they can't visualize the system from them. The customers may agree with the documentation but later come back and tell you that you've implemented the wrong system. If your requirements are unstable or not well understood, then you may design the perfect solution to the wrong problem!

Another point worthy of note is that models can be wrong. John Daniels once said to me, "No one ever got sacked for getting a model wrong." The point he was making was that code has to actually run—and therefore be testable—whereas models don't. There is always an inherent risk that the models may actually be incorrect and that once in a while, at least, we need to "prove it in code" and get some concrete feedback.

So there is a dilemma. On the one hand, a small window of design look-ahead can cause a lot of unnecessary refactoring later on. On the other hand, a large window of design look-ahead offers the prospect of less refactoring but at the risk of getting it wrong in one way or another.

So the answer to your question is, "Do as much design up front as you can given your confidence level in the stability and correctness of the requirements, the ability of the team to model effectively, the team's understanding of the technology base, how much the customer actually trusts you, and myriad other issues. It boils down to you making a judgment call.

Being Agile Means You Don't Need to Plan Ahead or Worry About the Future (You Can't Plan Anything Because You Don't Know What's Going to Happen)

Mark: Fiction. Agile projects certainly require some planning, but it's important to bear in mind that the effort you put in and level of detail you go into should be based on how far into the future you're looking. Plan in detail for the short term (current increment) and in broad strokes for the long term (tentative increment use case or feature list).

Doug: Fiction. You may not (and probably won't) be able to plan perfectly. The future always brings uncertainty. But that doesn't mean you shouldn't take your best shot at anticipating, because there are usually many things that can be (and should be) anticipated.

Matt: Fiction, and fact. You definitely do need to plan ahead, but it's true that you don't know what's going to happen. So what use is a plan? A plan would be useless if its purpose was to set in stone precisely what will happen and when. This would mean binding the project plan very closely to the design ("Bob will take 3 days to write the SQL mapping for XYZ module," etc.), and we all know that the design will shift and warp throughout the project. So what we need (and what agilists have already recognized) is that our projects need to be *planning driven* rather than *plan driven*.

Being Agile Means You Don't Need to Try to Get It Right the First Time

Doug: Fiction. Again, if you strive for perfection, you'll probably wind up with high quality. If you don't strive for perfection or high quality, you'll probably wind up with crap. This is true with pretty much everything in life.

Mark: Fiction. While I'm certainly not against refactoring in principle when it's really necessary, one of the biggest fears I have about a culture of continuous refactoring is that it can give developers an excuse to be sloppy ("We don't need to think about this very much because if we get it wrong, we can always refactor it later"). There's a danger of putting your project into continuous prototype mode ("We'll sort that out later") and ignoring real issues. You should always try to get it as right as possible first time.

Matt: I'll go against the grain here and say fact, because you basically know that the design is going to change, so why even bother trying to get it right first time? Just kidding—I think Doug and Mark were worried there for a second! Seriously, though, this is at the heart of agile design, so we shouldn't dismiss it outright. Even the most die-hard agilists will at least try to get a good design the first time, but they might not spend, say, 6–12 months sweating over it.

Even though it's important to absolutely try to get the design right the first time, it's equally important to recognize that the first design you create will never be 100% correct, and it may even be completely wide of the mark, so you can limit the damage by spending less time on the design before you see source code. That's not the same as saying "Leap straight into coding" or "Do 10 minutes of up-front design," though, even if you're following TDD (see Chapter 12). Instead, break the project into smaller sections and design in detail for each subsection before coding.

Being Agile Means You Mustn't Do Any Design Up-Front

Doug: [*Screams "Noooooooooooo!" quietly under his breath*] Fiction.

Matt: Fiction, but this is one of those situations where agilists and nonagilists talk at cross-purposes. One side says, "Agile method A is bad because it doesn't involve any up-front design." The other side responds, "What rubbish! We do up-front design all the time—usually for 10 minutes at the start of each day's programming." So, of course, it all depends on your definition of "up-front design." *Big Design Up Front* (BDUF) usually means 6+ months of design during which no programming takes place. That's bad. *Up-front design* might mean a month of intensive design work, or a week, or 10 minutes at the start of each day. There's a definite cut-off point where the more up-front design work you do, you suddenly stop being agile because the customer has to wait too long before he sees any working software—the feedback loop isn't small enough. I would say that before a large-ish project, a month of design work (including rapid prototyping to prevent the designs getting too naïve) is essential. It helps to arrange all your ducks in a row before you get started. After that, then design as you go along, module by module.

Mark: Fiction. This relates directly to the last point. If you've agreed on the contents of your current production increment, and you're confident they're stable, then why wouldn't you undertake some design and try to get it right first time? You may make some mistakes (as you haven't proven your design in code yet), but by undertaking some up-front design, you're going to reduce the amount of refactoring you need to do—assuming you have the skills to do so. But do note, however, that there's nothing to stop you from doing some coding as part of your design phase if you need to, if you're not sure if you have it right.

Being Agile Means You Should Never Design Flexibility into Your Software

Mark: It depends on what your definition of "flexibility" is. I think there's an implication in this question that the "flexibility" being talked about isn't actually needed in the current increment—that it is there for some future, as yet undefined purpose. Some software developers have a tendency to drastically overengineer solutions based on guesswork about the future. Given this, I'd say fact. Flexibility should be driven by known needs.

Doug: Fiction. While none of us may be able to correctly predict the future on a consistent basis, this doesn't mean that we should pretend the future won't happen.

Matt: This is definitely not what agile processes are telling us, although it isn't a million miles away either. Spending ages creating complex layers of indirection ironically makes the software more difficult to change (given that layers of indirection are supposed to make the design more flexible). Instead, agilists tell us to make the software easy to change by keeping it simple, which is more realistic.

Concluding Fact or Fiction

As you can see, when it comes to defining what agility is or isn't, and what it should or shouldn't be, some differences of opinion arise—even in a group of people who for the most part agree on how software should be developed. The definition of agility has become quite nebulous, and people in our industry risk losing sight of some "traditional" core principles that remain valid, even with the advent of agility.

Agility doesn't make up-front design obsolete. It also doesn't make in-depth requirements analysis unnecessary. If anything, we rely on these disciplines more than ever so as to better achieve the agile goals.

Software agility boils down to simply giving the customer what he wants, safely, and in a reasonable time frame. If the requirements change, we need to change with them—even late in the project—so that we're still delivering what the customer wants. (But see the caveat in the sidebar "Change Is Good, but It's Also Expensive" earlier in this chapter.)

Summary

In this chapter we defined a core subset of the many practices that are out there and variously defined as agile. These core practices used together complement each other and are particularly apt for use with the ICONIX object modeling process.

We also analyzed the reality of software agility versus the perception of software agility people have grown accustomed to. If an agile practice doesn't contribute to the core goals of software agility, then it can't reasonably be considered an agile practice. It might be important, but it's something other than agile.

In the next section of the book, we examine the core agile practices in action and show how to combine them with ICONIX Process, itself a core subset of UML modeling techniques. This won't be a theoretical discussion, but a very practical example: a real-life C#/.NET application.

PART 2

Agile ICONIX Process in Practice: The Mapplet Project

This part of the book features a running example project that will thread through the various chapters. We'll illustrate many of the points we made in Part 1 using this example project. The project is real—it's not an academic exercise—and we've taken snapshots during the various iterations of modeling, prototyping, and coding.

This being a book about agile development (i.e., adapting to changing requirements over time), our idea is to present the original project requirements and show that even though the requirements evolved over the course of the project, we were still able to incorporate up-front modeling into the development process. The story that unfolds is very much the story of how to approach this situation.

The use case text and diagrams shown in this part's chapters were taken directly from the project, so you'll notice some (minor) inconsistencies at times between the use cases and the text in the diagrams. This also reflects the "agile spirit": the analysis and design artifacts need to be just good enough to get us to the next stage of development. (Or, to put it another way, they need to be *minimal yet sufficient*. The team should always try to avoid spending ages polishing the diagrams until they're perfect.)

CHAPTER 5

Introducing the Mapplet Project

This project tells the story of a feedback-driven process that causes the design and the code to become more tightly in sync as the project progresses. To us, this is the essence of successful agile development. In most cases where modeling is done up-front, the model and the code quickly diverge, never to meet again. Agile ICONIX, on the other hand, encourages developers to keep the model and the code tightly synchronized, by revisiting and reviewing the model at the end of each iteration (and at the start of each new release phase), as well as by placing an emphasis on early feedback at every stage of the process. We revisit this concept in more detail in Chapters 6 and 7.

Our example project is a map-based hotel finder for a travel website, which was developed using the agile development approach described in this book. We'll show the evolution of the model and the code that goes with it.

The finished product is available for you to interact with at this web address: `http://smartmaps.vresorts.com`. Just drill down into any of the map destination pages from the main U.S. map, and then click the Show Map button to see the mapplet in action. You might find it interesting to compare the finished product with the use cases presented in this book.

The mapplet is a web-based application that is built on top of ESRI's[1] ArcGIS Server platform. The ArcGIS[2] platform enables the development of Geographic Information System (GIS) or map-based applications using state-of-the-art OO (e.g., C#/.NET) environments. To fully leverage the power of these modern development environments, it's helpful to adopt an OO approach from front to back. ICONIX Process, being a low-ceremony, minimalist, use case–driven design approach, is ideal for developing OO GIS applications. The mapplet example is actually an ArcGIS Server application that has been developed by ESRI's Professional Services organization.

The mapplet example shows how to run from requirements and use cases through detailed OO design, to C#/.NET source code and fully working software that meets the project requirements. A key element of the approach is the "agile" strategy of interleaving modeling and coding through multiple releases of the design.

So, What's a Mapplet, Anyway?

The mapplet project is a mapping application—a hotel-finder street map that is hosted on our favorite travel website (okay, it's Doug's site). As a reader, you'll have the opportunity to read through the use cases, look at the sequence and class diagrams, and interact with the application.

As you've probably gathered from the title of this chapter, our nickname for the example project is "mapplet," even though it's not really a Java applet. We apologize most profusely for confusing our readership, but the name just sort of stuck and now we're used to it . . .

This being a book about agile development, we didn't write a 500-page requirements document before coding, but instead "grew" the mapplet a few use cases at a time as a series of small releases. Over the various chapters of this book, you'll learn how the design evolved across these releases. You'll see some design errors that we corrected before coding, you'll see how (and if) the code matches the design, and you'll see how the actual running program matches the use cases we started with (aka use case–driven acceptance testing).

1. See `www.esri.com`.
2. See the sidebar "What Is ArcGIS?" later in this chapter.

Just for fun (and to enhance the real-world flavor of the example), the mapplet was built with a brand-new (still in beta as this paragraph is being written) version of the GIS server software,[3] and it was thus the first experience the development team had with this new server product. So, you'll see some exploratory coding to figure out how the beta software fits into the process as well.

WHAT IS ArcGIS?[4]

The core technology being used by the mapplet is a map server product called ArcGIS Server, from ESRI. ArcGIS[5] is a platform for building enterprise GIS applications.

At its core, a GIS is a system for the management, analysis, and display of geographic information. Geographic information is represented by a series of geographic datasets that model geographic information using generic data structures. A GIS includes a set of comprehensive tools for maintaining geographic data, visualizing geographic data, and analyzing relationships between geographic features on the earth's surface. Various map views of the underlying geographic information can be constructed and used as windows into the database to support queries, analysis, and editing of the information.

ArcGIS is used by thousands of different organizations and hundreds of thousands of individuals to access and manage a massive variety of geographic information. There are a number of books available that cover the ArcGIS suite of products, most notably *Getting to Know ArcGIS Desktop*,[6] *Mastering ArcGIS*,[7] and *Getting to Know ArcObjects*.[8] Also, a particularly nice book on GIS science in general (not specifically about ArcGIS) is *Geographic Information Systems and Science*.[9]

ArcGIS solves a particularly difficult challenge: representing in digital form a model of geographic information such as the earth's surface; breaking these aspects down into a database of specific searchable features, such as cities, landmarks, or (in our case) hotels; and mapping addresses and zip codes to geospatial coordinates (and vice versa).

ArcGIS Server is the enterprise server of the ArcGIS platform, which includes a shared library of GIS software objects to build server-side GIS applications in an enterprise and web computing framework. ArcGIS Server provides the ability to publish GIS web services. It's a platform for building enterprise GIS applications that are centrally managed, support multiple users, and include advanced GIS functionality. ArcGIS Server manages geographic resources, such as maps, locators, and GIS software objects, for use by applications.

Developers can use ArcGIS Server to build focused web applications, web services, and other enterprise applications, including those based on J2EE or .NET. Developers can use ArcGIS Server to build desktop applications that interact with the server in client/server mode. ArcGIS Server also supports out-of-the-box use by ArcGIS desktop applications for server administration, simple mapping, and geocoding over a local area network (LAN) or the Internet.

ArcGIS Server, like the entire ArcGIS system, is built and extended using software components called ArcObjects, as shown here:

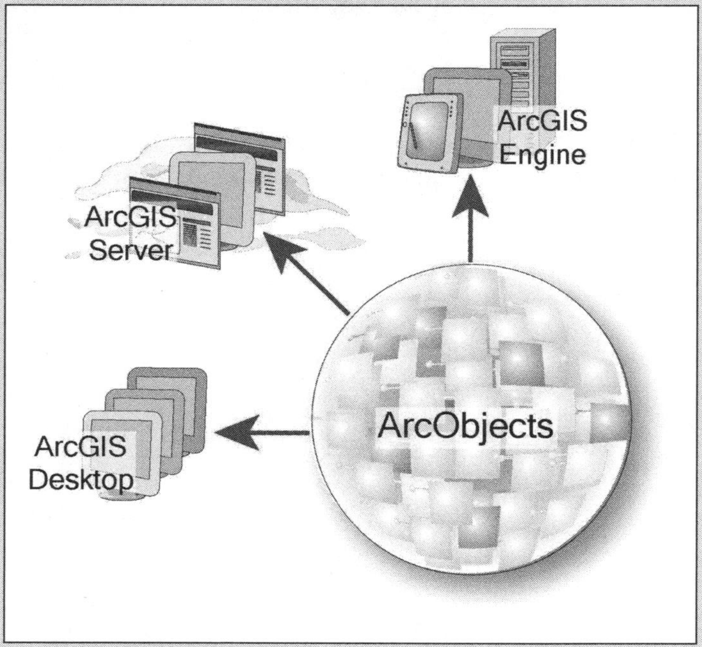

The ArcGIS Server ArcObjects are the same ArcObjects that are at the core of all the ArcGIS products: ArcGIS Desktop, ArcGIS Engine, and ArcGIS Server.

ArcGIS Server consists of two primary components: a GIS server and an Application Development Framework (ADF) for .NET and Java. The GIS server hosts ArcObjects for use by web, enterprise, and desktop applications. It includes the core ArcObjects libraries and provides a scalable environment for running ArcObjects on a server. ADF allows you to build and deploy .NET or Java desktop and web applications that use ArcObjects running within the GIS server.

ADF includes a software developer kit (SDK) with software objects, web controls, web application templates, developer help, and code samples. It also includes a web application runtime, which allows you to deploy web applications without having to install ArcObjects on your web server.

The following image is an example screenshot of an ArcGIS Server–based web application:

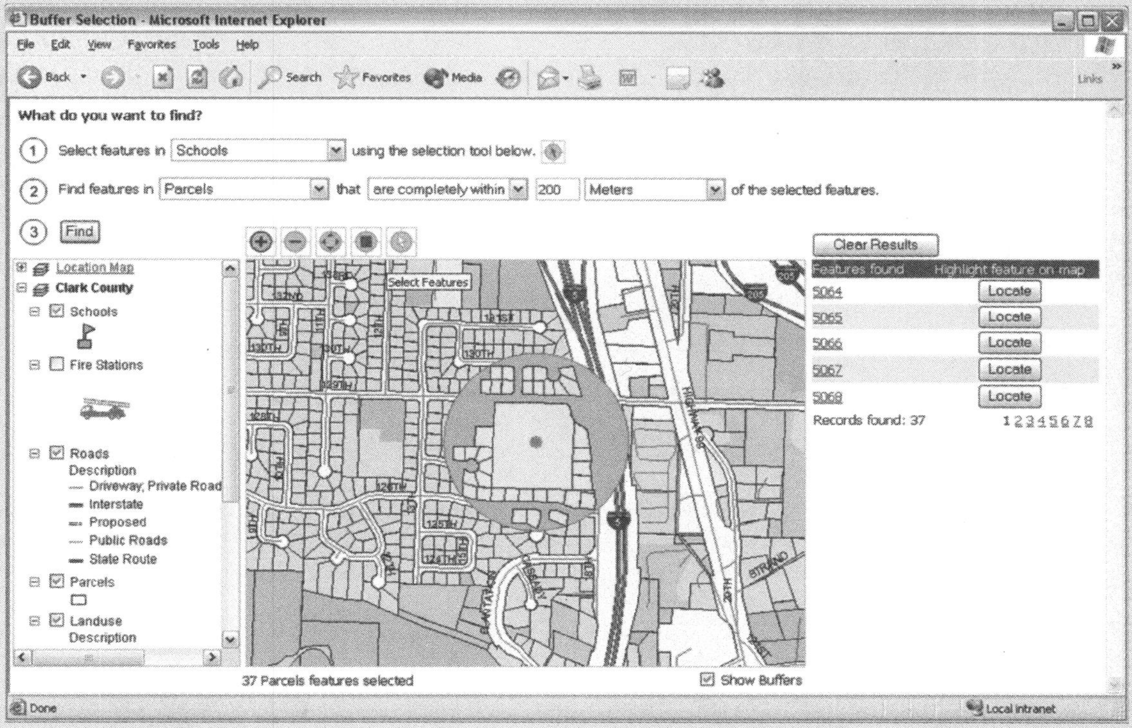

3. ArcGIS Server is now a fully released product. The first release of ArcGIS Server came with the release of the ArcGIS 9.0 software suite in May 2004. The mapplet development occurred on a beta release for the software; however, the final installation was released using ArcGIS 9.0.

4. Thanks to the ESRI marketing department and to Dave Lewis of ESRI for providing us with material for this section.

5. See `www.esri.com/software/arcgis`.

6. Tim Ormsby, Eileen Napoleon, Robert Burke, Carolyn Groessl, and Laura Feaster, *Getting to Know ArcGIS Desktop: The Basics of ArcView, ArcEditor, and ArcInfo Updated for ArcGIS 9* (Redlands, CA: ESRI Press, June 2004).

7. Maribeth Price, *Mastering ArcGIS* (New York: McGraw-Hill, September 2003).

8. Robert Burke, *Getting to Know ArcObjects* (Redlands, CA: ESRI Press, October 2003).

9. Paul A. Longley, Michael F. Goodchild, David J. Maguire, and David W. Rhind, *Geographic Information Systems and Science* (West Sussex, England: John Wiley & Sons, August 2001).

Mapplet Goals

The primary purpose of the mapplet is to provide a map-based interface that allows users to easily and quickly find hotels in specific areas of a destination city; refine their choices by price band, amenities, and so forth; and use an interface to a hotel "booking engine" that can display brochure pages about specific hotels. As you'd probably hope for this type of application, the mapplet also provides a booking capability so that users can make hotel reservations online.

The first release of the mapplet will work for all cities within the United States. Future releases may support major international cities as well. The existence of the mapplet is expected to allow scaling of traffic through the website by a couple of orders of magnitude from its current state, so performance requirements related to scalability of the number of concurrent users are very important. For that reason (among others) we're not Doing The Simplest Thing That Could Possibly Work (DTSTTCPW), nor are we "turning a blind eye toward future requirements." Rather, we're making a concerted effort to think ahead, make smart design decisions, and put an architecture in place early that won't result in severe performance degradation as the number of users increases.

Another major goal of the mapplet is to make it easy to construct web pages for destinations with local, street-level hotel maps featured on them.

The mapplet's goals can be summed up in the following list:

1. Allow scalability of traffic by allowing map-centric destination pages (and associated pay-per-click advertising) to be produced rapidly for any city in the United States (related feature: pass in a hotel ID as a parameter to the mapplet on startup).

2. Build a repeat clientele (related feature: save user preferences in a cookie).

2.1. Increase the "wow" factor of the website (related feature: very fast display filtering by price band).

3. Make the site more useful to business travelers (related features: search by chain and driving directions).

4. Make the site more useful to vacationers (related features: search by amenity, search by price band, etc.).

It's useful to define a small set of high-level goals at the start of a project. Then if one of these goals changes midproject, we get a good idea of how much of the requirements and design need to change to accommodate the shift in direction. Essentially, this means that we can *manage* change rather than embrace it.

Mapplet Requirements

As is typical with software requirements, the mapplet requirements are a mixture of high- and low-level functional requirements and ad-hoc implementation details.

Normally, you try to keep design and implementation details out of the requirements. However, with this example, the project is extending an existing website using an existing technology (ArcGIS Server). Therefore, the design is constrained by the website that the project must fit into, and some of the requirements are about how the product should leverage ArcGIS' out-of-the-box functionality. So (within reason) it's important to include some of these design details in the requirements.

The complete set of mapplet requirements is shown in the "Mapplet Requirements" sidebar. We've presented these requirements exactly as they were written for the project; there's been a small amount of tidying up and reformatting, but the essence is basically the same.

MAPPLET REQUIREMENTS

1. ArcGIS Server will be used to create a set of one or more Java applets that may be hosted on web pages within VResorts.com.

2. The applet(s) will provide map-based capability to locate and reserve hotels online within the US.

2.1. Within the US, hotels will be displayed on the ??? base map.

2.2. When loaded on a web page, the applet will read in its initial Region Of Interest (ROI) coordinates from an external source, which may be specified on the HTML of that web page or from the web page itself. The applet will access a hotel database that contains geocoding/location information for hotels, and use this information to locate and display hotels on the map.

2.2.1. Hotel database format. The hotel database is provided as a comma-separated flat file with the following fields:

```
id, brand, name, address1, address2, city, state, country, zip, latitude,
longitude, phone, online_bookings, hotrates, video, brochure, overview, map,
price_band, star_rating, amenities
```

An example record (4-star hotel in Luxury price band) follows:

```
10204567,HY,Park Hyatt Washington,24th & M Street NW 1201 24th
Street,,Washington,DC,US,20037,38.897500,-77.050700,202-789-1234,Y,N,N,N,Y,Y,L
,4,128 106 100 104 107 113 125 134 115 126 108 114 132 121 123 117 120 111 129
135 109 130 118 124
```

2.3. Users will have the option to modify the active ROI by panning and zooming in or out.

2.4. The applet will provide a variety of display options to the user, which will result in icons that represent hotels within the active ROI being displayed on the map.

2.4.1. Display any combination of price band searches from the sets "Luxury," "Upscale," "Midrange," and "Economy." Different icons will be used to represent each price band.

2.4.2. Display the "Star Rating" of the hotels next to the hotel icons, either based on the zoom level or upon mouse rollover.

2.4.3. Display the Names of the hotels next to the hotel icons, either based on the zoom level or upon mouse rollover.

2.4.4. [Optional] The applet will access the reservations database dynamically using an XML interface to determine rates and availability for a given date range, and display this information on the map.

2.4.4.1. [Optional] "Specify date range using calendar": The applet will provide a visual calendar-based interface for specifying date ranges.

2.5. "Find hotels near address": The applet shall provide the ability for the user to type in an address and display hotels on a map within some distance of that address. The default distance will be a 5 mile radius.

2.5.1. The applet will provide the user the ability to change the distance for "nearby hotel" display.

2.6. "Find hotels by zip code": The applet will provide the ability for a user to enter a zip code, and will display hotels within that zip code and all immediately adjoining zip codes on a map.

2.7. "Search by city": If the user clicks on the name of a city on the map, the applet will set the active ROI appropriately to that city's boundary and display a map showing all hotels within the price bands specified in 2.4.1.

2.8. "Search by state": If the user clicks on the name of a state on the map, the applet will set the active ROI appropriately to that state's boundary and display a map showing all hotels within the price bands specified in 2.4.1.

2.9. "View hotel information": If the user clicks a hotel icon on the map display, the applet will display a new browser window containing the hotel's detailed information.

2.9.1. Syntax for accessing hotel information: The applet will construct a URL to access hotel information according to the following rules. The applet will display a brochure page if one is available, otherwise display a property overview page.

2.9.1.1. Prefix: The URL shall begin with the string "`http://reservations.vresorts.com/hotel/10004663-`".

2.9.1.2. Property ID: The applet shall look up the hotel's property ID in the database. An example property ID is "10215820". The property ID is concatenated to the prefix.

2.9.1.3. Suffix: "O", "B", "V", or "M" .html.

* The string "O.html" results in the display of a property overview page when concatenated to the prefix and property ID.
* The string "B.html" results in the display of a property brochure page when concatenated to the prefix and property ID.
* The string "V.html" results in the display of a hotel video when concatenated to the prefix and property ID.
* The string "M.html" results in the display of a hotel map page when concatenated to the prefix and property ID.

2.9.1.4. [Optional] Right-click options. The user may right-click on a hotel icon and get a pop-up menu that provides options to display Overview, Brochure, Video, and Map pages if available for a given property. The user may also choose to check rates and availability from this menu, using the XML interface.

2.10. Filter hotels displayed by available amenities: The applet shall provide the capability to filter hotel searches via the selection of a set of amenities from a set of check boxes on a dialog box. For example, the user may choose to show only hotels with spas and pools. These filter selections will apply to all hotel/map displays above.

3. The applet(s) will provide map-based capability to locate and reserve hotels online outside of the US. Most hotels outside of the US are not geocoded, and therefore the applet will behave differently outside the US.

3.1. Outside the US, the data used should be vendor neutral.

3.2. When loaded on a web page, the applet will read in its initial Region Of Interest (ROI) coordinates from an external source, which may be specified on the HTML of that web page or from the web page itself.

3.3. Users will have the option to modify the active ROI by panning and zooming in or out. This will cause country and city names to appear on the map.

3.4. Search by country/city: When the user clicks on the name of a country or city on the map, a database query is generated in the form of a URL. The result set of the query is displayed in a new window.

3.4.1. Database query syntax: The query URL is a string composed of the following elements: Prefix, Country, City, and Sort Order.

3.4.1.1. Example: The following URL returns a list of hotels in Mazatlan, Mexico, sorted by star rating:

```
http://reservations.vresorts.com/nexres/search/power_results.cgi?src=10004663&la
ng=ENG&country=MX&city=MAZATLAN&sort_order=Stars
```

3.4.1.2. Prefix: All search URLs will begin with the prefix

```
http://reservations.vresorts.com/nexres/search/power_results.cgi?src=10004663&la
ng=ENG
```

3.4.2.2. Country Codes. A list of 2-character country codes will be provided in a separate document. In the example above, MX is the code for Mexico.

3.4.2.3. City name: The city name is read from the base map and added to the search query. For cities with names separated by spaces, the names are concatenated together using a "+". For example: "&city=PUERTO+VALLARTA" will return hotels in the city of Puerto Vallarta.

3.4.2.4. Sort Order: If left blank, the hotel database returns an alphabetic sort by hotel name. This applet will use the "sort by star rating" option, which is the string "&sort_order=Stars" concatenated to the Prefix, Country, and City.

An example of how we've left the original style/formatting in the preceding requirements is the way in which the requirements meander from formal "the system shall" wording to brief, informal note form. This is an important agile principle: if the customer is happy with this form of requirements, then we can save a lot of time by not having to dot every "i" and cross every "t." Whatever gets the point across. The requirements aren't the finished product, and they're not the goal in themselves—they just describe the goal, so we shouldn't spend ages perfecting them.

You'll also notice that the requirements talk about "applets" rather than "mapplets," because the original idea was to create a Java applet to perform the map-based hotel search functions. This was partly because the customer's website already has a hotel search applet that the new system will replace. However, it was soon decided that a web-based user interface (making heavy use of DHTML in the browser) would be more suitable, so the mapplet was born.

At this stage, we haven't decided which requirements will go into which release. Once we've done a small amount of initial use case modeling (where the use cases are derived from the requirements), we'll prioritize the use cases and divide them into different releases (we show this process later in this chapter). Further into the project, new requirements will be added and some of the existing requirements will change (or they'll be dropped altogether). It's a fluid process, but it's still important to get the requirements written down so that we have a baseline from which to work.

Project Inception: A JumpStart Workshop in Action

The mapplet project started out as a not entirely fictitious training example for ESRI developers, which resulted in a preliminary model with use cases, domain objects, and robustness and sequence diagrams. The idea of using the project as our central book example didn't transpire until several months (nearly a year) had elapsed after this training workshop. The first domain model that we show in the second image in the "What Is ArcGIS?" sidebar earlier in the chapter (which is more detailed than the subsequent ones) was actually a result of the JumpStart workshop.[10]

The workshop was run by Doug, who had a dual role as instructor and mapplet "customer" for his website. The initial set of requirements (which we show in this chapter) were written by Doug in preparation for the JumpStart class, at which time the team was anticipating using a different version of the ESRI map server software (ArcIMS instead of ArcGIS) and building a Java applet (hence the name "mapplet") instead of an ASP.NET application. Interestingly, the requirements and use cases (and project nickname) survived these technology changes pretty much intact.

Because the JumpStart class included hands-on development work, it doubled as a timeboxed investigative modeling spike (i.e., prototype) performed by teams with a coach and an on-site customer. Once the requirements were mapped onto use cases (behavior requirements) and the alternative courses were explored in detail, the on-site customer (Doug) wasn't really needed, so his time was freed up from the project. Speaking from one customer's perspective, it's important to note that this project would never have happened if Doug had to be a full-time on-site customer. Like many customers, he is just too busy. We've always felt that this over-reliance on an on-site customer was a significant flaw in some agile approaches.

10. See www.iconixsw.com/JumpStart.html.

Mapplet Architecture

Figure 5-1 shows a high-level architectural view of the ArcGIS Server architecture as it relates to web-based applications. We can see from this image how the mapplet application will need to fit into the ArcGIS architecture.

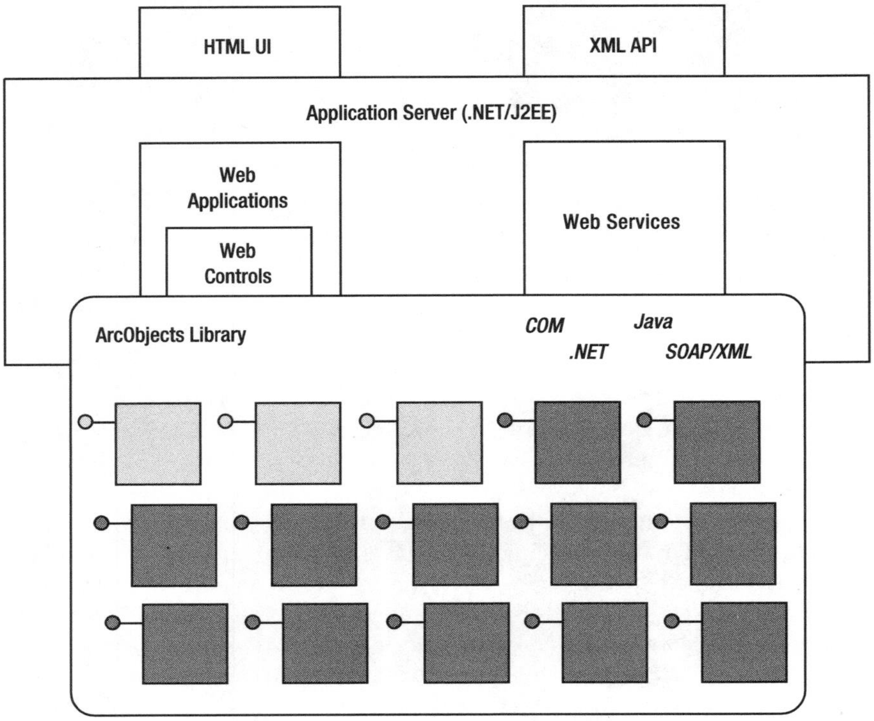

Figure 5-1. *ArcGIS Server architecture diagram*

We can think of the mapplet as a multilayer application. There are three major server objects deployed within the ArcGIS Server. The Map Server and Geocode Server are coarse-grained ArcObjects that are provided by the ArcGIS Server out of the box. These coarse-grained objects consist of hundreds of pre-existing COM objects that perform a multitude of GIS-related functionality. These server objects access map data stored in a variety of ESRI data formats. The other object is the Hotel Server, which wasn't provided out of the box. The Hotel Server is a utility COM object created using Visual Basic code, and it was written to access the hotel data in an SQL Server database. The Server Object Manager (SOM) manages the life cycle of the Map Server and Geocode Server, and brokers the requests to these server objects.

The web application layer of the mapplet is written in C# and deployed as ASP.NET pages. The ASP.NET web pages use the ESRI-provided WebMap control for ASP.NET applications. For mapping- and geocoding-related functions, the WebMap control accesses the Map Server and Geocode Server objects. For hotel-related queries, the C# classes interact with the compiled Visual Basic object Hotel Server on the server side, which in turn makes calls to the hotel database.

Most of the classes you'll see in the UML models that we present in this book are implemented as C# classes to encapsulate the business logic of the application. The ASP.NET code runs on the server side within the IIS web server, and generates the HTML and JavaScript code that is sent to the browser. Some data is cached in the web browser, and some functionality is implemented in the browser via HTML and JavaScript.

Initial Use Case Modeling for the Mapplet

As this is an iterative and incremental agile project, we'll go through many rounds of object modeling, coding, and testing before the project is complete. Because the planning in an Agile ICONIX project is driven by use cases, we need an initial set of use cases before we can begin planning at the use-case level. This stands to reason, of course: it would be difficult to plan *when* to deliver something to the customer without first determining *what* we're delivering to the customer!

The list of use cases is likely to change fairly quickly as the project continues its inception and exploration phase. Naturally, we'll need to revisit the plan frequently. Therefore, it's important not to have to produce a complicated plan that is difficult and time consuming to maintain. The iteration plan that we use is nice and simple, and shows just enough information to allow us to proceed.

We should expect to see the list of use cases settle down by the time we begin the production phase. By this stage, most of the hard work will have been done. We'll have a domain model for the whole system and a reliable set of use cases from which we can begin to design the system.

Recall from Chapter 3 that before we produce our use cases, we need to create a domain model. An early version of the domain model for the mapplet project is shown in Figure 5-2. As you can see, this version is rough around the edges and definitely needs more work. One issue with this diagram is that the team earnestly began to identify fields and operations on the classes, when it was really a bit too early in the project to do this. (Actually, this diagram was produced during the JumpStart class and had thus been fleshed out to a certain extent, but it served as the starting place for the mapplet team.) Generally the domain model (at least at this early stage) should consist of just the domain object names and the relationships between them. The rest of the details will be filled in later during the design process.

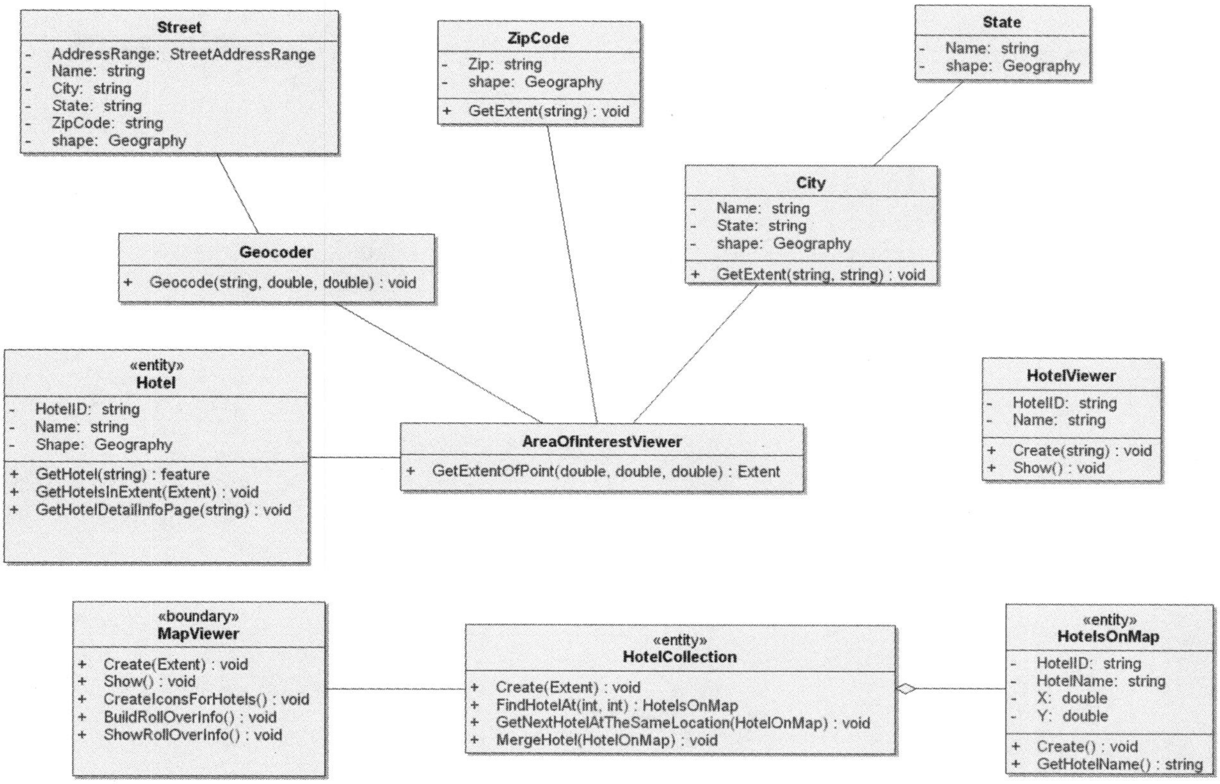

Figure 5-2. *Domain model after the original JumpStart workshop*

Having said that, we'd certainly expect the domain model to be quite rough around the edges at this stage. The main thing is that the team created one and provided a foundation from which to begin the project. So it should be sufficient for us now to begin identifying the use cases.

The initial use case diagram is shown in Figure 5-3. Again, this is going to need a lot more work, but it's good enough for us to produce the first release plan.

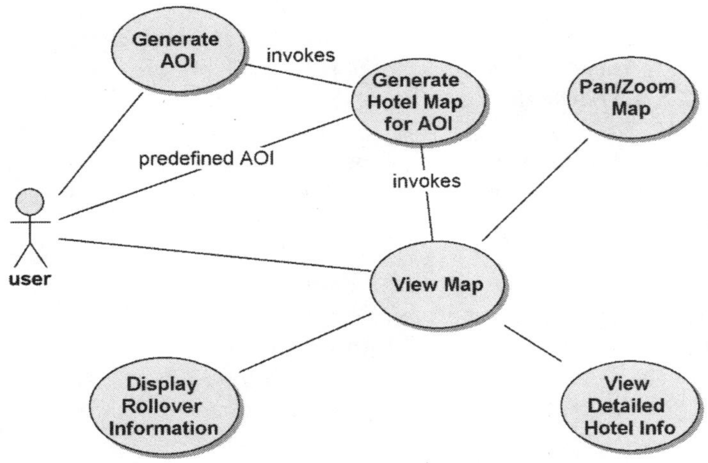

Figure 5-3. *Use case diagram early in the project*

We'll review the domain model and use case diagram in Chapter 6. For now, let's use what we have so far to take our first stab at the release plan.

First Release Plan

What we haven't yet done is divide the requirements and use cases into separate releases. Currently, they're a relatively unstructured list of things that we want the new system to be able to do. The next stage, then, is to start to prioritize these. We can then divide the project into smaller releases.

The original release plan for the mapplet project (totally unaltered from the version that the team used) is shown in Table 5-1.

Table 5-1. *The Initial Release Plan*

Release	Use Case	Comments
1	Create AOI for Address	
	Generate Hotel Map for AOI	
	View Map	
	Pan/Zoom Map	Basic
	View Hotel Information	Basic
	Create Shapefile	
2	Display Rollover Information	Basic
	Pan/Zoom Map	Progressive disclosure
	View Hotel Info	Multiple hotels found at click coordinates
3	Generate Query by Country from Map	Subsumes functionality of existing mapplet
	Generate Query by City from Map	Subsumes functionality of existing mapplet

continued

Table 5-1. *The Initial Release Plan (continued)*

Release	Use Case	Comments
4	Check Room Availability	Anything that requires "XML for Travel"
	Specify Reservation Dates	
	Set Up Display Filter	
	Display Rollover Information	Including availability/rate data

Of course, it doesn't get much simpler than that. We've simply taken the requirements, broken them down into use cases, and decided which use cases will go in which release.

The release plan isn't set in stone by any means. We'll revisit the plan several times as the project continues to take shape. The release plan after the first release is done will look different from this version. We'll evolve the requirements as the software gets partially completed, and our estimates should become more accurate the further we progress in the project.

The planning is done in an iterative, incremental, feature-driven, model-driven manner:

- It's *iterative* because each release is broken down into smaller, fixed-size planning iterations.
- It's *incremental* because each release builds incrementally on top of the previous release.
- It's *feature driven* because we're deriving the plan from specific features that we want to see delivered. (In the same sense, it's *use case driven* because we're driving the release plan directly from the use cases.)
- It's *model driven* because the estimates are derived from engineering tasks that we identify via the object model.

More Information on ArcGIS As Used by the Mapplet

This section provides some more technical background information on how the mapplet project will use the underlying technology. It's quite specific to ArcGIS, so if you're not expressly interested in ArcGIS, it probably wouldn't do any harm to skip this section.

Tip You can find a lot of useful information on developing with ArcGIS at the ArcGIS Developer Online website at `http://arcgisdeveloperonline.esri.com`.

ArcGIS Software Developer Kit

The ArcGIS SDK is geared toward helping developers implement custom ArcGIS functionality. It consists of the following:

- *Developer tools*: These are executables provided by ESRI for developing applications that use ArcObjects. For example, the Component Category Manager tool (`Categories.exe`) registers components in different component categories, and the Library Locator tool identifies an object library containing a specified interface. The developer tools are installed under the DeveloperKit\tools folder. There is one exception to this: the Component Category Manager tool is located in the ArcGIS\bin folder.
- *Add-ins*: These add-ins plug into the integrated development environment (IDE) that you use for developing on top of ArcGIS (e.g., there are add-ins for Visual Basic 6 and Visual Studio .NET).
- *Help system*: The help system provides a gateway to all the SDK documentation, including help for all the add-ins, developer tools, and samples. The help system organizes samples by functionality (e.g., all the Geodatabase samples are grouped under Samples\Geodatabase).
- *Code samples*: There are over 600 code samples to try out.

ArcGIS Server Terminology

The following list provides an overview of the terms and concepts you'll encounter during ArcGIS development. We also use some of these terms in the next few chapters to describe the mapplet project.[11]

- *GIS server*: The GIS server is responsible for hosting and managing server objects. The GIS server is the set of objects, applications, and services that make it possible to run ArcObjects components on a server. The GIS server consists of the Server Object Manager and one or more Server Object Containers.
- *Server Object Manager (SOM)*: The SOM is a Windows service or a UNIX daemon that manages the set of server objects distributed across one or more container machines. When an application makes a connection to an ArcGIS Server over a LAN, it is making a connection to the SOM.
- *Server Object Container (SOC)*: An SOC is a process in which one or more server objects are running. SOC processes are started up and shut down by the SOM. The SOC processes run on the GIS server's container machines. Each container machine is capable of hosting multiple SOC processes.
- *Server object*: A server object is a coarse-grained ArcObjects component—that is, it's a high-level object that simplifies the programming model for doing certain operations and hides the fine-grained ArcObjects that do the work. Server objects support coarse-grained interfaces that have methods that do large units of work, such as "draw a map" or "geocode a set of addresses." Server objects also have SOAP interfaces, which make it possible to expose server objects as web services that can be consumed by clients across the Internet.
- *Web server*: The web server hosts web applications and web services written using the ArcGIS Server API.
- *Pooled server object*: ArcGIS Server allows you to pool instances of server objects such that they can be shared between multiple application sessions at the per-request level. This allows you to support more users with fewer resources. Pooled server objects should be used by applications that make stateless use of the GIS server.
- *Nonpooled server object*: Nonpooled server objects are created for exclusive use by an application session and are destroyed when returned by the application to the server. The creation of each object includes creating the object and loading up any initialization data (e.g., the map document associated with a Map Server object). Users of a server application that makes use of a nonpooled server object require an instance of that object dedicated to their session. Nonpooled server objects are for applications that make stateful use of the GIS server.
- *Application Developer Framework (ADF)*: The ADF is a collection of web controls, convenience classes and data objects, and application templates that make it easy to build and deploy .NET or Java web applications that use ArcObjects running within the GIS server. The ADF includes an SDK with web controls, web application templates, developer help, and code samples. It also includes a web application runtime that allows you to deploy applications without having to install ArcObjects on your web server.

Summary

In this chapter, we introduced the ESRI mapplet project, a Professional Services project being run at ESRI using their ArcGIS Server mapping software and ICONIX modeling to define the product in terms of use cases. We also showed the initial rough draft of requirements and the use case model for this project, and we spent some time up-front creating a domain model. The domain model provides a project glossary, so that all subsequent artifacts (use cases, design models, etc.) can be written using consistent names. We also gave an overview of the ArcGIS Server platform and indicated which parts of its APIs the mapplet will use.

For the rest of Part 2, we'll continue to follow the mapplet project and show how the team got from use cases to code over the first two successive releases.

11. Thanks again to ESRI for allowing us to reproduce this material.

CHAPTER 6

Modeling the Mapplet (Release 1)

This chapter continues the case study of a real-life project run at ESRI using Agile ICONIX. So far, we've created an early version of the project domain model, written a "first-pass" attempt at some use cases, and created a release plan from the use cases. We also broke down the use cases into estimable chunks of work so that we could plan and prioritize the work for the first release.

In this chapter, we'll see the core modeling aspect of ICONIX Process kick into action. We'll show how the use cases are turned into a concrete design over two very brief modeling iterations, followed by a coding iteration.

Beginning with a Prototype (and Just a Little Bit of Modeling)

Release 1 was to be an exploratory release, examining the new server technology. So it made a lot of sense at this stage for the team members to get their hands dirty and just write some code to familiarize themselves with the new technology. Without the requisite familiarity with the technology they were using, it would be unrealistic to expect anyone to produce a really robust up-front design. Therefore, early prototyping is a key aspect of up-front design, to keep the design grounded in reality.

However, what the team also wanted to avoid was simply leaping in and producing something that was a million miles away from what the customer wanted. So, as the customer already had a pretty good idea of what he wanted from the new system, a *little* up-front design work was warranted.

Of course at this stage, the team already had a set of use cases and a domain model, so the behavioral requirements of the new system had been thought through. That's a pretty good place to start, especially for a prototype.

As it embarked on the prototype, the team produced some sequence diagrams to describe the design at a slightly higher level than pure code. The team also revisited and refined the domain model. However, this being a prototype, the team skipped robustness analysis and also didn't spend time creating a detailed class diagram.

The result was a design that would meet the needs of a prototype, but not a production system, as much of the team's time was focused on getting an understanding of the underlying technology. To the team members' credit, they still produced the goods, in the sense that the end product matched the initial set of requirements. However, as you'll see in Chapter 7, the code and design review gave the team an opportunity to start release 2 (the first production release) from a clean design.

In this chapter, however, we chronicle release 1 exactly as it happened, because it provides a useful real-world indication of the issues that most teams will encounter during the early stages of a project. At this point, the team is prototyping, exploring the technology, and looking for a way to match up the problem with a suitable solution.

PROVING IT WITH CODE

Early prototyping in this context is a key agile concept that fits neatly into ICONIX Process: *prove it with code*[1] as early in the project as possible.

The code doesn't have to be "industrial grade" (or even just plain old production-worthy). The important thing is that the team writes some code as soon as possible. As many teams have discovered, this can have an almost miraculous effect on their understanding of both the problem domain and the optimal design path that they should follow. This "miraculous effect" isn't the product of any particular development process or design methodology; it's simply that when programmers start thinking in code, they automatically put their design hats on and quickly discover which solutions will work and which ones won't. This is valuable early feedback, and it's the reason early prototyping is so important in an up-front design process.

Visual Acceptance Testing

A key part of ICONIX Process is to begin with a prototype of the UI. As we discuss in Chapter 7, this is a good opportunity to apply some interaction design techniques, to help produce a UI that's eminently focused on the needs of a particular target user. For now, though, let's take a look at our mock-up for the mapplet web page (see Figure 6-1).

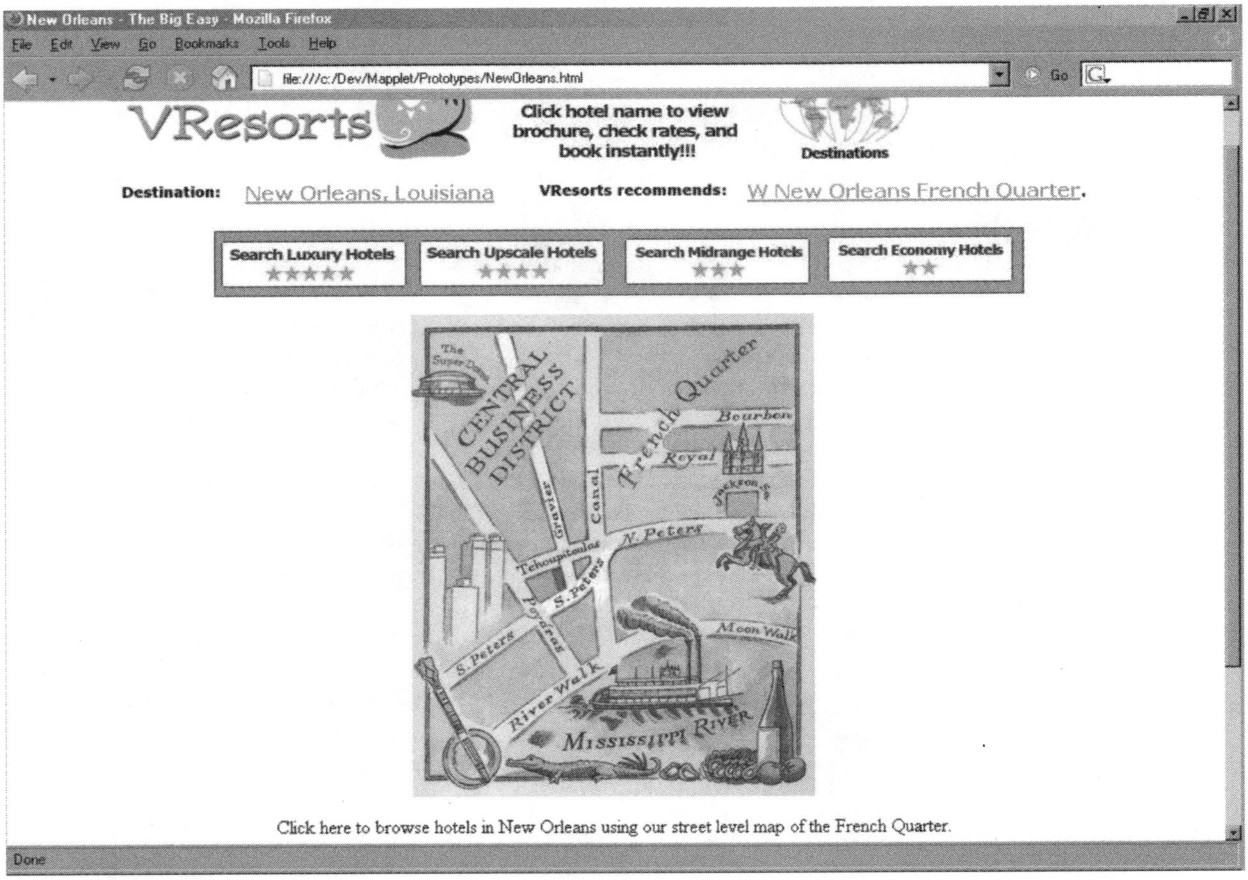

Figure 6-1. *A web page mock-up for the ESRI mapplet project*

1. Scott W. Ambler, *Agile Modeling: Effective Practices for eXtreme Programming and the Unified Process* (New York: John Wiley & Sons, 2002), p. 59.

It's important to note that the screenshot in Figure 6-1 was produced as quickly as possible. It doesn't need to be perfect, glossy, or fine-tuned—it isn't a final product, and it might not end up being entirely similar to the final product. But it gets the team thinking at an early stage about what the product will look like, how it will behave, how the user will interact with it, and so on. With this in mind, the New Orleans destination page in Figure 6-1 was slapped together using graphics "borrowed" from a variety of sources, rather like a photofit. When the project begins to pick up steam, the drawing of the New Orleans map will be replaced by a preview JPEG of the map instance, which will link to a new page containing the active map.

UI prototypes like this one can be used as an informal kind of visual acceptance testing. When we replace the static map of New Orleans with a preview JPEG of the mapplet, and we can browse brochures and book hotels through the mapplet, then it passes the acceptance test.[2]

The following additional instructions were given to the team by the customer in an e-mail:[3]

> *In most cases I'll be looking for a street-level map centered on the recommended hotel, defaulted to display Luxury and Upscale hotels and with options to switch on Midrange and Economy hotels, etc.*
>
> *One other really useful feature that I'm envisioning on every map page is the ability to just enter a zip code anywhere in the US and set the map to the zip code boundaries. Unless I miss my guess, this is "low-hanging fruit" (i.e., very easy for you to build) . . . so if I'm right, maybe we can go for it. This way, if you had a business meeting in New Orleans that was not in the French Quarter, you could just jam in the zip code and boom, there's the map. Also, if you were looking at the New Orleans map and suddenly remembered you had another meeting in Chicago, you just jam in that zip code and you're zapped into a Chicago map.*

After the first modeling iteration (which we cover in the next section), the team was due to create a working prototype of the hotel mapplet.[4]

First Pass Modeling Efforts (and Some Typical Modeling Mistakes)

During the prototyping release of the software, the team members began to get their feet wet with a little bit of modeling. Mostly they were figuring out how to program the new release of ArcGIS Server, but they also wanted to learn the Enterprise Architect (EA) modeling tool, and they generally tried to add a little bit of modeling into the mix. But at this point they weren't "modeling like they meant it"—that is, they weren't trying to drive the design and the code from the model. So, as you'll see over the next few chapters, the initial models weren't very "tight," but they definitely got better over time.

For the first-cut modeling activity during the prototype release, the team just grabbed the domain model that was left over from the JumpStart workshop, which was discussed in the last chapter. They used this domain model to help build the prototype and to help focus on the end product that the customer ultimately wanted.

Release 1 had a set of deliverables associated with it (i.e., the minimum functionality that the customer would want to see in the first release). It had also been agreed, however, that this first release wouldn't go into production—a second release would follow shortly afterward.

These functional requirements can come from a variety of sources: conversations with the customer, e-mails like the one shown in the previous section, and formal requirements specifications. Whatever the format of the requirements, the team needs to extract a useful domain model from them, and in so doing lay the groundwork for writing a set of use cases describing the system behavior.

---

2. If the suspense is really killing you, feel free to check ahead to Figure 6-12 to see if the finished screenshot for release 1 passes our visual acceptance test.

3. Note that in this case, "optimizing for communication" involved allowing the (very busy) off-site customer to supply direction to the programmers via e-mail.

4. Interestingly, this was written at around the time wildfires were spreading through the state of California in October 2003. At one stage, the fires had spread to within 10–15 miles of the ESRI offices—so it was touch and go for a while whether we were going to see the next iteration at all!

Let's zero in on the use case "Generate Hotel Map for AOI."

Use Case: "Generate Hotel Map for AOI" (First Version)

The user clicks a hyperlink for a predetermined AOI or an AOI is created via the "Generate AOI" use case. The system passes the geographic extent of the AOI to the Map Viewer. The Map Viewer queries ArcGIS Server for a base map within the geographic extent.

The Map Viewer queries ArcGIS Server again and asks for all hotel attributes and locations within the map extent. The Map Viewer gets the results and stores them in local memory.

The system shows the map on the screen and puts an icon on the map for each hotel. When the user moves the mouse over a hotel, the system shows the hotel name in a tip window. When the user clicks a hotel icon, the system calls the "Display Rollover Information" use case. When the user clicks the map, or when the user clicks the Zoom In button and drags a rectangle on the map, the system calls the "Pan/Zoom Map" use case. When the user clicks the hotel hyperlink on the rollover window, the system calls the "View Detailed Hotel Info" use case.

Although this use case looks fine, it should start a small alarm bell ringing somewhere in the back of your head. The text is fine, because it's written in active voice, present tense, and generally uses "user action/system reaction" couplets. However, the use case shows only the basic course. The absence of any alternative courses is a useful warning sign that this use case and its associated sequence diagram need more work.

With the domain model and first use case description in place, the team next created a robustness diagram for the "Generate Hotel Map for AOI" use case (see Figure 6-2).

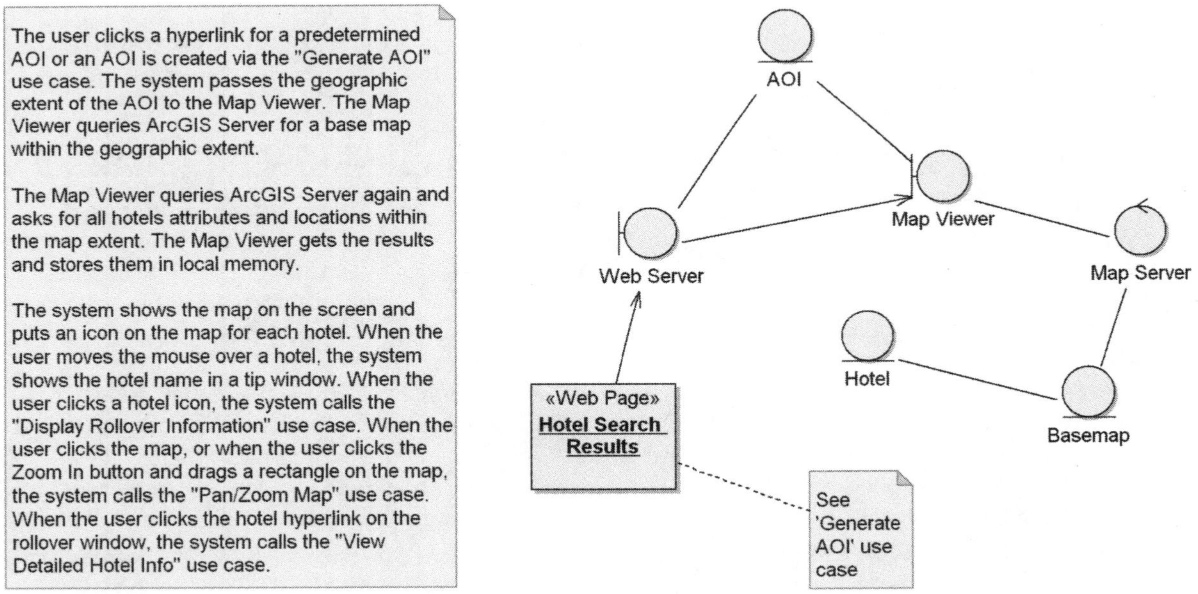

Figure 6-2. *In-progress robustness diagram for the "Generate Hotel Map for AOI" use case*

It's worth noting a few modeling issues with this robustness diagram:

- It isn't drawn to the same level of detail as the use case text.
- The use case text has "ArcGIS Server" whereas the robustness diagram has "Map Server." These are ambiguously used names for the same thing (i.e., ArcGIS Server is the product name of the Map Server).
- Neither ArcGIS Server nor the Map Server exists on the domain model.
- Neither ArcGIS Server nor the Map Server appears on the sequence diagram (see Figure 6-3).

The use case text states

The Map Viewer queries ArcGIS Server again and asks for all hotel attributes and locations within the map extent. The Map Viewer gets the results and stores them in local memory.

What does this sentence imply on the sequence diagram (which we show later, in Figure 6-3)? It implies an operation called `GetHotelsInExtent`, which should be an operation of the Map Server. `GetHotelsInExtent` should also be a controller on the robustness diagram. Instead, we can see in Figure 6-3 that `GetHotelsInExtent` is (erroneously) an operation on the Hotel object.

It's worth pausing to analyze exactly why this error occurred, because (as it turns out) it reveals a common modeling issue. Put simply, the various parts of this model that should be tightly coupled together are not. The use case text and robustness diagram don't match, and (more important) the robustness diagram hasn't been used to disambiguate the use case text and make it match the domain model. Since the robustness diagram wasn't detailed enough, it wasn't used to create the skeleton sequence diagram following the steps defined in ICONIX Process (i.e., copy the boundary and entity classes from the robustness diagram, etc., as described in Chapter 3). The result? When the designer went to draw the message arrow for `GetHotelsInExtent`, the correct target object wasn't on the diagram. This resulted in an error: the `GetHotelsInExtent` operation got assigned to the Hotel class.[5] These errors are tremendously easy to make! That's why the step-by-step "cookbook" guidance exists.

Let's feed this back into the diagrams that we have so far. First, we need to add "Map Server" to the domain model, and then stop using the term "ArcGIS Server." Next, we rewrite the sentence from the use case as follows:

The Map Viewer queries the Map Server for all the hotels within the map extent; the result is returned in a Hotel Collection.

This disambiguated sentence results in a clear and explicit robustness diagram and a correct sequence diagram, where the `FindHotelsInExtent` operation will naturally get assigned to the Map Server, where it belongs.

We'll revisit the "Generate Hotel Map for AOI" robustness diagram later in this chapter and see how this modeling feedback improves it.

Normally, we would aim to get the robustness diagrams to a level closer to completion before moving on to the sequence diagrams. However, this being a prototype release, the team was really focusing more on gaining an understanding of how to program the new server software and wasn't paying too much attention to all of the modeling details, as the team wasn't driving the design/code from the model. Using the robustness diagram in its current state (as shown in Figure 6-2), the team quickly moved on to the matching sequence diagram (see Figure 6-3). The result is obvious: the sequence diagram contains all the same ambiguities and "classic" modeling errors as the robustness diagram.

5. This type of error (a `GetHotels` method on a Hotel class) sometimes happens if the designer is thinking that Hotel represents a Hotel Table in a DBMS as opposed to a Java or C# class representing a single hotel. Getting the hotels out of a hotel table is a fairly typical occurrence. But it's important to keep the distinction clear between classes and tables, as they aren't the same thing.

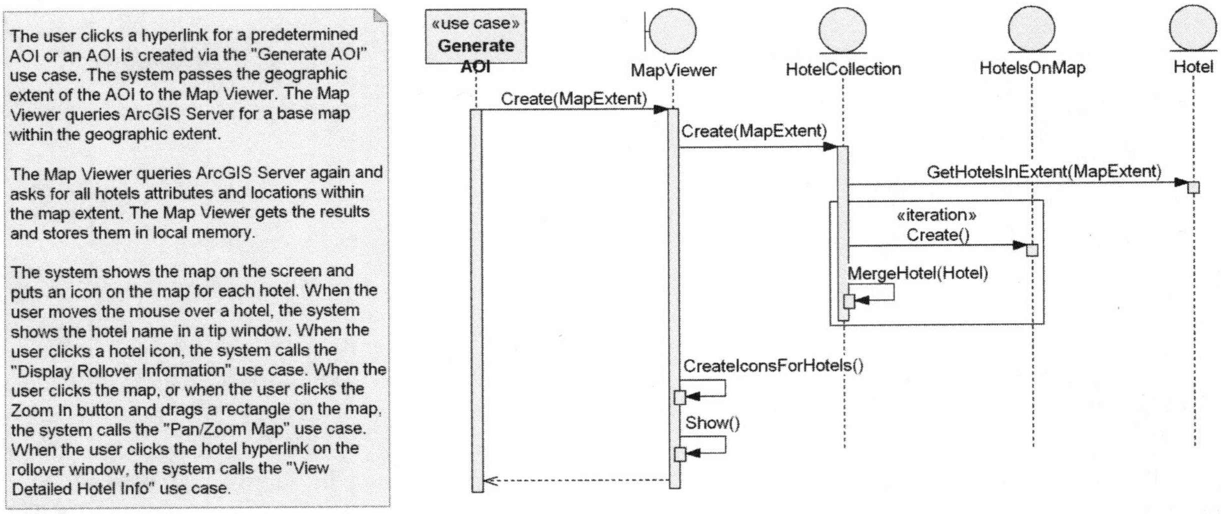
The user clicks a hyperlink for a predetermined AOI or an AOI is created via the "Generate AOI" use case. The system passes the geographic extent of the AOI to the Map Viewer. The Map Viewer queries ArcGIS Server for a base map within the geographic extent.
The Map Viewer queries ArcGIS Server again and asks for all hotels attributes and locations within the map extent. The Map Viewer gets the results and stores them in local memory.
The system shows the map on the screen and puts an icon on the map for each hotel. When the user moves the mouse over a hotel, the system shows the hotel name in a tip window. When the user clicks a hotel icon, the system calls the "Display Rollover Information" use case. When the user clicks the map, or when the user clicks the Zoom In button and drags a rectangle on the map, the system calls the "Pan/Zoom Map" use case. When the user clicks the hotel hyperlink on the rollover window, the system calls the "View Detailed Hotel Info" use case.
«use case» Generate AOI
MapViewer
HotelCollection
HotelsOnMap
Hotel
Create(MapExtent)
Create(MapExtent)
GetHotelsInExtent(MapExtent)
«iteration» Create()
MergeHotel(Hotel)
CreateIconsForHotels()
Show()

Figure 6-3. *The "Generate Hotel Map for AOI" sequence diagram at an early stage*

Iterating between diagrams can have its benefits, though. In this case, it was obvious that the sequence diagram in Figure 6-3 wasn't sufficient to code from. So the team needed to take a couple of steps back and review what was going wrong. Sometimes venturing ahead slightly can provide useful warning signs that more preparatory work needs to be done first.

CUSTOMER REVIEW MEETING BETWEEN THE FIRST AND SECOND MODELING ITERATIONS

Before the second modeling pass began, Doug visited the ESRI offices to exercise his "agile stakeholder rights" to add new requirements in the middle of the release, and also to do a little modeling coaching.

The resultant notes from the project review meeting provide some insight into this role. In particular, they show how an off-site customer can overcome some of the hurdles that naturally stand in his way if he can't be on-site with the project team 100% of the time (we discuss these hurdles in the section "Challenges of Being Agile" in Chapter 1).

- MEETING NOTES -

AMWIP PROTOTYPE AND MODEL REVIEW

ESRI ATTENDEES: DAVID LEWIS, AMIR SOHEILI
ICONIX ATTENDEES: DOUG ROSENBERG
Date: 11/11/03

1. *Mapplet prototype review and feedback*

Doug requested that display filters for AOI and Hotel Price Band should be part of the URL. The following name/value pair examples were discussed to define AOI:

AOI Name/Value Pairs
...ZipCode='92373'...
...HotelID='123456'...
...StreetName='380 New York Street'City='&Redlands'&State='CA'&ZipCode='92373...
...X='34.4567'&Y='-117.1345'...
...X1='34.4567'&Y1='-117.1345'&X2='36.4567'&Y1='-118.1345'...

Hotel Price Band Name/Value Pairs
...PB='L' (Luxury)
...PB='UL' (Upscale, Luxury)
...PB='MUL' (Midrange, Upscale, Luxury)
...PB='EMUL' (Economy, Midrange, Upscale, Luxury)

Preview JPEG on VResorts site will link to new web page of map viewer. Mapplet will display default settings based on name/value pairs above. Note: Mapplet should cache all hotel price bands locally on the client; however, it should only display by defaults defined in name/value pairs.

Map tips on mouse hover should be a little bigger.

Size of Hotel icon should reflect price band. Graduated circle symbols, as opposed to beds, may be used for display. Coloring should make Luxury stand out most, followed by Upscale, etc.

"Zoom to Zip Code" text box and "Click Here To Enter Address" link should be available below the mapplet.

Price Band legend should include a title and price band descriptions.

In the Hotel pop-up, three links will be provided (if available): "View hotel brochure...", "View hotel overview...", and "Check rates...". These links will be to the predefined URL appended with the HotelID and associated suffixes B, O, or R. The link will display only if these pages are available as defined in the hotel database.
Example URL: `http://reservations.vresorts.com/hotel/10004663-102034663B.html`

Overview Map at the bottom of the screen would be a nice-to-have; however, it is a low priority at this point.

2. *Overview of current model*

Revisited use case "Generate Hotel Map for AOI." Rewrote use case, robustness, and sequence diagrams.

ESRI will provide a high-level architecture diagram of ArcGIS Server/.NET interaction for inclusion in the book.

ESRI to revisit remaining use cases and provide update before making further code changes.

3. *Mapplet iteration 2*

Was briefly discussed that the second iteration should focus on more sophisticated display filtering and saving personal profiles of users as a client-side cookie for default displays.

Mentioned the potential of also adding routing functionality.

ESRI may recommend some additional use cases/upgrades that may be applicable.

Tightening Up the Model

This time around, the modeling effort is starting to zero in on a more refined, detailed design. The overall model is beginning to take shape, and we're seeing some of the benefits of putting more effort into the up-front design stage.

The team has refined the domain model (see Figure 6-4).

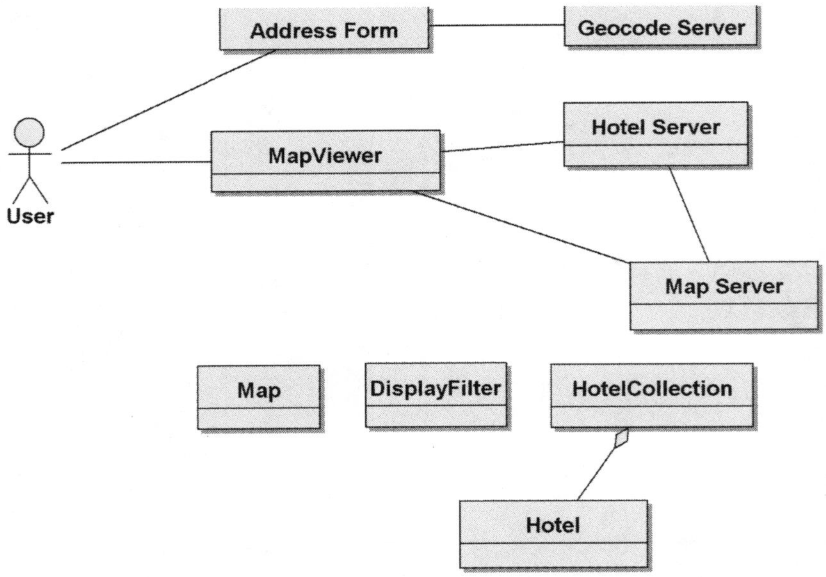

Figure 6-4. *The domain model the second time around*

During the prototype and model review meeting, the team found that it needed to update the terminology used on the domain model. This was because, back when the project was just getting started, the team had anticipated using an older version of the ESRI technology. Since then, the team had opted to use the mapplet as a way to perform some tests on its new high-end mapping server, ArcGIS Server.

So the team needed to bring the model into closer synchronization with the architecture of the new map server. In the new architecture, we see, for example, conceptual entities for "Geocode Server" and "Map Server" (both of these are predefined objects residing in ArcGIS Server). There's also a "Hotel Server," which is in reality part of the more generic Map Server, as Hotels are just one of the data layers that we query in the Map Server.

In any project, it's vitally important that the domain model be kept up to date throughout, as it forms a kind of object-oriented glossary of terms. It's the Babel fish[6] that keeps everyone talking the same language.

---

6. A *Babel fish* (according to *The Hitchhiker's Guide to the Galaxy* by Douglas Adams) is "small, yellow, and leech-like" but has the bonus of behaving like a universal translator if you stick one into your ear.

The "Generate Hotel Map for AOI" Use Case

Figure 6-5 shows the "Generate Hotel Map for AOI" use case being edited in the team's CASE tool (Enterprise Architect [EA] from Sparx Systems[7]).

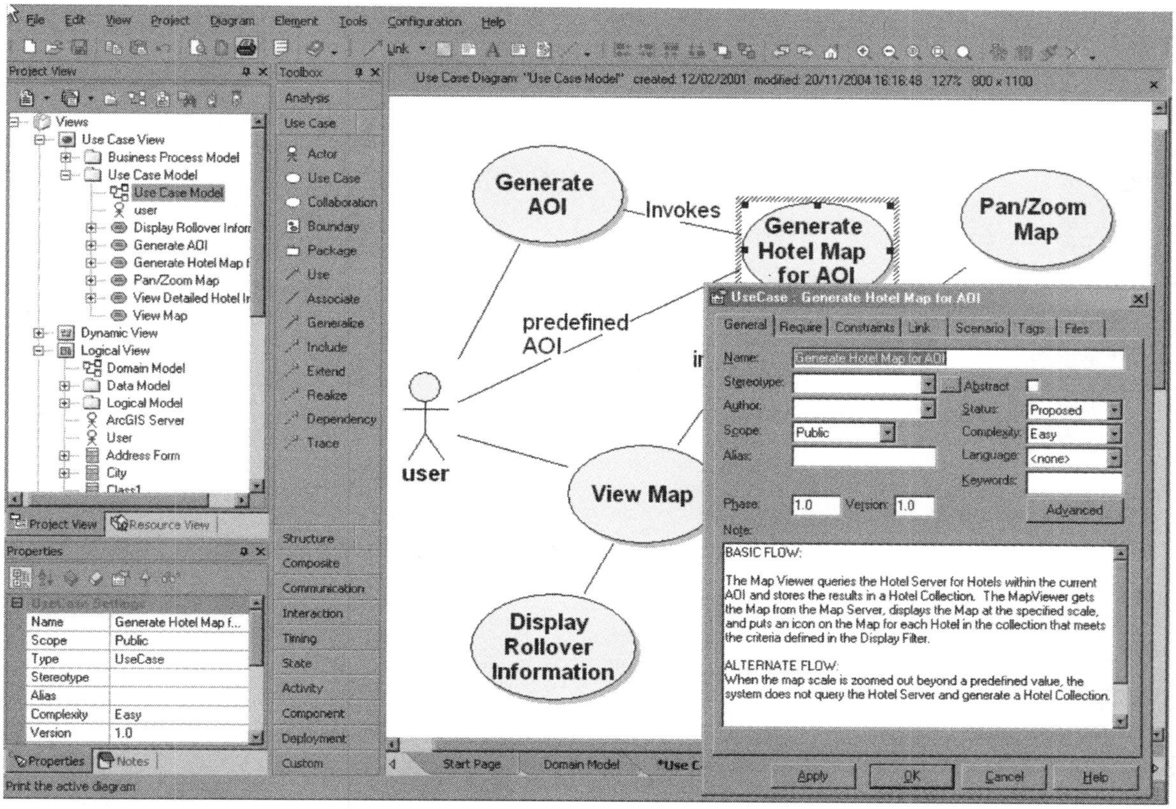

Figure 6-5. *Editing the "Generate Hotel Map for AOI" use case*

Revised Use Case: "Generate Hotel Map for AOI"

BASIC FLOW:

The Map Viewer queries the Hotel Server for Hotels within the current AOI and stores the results in a Hotel Collection. The Map Viewer gets the Map from the Map Server, displays the Map at the specified scale, and puts an icon on the Map for each Hotel in the collection that meets the criteria defined in the Display Filter.

ALTERNATE FLOW:

When the map scale is zoomed out beyond a predefined value, the system does not query the Hotel Server and generate a Hotel Collection.

Contrast this with the original version of the use case. The most noticeable improvement is that the use case has been divided into "Basic Flow" and "Alternate Flow" sections. The scope of the use case has also been trimmed down—that is, it no longer starts at the UI, but instead picks up the story from the point of interaction between the Map Viewer and the Hotel Server. The result is a more focused, more manageable chunk of functionality from which to drive its sequence diagram.

7. See `www.sparxsystems.com`.

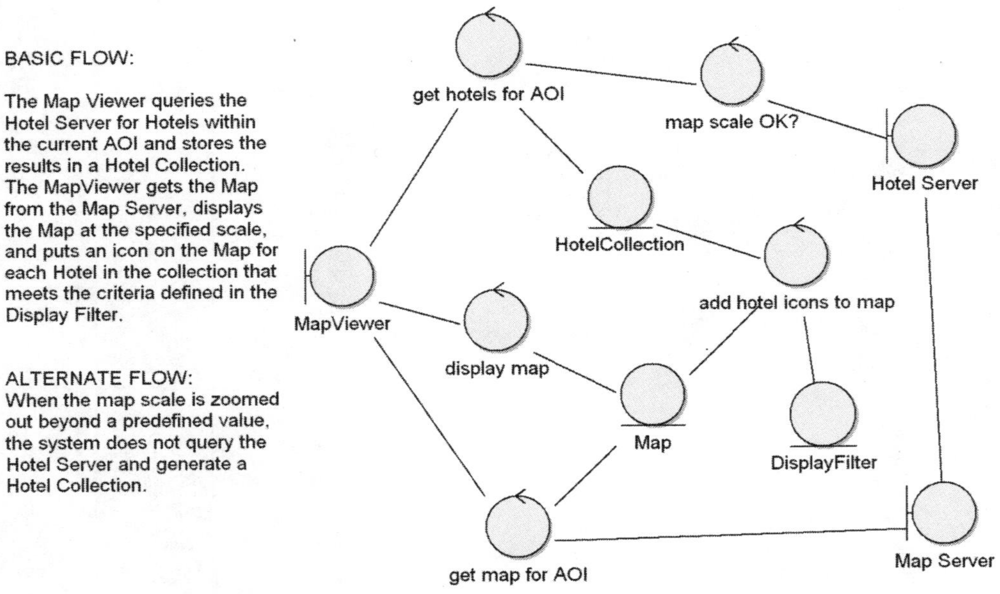
BASIC FLOW:
The Map Viewer queries the Hotel Server for Hotels within the current AOI and stores the results in a Hotel Collection. The MapViewer gets the Map from the Map Server, displays the Map at the specified scale, and puts an icon on the Map for each Hotel in the collection that meets the criteria defined in the Display Filter.
ALTERNATE FLOW:
When the map scale is zoomed out beyond a predefined value, the system does not query the Hotel Server and generate a Hotel Collection.
get hotels for AOI
map scale OK?
Hotel Server
HotelCollection
add hotel icons to map
MapViewer
display map
Map
DisplayFilter
get map for AOI
Map Server

Figure 6-6. The robustness diagram for the "Generate Hotel Map for AOI" use case

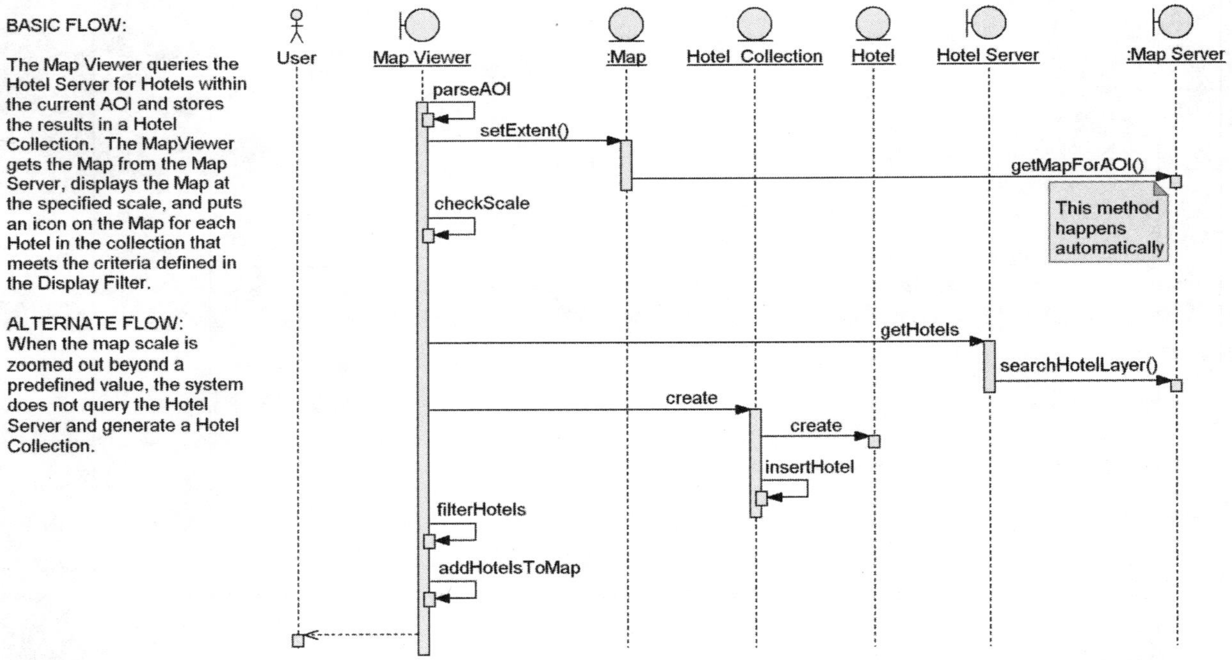
BASIC FLOW:
The Map Viewer queries the Hotel Server for Hotels within the current AOI and stores the results in a Hotel Collection. The MapViewer gets the Map from the Map Server, displays the Map at the specified scale, and puts an icon on the Map for each Hotel in the collection that meets the criteria defined in the Display Filter.
ALTERNATE FLOW:
When the map scale is zoomed out beyond a predefined value, the system does not query the Hotel Server and generate a Hotel Collection.
User
Map Viewer
:Map
Hotel Collection
Hotel
Hotel Server
:Map Server
parseAOI
setExtent()
getMapForAOI()
This method happens automatically
checkScale
getHotels
searchHotelLayer()
create
create
insertHotel
filterHotels
addHotelsToMap

Figure 6-7. *The sequence diagram (revisited) for the "Generate Hotel Map for AOI" use case*

Also, as a result of the team's model review activities (particularly the discovery of the ambiguous domain objects during robustness analysis), the text has been effectively disambiguated.

Figure 6-6 shows the robustness diagram for the "Generate Hotel Map for AOI" use case. Note that the new robustness diagram more accurately reflects the technical architecture of the ArcGIS product: Maps are "served" by the Map Server, while Hotels are "served" by the Hotel Server (although strictly speaking, the Hotel Server is part of the Map Server).

In this release of the software, we are not yet attempting to do a proximity search near an address, so there is no use of the "Geocode Server" on the robustness diagram.

Figure 6-7 shows the sequence diagram for the "Generate Hotel Map for AOI" use case. Notice how the use case text has been pasted directly into the left border of the diagram. This helps to keep the sequence diagram and the use case tightly bound. If one or the other starts to stray, then it's easily noticeable and its twin view can be updated. This practice can also make a huge difference in the accuracy of any team's modeling efforts, because the team is designing the program directly from the system behavior defined in each use case.

If we think of the use case scenario text and the sequence diagrams as being different views of the same activity, then we can see why they're so closely interrelated. They're actually different representations of the same sequence of steps (in addition, the sequence diagram shows the system's internal workings).

This sequence diagram took a while to figure out, and it involved a fairly detailed discussion of how the C# code actually worked, along with a discussion of what information was kept in cached HTML inside the web browser (price-band filtering information) for performance reasons and what queries would be done by hitting the database (amenity filtering). We came up with a design that used both a *display filter* for changing price bands (operating on cached HTML within the browser) and a *query filter* for amenity filtering, which hits the server (e.g., when we're only looking for Hilton hotels with 24-hour room service).

Note that query filtering did not get implemented in the first release of the mapplet. Even though the sequence diagram might not precisely match the code, working through it proved to be a very valuable exercise for the insight it gave the team into how the design needed to work.

Use Case: "Display Rollover Information"

This particular use case didn't change during the first two modeling passes (however, we'll improve it substantially in the next chapter). Here's the use case text for "Display Rollover Information."

Basic Flow:

The user positions the mouse cursor over a hotel icon in the map display. The mouse icon changes to "selection hand" and the hotel icon changes to "selected hotel." The system displays a map tip, displaying the hotel name. The user may click the hotel icon to display a hotel information pop-up that displays the hotel's attributes for all of the fields in the hotel pop-up fields collection. The system queries the hotel attributes to determine which hotel details are available for the hotel. Within the hotel pop-up, the system displays hyperlinks for available hotel details. The user may click these to invoke the "View Detailed Hotel Info" use case.

Alternate Flow:

If no hotels are found at click coordinates, do nothing.

If multiple hotels are found at click coordinates, the system constructs a list of the selected hotels' names and displays them in a pop-up. The user may select a hotel from the list to display the associated hotel information pop-up.

The robustness diagram for this use case is shown in Figure 6-8. Note that the robustness diagram takes into account the alternative course of "If multiple hotels are found at click coordinates."

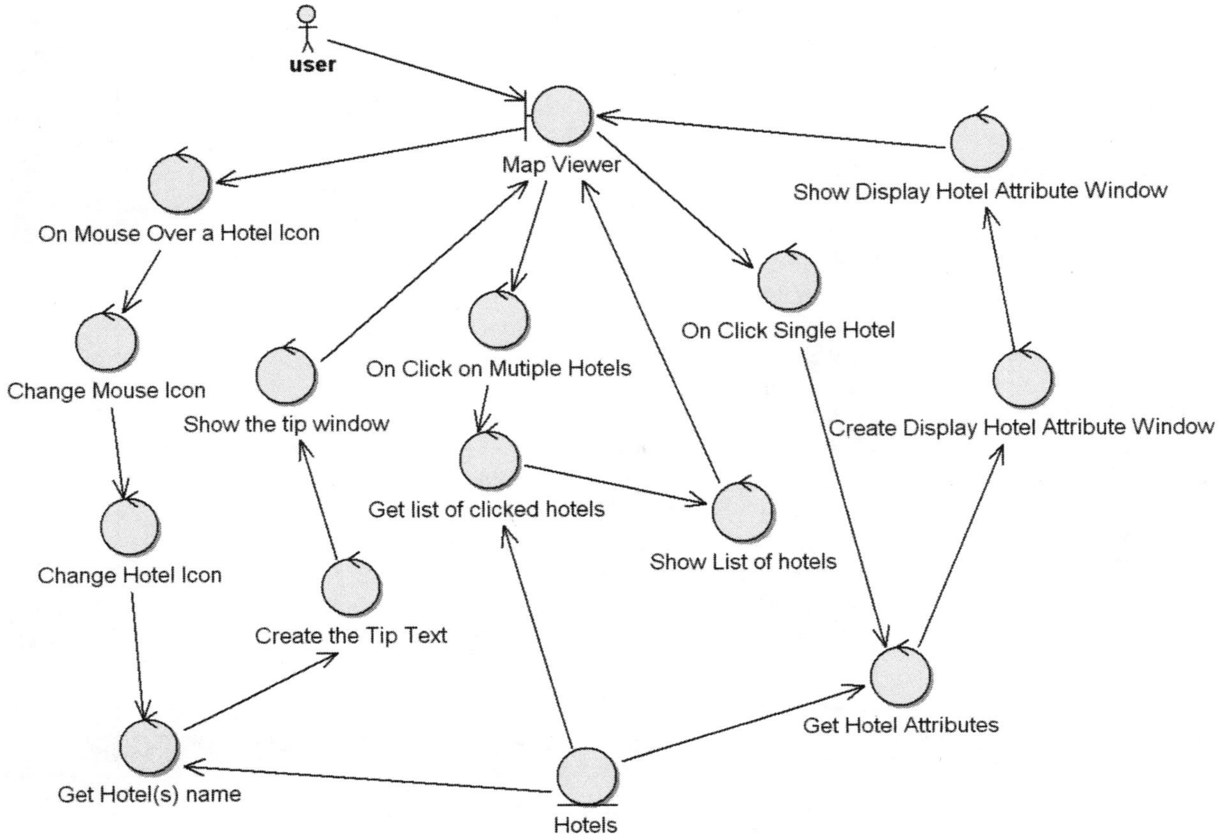

Figure 6-8. *The initial robustness diagram for the "Display Rollover Information" use case*

There's actually quite a lot that can be done to improve both this diagram and the ensuing sequence diagram (see Figure 7-3 if you'd like a peek at the "decluttered" and disambiguated version). However, this being a prototype, the team opted to move quickly on to the sequence diagram, and thenceforth to the code. We'll return to both of these diagrams in Chapter 7 to give them a serious roughing up (or should that be "smoothing over"?). You'll be surprised at the result!

The sequence diagram for this use case is shown in Figure 6-9.

As we described earlier, during this prototype-intensive stage of the project, the team actually breezed over robustness analysis and also skipped the detailed class diagram entirely. As we hope you're starting to suspect, *insufficient modeling results in the need for code-level refactoring*. So, in the next section, we show some of the prototype source code, because it's useful to see what can happen when crucial parts of the design modeling stage are skipped. We then do some minor refactoring to the code in preparation for the next release.

Refactoring is a useful fallback position if your team has skimped on the up-front design. In other words, if a less-than-optimal design has been coded up, it's not the end of the world: refactoring provides a handy escape route. However, as we discuss in our book *Extreme Programming Refactored: The Case Against XP*, refactoring can be a serious resource drain—it is not the most efficient way to design software. It really is better to focus on getting the design right as early as possible.

In Chapter 7, we return to the robustness and sequence diagrams, and examine some improvements that could have been made prior to coding.

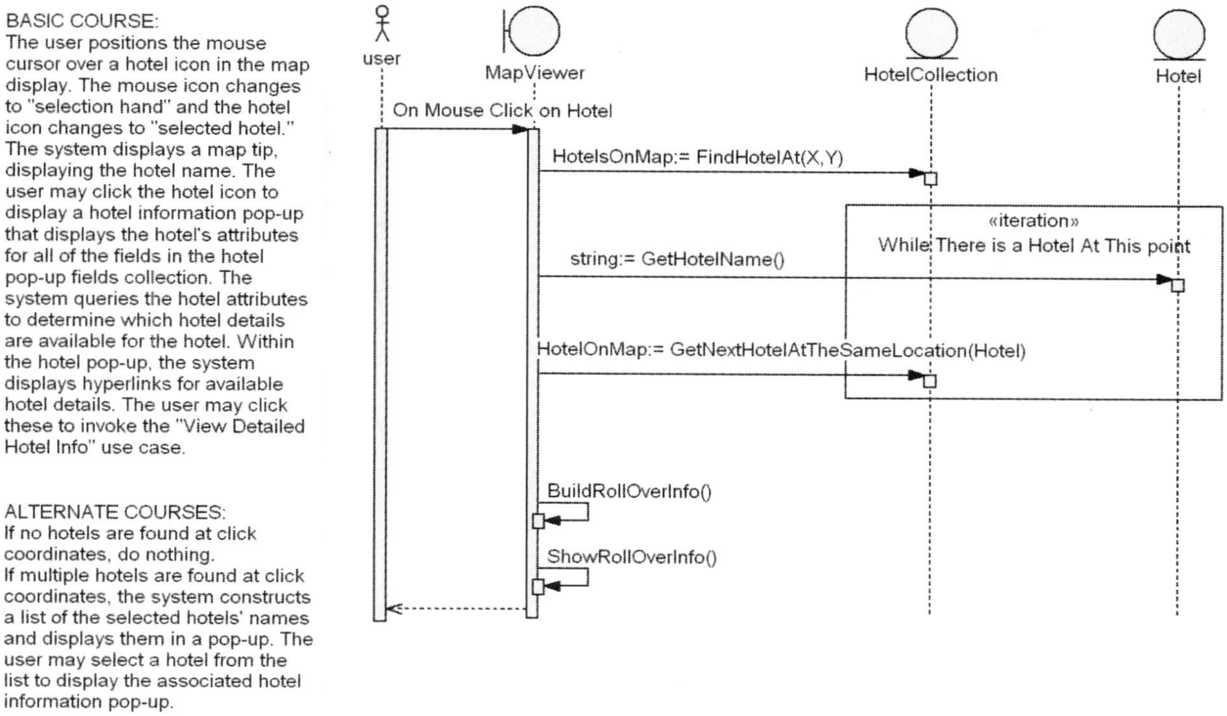
BASIC COURSE:
The user positions the mouse cursor over a hotel icon in the map display. The mouse icon changes to "selection hand" and the hotel icon changes to "selected hotel." The system displays a map tip, displaying the hotel name. The user may click the hotel icon to display a hotel information pop-up that displays the hotel's attributes for all of the fields in the hotel pop-up fields collection. The system queries the hotel attributes to determine which hotel details are available for the hotel. Within the hotel pop-up, the system displays hyperlinks for available hotel details. The user may click these to invoke the "View Detailed Hotel Info" use case.
ALTERNATE COURSES:
If no hotels are found at click coordinates, do nothing.
If multiple hotels are found at click coordinates, the system constructs a list of the selected hotels' names and displays them in a pop-up. The user may select a hotel from the list to display the associated hotel information pop-up.
user
MapViewer
HotelCollection
Hotel
On Mouse Click on Hotel
HotelsOnMap:= FindHotelAt(X,Y)
«iteration»
While There is a Hotel At This point
string:= GetHotelName()
HotelOnMap:= GetNextHotelAtTheSameLocation(Hotel)
BuildRollOverInfo()
ShowRollOverInfo()

Figure 6-9. *The sequence diagram for the "Display Rollover Information" use case*

Let's Take a Look at Some Code

In this section, we show the prototype source code that the ESRI team wrote to implement the "Generate Hotel Map for AOI" use case. It's important to keep in mind that this is real-life code—not written for a dusty textbook showing a fictitious, contrived example.

As mentioned earlier, while busy learning how the new server software worked, the team skipped the detailed class diagram (the static model), making do instead with the domain model and the other up-front design diagrams created so far. This is a useful example of the trade-offs involved in deciding whether to stray from the process path (especially when up against a tight deadline, which is the point at which such dilemmas usually occur).

Luckily, the team had done enough up-front design on this project that skipping one design step didn't cause any major issues. There's always a judgment call involved: do you do it "by the book" or skip a step to save time and take the risk that it might store up trouble for later? In this case, the team skipped the class diagram (because this release is just a prototype) and as a result needed to do some refactoring of the code to get it ready for the next release. (We show some of these refactorings in this section and in Chapter 7.)

The existence of a comprehensive design spec allows us to easily determine what code will benefit from refactoring and what code should simply be left as is. When programmers begin coding, particularly in the early stages of product development, the code can be somewhat less than perfect. Modeling the design up-front goes a long way toward improving the initial state of the code, especially when the design process is followed stringently. But there's often still room for improvement. Later we'll show how to bring the code and the design documentation back in sync with each other.

Anyway, back to the source code. We don't show the entire source code for each class here—just the parts relevant to the "Generate Hotel Map for AOI" sequence diagram in Figure 6-3 (which is revisited in Figure 6-7). This should give you a flavor of the extent to which the sequence diagrams drive the code-level design.

ARCGIS SERVER WEB CONTROLS

It's worth giving a little background information here about the framework that the mapplet was developed on. As we described in Chapter 5, the mapplet is a web-based application developed with ArcGIS Server, using Microsoft's .NET Framework. ArcGIS Server includes an Application Developer Framework (ADF) built on top of .NET, which the mapplet team used to integrate GIS functionality into the web application.

When you create a new project in Visual Studio .NET, you're presented with a set of templates that you can use as a starting point to create an application. Visual Studio .NET is highly extensible—for example, when you install the ArcGIS Server ADF, it adds a folder to Visual Studio containing an array of templates and custom web controls. Some of these predefined templates were used directly in the mapplet application, for example:

- *Map Viewer template*: Offers basic map navigation and display
- *Search template*: Finds features by attributes
- *Geocoding template*: Locates places by address

The Map Viewer template provides basic map display capabilities. It consists of a main map, an overview map, a table of contents, a North arrow, and a scale bar. The template also contains a toolbar with built-in tools for panning and zooming. For any map-centric application, the Map Viewer template offers a good starting point. (Alternatively, you can use the web controls directly to create your own specialized application in a style that conforms to your existing website.)

The following image shows a conceptual object model diagram for the .NET ADF web controls.

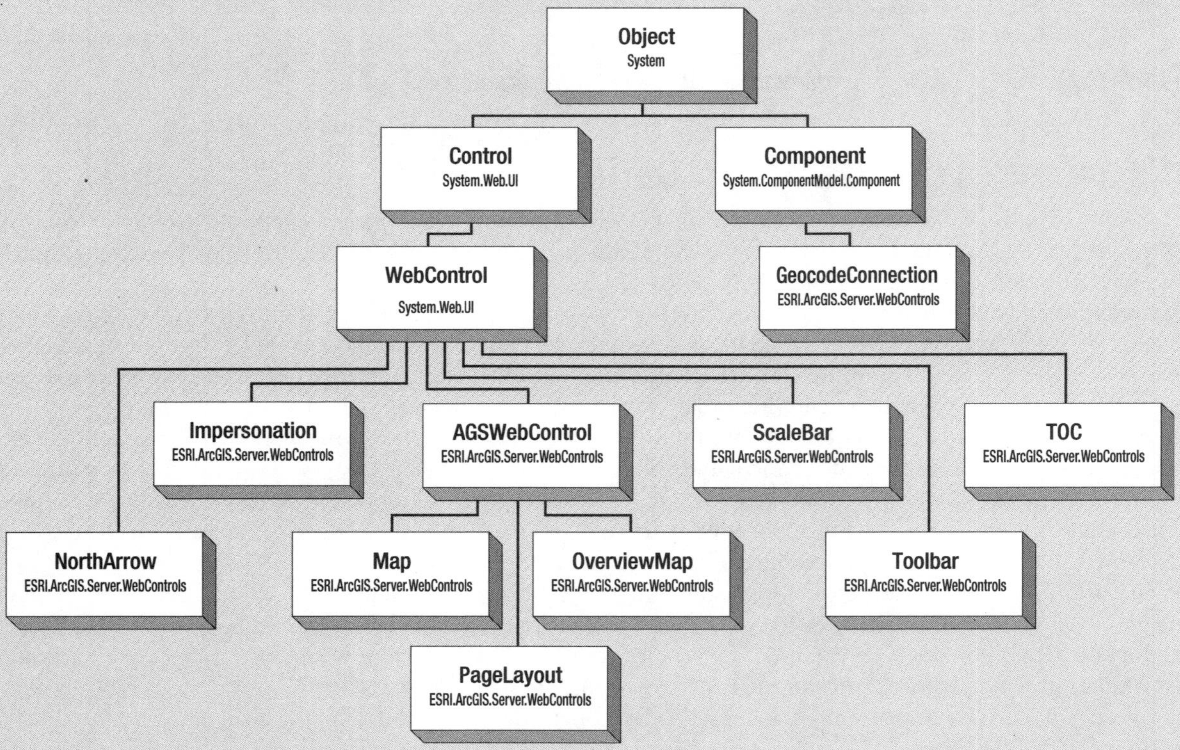

Source Code for the "Generate Hotel Map for AOI" Use Case

This use case can be considered to be a "system use case" because the user doesn't directly trigger it. Instead, it is triggered by other use cases. For example, if the user opts to search for a hotel by zip code, or zoom in to the current map, then the AOI would change and the map would need to be updated (hence the name "Generate Hotel Map for AOI").

We'll trace through the source code for the search by zip code example.

Search by Zip Code

The following code declares the ASP.NET Web Forms UI components for searching by zip code:

```
protected System.Web.UI.WebControls.Panel pnlZipCode;
protected System.Web.UI.WebControls.Label lbZipCode;
protected System.Web.UI.WebControls.TextBox txtZipCode;
protected System.Web.UI.WebControls.Button btnSearchZipCode;
```

Figure 6-10 shows how those components look on the web page (see the four page elements in the middle of Figure 6-10: the Zip Code label, the text field, the Go button, and the shaded area that contains them).

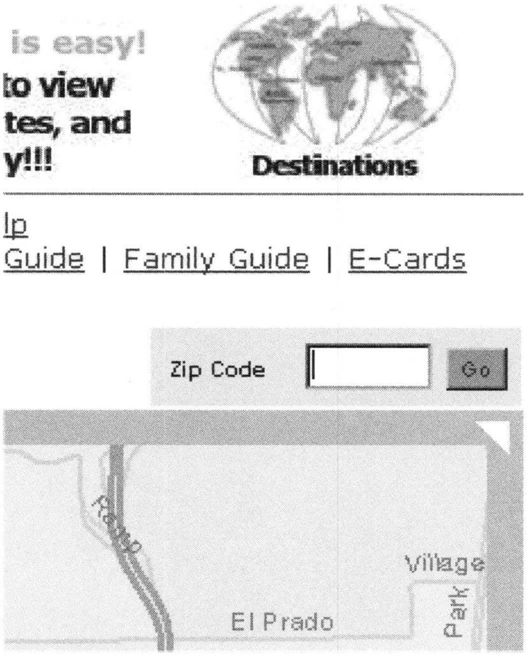

Figure 6-10. *The four controls as they appear on the web page*

When the Go button is clicked, an HTTP request needs to be sent to the web server, which is then picked up by a server-side event handler. The event handler is set up using this line of code (when the component is initialized):

```
this.btnSearchZipCode.Click += new System.EventHandler(this.btnSearchZipCode_Click);
```

When the request comes in, the zip code is contained in an HTTP request parameter called `ZIP`. The request handler simply copies this into a local variable called `zip`, which is then checked for in a method called `CalcNewExtent` in the MapViewer object. Here's a small part of this method:

```
private bool CalcNewExtent (out double XMin,
                                                          out double YMin,
                                                          out double XMax,
                                                          out double YMax,
                                                          out string ErrMsg)
{
    // . . . .

    #region Check Zip Code
        if (zip.Length > 0)
        {
            try
            {
                GetZipCodeExtent (zip, out XMin, out YMin, out XMax, out YMax);
            }
            catch
            {
                ErrMsg = "Cannot find the zip code.";
                return false;
            }
            return true;
        }
    #endregion}
```

The preceding code calls the `GetZipCodeExtent` method with the zip code, and gets in return the values for `XMin`, `YMin`, `XMax`, and `YMax`—in other words, the new AOI (the area of the map that needs to be displayed to the user).

The `GetZipCodeExtent` method in turn calls the actual Map Server to retrieve an AOI that includes the zip code. Here is the method in full:

```
private IEnvelope GetZipCodeExtent (string zip, out
double XMin, out double YMin,
out double XMax, out double YMax)
{
    XMin = 0;
    YMin = 0;
    XMax = 0;
    YMax = 0;

    int ZipLayerIndex = int.Parse (
                ConfigurationSettings.AppSettings ["ZipLayerIndex"]);
    IServerContext sc = getSOM().CreateServerContext (
                ConfigurationSettings.AppSettings ["ServerObject"], "MapServer");

    try
    {
        IMapServer ms = (IMapServer)sc.ServerObject;
        String MapName = ms.DefaultMapName;
        IMapServerObjects mso = (IMapServerObjects) ms;
        IMap map = mso.get_Map(MapName);
```

```
            IFeatureLayer fl = (IFeatureLayer) map.get_Layer (ZipLayerIndex);
            IFeatureCursor fc = null;

            IQueryFilter qf =
                        (IQueryFilter) sc.CreateObject ("esriGeodatabase.QueryFilter");
            qf.WhereClause = "ZIP = '" + zip + "'";
            fc = fl.Search (qf, false);

            if (fc == null)
                return null;

            IFeature f = fc.NextFeature ();
            if (f == null)
                return null;

            XMin = f.Shape.Envelope.XMin;
            XMax = f.Shape.Envelope.XMax;
            YMin = f.Shape.Envelope.YMin;
            YMax = f.Shape.Envelope.YMax;
            return f.Shape.Envelope;
        }
        finally
        {
            sc.ReleaseContext ();
        }
    }
```

Something that springs to mind about this source code so far is that it could probably do with a bit of refactoring. The code does its job, and (we're proud to report) is stable and doesn't seem to contain any bugs. But code quality isn't just about the bug count for the current iteration. It's also about whether the code can be maintained and the demands that it will place on future code that must coexist with it.

In the example code so far, we've seen two methods that take a series of numeric types (doubles) as an output parameter. These doubles (`XMin`, `YMin`, `XMax`, and `YMax`) are actually the left, top, right, and bottom coordinates for the AOI. As well as cluttering the interface, this approach is also error-prone, as the four doubles could easily be typed out of sequence ("Now should that have been 'XMin, YMin, YMax, XMax,' or was it 'XMin, XMax, YMin, XMin' . . . oh, hang on!").

DUPLICATE NAME POLICE

At this point, you might be wondering where the term "extent" has come from. We've seen "area of interest" (AOI) used quite a lot. As it turns out, "AOI" and "extent" are basically different names for the same thing. The term "extent" is used extensively in GIS applications, and ArcGIS Server also has an object called Extent.

Normally, the domain model helps to prevent this sort of duplicate naming. Having identified duplicate objects in the model, the team should choose one term or the other and stick with it. Occasionally, of course, a duplicate term slips through the cracks and ends up in the code. It's important to eradicate these duplications as soon as they're discovered.

In this instance (as we'll see in the next chapter), the team eradicated "extent," going instead with "AOI" in the early stages of the next release.

Our personal feeling about output parameters in C# is that they encourage programmers to pollute their code interfaces with additional parameters, when it's much more likely that what's needed is a new class to group the parameters together. In our example, an AOI class could be defined as follows:

```
public class AOI
{
    public double XMin = 0;
    public double XMax = 0;
    public double YMin = 0;
    public double YMax = 0;

    public AOI()
    {
    }

    public AOI(IEnvelope envelope)
    {
        XMin = envelope.XMin;
        YMin = envelope.YMin;
        XMax = envelope.XMax;
        YMax = envelope.YMax;
    }

    public double XMin
    {
        get
        {
            return XMin;
        }
        set
        {
            XMin = value;
        }
    }    // same again for XMax, YMin and YMax . . . .

}
```

Note the optional constructor, which takes a parameter of type IEnvelope. IEnvelope is a class defined by the ESRI Map Server, similar to AOI.

Then the previous method signatures would be changed to

```
private bool CalcNewExtent (out AOI aoi, out string ErrMsg)
```

and

```
private IEnvelope GetZipCodeExtent (string zip, out AOI aoi)
```

That's better! Now we have a nice, clean interface with the implementation details (coordinates, in this case) encapsulated away.

If we check back to the domain model shown in Chapter 5, we see that there was actually a class called AreaOfInterestViewer defined. Somewhere along the way, AOI as an independent entity sort of slipped through the cracks. In fact, AOI does get mentioned a lot in the robustness and sequence diagrams shown in this chapter, but (considering it's a pretty obvious noun) it should also have been a "first-class" object on the sequence diagrams.

What the object model gives us is a blueprint to check back and validate that all the classes that are supposed to be there actually are there. If there's anything missing or different, then we either update the object model to bring it in line with the code or update the code to bring it in line with the object model. In the example, it's blindingly obvious that the code will benefit from the additional AOI class, so in this instance we update the code to bring it in line with the object model.

Another refactoring that can be made to the example code is to simplify the `GetZipCodeExtent` method. Currently the method does a lot of things, and the golden rule of program cohesion (well, okay, one of them!) is that each method should only do one thing.

While we're at it, we could also rename some of the variables so that they're more meaningful. Names like `qf` and `f` don't stand up well on their own; you have to scan some more code to decipher what they mean. They're also difficult to search for (try doing a text search for `f`!). Names like `QueryFilter` and `Feature` convey much more information.[8]

We notice that in addition to its AOI output parameter, `GetZipCodeExtent` is returning an IEnvelope object (basically the equivalent of the AOI). We can eliminate this duplication by making AOI the return type and removing AOI from the parameter list.

It's worth showing the `GetZipCodeExtent` method again in full, using the new AOI class, and refactored with improved naming and extracted methods:

```
private AOI GetZipCodeExtent (string zip){
    IServerContext context = getSOM().CreateServerContext(
                ConfigurationSettings.AppSettings ["ServerObject"], "MapServer");

    try
    {
        IMap map = FindDefaultMap (context);
        IFeatureLayer FeatureLayer = FindFeatureLayer();
        IFeatureCursor FeatureCursor = FindFeatureCursor(zip, context);

        if (FeatureCursor == null)
            return null;

        IFeature feature = FeatureCursor.NextFeature ();
        if (feature == null)
            return null;

        return new AOI(feature.Shape.Envelope);
    }
    finally
    {
        context.ReleaseContext ();
    }
}


private IMap FindDefaultMap (IServerContext context)
{
    IMapServer server = (IMapServer) context.ServerObject;
    IMapServerObjects mso = (IMapServerObjects) server;
    return mso.get_Map(server.DefaultMapName );
}
```

8. We're also dead set against the opposite affliction: variable names that are too long. Names like `ServerLayerAppendedFollowingAdjustmentInt` take ages to read (not to mention ages to type) and just annoy people. Avoid!

```
private IFeatureLayer FindFeatureLayer()
{
    int ZipLayerIndex = int.Parse (
                            ConfigurationSettings.AppSettings ["ZipLayerIndex"]);
    return (IFeatureLayer) map.get_Layer (ZipLayerIndex);
}

private IFeatureCursor FindFeatureCursor(string zip, IServerContext context)
{
        IQueryFilter QueryFilter = (IQueryFilter) context.CreateObject
                                            ("esriGeodatabase.QueryFilter");
        QueryFilter.WhereClause = "ZIP = '" + zip + "'";
        return FeatureLayer.Search (queryFilter, false);
}
```

In this version, notice how much easier it is to quickly read through the `GetZipCodeExtent` method. There are still some refactorings that could be done to this code, but it's certainly a start.

■ **Note** Of course, when we're refactoring, we also need a decent set of unit tests. We discuss how to combine Test-Driven Development (TDD) with ICONIX Process in Chapters 11 and 12.

The Class Diagram

Figure 6-11 shows the class diagram reverse-engineered from the C# source code. In Chapter 7, we'll revisit the design and present a refactored version of this class diagram. It should be interesting to compare the two.

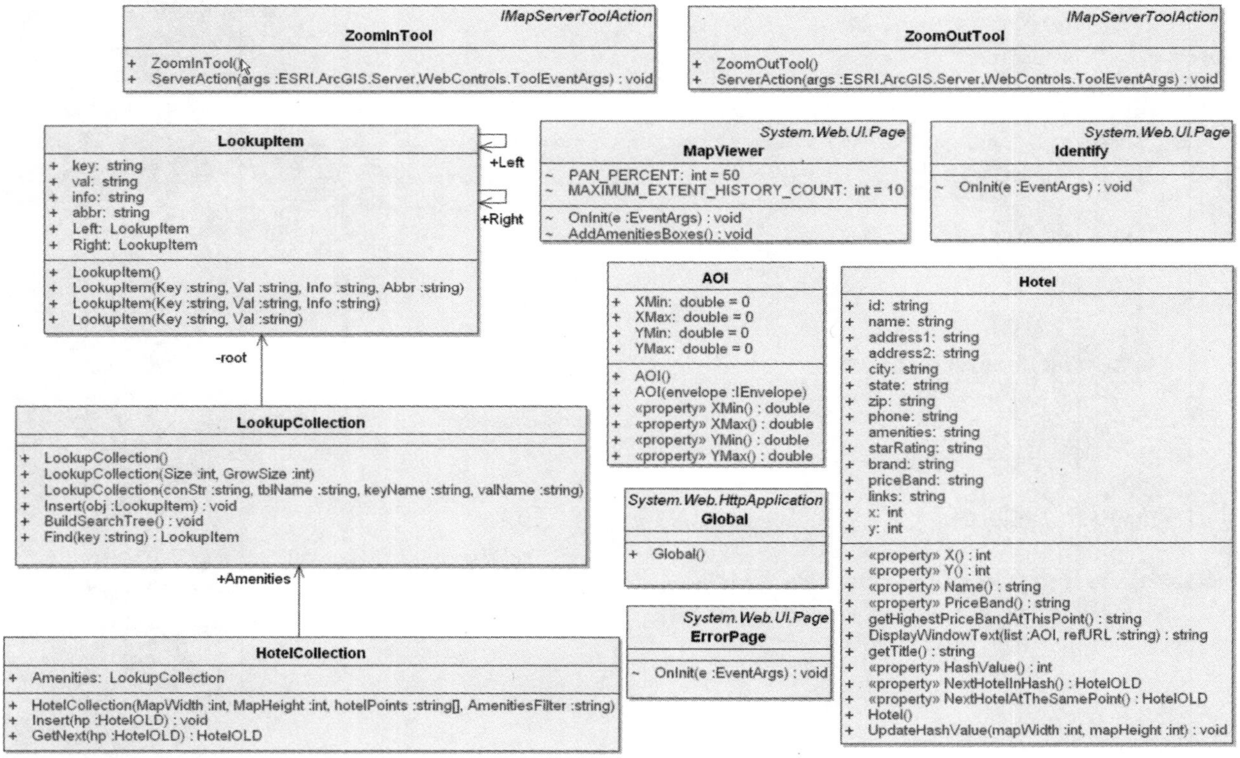

Figure 6-11. *The class diagram reverse-engineered from the C# source code*

Et Voila! The First (Working Prototype) Release

Figure 6-12 shows the product of all our hard work: the alpha version of the mapplet release 1. As you can see, the core functionality is in place. The user can browse the map, zoom in, pan the map around, and so forth. The user can also select individual hotels and view basic information (hotel name, address, and so forth) in a pop-up window. The pop-up behaves like a GUI tool tip, so we'll refer to it as a *map tip*.

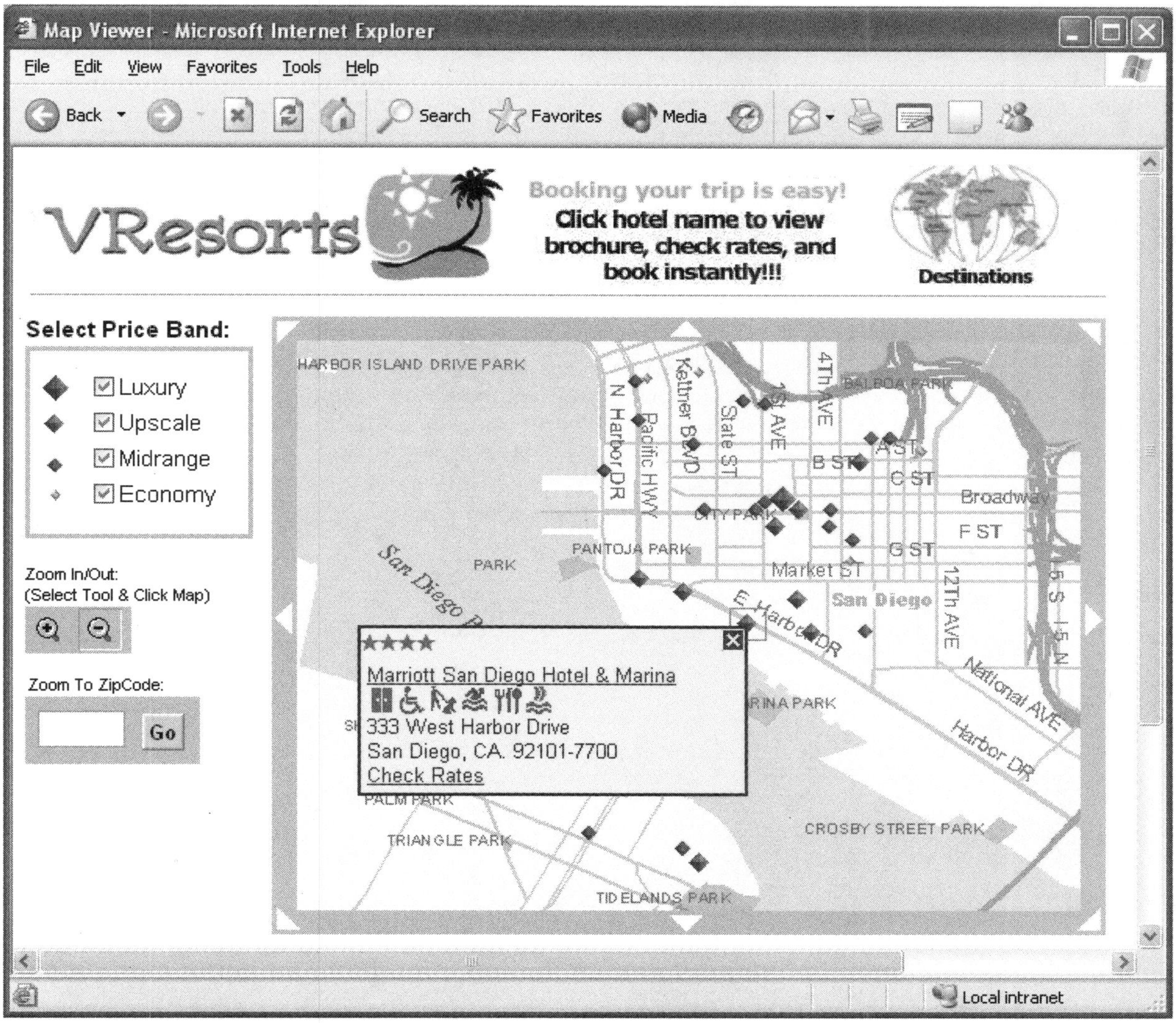

Figure 6-12. *The mapplet gets its first airing. Not bad for a prototype!*

Each hotel is represented on the map by a small diamond (as shown in the key at the left of Figure 6-12).

In this version of the mapplet, each hotel actually has two map tips: a small, relatively nonintrusive *hover tip* that appears when the mouse cursor is hovered over the hotel diamond, and a larger, more detailed pop-up (as shown in Figure 6-12). This UI behavior was specified by the "Display Rollover Information" use case (see earlier in this chapter).[9]

9. And, of course, if you go online to `http://smartmaps.VResorts.com` (and please do), you can try this out for yourself!

The larger pop-up behaves more like a floating dialog window than a tool tip. For example, it's more *persistent*, meaning it doesn't disappear when the mouse is moved away, but must be closed using the "close" button at the top-right corner. The pop-up also contains hyperlinks, which can be clicked to show hotel details in a separate browser window.

Why have two distinct classes of map tip for each hotel? It might seem a little odd at first, but there are some good reasons. Probably the most important reason is that the larger pop-up shows more information and therefore takes up more space. Having a map tip of that size pop up just by moving the mouse around would be seriously annoying for the user. The user might be moving the mouse to a different hotel, which is suddenly obscured by the giant map tip that pops up uninvited.

So it's better to keep the hover tip small and unobtrusive (little more than a tool tip). Then, if the user wants more details, she performs a deliberate action (clicking the mouse on the hotel diamond) to bring up the larger pop-up window. Similarly, the pop-up window must be closed using a deliberate action.

Summary

In this chapter, we told the story of a project team beginning to adapt to ICONIX Process, with the prototype release of the mapplet project. We showed how the initial set of use cases was analyzed and broken down into an object-oriented design using a cookbook-style, step-by-step process.

This first release was intended as a way of testing ESRI's new server product, so release 1 was earmarked very much as a prototype. While the team did do some modeling, the emphasis was on writing prototype code and getting familiar with the new technology. As a result, the team skipped some of the initial design efforts. However, to the team's credit, the deliverable software for this first release matched up to the requirements pretty well.

We also showed one of the safety nets (namely, code-level refactoring) that Agile ICONIX puts in place for when the team strays from the process path. (This does occur, particularly early in a project when the team is still adapting to the new design process, so expect it to happen and be prepared!)

Finally, we saw the end result of this first release: the alpha release of the mapplet.

Having seen the first release, the team now has a much better idea of what works and what doesn't, design-wise. So in the next chapter, we revisit the design and give it a serious going-over in preparation for release 2.

CHAPTER 7

Synchronizing the Model and Code: One Small Release at a Time

If release 1 marked the end of the project, then that would be fine: our work here would be done. If the product works, it meets the requirements, and there's no more development to be done, then there's simply no need to spend time tidying up the design.[1] For the mapplet project, however, we're really just getting started. So to prepare for the next release, we need to transform the prototype alpha design into a production-quality design that's more maintainable, reusable, and extensible.

In this chapter, we analyze the robustness and sequence diagrams that the team produced (i.e., the design the team coded from) and show how that design could have been improved. This should prove useful, as the diagrams reveal some common issues that it pays to be aware of. These issues typically appear early in a project when the team is still working to create an understanding of the product that it's going to build.

In the early stages of a project, you'd normally expect design errors to be made and for the source code to not be precisely aligned with the diagrams. As subsequent releases are embarked upon, however, you should expect to see the diagrams and the source code converge more and more. Having the design model and the code in sync allows the project to be much more agile, as it's easier to design for the next release, building on the design work that was done for the previous release.

Keeping It Agile

A truly agile project will produce lots of short software releases, unleashing them on the world in quick succession (with each release lasting anywhere from a week up to a month or two[2]). If we end each release with a design review, then the design is reined in before it has a chance to get out of control.

The design review is actually a code *and* design review, because we also compare the code with the design (once the design has been reviewed) and bring the code back in sync with the design.

Tip Bringing the model and the source code back in sync is an important Agile ICONIX practice. We need the model and the source code to be tightly coupled so we can reuse these diagrams for the next release. In other words, we're going to drive the code from the model, so we'd better have the model in good shape.

---

1. In such cases, however, it does pay to spend a little time "mothballing" the project—that is, updating the documentation so that if the project does happen to be revisited sometime in the future, the documentation actually matches the code. Think about the maintenance team that will have to work with your legacy. Be nice to them!

2. Our preference is for a 1- or 2-month release cycle (3 months as an absolute maximum). Anything less than 1 month creates too much admin overhead, and anything longer than 2 months greatly increases the risk of delivering something the customer wasn't expecting. (We discuss this idea further in the "Release Planning" section in Chapter 9, and also in Chapter 4.)

This also works the other way: when we review the code, it will probably remind us why the design followed a particular route. So this prevents us from taking the design in a direction that just isn't going to work with our chosen solution.

The first design review (between release 1 and release 2) is also the most important. It gives us a chance to radically alter the design if need be, before so much code has been written that it would be prohibitively expensive to make such sweeping design changes. In this chapter, we pay very careful attention to reviewing the mapplet design as we prepare for release 2.

Divergence of Code and Design over Time

As Figure 7-1 shows, some divergence between the design and the code is normal and should be expected, and the "idealized" case of 100% conformance between the design and the code will rarely be achieved. "Traditional" ICONIX Process uses the Critical Design Review (CDR) to make sure the design is specified at an appropriate level of detail that the code headers can be generated from the classes. With a low-ceremony approach, the CDR might get skipped, or at least not be as rigorous. By introducing code reviews at the end of each release in Agile ICONIX, we have another opportunity to bring the design and the code back into sync. If refactoring is used to "clean up" the code, this refactoring should be reflected in the sequence and class models so that these models can continue to be useful during the successive releases. The code review is really a code and design review.

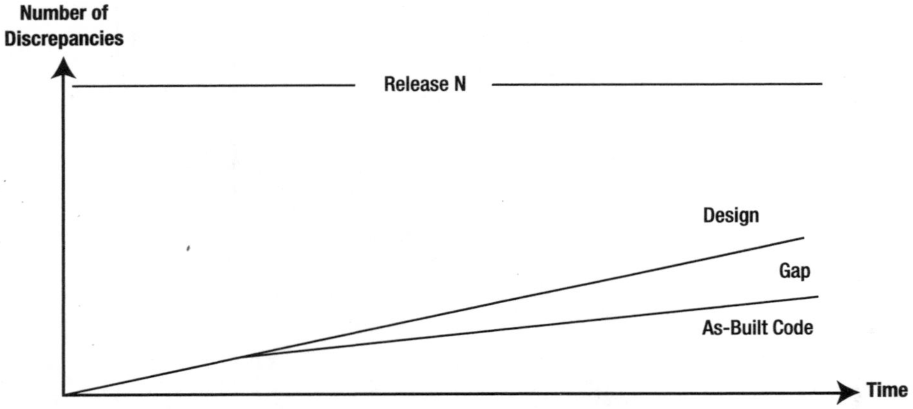

Figure 7-1. *Combating the gap between code and design*

As the software evolves over multiple releases, we'd hope to see the gap between the design and the as-built code growing progressively smaller. If the gap between the design and the code is large in one iteration, this should be an indicator to pay closer attention to CDR during the next release.

The gap between the design as specified on sequence and class diagrams and as-built code can be minimized by aggressively driving the code from the design (allocating operations to classes from sequence diagrams and generating code headers from the modeling tool), and by aggressively reviewing the detailed design (via CDR; see Chapter 3 for more details). If the as-built code diverges from the design, it can be brought back into sync after each release during a code review.

Design Review

Now that we've covered why the design and code review stage is so important, let's get started with the review! For the purposes of this chapter, we'll focus on the diagrams for the "Display Rollover Information" use case, because this use case happens to expose some areas where the design of the prototype code could be improved. Note that we're not updating these diagrams in order to have a pristine document; we're going to improve the code by revisiting the design. Along the way, we hope you'll learn a bit about how to "model like you mean it," as the team did.

"Display Rollover Information" Robustness Diagram Revisited

It quickly became obvious from looking at the sequence diagram for "Display Rollover Information" (see Figure 6-9) that the design was less than ideal. We traced the problem back to the robustness diagram and, in the course of reviewing it, discovered several issues that we felt could lead to a better design if addressed.

The robustness diagram that the team used as the basis for the design is shown back in Figure 6-8. In this section, we'll critique this diagram, working through the improvements one by one. We'll show some snapshots of the diagram as it's being improved. And then, using our new and improved robustness diagram, we'll create a new version of the sequence diagram and rework the code to match.

Step 1: "Decluttering" the Diagram

The robustness diagrams should be drawn at a fairly high level of abstraction so that they're uncluttered and easy to follow. This means showing less detail than what we'll be showing in the sequence diagrams. With this in mind, we can make several refinements in this diagram:

- All of the "On Click" and "On Mouse Over" controllers can be removed, and instead the controller name can simply be placed on the arrow. (We can safely do this, because, as drawn, these "On Click" controllers have no real behavior—the software behavior is in the controllers that are linked to these. As a general rule, *if a controller has no behavior, don't draw it.*) For example, the On Click on Multiple Hotels controller (near the center of the diagram) could be removed, and we could instead have an arrow going from Map Viewer to "Get list of clicked hotels." The arrow would then be labeled On Click on Multiple Hotels.

- Similarly, we can get rid of the On Mouse Over a Hotel Icon controller, by just labeling the arrow coming from the Map Viewer.

- Also, is the Change Mouse Icon operation major enough to warrant being on this diagram? We can combine Change Mouse Icon and Change Hotel Icon into something like "Change mouse icon and highlight Hotel icon" on the robustness diagram, even though these would be two different operations on a sequence diagram.

- We can also rename "mouse icon" to "cursor," as the term "cursor" is more intuitive than "mouse icon." So the renamed operation would be "Change cursor and highlight Hotel icon."

The result of these analysis-model refactorings should be a robustness diagram that's simpler and easier to read. The new and improved robustness diagram (so far) is shown in Figure 7-2.

We've also jiggled the objects around a bit to improve the readability, and as you can see, the straight-line police paid a visit to this diagram. Note, however, that in most cases it just isn't worth spending ages perfecting a diagram's layout. In certain cases when presentation is important (like, hey, for a book!), it's worth doing, but usually the main purpose of a diagram is to get you to the next stage of development (in this case, the sequence diagrams), not to spend ages making every line perfectly straight.

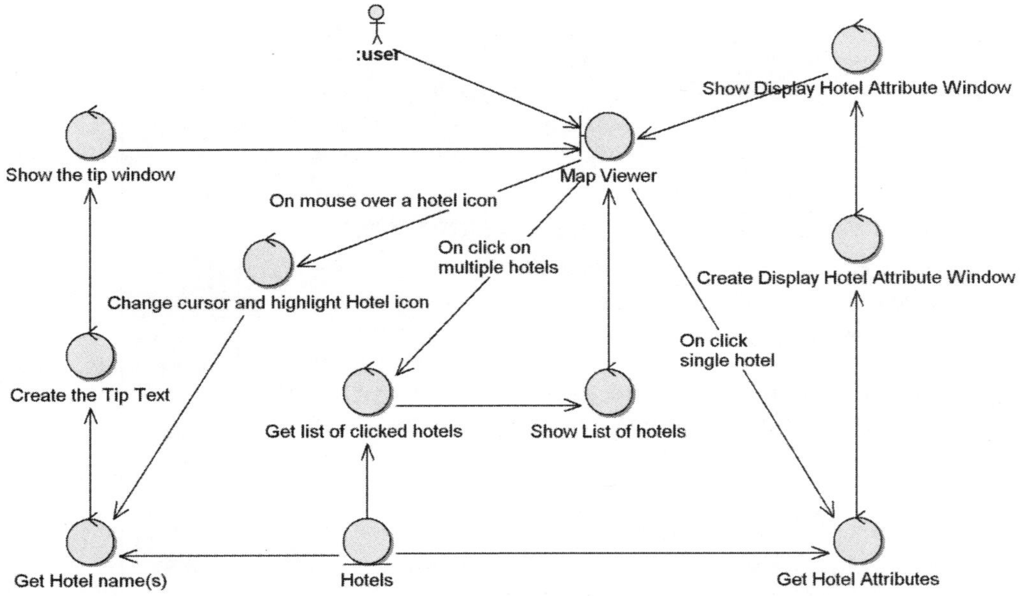

Figure 7-2. *New and improved "Display Rollover Information" robustness diagram. It's looking better already!*

On discussing these changes with the ESRI team, we realized that Change Mouse Icon is never really explicitly called. The cursor graphic is just a parameter of the HTML image map, and the browser automatically does this for us. However, the Change Hotel Icon operation is explicitly called when the `onMouseOver` or `onMouseExit` events occur for a particular image.

So at this stage, we could either revisit the diagram and change it again or leave this part of it unaltered. We opted to leave the operation as "Change cursor and highlight Hotel icon," because that's what actually happens. (At this stage, we're not so concerned with *how* things happen—much of that thought process can be left to the design stage.)

Step 2: Disambiguating the Diagram

Now that the diagram has been "decluttered", we instantly begin to see some other improvements and corrections (aka disambiguations) that we can make.

The two controllers at the top-right of Figure 7-2, Create Display Hotel Attribute Window and Show Display Hotel Attribute Window, could probably be merged into a single controller. Their purpose is similar enough that we don't gain anything from them being shown separately. Remember that robustness diagrams are high-level analysis tools.[3]

3. Of course, when we get to the sequence diagram, it will be a different matter. Sequence diagrams are all about low-level design, so at that stage we *will* want the extra detail on the diagram.

While we're at it, where did the Display Hotel Attribute Window name come from in the first place? It doesn't appear in the domain model or the use case, so at this point alarm bells should be ringing—we have a rogue controller on our diagram! If we check back to the "Display Rollover Information" use case, the following sentence provides the answer:

> *The user may click the hotel icon to* ***display a hotel information pop-up*** *that displays the hotel's attributes for all of the fields in the hotel pop-up fields collection.*

So Show Display Hotel Attribute Window should be renamed as Show Hotel Info Pop-up. (You might think this sort of thing is too trivial to bother with, but it's not. It's amazing how many bugs get introduced into software because elements are named ambiguously.)

Tip Let's boil this down to a simple rule of thumb. The use case text has to match the robustness diagram, and the robustness diagram has to match the class diagram, and the class diagram has to match the code. In short, that's how you can drive code from use cases.

A question that arose during the design review was, "Should 'Hotel Info Pop-up' also appear on the domain model, as it's an entity, a noun?" Although it should be a Boundary object on the robustness diagram, we chose not to put it on the domain model. Nouns for "GUI stuff" stay off the domain model because they're solution space in nature (i.e., we would have built a different solution for hotel map finders that didn't use this particular GUI widget). Another reason we avoid putting GUI stuff in the domain model is because it would very quickly get all cluttered up. Starting to include GUI stuff on the domain model is really opening Pandora's box, and it should be avoided.

MapTip could also be a Boundary object on the robustness diagram. When you look at the finished diagram (skip ahead to Figure 7-4 if you can't wait!), you'll see how the robustness diagram really "tells the story" of the behavior requirements written in the use case.

OBJECT DISCOVERY IN ACTION: INTRODUCING MULTIPLEHOTELCLUSTER

At this point, the question arose about whether Hotels (the entity) should be Hotel (the domain class) or HotelCollection (the domain class). The issue arises because when a map is zoomed out far enough, a single icon is used to represent a cluster of hotels that are very close together, and the code needs to make this all work correctly (meaning the design needs to account for it). Our first inclination was that it should probably be HotelCollection, not Hotel (because it was providing a list of hotels). We were seeing basically the same disconnect error between static and dynamic parts of the model that we saw at the beginning of Chapter 6.

Our second inclination (on rubbing bleary eyes and staring again at the diagram) was . . . wait . . . that it should actually be the reverse—it should be Hotel and not HotelCollection (because it was providing hotel attributes)!

In a situation such as this, where you find yourself switching back and forth between two options, consider strongly the possibility that there should in fact be a *third* class involved. In this case, the confusion arises because Hotel is schizophrenic and doesn't know if it's one hotel or several hotels (and because there's a disconnect between the static and dynamic models). So the solution is to introduce a new class that can be both Hotels and HotelCollections. Let's call the new class MultipleHotelCluster.

"Hotel" on this diagram really means "all the hotels that are too close together to resolve as individual hotels." So our new MultipleHotelCluster class is a HotelCollection within which all the hotels are, for practical purposes, at the current map scale, geographically coincident.

If you're an avid design-pattern spotter, you'll recognize that we've just described the Composite pattern. We'll revisit this part of the design later in the chapter, when we get into the nitty-gritty aspects of the design. We just mention it now because it figures in the robustness diagram (see Figure 7-3) and has some bearing on the analysis thought process at this stage.

Figure 7-3 shows the updated version of the robustness diagram. It's very nearly complete, but there are still one or two improvements that can be made.

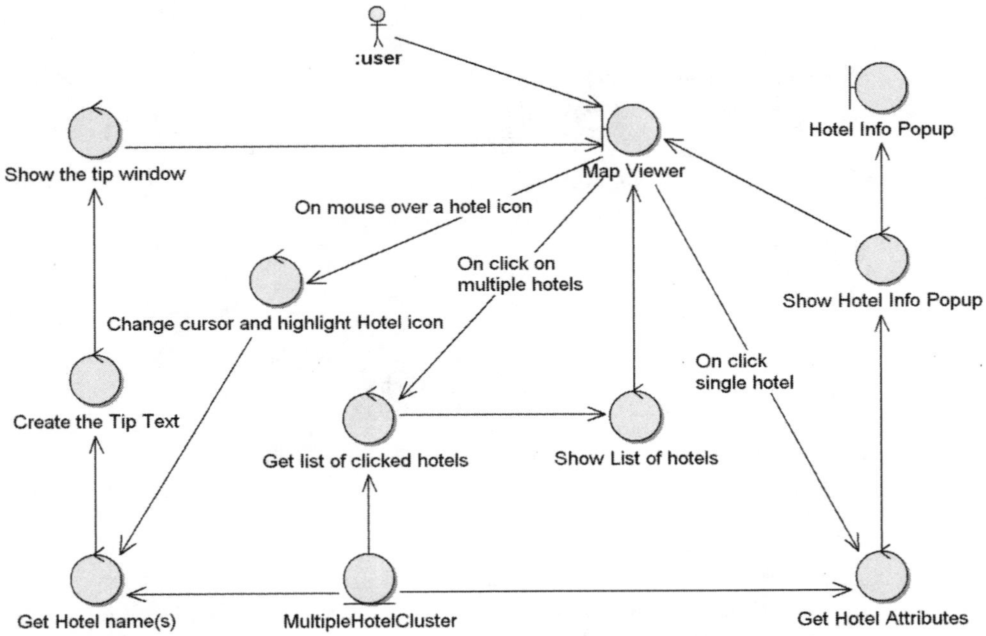

Figure 7-3. *Updated "Display Rollover Information" robustness diagram*

Step 3: Fine-tuning the Diagram

Let's take a look at the Entity objects in Figure 7-3 and give those a good going-over next.

1. The diagram now shows MultipleHotelCluster, but it also needs to show Hotel.
2. Hotel attributes come from a Hotel and are displayed in a Hotel Info Popup when a single hotel is clicked (via the "On Click single hotel" connector). Ergo, Get Hotel Attributes needs to be connected to . . . Hotel (not to MultipleHotelCluster).
3. The class MultipleHotelCluster has no hotel attributes; it's merely a container for Hotels that happen to be geographically close together. So it makes no sense to have a connection between MultipleHotelCluster and Get Hotel Attributes. This is because Get Hotel Attributes is going to be a method on the Hotel class. Therefore, the arrow at the bottom right of the diagram needs to be deleted, an entity (Hotel) needs to be added to the right of MultipleHotelCluster, and that entity (Hotel) needs to be connected to Get Hotel Attributes.

Now on to the Boundary objects:

1. Currently the diagram shows two boundaries: Hotel Info Popup and Map Viewer. We could do with a third: Map Tip Window. This third Boundary object is really just for symmetry (and, of course, to make the robustness diagram match the use case text). If there's a boundary for the pop-up, why not also have one for the map tip? (Recall from the UI description that pop-ups and map tips are very similar beasts, so they should be modeled consistently.) So . . .

2. We need to add a boundary called Map Tip Window toward the upper left of the diagram.

3. We then disconnect "Show the tip window" from Map Viewer and connect it to Map Tip Window. The result of the last few steps is that on the right side of the diagram, Show Hotel Info Popup is connected to Hotel Info Popup, and on the left side of the diagram, "Show the tip window" is connected to Map Tip Window.

4. Finally, on refactoring this diagram, we noticed that the "Show List of hotels" controller isn't actually needed at all. This is because it's redundant with the "Get Hotel name(s)" controller. So "Show List of hotels" can safely be removed altogether.

Figure 7-4 shows the final version of the robustness diagram, before we move on to the sequence diagram.

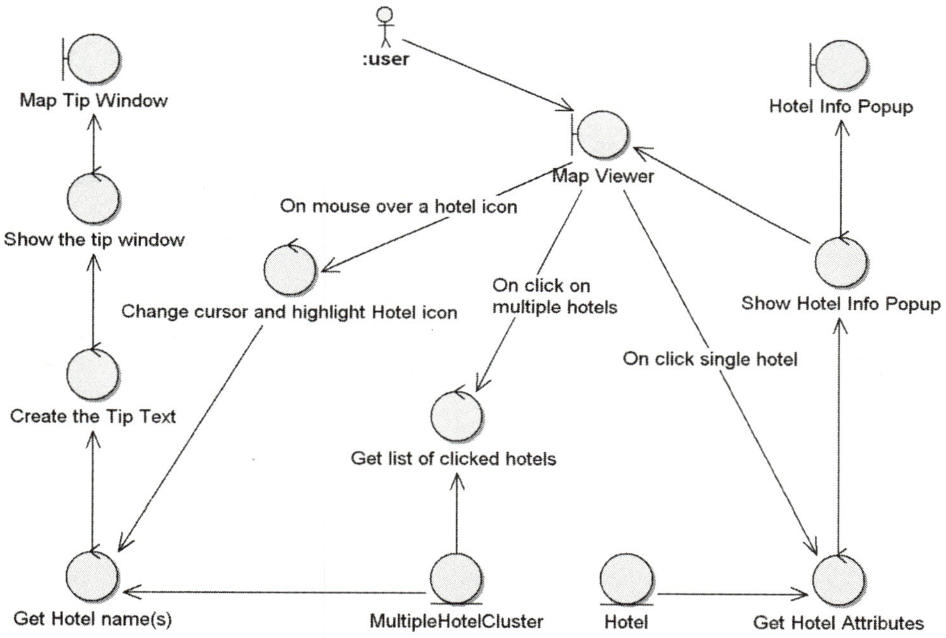

Figure 7-4. *Final "decluttered" and disambiguated "Display Rollover Information" robustness diagram*

As you can see, a lot has changed between this version of the diagram and the original version shown in Figure 6-8. You'll often see robustness diagrams produced that are more like Figure 6-8 than the disambiguated diagram shown in Figure 7-4. There's a reason for this, which we discuss back in Chapter 3 in the section "Is Robustness Diagramming an Art or a Science?"

Remember that with robustness diagrams, we're producing a conceptual design. This gives us a great opportunity to spend a little time getting the conceptual (high-level) design right, creating a solid foundation from which to design the implementation.

Code-level refactoring is often the result of code that has been written to the wrong conceptual design. For example, we never imagined the need for a Hotel Cluster object, so we just jammed the behavior for multiple hotels into the Hotel object, giving Hotel a bad case of schizophrenia because it didn't know if it was one Hotel or several.

However, even for people who initially find robustness diagrams difficult to get right, it really does become much easier with practice. Doug's experience from teaching hundreds of JumpStart workshops is that it takes working through about a half-dozen robustness diagrams to get good at it. Your first one might take an hour, but by the time you've worked through five or six of them and gotten the hang of it, you'll be able to knock them out in about 5 minutes. It's a lot like riding a bicycle: once you figure it out, it's really quite easy. The benefit you gain from this perseverance is the ability to design systems that are highly modular and easy to maintain, and that stand a much better chance of being correct.

■ **Modeling Tip** Use the *highlighter test* to check if your robustness diagram is right. Remember that the robustness diagram is an "object picture" of your use case. Check the robustness diagram against the use case text by using a highlighter pen to go through your use case one sentence at a time, and highlight the corresponding objects and links on the robustness diagram. If they don't match, make them match. This will often mean rewriting (disambiguating) the use case.

"Display Rollover Information" Sequence Diagram Revisited

Now that we've corrected the robustness diagram, we can safely move on to the next stage: the sequence diagram (the original version is shown back in Figure 6-9). In fact, producing the new version of the sequence diagram should now be smooth sailing, using the ICONIX cookbook-style process (refer back to Chapter 3):

1. Use the boundaries, actors, and entities.[4]
2. Copy the use case text.
3. Work through the controllers one at a time.

What we actually find is that as we start to produce the sequence diagram, new design concerns become apparent. In general, you'll often find that these concerns feed back into the robustness diagram, and sometimes they even go as far back as the use case and domain model.

For this particular example, we'll see the sequence diagram develop over several short, fast passes. We'll see the diagram split into three separate diagrams. Then, as our understanding of the design improves, two of these diagrams get merged. Finally, we converge on a design (with the active involvement of the programmer responsible for this area of the code). This is not dissimilar to the way that a programmer refactors code, evolving his way to a cleaner design. However, the approach we're taking is faster because there are no unit tests to write and rewrite, and no source code to slow us down (yet).

Let's walk through this process in more detail.

---

4. For example, using Enterprise Architect, this literally means "drag the boundaries, actors, and entities from the browser window into the sequence diagram."

"Display Rollover Information" Sequence Diagram: The First Refactoring

As we began refactoring the sequence diagram from Figure 6-9, we realized that the use case is really describing three different events:

- What happens when the user hovers the mouse over a Hotel icon
- What happens when the user clicks a Hotel icon
- What happens when the user clicks a Multiple Hotels icon

MODELING QUESTION: IS THIS ONE USE CASE OR THREE?

The fact that this use case is describing three different events could theoretically justify creating three separate use cases. However, this really is just a single use case.

The use case is the conceptual activity that the user is doing: she's rolling the mouse over the icons on the map and the system is displaying details about what she rolls over. Whether it's one hotel or a cluster that she happens to roll over doesn't make it a different use case—it's just different behavior within the "Display Rollover Information" use case.

For the purposes of displaying the sequence diagram in this book, we've divided it into three. Normally, however, the basic course and the alternate courses should all be shown on the same sequence diagram, with the message arrows lined up opposite the text (see Chapter 3). Figures 7-5, 7-6, and 7-7 show the three parts of the sequence diagram.

In the use case (shown at the left of Figure 7-5), the text that's relevant to the sequence diagram is as follows:

The user positions the mouse cursor over a hotel icon in the map display. Mouse icon changes to "selection hand" and the hotel icon changes to "selected hotel." The system displays a map tip, displaying the hotel name.

BASIC COURSE:

The user positions the mouse cursor over a hotel icon in the map display. Mouse icon changes to "selection hand" and the hotel icon changes to "selected hotel." The system displays a map tip, displaying the hotel name. The user may click on the hotel icon to display a hotel info popup that displays the hotel's attributes for all of the fields in the hotel popup fields collection. The system queries the hotel attributes to determine which hotel details are available for the hotel. Within the hotel pop-up, the system displays hyperlinks for hotel details. The user may click these to invoke the "View Detailed Hotel Info" use case.

ALTERNATE COURSES:

No hotels are found at click coordinates: do nothing.

Multiple hotels found at click coordinates: System constructs a list of the selected hotels' names and displays them in a popup. The user may select a hotel from the list to display the associated hotel info popup.

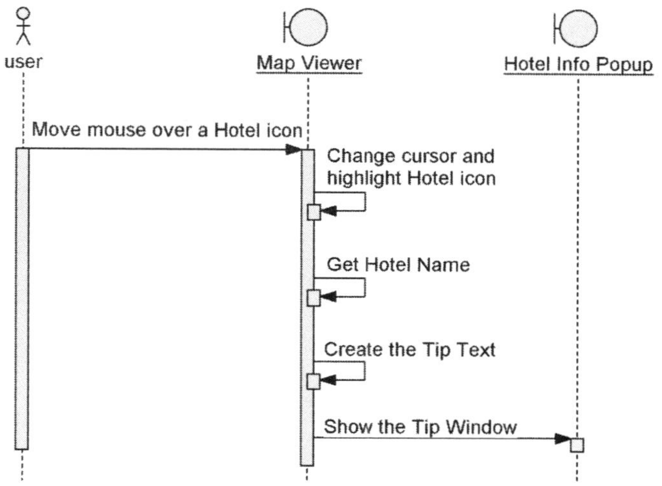

Figure 7-5. *"Display Rollover Information," zeroed in on the "Move mouse over a Hotel icon" event*

In the use case text (shown in the text at the left of Figure 7-6), the text that pertains to the sequence diagram is as follows:

> *The user may click on the hotel icon to display a hotel info popup that displays the hotel's attributes for all of the fields in the hotel popup fields collection . . . [and so on to the end of the basic course].*

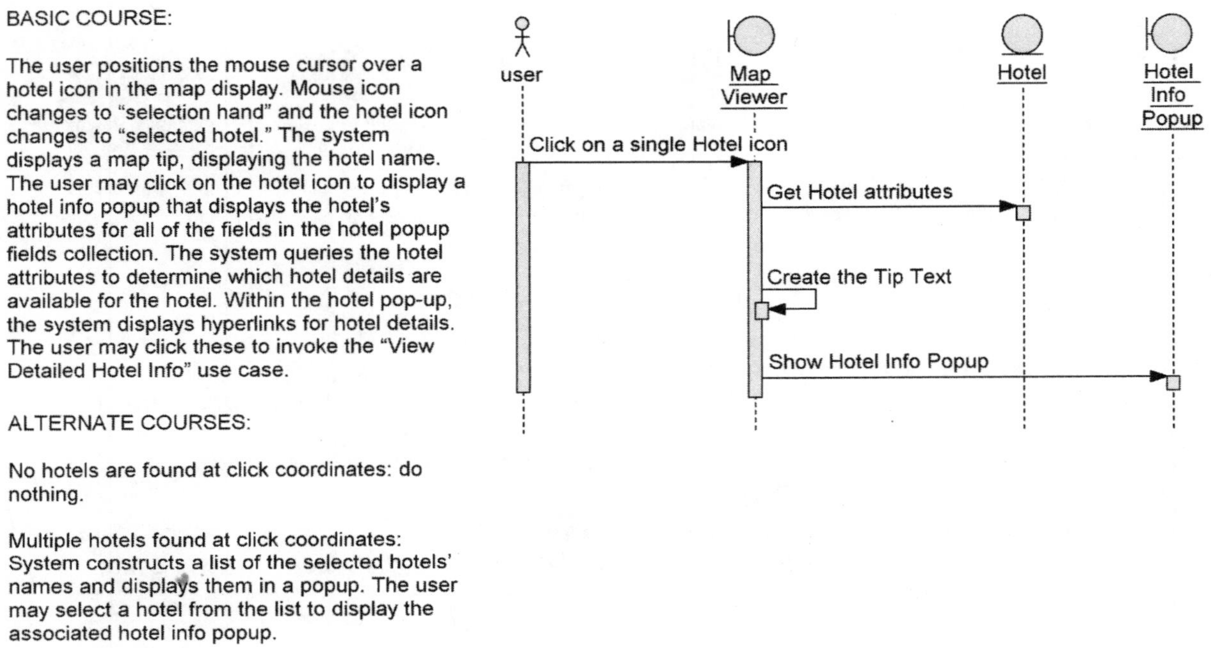
BASIC COURSE:
The user positions the mouse cursor over a hotel icon in the map display. Mouse icon changes to "selection hand" and the hotel icon changes to "selected hotel." The system displays a map tip, displaying the hotel name. The user may click on the hotel icon to display a hotel info popup that displays the hotel's attributes for all of the fields in the hotel popup fields collection. The system queries the hotel attributes to determine which hotel details are available for the hotel. Within the hotel pop-up, the system displays hyperlinks for hotel details. The user may click these to invoke the "View Detailed Hotel Info" use case.
ALTERNATE COURSES:
No hotels are found at click coordinates: do nothing.
Multiple hotels found at click coordinates: System constructs a list of the selected hotels' names and displays them in a popup. The user may select a hotel from the list to display the associated hotel info popup.
user
Map Viewer
Hotel
Hotel Info Popup
Click on a single Hotel icon
Get Hotel attributes
Create the Tip Text
Show Hotel Info Popup

Figure 7-6. *"Display Rollover Information," zeroed in on the "Click on a single Hotel icon" event*

In the use case text (shown in the text at the left of Figure 7-7), the text that pertains to the sequence diagram is the alternate course:

> *Multiple hotels found at click coordinates: System constructs a list of the selected hotels' names and displays them in a popup.*

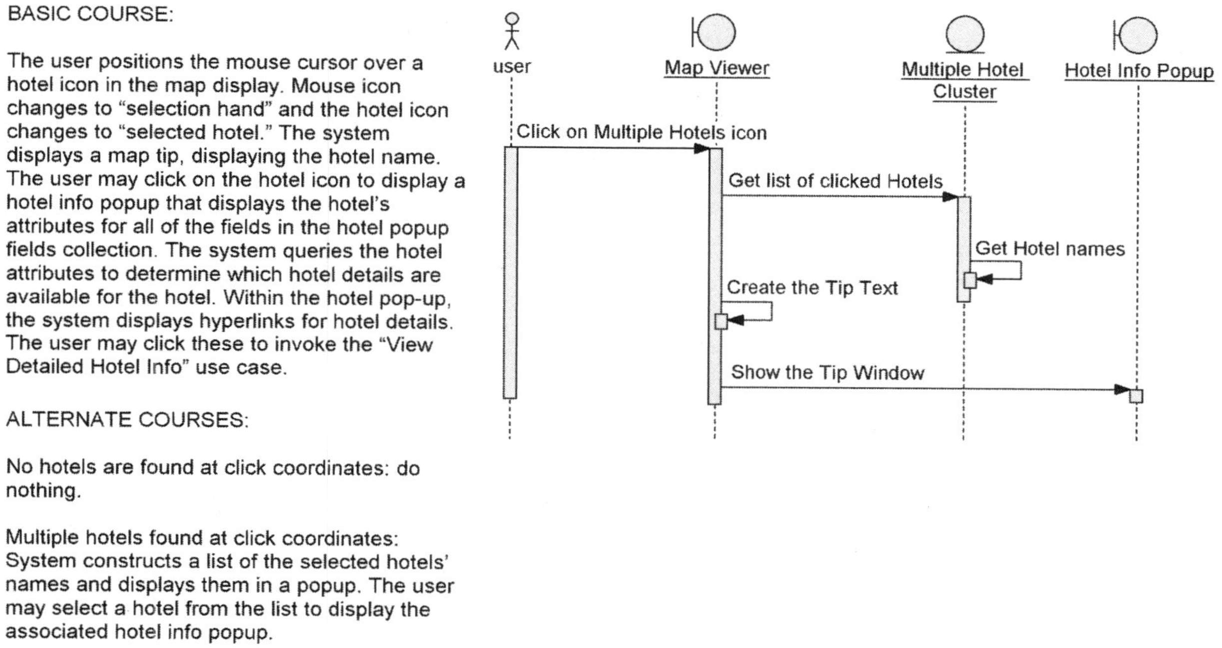
BASIC COURSE:
The user positions the mouse cursor over a hotel icon in the map display. Mouse icon changes to "selection hand" and the hotel icon changes to "selected hotel." The system displays a map tip, displaying the hotel name. The user may click on the hotel icon to display a hotel info popup that displays the hotel's attributes for all of the fields in the hotel popup fields collection. The system queries the hotel attributes to determine which hotel details are available for the hotel. Within the hotel pop-up, the system displays hyperlinks for hotel details. The user may click these to invoke the "View Detailed Hotel Info" use case.
ALTERNATE COURSES:
No hotels are found at click coordinates: do nothing.
Multiple hotels found at click coordinates: System constructs a list of the selected hotels' names and displays them in a popup. The user may select a hotel from the list to display the associated hotel info popup.
user
Map Viewer
Multiple Hotel Cluster
Hotel Info Popup
Click on Multiple Hotels icon
Get list of clicked Hotels
Get Hotel names
Create the Tip Text
Show the Tip Window

Figure 7-7. *"Display Rollover Information," zeroed in on the "Click on Multiple Hotels icon" event*

Notice that this part of the sequence diagram uses MultipleHotelCluster instead of Hotel, as it's dealing with multiple hotels.

"Display Rollover Information" Sequence Diagram: The Second Refactoring

Having separated out the diagrams, we began to think some more about the Composite design pattern (discussed earlier in this chapter; see the sidebar titled "Object Discovery in Action: Introducing MultipleHotelCluster") and how this could help to simplify the design. The essence of the Composite design pattern is that to the client code, it makes no difference whether it's dealing with a single object or a cluster of similar objects. For our example, this translates to a single Hotel or a MultipleHotelCluster.

To describe the pattern in UML parlance

> *AOI **has** a HotelCollection, which **has** MultipleHotelClusters and Hotels. MultipleHotelCluster **is a** HotelCollection, and it **has** Hotels.*

(Note that we can read *has* as a UML Aggregation relationship, and ***is*** as a UML Generalization relationship).

We began to put this into a class diagram to clarify the design in our minds. The initial version that we produced is shown in Figure 7-8.

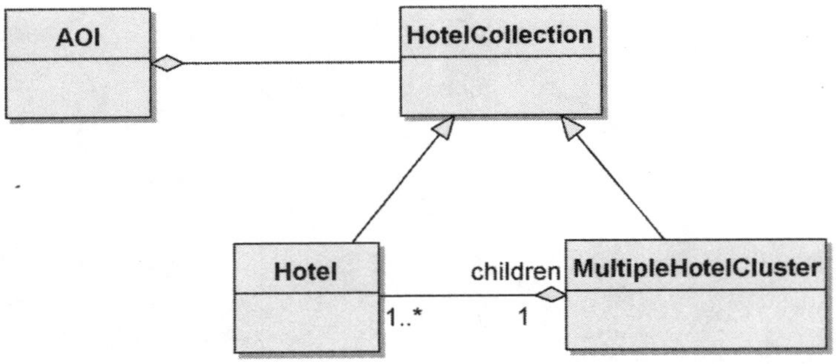

Figure 7-8. *Refactoring Hotel and HotelCollection into an (almost) Composite design pattern*

Strictly speaking, this isn't a 100% conformant Composite pattern. If it was, then the "children" relationship between Hotel and MultipleHotelCluster would instead be pointing from MultipleHotelCluster back to HotelCollection. This would allow HotelCollection (theoretically at least) to be composed of an infinite number of nested Hotels and MultipleHotelClusters. For our purposes, however, this is overkill; we want the collection to be only one level deep. That is, a HotelCollection may be a single Hotel or a cluster of Hotels, but not a cluster of clusters. So for our purposes, it makes sense for "children" to point directly to Hotel (effectively closing off the loop and preventing recursion) rather than back to HotelCollection.

As we produced this class diagram, we began to think about the class names we were using. If HotelCollection was a single Hotel, then it didn't seem to make sense for it to be a "collection" as such. We also agreed that MultipleHotelCluster was a bit of a mouthful, so we began to refactor the class names. What we ended up with is in Figure 7-9. As you can see, HotelCollection became HotelComposite (in tribute to the Composite pattern that we borrowed and then mangled shamelessly for our own purposes). And MultipleHotelCluster became simply HotelCluster (which takes fewer brain cycles to read but conveys basically the same information).

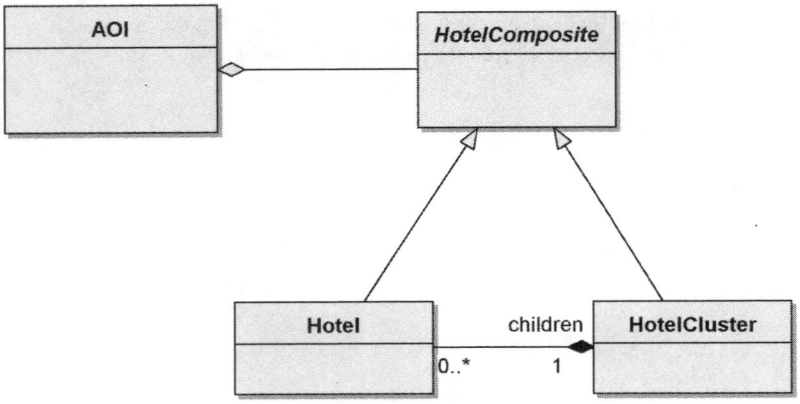

Figure 7-9. *Our semi-Composite design with some of the classes renamed*

Although we don't normally split hairs about such things, note that AOI and HotelComposite have an *aggregation relationship* (meaning AOI contains some HotelComposites), whereas HotelCluster and Hotel have a much stronger *composition relationship* (meaning essentially that a HotelCluster consists purely of Hotels. Building a HotelCluster without Hotels would be like building a brick house without bricks).

Now that we have our HotelComposite all sorted out, we can examine how it affects the rest of the design. Recall from earlier that we had modeled the use case as three separate sequence diagrams (shown in Figures 7-5, 7-6, and 7-7) to cover each of the scenarios. Two of these were "Click on a single Hotel icon" and "Click on Multiple Hotels icon." But of course, the whole point of adopting the Composite pattern is that the design doesn't need to differentiate between single and multiple hotels. So we should, in that case, be able to combine Figures 7-6 and 7-7.

This will leave us with two sequence diagram "fragments": Click HotelComposite and Mouse Over HotelComposite. Figure 7-10 shows the "final" refactored sequence diagram for this use case, including the Mouse Over event and Click Hotel/HotelComposite events.

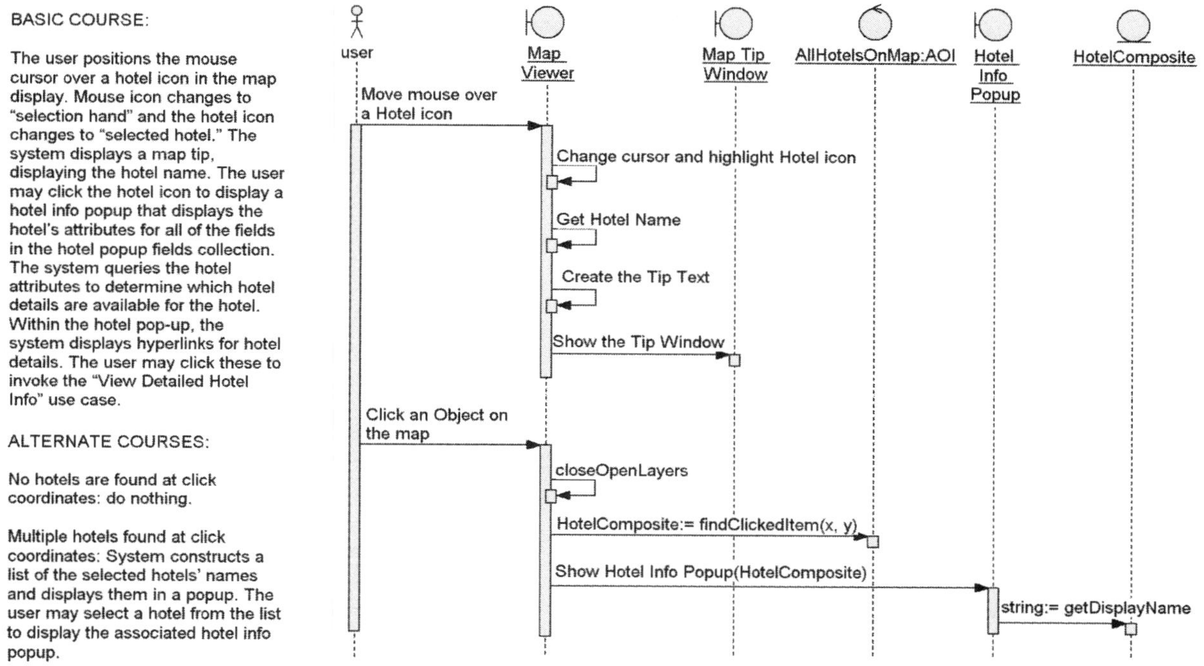
BASIC COURSE:
The user positions the mouse cursor over a hotel icon in the map display. Mouse icon changes to "selection hand" and the hotel icon changes to "selected hotel." The system displays a map tip, displaying the hotel name. The user may click the hotel icon to display a hotel info popup that displays the hotel's attributes for all of the fields in the hotel popup fields collection. The system queries the hotel attributes to determine which hotel details are available for the hotel. Within the hotel pop-up, the system displays hyperlinks for hotel details. The user may click these to invoke the "View Detailed Hotel Info" use case.
ALTERNATE COURSES:
No hotels are found at click coordinates: do nothing.
Multiple hotels found at click coordinates: System constructs a list of the selected hotels' names and displays them in a popup. The user may select a hotel from the list to display the associated hotel info popup.
user
Map Viewer
Map Tip Window
AllHotelsOnMap:AOI
Hotel Info Popup
HotelComposite
Move mouse over a Hotel icon
Change cursor and highlight Hotel icon
Get Hotel Name
Create the Tip Text
Show the Tip Window
Click an Object on the map
closeOpenLayers
HotelComposite:= findClickedItem(x, y)
Show Hotel Info Popup(HotelComposite)
string:= getDisplayName

Figure 7-10. *"Display Rollover Information," using the Composite pattern to combine the single hotel and multiple hotel scenarios*

Notice that the use case text has been split up so that the text lines up more or less with the messages in the diagram (the exception to this is the "No hotels are found at click coordinates" alternate course, which isn't shown).

Figure 7-10 also introduces a new controller object, AllHotelsOnMap. This is simply an instance of the AOI class.

To sum up, this is the essence of model refactoring: iterating through various design possibilities until we zero in on the design that works for everyone involved. We believe (and we hope you'll agree) that this is far more efficient (and leads to a higher quality product) than coding "the simplest thing that could possibly work" and refactoring the design into shape later. We believe that a concerted effort to get the design right the first time is worth its weight (figuratively speaking) in gold.

Class Diagram

Cast your mind back to the reverse-engineered diagram in Figure 6-11. Let's compare that with our new class diagram in Figure 7-11, the product of our analysis-level and design-level refactorings so far.

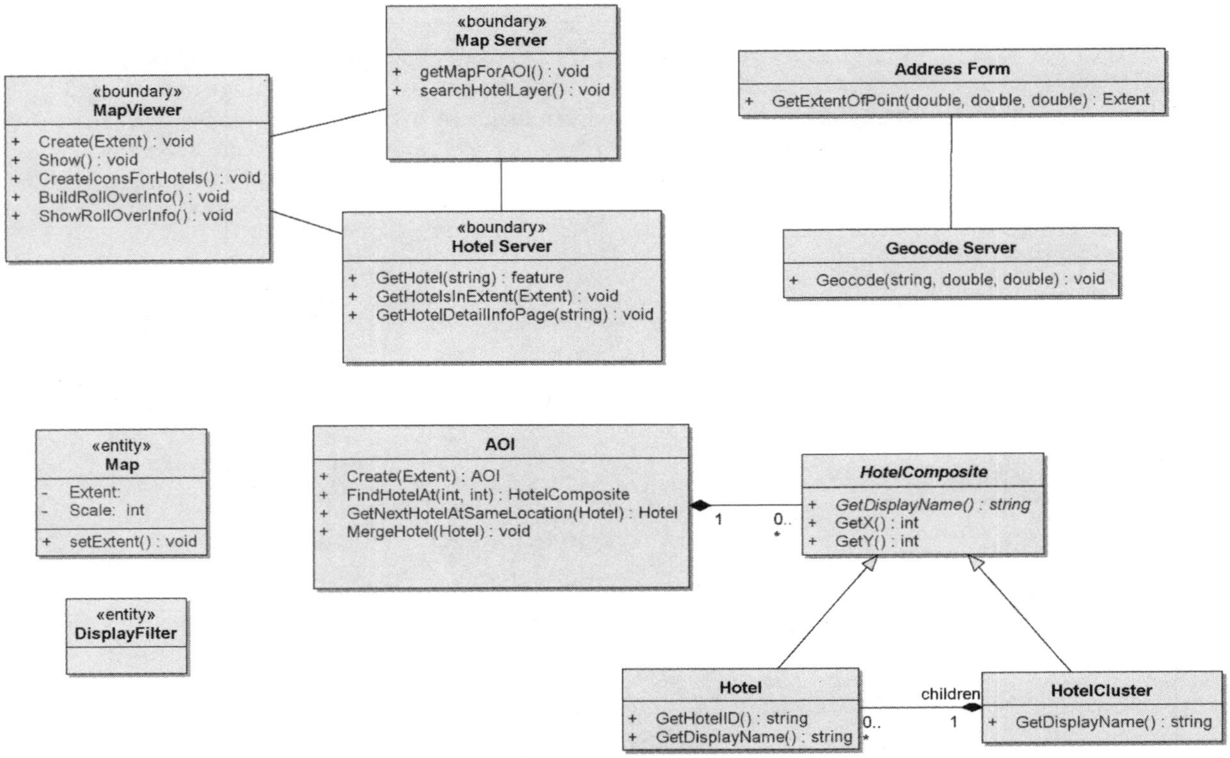

Figure 7-11. *Refactored class diagram for the mapplet prototype*

As you can see, Figure 7-11 still needs work. We deliberately show it here in an unfinished state, because we're going to delve into the source code for the prototype and refactor parts of it. This will be fed back into the class diagram, so there would be little point in trying to perfect the diagram at this stage.

MODELING VS. DOING THE SIMPLEST THING THAT COULD POSSIBLY WORK AND THEN REFACTORING

It's worth pausing for a moment here to reflect on what we've just done in our model. We started out with a very simple model: a Hotel class that was hiding a dual personality by doing the work of both a single hotel and a cluster of hotels. This was in fact, exactly "the simplest thing that could possibly work," because the prototype release was actually coded that way, and it ran. But it was far from the best design. We then went through a number of refactorings of the design and saw Hotel become Hotels, MultipleHotelCluster, and HotelCluster, before finally arriving at the Composite pattern.

Could these refactorings have been done in code, without modeling? Sure they could have. But they would have carried the additional overhead of writing and running unit tests every step of the way. We believe it's much more efficient to learn how to manipulate the design using UML. But here's the lesson we hope this example teaches you: *myopically Doing The Simplest Thing That Could Possibly Work (DTSTTCPW) and "just coding what we need today" will almost always generate the need for massive amounts of refactoring.* This "continual rework because we didn't get it right the first time syndrome" (i.e., Constant Refactoring After Programming) can be avoided by using a little bit of foresight. In this case, one (highly questionable) agile practice (DTSTTCPW) generates the need for another compensatory agile practice (refactoring). We discuss this sort of thing at great length in *Extreme Programming Refactored: The Case Against XP.*

Source Code for the Refactored Design

Here's the source code for the refactored design using our adapted version of the Composite pattern.

Source Code for HotelComposite

We'll start with the abstract class HotelComposite (refer to Figure 7-11):

```
public abstract class HotelComposite
{
    protected int X;
    protected int Y;

    public HotelComposite (int aX, int aY)
    {
        X = aX;
        Y = aY;
    }


    public int GetX ()
    {
        return X;
    }

    public int GetY ()
    {
        return Y;
    }


    public abstract string GetHint ();
    public abstract string GetTitle ();
    public abstract string GetHighestPriceBand ();
    public abstract int GetHotelCount ();
    public abstract string GetRolloverInfo (
                              int ImageIndex,
                              LookupCollection Amenities,
                              string refURL);
    public abstract string GetPriceBand ();
}
```

The `X` and `Y` member variables are simply the HotelComposite's `X` and `Y` coordinates on the map.

Some of the abstract methods in HotelComposite didn't appear in Figures 7-10 and 7-11, because the methods are derived from the other use cases (which we've left out for brevity). But there's also a method, `GetHotelCount()`, which we forgot to include in the sequence diagrams and class diagram. That sort of thing is to be expected: *the code verifies the design equally as much as the design verifies the code.* As soon as the programmer really gets down to the source code level, he'll discover parts of the design that need to be changed. If he's followed a stringent design process, these changes should be minimal, but it's important to recognize that they do still occur and to bring the design diagrams back in sync as quickly as possible.

As this code was written, it quickly became obvious that our `GetDisplayName()` method wasn't quite right. For the purposes of constructing the web page, simply showing a display name wasn't sufficient. Instead, we need a method that returns the entire rollover information. And so the replacement for `GetDisplayName()`, at least in spirit, is `GetRolloverInfo()`.

GetRolloverInfo() actually returns a small snippet of HTML that gets added to the web page. We'll focus on GetRolloverInfo() as we explore the remainder of the source code, because this gives us the essence of the Composite pattern that is at the heart of our design refactoring efforts in this chapter.

Source Code for Hotel

Here's the concrete Hotel class, focusing on the GetRolloverInfo() method (again, refer back to Figure 7-11):

```
public class Hotel : HotelComposite
{
    private string id;
    private string name;
    private string address1;
    private string address2;
    private string city;
    private string state;
    private string zip;
    private string phone;
    private string amenities;
    private string starRating;
    private string brand;
    private string priceBand;
    private string links;


    public Hotel (string aID,
        int aX,
        int aY,
        string aName,
        string aAddress1,
        string aAddress2,
        string aCity,
        string aState,
        string aZip,
        string aPhone,
        string aStarRating,
        string aAmenities,
        string aBrand,
        string aPriceBand,
        string aLinks): base (aX, aY)
    {
        id = aID;
        name = aName;
        address1 = aAddress1;
        address2 = aAddress2;
        city = aCity;
        state = aState;
        zip = aZip;
        phone = aPhone;
        amenities = aAmenities;
        starRating = aStarRating;
        brand = aBrand;
        priceBand = aPriceBand;
        links = aLinks;
    }
```

```
public string GetName ()
{
    return name;
}


public override string GetRolloverInfo (int ImageIndex,
                            LookupCollection Amenities,
                            string refURL)
{
    return DisplayWindowText (Amenities, refURL);
}


private string DisplayWindowText (LookupCollection Amenities,
                                  string refURL)
{
    string s;
    if (links.IndexOf ("O") < 0)
        s = name;
    else
    {
        string webPage = String.Format (refURL, id, "O");
        s = "<A HREF=\"" +
            webPage +
            "\" target=blank>" +
            name +
            "</A><BR>";
    }

    bool added = false;

    LookupItem item;
    string delimStr = " ";
    char [] delimiter = delimStr.ToCharArray();

    string [] a = amenities.Split (delimiter);
    foreach (string st in a)
    {
        if (st.Length > 0)
        {
            item = Amenities.Find (st);
            if (item != null)
                if (item.info != null)
                {
                    added = true;
                    s = s + "<IMG SRC='" +
                            item.info +
                            "' ALT='" +
                            item.val +
                            "'/>";
                }
        }
    }
```

```
            if (added)
                s = s + "<BR>";

            string Address = address1;
            if (address2.Length > 0)
                Address = Address + "<BR>" + address2;
            Address = Address + "<BR>";
            if (city.Length > 0)
                Address = Address + city;
            if (state.Length > 0)
                Address = Address + ", " + state;
            if (zip.Length > 0)
                Address = Address + ". " + zip;
            s = s + Address;

            if (links.IndexOf ("B") >= 0)
            {
                string webPage = String.Format (refURL, id, "B");
                s = s + "<BR><A HREF=\"" +
                        webPage +
                        "\" target=blank>View hotel brochure</A>";
            }

            string wp = String.Format (refURL, id, "R");
            s = s + "<BR><A HREF=\"" +
                    wp +
                    "\" target=blank>Check Rates</A>";

            return s;
        }


        public override int GetHotelCount ()
        {
            return 1;
        }

    }
```

Notice the GetHotelCount() method, which we discussed earlier. You can see here how it works in the context of the Composite pattern. GetHotelCount() is defined as an abstract method in HotelComposite. In Hotel, it simply returns 1, as Hotel is obviously just the one hotel itself. However, as we'll see in a moment, HotelCluster will instead return a count of all its Hotels.

Taking a look at the source code for Hotel, one question that springs to mind is why the DisplayWindowText() method needs to be a separate method from the one-line GetRolloverInfo(). In fact, we'd better not let the refactoring police get too close to this code, as they would immediately want to break the fairly large DisplayWindowText() into a series of smaller, more fine-grained methods (and rightly so!). For example, the code (halfway through the method) that concatenates various strings to make an Address is a prime contender for being extracted into a separate method, somewhat like this:

```
public string ConcatAddress ()
{
    string Address = address1;
    if (address2.Length > 0)
        Address = Address + "<BR>" + address2;
```

```
    Address = Address + "<BR>";
    if (city.Length > 0)
        Address = Address + city;
    if (state.Length > 0)
        Address = Address + ", " + state;
    if (zip.Length > 0)
        Address = Address + ". " + zip;
    return Address;
}
```

Also, the DisplayWindowText() method starts very cryptically:

```
string s;
if (links.IndexOf ("O") < 0)
    s = name;
else
{
    string webPage = String.Format (refURL, id, "O");
    s = "<A HREF=\"" +
        webPage +
        "\" target=blank>" +
        name +
        "</A><BR>";
}
```

Someone trying to find her way around this code would likely be scratching her head, wondering about the significance of the links string containing the letter "O," and to whom the letter "O" might be important. Let's briefly explore what the "O" check means. Then we can decide whether it's worth refactoring and feeding back into the model. At the very least, we could add a comment to the code, so that the next person who arrives at this class won't need to do the same rooting around to work out what it's doing.

There are three fields in the hotel database that have a Y/N value: Brochure, Overview, and Rate. A Visual Basic DLL running on the server queries the database and returns a string of which info pages are available for each hotel. These are returned to the .NET application in the form of a string (e.g., BOR means "Brochure, Overview, and Rate," and BR means "Brochure and Rate"). So by checking for the letter "O," the code is actually checking whether this Hotel object has an Overview available for it.

It's worth reiterating the point that the team was prototyping at this stage, so it's not surprising that this implementation detail wasn't picked up in the up-front design. However, we're now at the stage where we're bringing the code and the design into sync (so that we can do a proper design for the next release), so we need to decide whether it's worth refactoring this now, or simply add a note to the code (or to our UML model) so that when we return to the model for the next iteration, we'll know to address this area. Because we happen to be staring at the code at the moment, let's examine what would be needed to tidy up this area of the code and make it more self-explanatory.

Coding by intention is an important agile principle—that is, write the code in terms of what you want it to do, not how you want it to do it. Following this principle results in code that is self-explanatory and needs fewer code comments. For our mysterious letter "O" example, we could replace the check with a function call whose name actually states what the check is doing, for example:

```
string s;
   if ( !HasOverview() )
   {
    s = name;
else
{
      // . . .
```

The `links` variable is a member of the Hotel class, so we don't need to pass it in to our new `HasOverview()` method. Our new method is as follows:

```
private bool HasOverview ()
{
    return links.IndexOf ("O") >= 0;
}
```

Notice that we've reversed the `links.IndexOf` check. Previously, it was returning true if links did *not* contain the letter "O." Now it returns true if there's a positive match, which in our minds is a little less brain-warping. You can also see the result of this in the code that calls the new method, `if ( !HasOverview() )`, in other words, if this Hotel does *not* have an Overview . . .

We would also add similar methods for HasBrochure and HasRate as and when we discover that we need them. We can now see much more easily what the code is doing (i.e., checking that this Hotel has an Overview), without needing to add code comments. In the previous version, this just wouldn't have been obvious from looking at the code.

This early prototyping is useful because it allows us to feed these methods back into the UML diagrams, having proven in the code that they're going to be needed. In fact, what often happens is that, as we feed back into the UML, we see an overall pattern taking shape, which we might otherwise have missed. This allows us to further streamline the design and feed the improvements back into the code, and so on.

Of course, this refactoring still leaves us with quite a lengthy `DisplayWindowText()` method overall. So perhaps this whole section could be moved into a separate method, something like this:

```
private string CreateOverviewLink ()
{
    if ( !HasOverview() )
       {
        return name;
       }
    string webPage = String.Format (refURL, id, "O");
    return "<A HREF=\"" +
           webPage +
           "\" target=blank>" +
           name +
           "</A><BR>";
}
```

Anyway, there's quite a bit more refactoring that could be done to this code (mainly involving breaking up the `DisplayWindowText()` method into smaller methods), but we'll leave that until release 2. At this stage, we're concentrating on enabling the next effort, not actually *implementing* the next effort, so it's important to not get too carried away changing things around.

Source Code for HotelCluster

Finally, here's the prototype implementation of the `GetRolloverInfo()` and `GetHotelCount()` methods in HotelCluster:

```
public class HotelCluster : HotelComposite
{
    private ArrayList hotels;

    public HotelCluster (int aX, int aY): base (aX, aY)
    {
        hotels = new ArrayList ();
    }
```

```
public override string GetRolloverInfo (int ImageIndex,
                            LookupCollection Amenities,
                            string refURL)
{
    string RolloverInfo = "";
    Hotel h;
    for (int HotelCount = 1;
         HotelCount <= hotels.Count;
         HotelCount++)
    {
        h = (Hotel) hotels [HotelCount-1];
        RolloverInfo = RolloverInfo +
               "<A HREF='javascript:updateTheLayer " +
               "(document.WebForm.hotel_" +
               ImageIndex.ToString () +
               ".getAttribute (\"Title_" +
               HotelCount.ToString ()
               + "\"), document.WebForm.hotel_"
               + ImageIndex.ToString ()
               + ".getAttribute (\"RolloverInfo_"
               + HotelCount.ToString ()
               + "\"))'>"
               + h.getName ()
               + "</A><BR>";
    }
    return RolloverInfo;
}

   public override int GetHotelCount ()
{
    return hotels.Count;
}

}
```

Not much to say here, except that, again, this code will be a prime candidate for refactoring when we get to the next release. For example, the block of code in the middle of the method that puts `RolloverInfo` together could be moved into a separate method called `BuildRolloverInfo()`. Again, this new method would be fed back into the appropriate UML diagram.

Feeding Our Changes Back into the Model

Because the purpose of this exercise is to bring the source code and the model into sync, we ought to feed these changes back into the class diagram (see Figure 7-13). If the behavior of our classes had significantly changed, we'd also want to update the sequence diagrams. But luckily, the relatively minor changes that we've made are mostly structural in nature.

Let's start with HotelComposite. To jog your memory, Figure 7-12 shows a "detail" of HotelComposite and its two subclasses from the class diagram.

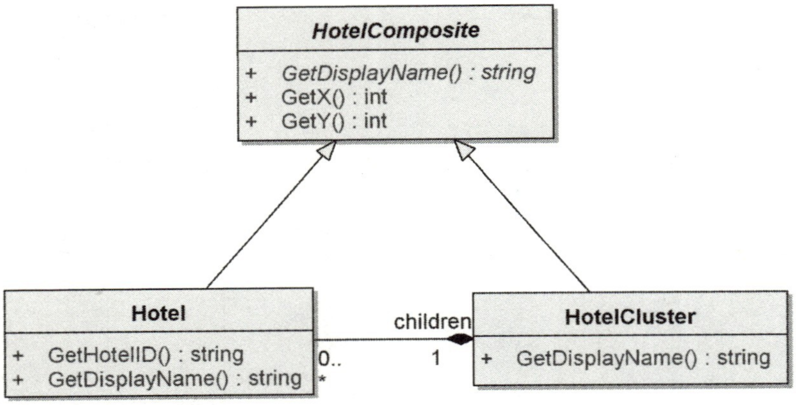

Figure 7-12. *HotelComposite and its subclasses before the code-level refactoring*

`GetDisplayName()` didn't actually make it as far as the code. Instead, two new methods were added at coding time: `GetTitle()` and `GetRolloverInfo()`. This was one of those cases where, at the time, it *seemed* like it would be sensible to have a `GetDisplayName()` method. But in reality, something else was needed, so we got rid of it. Never be sentimental with unused code. If it isn't used, get rid of it![5]

There's also a whole bunch of abstract methods in HotelComposite, which we didn't show in the original class diagram (because they're defined by the use cases that we left out for brevity's sake). These are `GetHint()`, `GetHighestPriceBand()`, and `GetPriceBand()`.

And finally, if you recall, `GetHotelCount()` was missing from the original class diagram but was discovered during coding. This seems like a good time to feed it back into the class diagram.

Next, let's move on to the Hotel class (a concrete subclass of HotelComposite). The original version of Hotel (just prior to coding) is also shown in Figure 7-12. An attribute that was added to Hotel is `Name` (with an associated `GetName()` accessor method). But hang on a second—this seems remarkably similar to the abstract method `GetDisplayName()`, which was removed from the parent HotelComposite. The reason `GetDisplayName()` was removed was because it was replaced with `GetRolloverInfo()`, which constructs a tool tip including the name. To confirm this, we can see that in Hotel's implementation of the `GetRolloverInfo()` method, it uses the `Name` attribute to construct part of the tool tip. So `Name` definitely belongs, and it serves a different purpose from the `DisplayName` attribute, which was removed. Whew—that seems like a lesson in minutiae, but sometimes it's worth checking these things in case they throw up a more deep-seated design issue (e.g., a misunderstanding might have arisen that resulted in a duplicate attribute).

We also did some refactoring on the Hotel class: we created a new private method, `HasOverview()`. Plus, we created `HasBrochure()` and `HasRate()` (waiting in the wings for when we need them). These are private methods, and they may be a bit too low level to warrant showing on the class diagram, so it's probably better not to show them.

Finally, let's move on to HotelCluster. We hinted at some refactorings that could be done on this class, but we didn't dive into them just yet, instead opting to leave them until release 2, when we'll need to revisit the code anyway. However, our earlier refactorings (the removal of `GetDisplayName()` and the addition of the abstract methods that need to be implemented by both Hotel and HotelCluster) do affect HotelCluster.

---

5. It should go without saying that all your source code is under version control (including prototype code), so if you later discover that you really did need that method you deleted, it isn't lost forever.

HOW TIGHTLY SHOULD THE UML BE BOUND TO THE CODE?

Knowing how tightly to bind the code and the design is a burning issue. If we reflect every last detail of the source code in the class diagrams and sequence diagrams, we'd still be finishing off the same diagrams in several years' time, probably after the customer has gone out of business. Conversely, if we draw the diagrams at such an abstract level that they're largely meaningless, then that's not much use either. So finding the "sweet spot" (and knowing it when you see it) is an important design skill.

Similarly, every change we make to our design diagrams needs to be justifiable. Simply saying, "We must do this because we're following a design process" isn't sufficient. It's important to be able to say, "We're making this change because it will help to make XYZ clearer later on."

In the Hotel example, it's doubtful that adding the private methods (`GetOverview()`, etc.) to the class diagram would add value, because we'd simply be replicating what's in the source code (and binding the class diagram *too tightly* to the code). This would mean that there's more diagram to maintain when we change the code.

In addition to generating code and importing code, the Enterprise Architect (EA) tool has the option to synchronize the model and source code. For example, say you've already generated some source code, but you've made subsequent changes to the model. When you generate again, EA will add any new attributes or methods to the existing source code, leaving intact what already exists. This means that developers may work on the source code and then generate additional methods as required from the model, without having their code overwritten or destroyed.

In another scenario, changes may have been made to a source file, but the model has detailed notes and characteristics you don't want to lose. By synchronizing from the source into the model, additional attributes and methods are imported, but other model elements are left alone. Using the two synchronization methods, it's simple to keep source code and model elements up to date and synchronized.

So that about wraps up our changes between release 1 and release 2. The updated class diagram is shown in Figure 7-13.

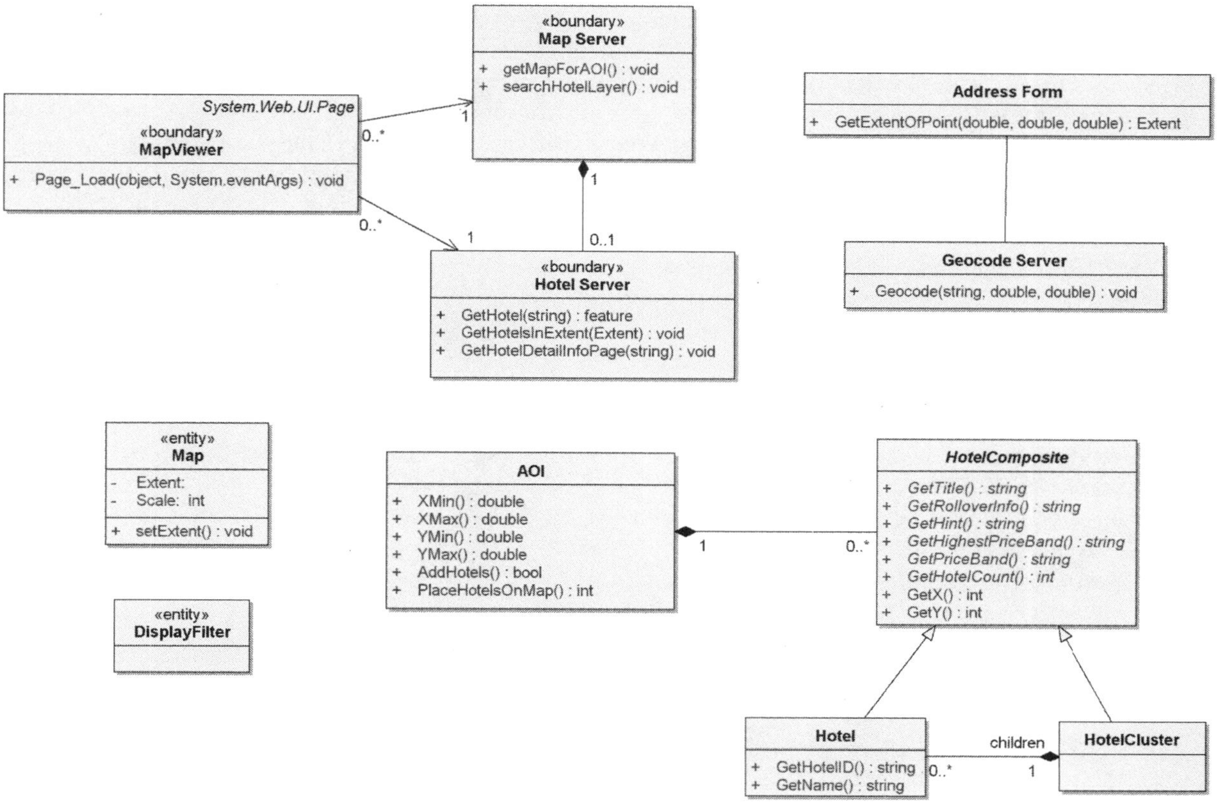

Figure 7-13. *Refactored class diagram*

As you can see, HotelCluster seems fairly empty now. In fact, it does implement all the methods that are shown as abstract in HotelComposite. We just haven't shown them on the diagram because it seems kind of obvious: HotelCluster is concrete, therefore any abstract methods in the parent class would have to be included. It's worth taking this sort of shortcut if you're *absolutely sure* that it won't cause confusion in the project. When in doubt, put the detail in!

As for the other classes on the diagram, we've updated some of the method names. MapViewer now looks much more streamlined, with only one public method. The other methods, it turned out, just weren't needed in the implementation; to fit into the Web Forms framework, just `Page_Load` was needed. So we've updated the diagram to show this. This will prove useful when we're designing the next release, because we have it on good authority (working source code!) that the MapViewer Boundary object works this way.

We've also updated the other classes' relationships to show the multiplicity. Earlier, this wasn't really necessary (plus we would have been guessing), but now that we have a solid prototype to refer to, we can add this information and be pretty confident that it's right.

And finally, we've updated the relationship between the Map Server and Hotel Server to show this as Composition, because (referring back to the architecture discussion earlier in this chapter) the Hotel Server is really a part of the Map Server.

The design shown in Figure 7-13 is the one that we'll build upon for release 2, which begins in earnest in the next chapter.

When to Keep the Model and the Code Tightly Interwoven

In Chapter 6, we walked through the source code for release 1 and refactored the code in a couple of places (e.g., we introduced a new AOI class). A natural consequence of this (which occurs in every single project that includes a documented design of some sort) is that the source code and the design model became out of sync.

The Agile Modeling (AM) guidance on the subject is to "update only when it hurts." That is, update the design diagrams only when you find that working from an out-of-date document is starting to affect the project. Our guidance is different because AM does not propose driving the code from the model (instead, the model is a marginally useful "document" that gets produced and is not maintained). ***In Agile ICONIX, we drive the code from the model.***

This is a hugely important distinction. AM drives the design of the code by refactoring. Agile ICONIX makes a dedicated effort to get the design right the first time, by "modeling like we mean it" (one small use case at a time) and using refactoring when minor cleanup is needed. Note that this doesn't mean we need to spend months redrawing sequence diagrams after the code has been changed around so that we can have a large stack of useless documentation. It means that we spend a little more time trying to get the sequence diagrams right before coding.

The nature of an agile project is that we're never really 100% sure where the requirements are going to drift. And so doing a bit of housekeeping on the model so that it can remain useful moving forward is just a good thing to do after each release. (Note that this is also in keeping with the AM core principle that "enabling the next effort is your secondary goal.")

In the spirit of "traveling light" (another AM core principle[6]), it's not necessary to redraw all the sequence diagrams. But the static model (class diagrams) should be cleaned up, and the classes in the model should match the classes in the code. If you update only when it hurts, you'll quickly toss out the model because it has become useless and obsolete.

The creation of the new AOI class was a result of revisiting the original design and finding that we'd missed it in the code. In this case, we were updating the code to keep it in sync with the design, which in this instance resulted in better, more tightly factored code. However, in other cases, the design has evolved during the programming iteration, and these changes need to be fed back into the design model.

Note, however, that updating every sequence diagram to reflect the code could end up being a waste of time if the diagrams are never going to be used again. The code has already been written, so to a large extent the sequence diagrams (the detailed, low-level design artifacts) have served their purpose.

To determine which parts of the model need to be updated, we refer to the plan for the next release (assuming the features for the next release increment have been picked already). We use this to determine which parts of the

6. From Scott Ambler's *Agile Modeling: Effective Practices for eXtreme Programming and the Unified Process* (Hoboken, NJ: John Wiley & Sons, 2002), p. 29: "Traveling light means that you create just enough models and documentation to get by."

project we're going to be extending in the next release. These are, of course, the areas that will need up-to-date design documentation.

Some of the other differences between the model and the mapplet code were because we didn't follow ICONIX Process 100% during coding, which resulted in source code that didn't precisely fit the design. This isn't a cardinal sin—at the end of the day, we're mostly interested in creating finished, working code that fulfills the original requirements. However, we do find that if the code and the design diverge too much, then it becomes more difficult to design the next iteration. If the code and the design are roughly similar, then we can reuse a lot of the design artifacts (the domain model, in particular) and also build on the original set of use cases for the next release.

"And Today's Lesson Is . . ."

There are a couple of important lessons that you can learn from this early release of the mapplet:

- Write your use cases carefully (include alternative courses, so it isn't DTSTTCPW[7]), and make the code match the use cases. This gets you a "good job" (passing grade) and means you're ahead of a lot of projects because your code meets the requirements.

- Drive the design from the use cases, and make the code match the design. This is the right way to do it, and it gets you a "great job" (A+ grade).

If you're under severe time constraints, you can still make sure the code meets the requirements by skipping certain stages of the design and then patching up the code through refactoring. Ironically, though, a team that skips design because of time constraints is also unlikely to write unit tests while coding, so patching up the code later is more likely to consist of debugging (hacking the design to get it to work) than refactoring (improving the design to enable the next effort).

So there's a judgment call about how much design can safely be skipped before the team's corner-cutting capers come back to bite it. In our mapplet example, the team probably did a bit too much design-skipping during the first release, meaning that some of the code needed to be refactored before release 2 development could really kick off. But then, that's also what the first release is all about: finding your feet and adjusting the parameters to tailor the process for this new project. Every project is different, after all, so we expect the first release to be slightly wide of the mark. Considering that the mapplet team members actually did meet the requirements for release 1, we think they did pretty well.

Summary

In this chapter, we revisited the mapplet design for release 1 and kicked it into shape, in preparation for release 2. There is often a bit of a lull between releases while the requirements are being sorted out for the next release. By keeping the releases short (no more than a month or two each), this lull is minimized—but it's often still there. Your development team members may spend this time fixing bugs, playing *Unreal Tournament*, or sharpening up their resumes. But this could instead be an ideal time for them to revisit the design and bring it and the code back in sync. This prepares them nicely for building upon the product in the next release. This is also an Agile ICONIX safety net: a chance to regroup and put all your ducks back in a row if they have started to wander off their line.

The mapplet release 1 was an early alpha release of the mapplet. It immediately generated some interesting feedback from the customer, which helped the team to formulate and prioritize the second release. But that's another story (. . .but luckily, it's in the next chapter).

The next chapter also introduces an interaction design technique that can be used in conjunction with ICONIX Process.

---

7. As mentioned earlier, DTSTTCPW stands for *Do The Simplest Thing That Could Possibly Work*. See `http://xp.c2.com/DoTheSimplestThingThatCouldPossiblyWork.html`.

CHAPTER 8

Mapplet Release 2

The mapplet example now begins development for its second release. We'll write some new use cases to define the new functionality that the customer wants added to the mapplet for this release. We'll also use an extension to ICONIX Process, persona analysis (described in detail in Chapter 10), to help drive the requirements. Then we'll drive the use cases all the way to code. For brevity's sake we'll focus on just one of the use cases, "Filter Hotels."

Customer Feedback on the First Release

With the first release of the mapplet in alpha (see the screenshot of the finished release in Figure 6-12), the customer (that would be our Doug) set up the new mapplet on a sectioned-off area of the VResorts website to test it out and generally play around with it. An interesting thing happened—something we've seen time and again after an initial release (or prototype) of a new system becomes available. The customer began to think of all sorts of new possibilities. His reaction went along the lines of "Hey, this is great! By adding the mapplet, I can now also do this, that, and the other with my website that I couldn't do before. I could also do these *other* things if the mapplet could be extended to do this stuff too . . ."

This type of feedback seems especially common when a project is extending an existing system. The project opens up new possibilities, not just in itself, but also in what the existing system is suddenly capable of.

Here are a couple of examples of the feedback Doug (in his customer role) e-mailed to the development team upon seeing the first release version:

> *This will definitely allow me to put up "mapplet-based destination pages" by the hundreds very quickly. But it does need to allow me to drill down and look at the hotel brochures.*

> *All these links use the* `?HotelID=11111111` *form of the URL. This allows me to preset the mapplet to the immediate neighborhood that I'm looking for centered on a specific hotel.*

This feedback proves useful in a couple of ways. First, it provides confirmation that the release has met the specific goals that we set out to achieve. Second, it comes in handy when planning the next release of the project. Quite often, the customer reprioritizes features based on what he now realizes is possible. He might have previously assumed that certain features would be too difficult or expensive (even if the developers had assured him that certain features would be easier to implement than others).

There is often a disconnect between the customer's preconception of whether something is technically difficult to achieve versus the programmers' assurance that something is actually not that difficult to implement. The customer may not realize that the programmers already have a powerful set of APIs at their disposal, so they actually don't need to do very much to implement an apparently difficult feature. Seeing something concrete produced in a relatively short amount of time in the first release should allow the customer to place some faith in the programmers' estimates. This will almost certainly affect the way the customer prioritizes subsequent releases, which therefore should become increasingly grounded in reality.

How Persona Analysis Was Used to Drive the Requirements

In this section, we describe briefly how persona analysis (an interaction design technique) was used to help drive release 2 and create a more focused product. Persona analysis (as an extension to ICONIX Process) is described in more detail in Chapter 10.

Using Personas to Identify Requirements

A *persona* is a description of a "typical" end user that the product is targeting, which focuses on her goals when using the product. The persona is fictional, but the end users' goals that we identify should be the result of in-depth research, including interviews with actual users.

For release 2 we began by defining two personas, Bob and Carol. We discuss both these personas in more detail in Chapter 10, but for now here's Carol's persona:

> *Carol is single and in her late twenties. She's heading over to this year's Mardi Gras in New Orleans. She knows that she's going to be out partying, and she wants a hotel with a spa (where she can get a massage), an indoor pool, and a Jacuzzi. Because she's on a budget, she wants to stay at a hotel in the midrange price band, and she wants it located on Bourbon Street. So she's interested in amenities, price, and location.*

We use this persona to write an *interaction scenario* (a detailed use case scenario that describes what the user is doing externally to the system). Here we define *external behavior* as being what the user is doing outside the system boundary and *internal behavior* as being what the system itself is doing. The interaction normally described in a software use case is the external behavior prompting responses from the internal system (as in, "The user clicks this button. The system responds with this list").

An interaction scenario is different from an ICONIX-style use case (for brevity's sake, let's call this type a *software use case*). An interaction scenario describes an equal or greater amount of external behavior than internal behavior. You'll find some examples of interaction scenarios and how they relate to software use cases in Chapter 10.

Describing external behavior is useful (from an interaction design standpoint) because it helps to keep us focused on the user's goals, what the user is trying to achieve and, above all, why the user is trying to achieve those particular goals. It's surprising how differently the use case can turn out. You may even discover that a completely different use case is needed.

This contrasts greatly with software use cases. Software use cases are much shorter and generally are more generic, and they describe purely the user's interaction with the system. This, of course, makes them both easier and quicker to write.

Our goal is to create a *few* of these detailed interaction scenarios and (eventually) to discard them in favor of smaller, more generic software use cases that define the user's interaction with the system in more precise terms. Once we get to this stage, the external behavior that had been so useful earlier on now becomes excess clutter, so we get rid of it.

So, using this analysis, we identified that Carol would benefit from being able to find the nearest hotel to Bourbon Street. The interaction scenario we created was called exactly that: "Find the Nearest Hotel to Bourbon Street." That's pretty specific, so the eventual software use case that we ended up with was a cut-down, more generic version called "Find a Hotel."

Upon further analysis, we discovered that a "typical" business user would also want to find a specific hotel chain in a city (e.g., a Hilton Hotel in San Diego). So the interaction scenario we created for this was called "Find a Hilton Hotel in San Diego." This eventually turned into a cut-down software use case called "Filter Hotels."

Was This the Right Time for Persona Analysis on the Mapplet Project?

Interaction design works best when applied to a project in its very early stages (ideally when the first use cases are being written). However, as the mapplet is a "real-life" project, not everything in it happens exactly by the book. In fact, because it's an agile project, we're adapting the process to the project's needs as we go along.

For example, the persona analysis was not part of the inception planning. It happened later (not until analysis began for the second release, in fact). Would the project have benefited from the persona analysis taking place right at the start? Possibly so. As we maintain in this chapter, the earlier you apply interaction design to your project, the better.

In our case, the functionality written in the first release was limited to the most basic feature set while the developers explored the features available in the (then beta) ESRI Map Server. So release 1 was essentially about grabbing the low-hanging fruit and getting something up and running on the VResorts site.

We got a working mapplet page connected to the mapplet server and hooked it all up to the "live" website. So in this way, the mapplet immediately began to provide business value to the customer. Additionally, we were able to treat this first release like an early prototype, and we used it to get a better idea of how the system should work. The value we gained from this first release was that we can now shape the website however we want in the second release.

HTML proved suitable for this purpose because it's relatively cheap to change. Other projects (e.g., rich-client GUI applications or enterprise workflow systems) may not have this luxury. The key is to tailor the process to fit the project.

Of course, this first release wasn't written blind to the user's requirements. We did some use case analysis and modeled the solution (over a couple of modeling iterations) before coding it up.

In the second release, we're starting to extend the mapplet's functionality and embed it further into the website. So before we go any further, we should definitely "put down our tools" for a moment and do some deeper analysis of the ways in which the user will want to interact with the system.

AGILE SCORECARD: GROWING PAINS

The approach we've taken on this project highlights the difference between a totally up-front project and an agile project. We don't have to do all the modeling up-front. We can make midcourse corrections to the model based on feedback from the already built earlier releases. A term for this that we first heard 20 years or so ago (long before "agility" existed) is that we're "growing" the software.

For example, 20 years ago in his book *The Mythical Man-Month*, Fred Brooks discussed the evolution of the software development metaphor (a necessity as the size and complexity of software systems increase and the expected time to market decreases), from "writing" a program, through "building" a program, to incrementally "growing" a program:

> *The building metaphor has outlived its usefulness. It is time to change again. If, as I believe, the conceptual structures we construct today are too complicated to be accurately specified in advance, and too complex to be built faultlessly, then we must take a radically different approach.*[1]

These days, feature-driven planning (as described in Chapter 9) and all the method constructs surrounding it allow us to "grow" software incrementally, without lapsing into the Constant Refactoring After Programming syndrome.

---

1. Frederick P. Brooks, Jr., *The Mythical Man-Month, Twentieth Anniversary Edition* (New York: Addison-Wesley, 1995), p. 201.

Planning the Second Release

Now that we have a good idea of where we want to take the mapplet in the second release, we can begin to identify specific features. These can then be broken down into *tasks* (estimable chunks of work).

Features can be high or low level. They're also an orthogonal concept to a use case: there may be a direct correlation between a feature and a use case, but it's more likely to be by coincidence than by design.

We can identify features before we spend time to identify use cases. However, to create a project plan with realistic cost estimates, we need to identify the use cases that will be defined in order to implement the features. And before we begin the process of discovering new use cases, we need an up-to-date domain model.

Luckily, it doesn't take a huge amount of time to do this (perhaps a morning, or a day at the most). But it's definitely worth spending the time up front creating (or updating, as this is the second release) the domain model first, to reflect our new requirements. But before we do even that, we need to define a set of high-level requirements.

High-Level Requirements for Release 2

Before we update the domain model and use cases, we need a list of requirements for release 2. We've done some interaction design prior to this, to help identify some of the new requirements. Other requirements were identified via e-mails flying back and forth between ESRI and the customer, and through face-to-face review sessions of release 1 with the customer.

The requirements are as follows:

- Use a different base map that shows major attractions and landmarks on the map (if this data is available)—for example, theme parks (e.g., Disneyland, Sea World, etc.), stadiums (e.g., Dodger Stadium), airports (e.g., O'Hare Airport), and so forth.
- Include a U.S. map with rollovers that allow the user to drill down to map destination pages. (See the next section, "The 'Uber' Use Case," for more information.)
- Implement driving directions (this was discussed as a possibility, but left as a potential enhancement to be implemented after this book is published).
- Highlight specially discounted (Hot Rate) hotels.
- Resolve Netscape compatibility issues.

The "Uber" Use Case

The following use case was dreamed up by the customer while taking a stroll through a cool, tree-shaded park on a sunny California day—just the sort of situation in which inspiration can strike! This use case turned into the second requirement (see the previous section). Also, during use case modeling and subsequent e-mail discussions with the developers, this use case was refined from this initial "Eureka!" version.

Basic Course:

The system displays a zoomable, clickable map of the United States, accompanied by the following radio buttons: Zoom In, Zoom Out, Pan, and Show Hotels. The map contains a shapefile layer shown as labeled red dots and consisting of the destinations defined in `www.vresorts.com/mapplet/340destinations+.html`. When the user moves the mouse over one of the destination dots, the system displays a rollover map tip with the name of the destination. If the user clicks the dot, the system displays a persistent "thumbnail" map tip, which is a reduced-scale map screenshot approximately 150 pixels wide that is shown underneath the name of the destination.

Underneath the thumbnail image are three links: Show Destination Page, Show featured hotel, and Browse hotel map. The links for Browse hotel map are the URLs linked to the Show Map links in `www.vresorts.com/mapplet/340destinations+.html`. The Show Destination Page links are simply links to static HTML pages. The Show featured hotel links are as shown on the `340destinations+` page.

Alternate Course:

If the user clicks in an "empty" (nondestination) area of the map with Show Hotels selected, the system performs a statewide hotel search and shows the search results in a new window.

The `340destinations+` page (defined originally as a test suite for the mapplet) is shown in Figure 8-1. As you can see, this is a basic list of U.S. states divided into cities, each with links to maps, hotel lists, and a featured hotel for each city. For release 2, the plan is to transcribe this basic text page to a much groovier, interactive mapplet page in which the user can zoom, pan, search, and so forth. (In fact, you can see the final result in Figure 8-8.)

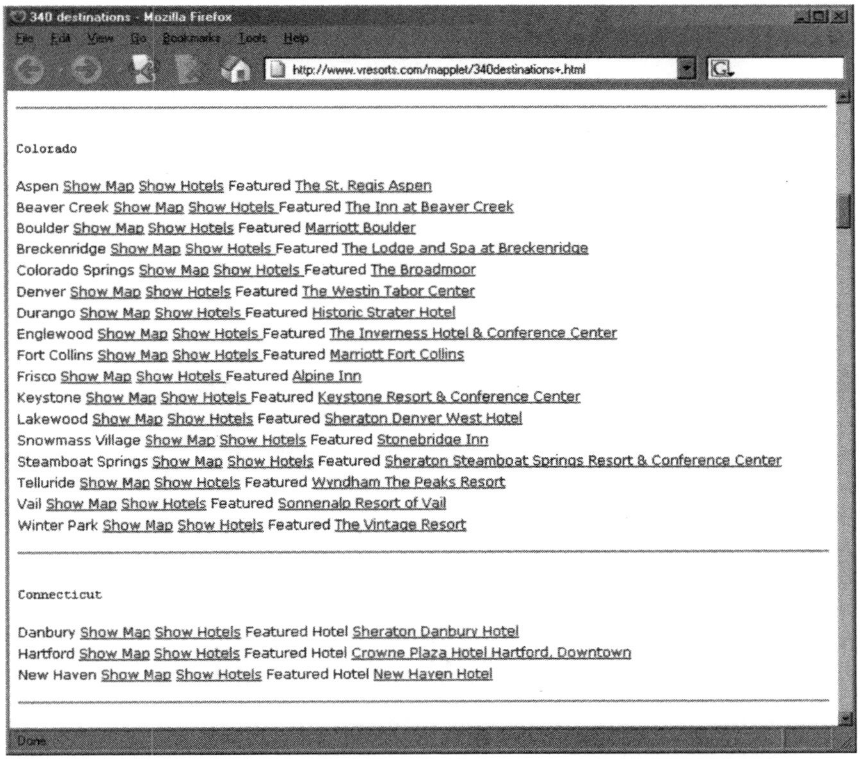

Figure 8-1. `340Destinations+` *page*

Updated Domain Model

The updated domain model is shown in Figure 8-2.

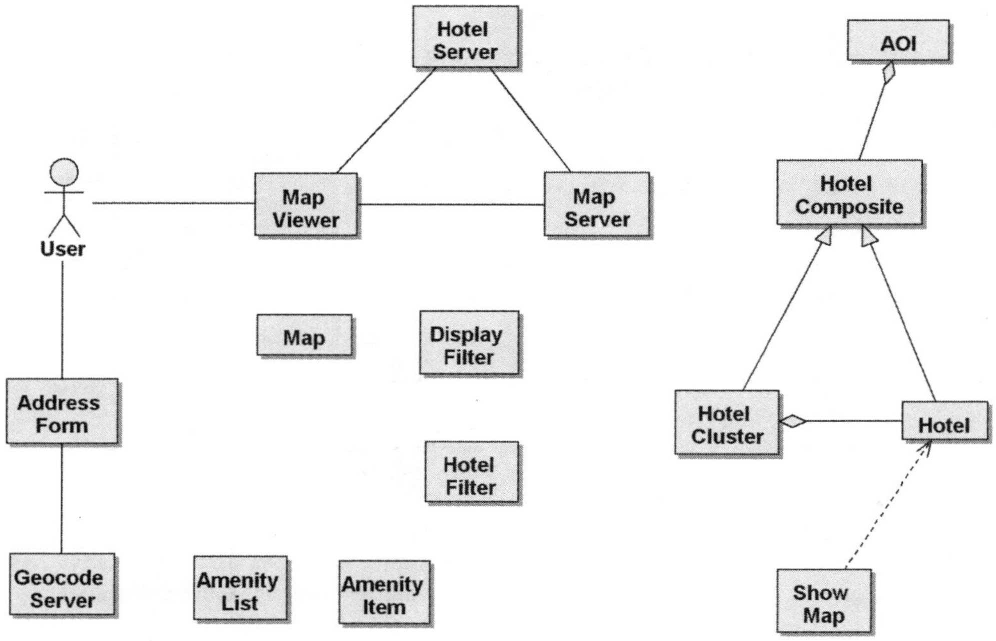

Figure 8-2. *Updated domain model for release 2*

There are a few changes between this version and the version for release 1 (see Figure 6-4):

- Hotel Filter has been added in addition to Display Filter.
- Amenity List and Amenity Item have been added.
- The old Hotel Collection/Hotel objects and relationship have been replaced with the Composite pattern that was discussed in Chapter 7.
- An AOI class was added. (This was a late but important addition—the domain model was incomplete without this central class!)
- The Boundary object Show Map was added. This object represents the `ShowMap.aspx` web page. It's the cornerstone of the mapplet, so it really needs to be on the domain model. It's shown in the final class diagram (jumping ahead to Figures 8-6 and 8-7) as having a dependency on Hotel, so we replicate that in the domain model. We wouldn't normally go into great detail on relationships among objects in the domain model, but this particular one is such an important relationship that it's worth emphasizing.

Updated Use Case Diagram

Figure 8-3 shows the use cases for release 2. We can compare this with the use case diagram for release 1 back in Figure 5-5. As you can see, there are two new use cases here: "Filter Hotels" and "Browse by US Map."

Because there are only the two new use cases, it's pretty easy to keep track of what's new for release 2. However, in a larger project, you'd almost certainly want to visually separate the new use cases in some way. A stereotype such as <<Release 2>> would be useful.

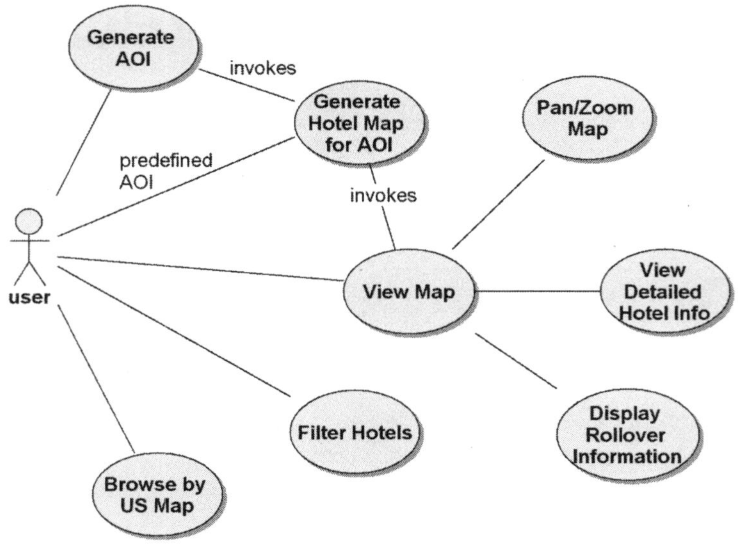

Figure 8-3. *Use cases for release 2*

■ **Modeling Question** *What if the project has hundreds of new use cases?* In this case, you could separate the use cases into different diagrams. But it would also be worth questioning why there are so many use cases in a single release. Remember, this is meant to be an agile project with short timescales for each release, so if you end up with hundreds of use cases, you need to do some more work prioritizing them and dividing them into separate, smaller releases.

Here are the two new use cases in detail. (The second one, "Browse by US Map," was rewritten from the customer's original use case shown earlier in this chapter during use case modeling.)

Use Case: "Filter Hotels"

Filter By Amenity:

The system displays the List of Amenities in the Amenity List. The user selects one or more amenities from the list and then selects Update Map. The MapViewer creates a HotelFilter based on the selected items in the Amenity List. The MapViewer queries the HotelServer for all hotels in the AOI and then filters the results with the HotelFilter. The map is refreshed and a label is placed adjacent to the map indicating the current selection criterion.

Filter by Hotel Chain:

The system populates a Hotel Chain pick list from the Hotel Chain table. The user selects one Hotel Chain from the pick list. The MapViewer creates a HotelFilter for the selected Hotel Chain. The MapViewer queries the HotelServer for all hotels in the AOI and then filters the results with the HotelFilter. The map is refreshed and a label is placed adjacent to the map indicating the Hotel Chain selected.

Alternate Scenario 1:

If there are no Hotels that meet the filter criterion, the following message is displayed: "No hotels meet selection criterion. Please expand search."

Use Case: "Browse by US Map"

Basic Scenario:

The Grouped Destination shapefile is shown as a set of points on an overview map of the United States. The user positions the mouse cursor over a Grouped Destination point. The mouse icon changes to a selection hand, and the icon changes to a selected icon. The system shows a map tip displaying the list of cities grouped in the region (e.g., "Birmingham, Huntsville, Montgomery, Mobile"). The user clicks the Regional Destination icon, and the associated URL opens in a new browser window.

Alternate Scenario 1:

If the user zooms in, the system will zoom in to a suitable scale to show the Destinations city layer. If the user positions the mouse cursor over a city, the city name is displayed in the map tip. If the user clicks the city, the system will zoom in to the city and display the hotels in that city.

Alternate Scenario 2:

If the user chooses to zoom in when the Destination city layer is shown, the map will display the hotels in the zoomed-in area.

Alternate Scenario 3:

If the user attempts to pan at the U.S. level, the system will not allow this action.

Alternate Scenario 4:

If the user attempts to zoom out at the U.S. level, the system will not allow this action.

Release 2 Plan

Let's review the release plan as it stands now. If you look back at the plan shown in Table 5-1 (which shows the use cases to be implemented for the first four releases), you can see that (now that release 1 is out of the way) this plan doesn't bear much resemblance to reality at all. This is understandable—release 1 was primarily an exercise in prototyping to gain a greater understanding of what's possible in the time frames involved and what (if any) dependencies exist.

So let's revisit the plan, and then correct it for release 1 so we can see what really happened (see Table 8-1).

Table 8-1. *Corrected Release Plan for Release 1*

Release	Use Case	Comments
1	Create AOI for Address	
	Generate Hotel Map for AOI	
	View Map	
	Pan/Zoom Map	Basic
	View Hotel Information	Basic
	Create Shapefile	
	Display Rollover Information	Basic
	Pan/Zoom Map	Progressive disclosure
	View Multiple Hotel Info	Multiple hotels found at click coordinates

So in fact, all the items that had originally been penciled in for release 2 were also implemented in release 1 and within the timescale that was originally estimated for release 1. Not bad, although we would certainly hope that the release plans will become more accurate over successive releases. It's unusual for a release to include significantly *more* than was originally planned! (Maybe there's something to this low-ceremony stuff after all.)

Release 2, then, simply consists of the two new use cases in Figure 8-3, plus the nonfunctional requirements listed earlier in this chapter. Let's put these together in a plan for release 2 (see Table 8-2).

Table 8-2. *Release Plan for Release 2*

Release	Use Case/Nonfunctional Requirement	Comments
2	Filter Hotels	
	Browse by US Map	
	Netscape compatibility	
	Automatically scale AOI	

Analysis Review

In this section, we zip through the modeling activities that took place to analyze the domain model and use cases for release 2 of the mapplet (focusing on the "Filter Hotels" use case).

Robustness Diagrams

Figure 8-4 shows the robustness diagram for the "Filter Hotels" use case.

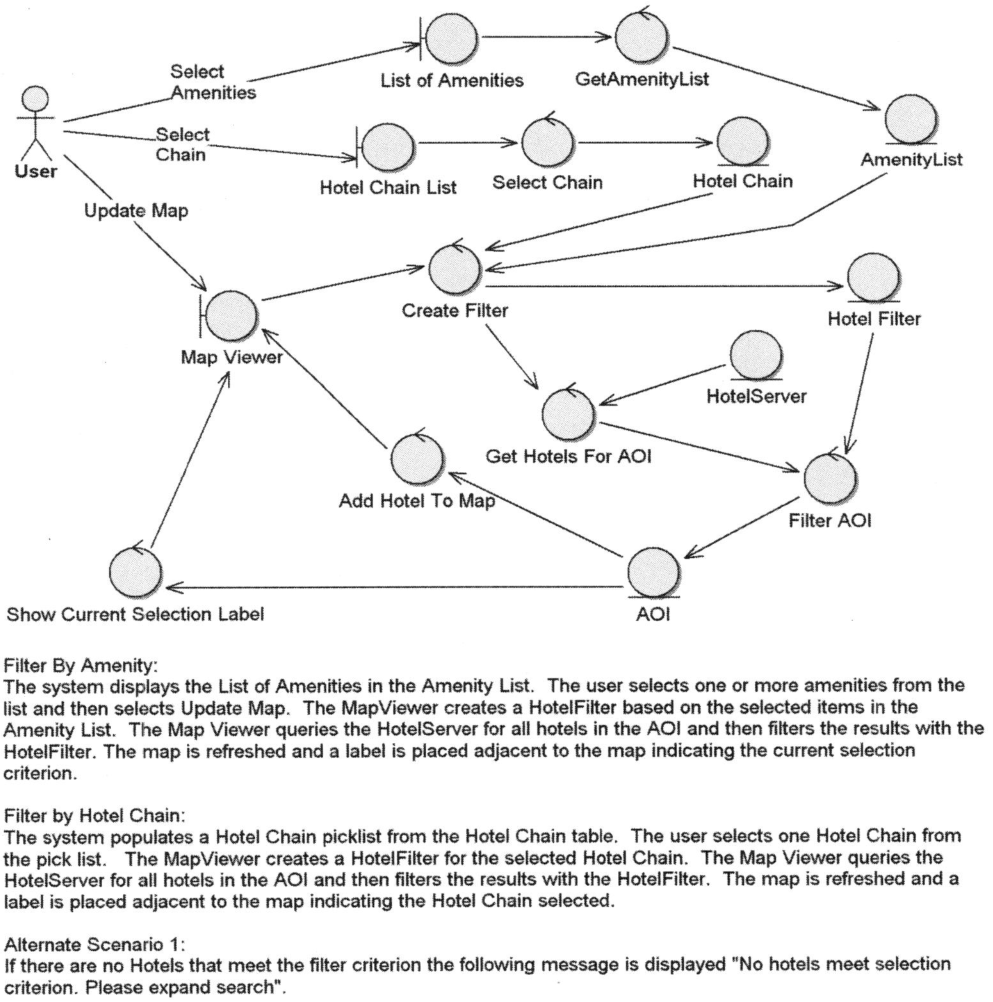
Select Amenities
List of Amenities
GetAmenityList
User
Select Chain
Hotel Chain List
Select Chain
Hotel Chain
AmenityList
Update Map
Create Filter
Hotel Filter
Map Viewer
HotelServer
Get Hotels For AOI
Add Hotel To Map
Filter AOI
Show Current Selection Label
AOI
Filter By Amenity:
The system displays the List of Amenities in the Amenity List. The user selects one or more amenities from the list and then selects Update Map. The MapViewer creates a HotelFilter based on the selected items in the Amenity List. The Map Viewer queries the HotelServer for all hotels in the AOI and then filters the results with the HotelFilter. The map is refreshed and a label is placed adjacent to the map indicating the current selection criterion.
Filter by Hotel Chain:
The system populates a Hotel Chain picklist from the Hotel Chain table. The user selects one Hotel Chain from the pick list. The MapViewer creates a HotelFilter for the selected Hotel Chain. The Map Viewer queries the HotelServer for all hotels in the AOI and then filters the results with the HotelFilter. The map is refreshed and a label is placed adjacent to the map indicating the Hotel Chain selected.
Alternate Scenario 1:
If there are no Hotels that meet the filter criterion the following message is displayed "No hotels meet selection criterion. Please expand search".

Figure 8-4. *Robustness diagram for the "Filter Hotels" use case*

As you can see, this diagram covers two basic scenarios: filtering by amenity and filtering by hotel chain.

MODELING QUESTION: WHAT IF A USE CASE CHANGES HALFWAY THROUGH A RELEASE INCREMENT?

Once development begins, a mid-development change would likely cause hacking of the code to shoehorn the last-minute changes into a system that was designed for something else. So an understandable reaction to this problem is to forbid changes to the requirements once the design and programming stages are under way. This is the dreaded *requirements freeze* that agile methodologies generally stick their noses up at.

In "old-school" waterfall projects with iterations of 6 months or more, requirements freeze would have been a serious problem (and often was, with large systems delivered that went wide of what the customer really wanted). But keeping the iterations short (a month or less) reduces the problem.

Agile methodologies handle this in different ways. In the Scrum process, for example, the requirements are absolutely not allowed to change during a monthly sprint. The requirements can be juggled around and changed only at the start of the next sprint. Alternatively, XP actively embraces change, whether midway through an iteration or not.

In ICONIX Process, use cases aren't frozen until you've completed robustness analysis. You expect that the first-draft use case will change (i.e., it will be revised and improved) during the disambiguation phase of design. So ICONIX Process not only allows the requirements to change, but also expects them to change (and pretty much demands that they have any ambiguity squeezed out of them) in the middle of each release increment.

In other words, in ICONIX Process, *you don't baseline the behavior requirements until you've done a bit of exploratory design—at the conceptual design level of abstraction.* When you're applying ICONIX Process in an agile context, each release includes requirements definition (first-draft use cases), requirements analysis/preliminary design (robustness analysis), and then detailed design (sequence diagrams).

You hope that the use cases don't change in the middle of detailed design—but if they have to, then they do, and this is still preferable to coding up incorrect requirements and then ripping out the incorrect code later.

Designing Release 2

In this section, we run through the modeling activities that took place to create the design for release 2 of the mapplet.

Sequence Diagrams

Figure 8-5 shows the sequence diagram for the "Filter Hotels" use case.

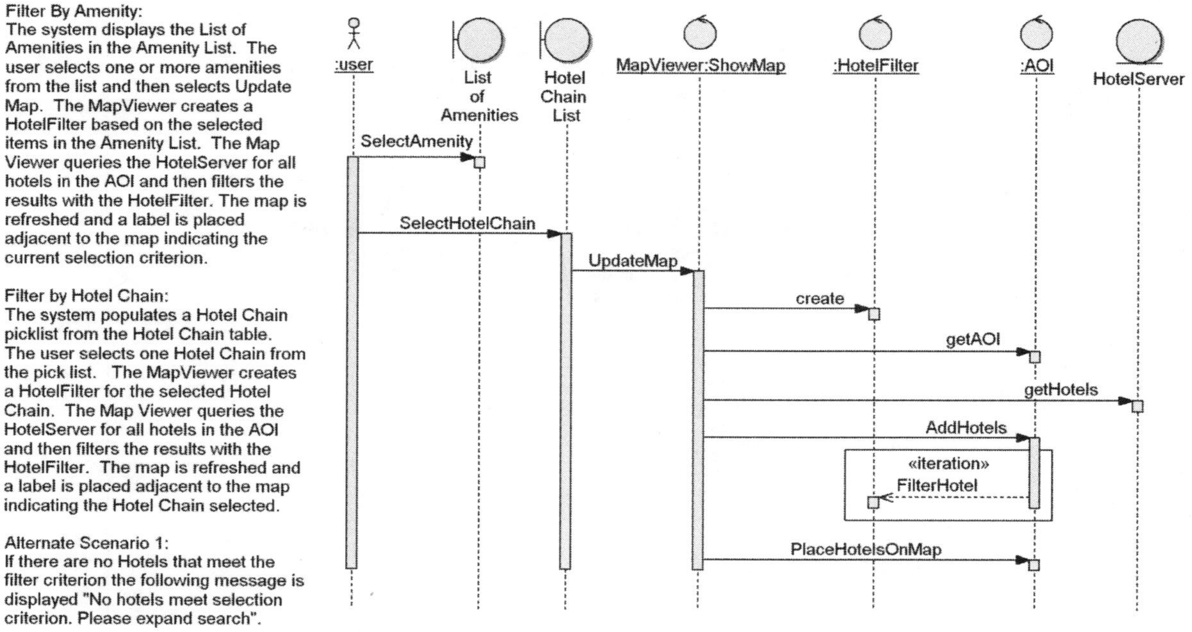
Filter By Amenity:
The system displays the List of Amenities in the Amenity List. The user selects one or more amenities from the list and then selects Update Map. The MapViewer creates a HotelFilter based on the selected items in the Amenity List. The Map Viewer queries the HotelServer for all hotels in the AOI and then filters the results with the HotelFilter. The map is refreshed and a label is placed adjacent to the map indicating the current selection criterion.
Filter by Hotel Chain:
The system populates a Hotel Chain picklist from the Hotel Chain table. The user selects one Hotel Chain from the pick list. The MapViewer creates a HotelFilter for the selected Hotel Chain. The Map Viewer queries the HotelServer for all hotels in the AOI and then filters the results with the HotelFilter. The map is refreshed and a label is placed adjacent to the map indicating the Hotel Chain selected.
Alternate Scenario 1:
If there are no Hotels that meet the filter criterion the following message is displayed "No hotels meet selection criterion. Please expand search".
:user
List of Amenities
Hotel Chain List
MapViewer:ShowMap
:HotelFilter
:AOI
HotelServer
SelectAmenity
SelectHotelChain
UpdateMap
create
getAOI
getHotels
AddHotels
«iteration»
FilterHotel
PlaceHotelsOnMap

Figure 8-5. *Sequence diagram for the "Filter Hotels" use case*

As in the robustness diagram, the sequence diagram covers two scenarios: filtering by amenity and filtering by hotel chain.

Class Diagram

The finished class diagram for release 2 is shown in Figures 8-6 and 8-7.

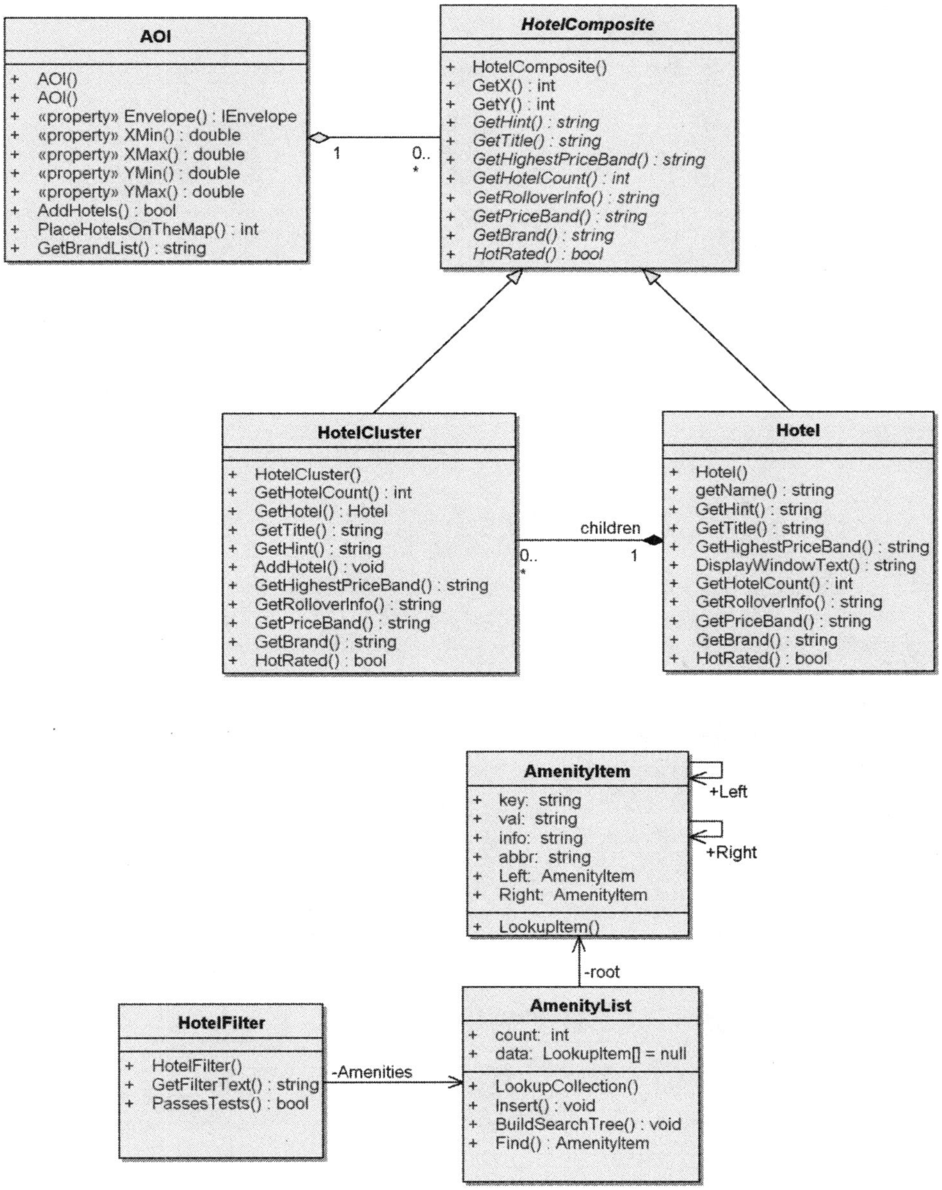

Figure 8-6. *Class diagram (part 1) for release 2*

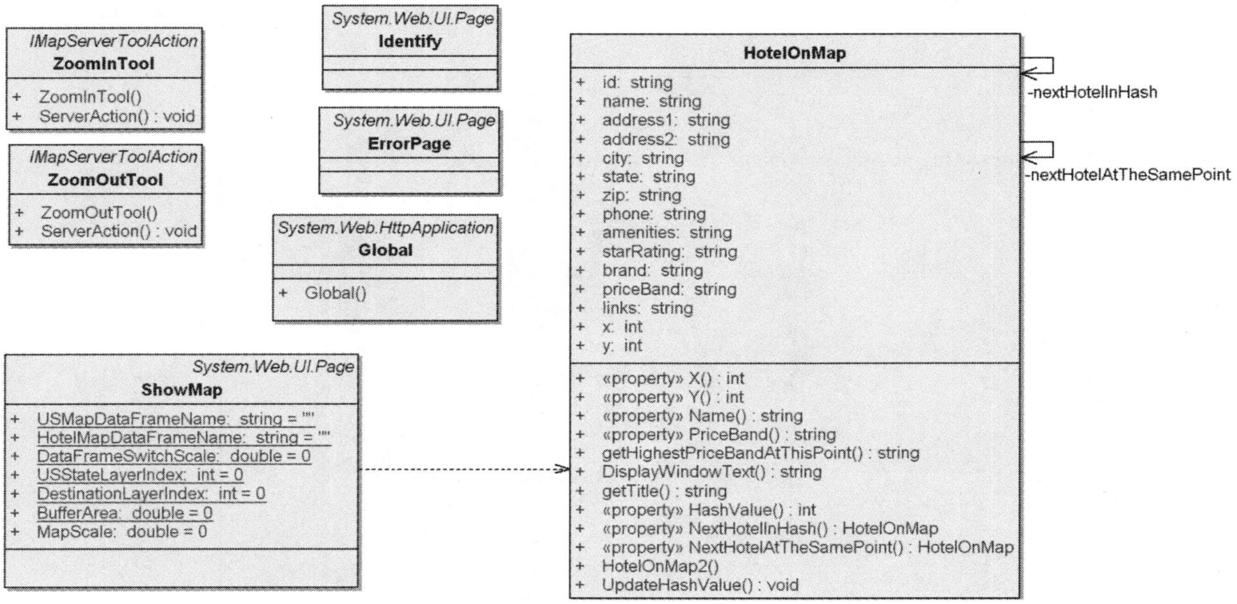

Figure 8-7. *Class diagram (part 2) for release 2*

CODE AND DESIGN: TO CONVERGE OR TO DIVERGE?

With release 2, it's noticeable that the developers have grown more accustomed to the ICONIX modeling process, and in fact they're starting to drive new features from the use cases and sequence diagrams. So (perhaps for the first time in recorded history?) we actually accomplished the feat of having the model and the code converge over time, as opposed to diverging over time. (Historically, models and code always have tended to diverge over time. Reverse-engineering tools have helped a little bit back at the class level, but nothing has really had much impact at the use case level.)

Perhaps another way to state this is that a feedback-driven process also has benefits in terms of improved modeling technique, with a short first release taken all the way through to code and then feedback on how the models could have been improved. The developers, seeing the resulting improvements in the code definitely took the modeling more seriously in the next iteration and avoided a lot of potential rework on both the models and the code. (Restated once again: "Eureka—it works!")

The issue of code/design divergence is discussed further in Chapter 7, in the section "Divergence of Code and Design over Time" (also see Figure 7-1).

Source Code: Refactoring Is Still Useful After Doing Use Case–Driven Modeling

If you check back to the "Filter Hotels" sequence diagram shown in Figure 8-5, you'll see the interaction between the MapViewer and the HotelFilter. The MapViewer creates a HotelFilter, and (after getting an AOI and a list of hotels) passes the HotelFilter into the AOI. The AOI then iterates through the list of hotel points (a *hotel point* is an amenity that we want to filter on), filtering the list using the HotelFilter.

Let's take a look at the AddHotels method in the AOI class, plus a worker method (Insert) that it delegates to:

```
// Get a list of hotels and their properties,
// create a list hotel composite objects
public bool AddHotels (string[] hotelPoints,
                       AmenityList Amenities,
                       HotelFilter hf)
{
    bool SomethingFound = false;

    if (hotels == null)
        hotels = new ArrayList ();

    // hotelPoints are list of
    //  0: ID
    //  1: X
    //  2: Y
    //  3: Name
    //  4: Address1
    //  5: Address2
    //  6: City
    //  7: State
    //  8: Zip
    //  9: Phone
    // 10: StarRating
    // 11: Amenities
    // 12: Brand
    // 13: PriceBand
    // 14: Links

    Hotel hp;
    long hiBound = hotelPoints.Length;
    string hotelAmenities = "";

    bool visible;

    for (int i=0; i < hiBound; i += 15)
    {
        try
        {
            visible = hf.FilterHotel (hotelPoints [i+12],
                                      hotelPoints [i+11],
                                      ref hotelAmenities);
            if (visible)
            {
                hp = new Hotel (hotelPoints [i+0],
                               int.Parse (hotelPoints [i+1]),
                               int.Parse (hotelPoints [i+2]),
                               hotelPoints [i+3],
                               hotelPoints [i+4],
                               hotelPoints [i+5],
                               hotelPoints [i+6],
                               hotelPoints [i+7],
                               hotelPoints [i+8],
```

```
                                hotelPoints [i+9],
                                hotelPoints [i+10],
                                hotelPoints [i+11],
                                hotelPoints [i+12],
                                hotelPoints [i+13],
                                hotelPoints [i+14]);
                    Insert (hp);
                    SomethingFound = true;
                }
            }
            catch (Exception ex)
            {
                string str = ex.Message;
                return false;
            }
        }
        return SomethingFound;
    }


    /// <summary>
    /// Insert a HotelOnMap into the hash.
    /// If the point is near another point
    /// then instead of inserting it into the hash,
    /// it inserts the point to the linked list of
    /// the HotelPoints that stores these points.
    /// </summary>
    /// <param name="hp"></param>
    private void Insert (Hotel hp)
    {
        if (hp == null)
            return;

        HotelComposite hc;
        for (int i = 0; i < hotels.Count; i++)
        {
            hc = (HotelComposite) hotels [i];
            if (Math.Abs (hc.GetX () - hp.GetX ()) <= 5 &&
                Math.Abs (hc.GetY () - hp.GetY ()) <= 5)
            {
                // Multiple hotels at the same point
                if (hc is HotelCluster)
                {
                    ((HotelCluster) hc).AddHotel (hp);
                    return;
                }
                else
                {
                    HotelCluster mhc =
                        new HotelCluster (hc.GetX (), hc.GetY ());
                    mhc.AddHotel (hc);
                    mhc.AddHotel (hp);
                    hotels [i] = mhc;
                    return;
```

```
                }
            }
        }

        hotels.Add (hp);
    }
```

We've shown hf.FilterHotel in bold because we'll drill down into the FilterHotel method in just a moment.

While this code is in better shape than the initial state of the code we saw in release 1, there's still some tidying up that we can do. We'll cover the finer points of combining refactoring (via unit testing) with ICONIX modeling in Chapter 12. For now, we'll just cover what needs to be changed and show the modified code.

KNOWING WHEN TO TIDY UP THE CODE

It's worth emphasizing that the code works just fine in its current state, so what we're doing here is tidying up to get it ready for the next release. If we knew that this was the final release, or that tidying the code at this stage wouldn't give us much return on our investment, then it wouldn't be worth doing. But in this case, the mapplet will (we hope) continue to go through several releases after this book is published, so keeping the code in trim is definitely a good idea.

The first part of this code that's crying out to be changed is the big list of array indices pointing into the hotelPoints array (where the code is creating a new Hotel object and passing in hotelPoints[i+4], hotelPoints[i+5], etc.). This code is linked to the big code comment just prior to it, which shows what each index in the array means (4 is address1, 5 is address2, etc.).

Whenever you see comments in code, you should immediately pause to think about how the code could be made clearer so that the comments aren't necessary. In this case, the obvious thing to do is turn the comments into actual constants and use these instead of the numeric literals. This gives us the added benefit of compile-time checking. While we're at it, here are some more refactorings that the code would benefit from:

- We could rename some of the variables so they're more closely tied in with the domain model (e.g., the variable hiBound could instead be numHotelPoints). Plus, the oddly cryptic variable name hp could instead be visibleHotel, and hf could instead be hotelFilter.
- The code contains the numeric literal 15. We could replace this with a constant so that it's a bit more meaningful (and less error-prone, for example, if the total number of defined hotel points changes), so 15 becomes TOTAL_HOTEL_POINTS (the total number of defined Hotel Points, as distinguished from numHotelPoints in the previous bullet point).
- The area of code that creates the visible Hotel could easily be separated into a separate method.

Implementing these refactorings, the code will change as follows:

```
// Hotel Points for AddHotels:

internal const TOTAL_HOTEL_POINTS = 15;

internal const int HP_ID = 0;
internal const int HP_X = 1;
internal const int HP_Y = 2;
internal const int HP_NAME = 3;
internal const int HP_ADDRESS1 = 4;
internal const int HP_ADDRESS2 = 5;
internal const int HP_CITY = 6;
internal const int HP_STATE = 7;
```

```
internal const int HP_ZIP = 8;
internal const int HP_PHONE = 9;
internal const int HP_STAR_RATING = 10;
internal const int HP_AMENITIES = 11;
internal const int HP_BRAND = 12;
internal const int HP_PRICE_BAND = 13;
internal const int HP_LINKS = 14;


// Get a list of hotels and their properties,
// create a list hotel composite objects
public bool AddHotels (string[] hotelPoints,
                       AmenityList Amenities,
                       HotelFilter hotelFilter)
{
    bool SomethingFound = false;

    if (hotels == null)
        hotels = new ArrayList ();

    Hotel visibleHotel;
    long numHotelPoints = hotelPoints.Length;
    string hotelAmenities = "";

    bool visible;

    for (int i=0; i < numHotelPoints; i += TOTAL_HOTEL_POINTS)
    {
        try
        {
            visible = hotelFilter.FilterHotel
                      (hotelPoints [i+HP_BRAND],
                       hotelPoints [i+HP_AMENITIES],
                       ref hotelAmenities);
            if (visible)
            {
                visibleHotel = createVisibleHotel(hotelPoints);
                Insert (visibleHotel);
                SomethingFound = true;
            }
        }
        catch (Exception ex)
        {
            string str = ex.Message;
            return false;
        }
    }
    return SomethingFound;
}

private Hotel createVisibleHotel(string[] hotelPoints)
{
    return new Hotel(hotelPoints [i + HP_ID],
                     int.Parse (hotelPoints [i + HP_X]),
                     int.Parse (hotelPoints [i + HP_Y]),
                     hotelPoints [i + HP_NAME],
```

```
                        hotelPoints [i + HP_ADDRESS1],
                        hotelPoints [i + HP_ADDRESS2],
                        hotelPoints [i + HP_CITY],
                        hotelPoints [i + HP_STATE],
                        hotelPoints [i + HP_ZIP],
                        hotelPoints [i + HP_PHONE],
                        hotelPoints [i + HP_STAR_RATING],
                        hotelPoints [i + HP_AMENITIES],
                        hotelPoints [i + HP_BRAND],
                        hotelPoints [i + HP_PRICE_BAND],
                        hotelPoints [i + HP_LINKS]);
        }
```

A really "classy" refactoring (excuse the pun) would be to do away with the way in which the `hotelPoints` array must be parsed by any code that wants to extract anything from it, and instead encapsulate this behavior in a HotelPoints class. This would tidy up the code immensely, increase its reusability, and so forth. To do this, the first stage would be to move all the `HP_` constants (`HP_CITY`, `HP_STATE`, etc.) into the new class; make the constants external (so any other class can read them); and create a method called something like `CreateHotel()`, which would take a string array of hotel point characters. All this really does is move the same code from one class to another. Now that we've liberated the code and given it its own class, the next stage would be to make HotelPoints hide away the whole arrays and `HP_` constants thing altogether.

Doing this, we'd probably also notice some other areas of the code that could be encapsulated away. We won't take this particular refactoring any further here, but you get the point.

Tip Normally, following ICONIX Process will get the code into a nicely factored state, so there shouldn't be a need to do further refactoring. Sometimes, though, it's only when you see the code that you realize the design could be tidied up a bit, so in Chapter 12 we describe how ICONIX Process can be used in conjunction with Test-Driven Development (TDD), a code-centric design process.

Next, let's take a look at the HotelFilter class, which `AOI.AddHotels` uses to filter out the Hotels that are going to be shown to the user.

```
public class HotelFilter
{
    private string AmenityFilter;
    private string HotelChainFilter;
    private string HotelChainName;
    private AmenityList Amenities;
    private char [] delimiter;

    public HotelFilter(AmenityList aAmenities,
                       string aAmenityFilter,
                       string aHotelChainFilter,
                       string aHotelChainName)
    {
        Amenities = aAmenities;
        AmenityFilter = aAmenityFilter;
        HotelChainFilter = aHotelChainFilter;
        HotelChainName = aHotelChainName;

        string delimStr = " ";
        delimiter = delimStr.ToCharArray();
    }
```

```
public string GetFilterText ()
{
    if (HotelChainFilter.Length > 0)
        return "Currently displaying " + HotelChainName;
    if (AmenityFilter.Length > 0)
    {
        string res = "";
        AmenityItem p;
        for (int j = 0; j < Amenities.count; j++)
        {
            p = Amenities.data [j];
            if (p.abbr != null)
                if (AmenityFilter.IndexOf (p.abbr) >= 0)
                {
                    if (res.Length > 120)
                    {
                        res = res + ", ...";
                        break;
                    }
                    if (res.Length > 0) res = res + ", ";
                    res = res + p.val;
                }
        }
        return "Currently displaying hotels with " + res;
    }
    return "";
}


public bool FilterHotel (string aHotelChain,
                         string Amenity,
                         ref string hotelAmenities)
{
    string [] sp;
    AmenityItem p;

    if (HotelChainFilter.Length > 0)
        return HotelChainFilter.ToUpper ().
                    Equals (aHotelChain.ToUpper ());
    else if (AmenityFilter.Length > 0)
    {
        sp = Amenity.Split (delimiter);
        hotelAmenities = "";
        for (int j = 0; j < sp.Length; j++)
        {
            p = Amenities.Find (sp [j]);
            if (p != null)
                hotelAmenities = hotelAmenities + p.abbr;
        }

        for (int j = 0; j < AmenityFilter.Length; j++)
        {
            if (hotelAmenities.IndexOf
                   (AmenityFilter.Substring (j, 1)) < 0)
```

```
                    return false;
                }
            }
            return true;
        }

    }
```

To sum up, it's a good time to ask if this refactoring is worth it, or if we're fiddling too much with working code. As we mentioned earlier in the sidebar titled "Knowing When to Tidy Up the Code," we're actually preparing the way forward for the next release, so from that perspective it's worth doing—but in some respects, it's borderline tinkering.

The ICONIX forward-engineered design got us a pretty clean and fully functional piece of code. But we were still able to find a useful refinement using refactoring principles. If both the following points hold true . . .

- The code is written but you see a way to improve it.
- The product (and especially the customer) will benefit from you refactoring the code. That is, there are appreciable business benefits from refactoring the code, such as keeping the design in good shape so the next release will go more smoothly.

. . . then definitely go for it.

Screenshots of the Finished Product

Let's begin with the U.S. map that resulted from the "uber" use case (see Figure 8-8).

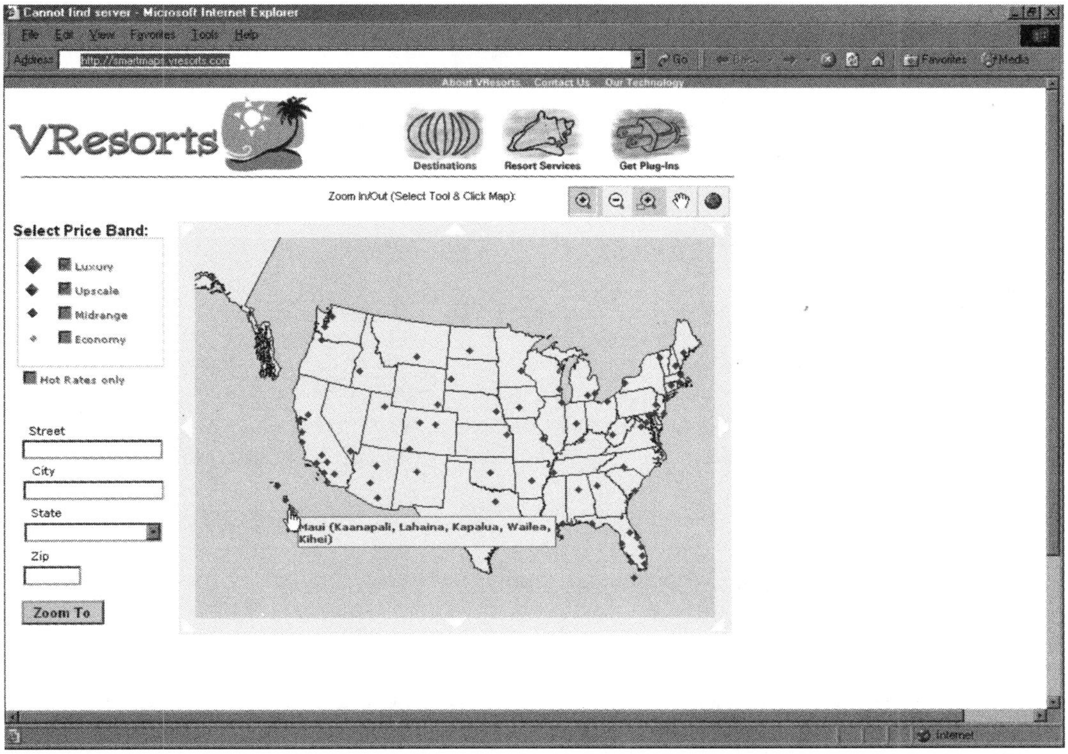

Figure 8-8. *Result of the "uber" use case*

Using this map, the user can hover the mouse over individual cities, and then drill down into any part of the United States. Clicking a city (or area or island) actually takes the user to a map destination page for that region, showing a list of hotels plus a featured hotel for each district (see Figure 8-9). Each district also has a prominent Find Hotels button and a Show Map button, which takes the user to the mapplet. If you check the use case back at the start of this chapter, you'll see this is exactly the behavior that the customer was asking for. This is an important aspect of use case–driven design: the finished product exactly fits the behavior defined by the use cases.

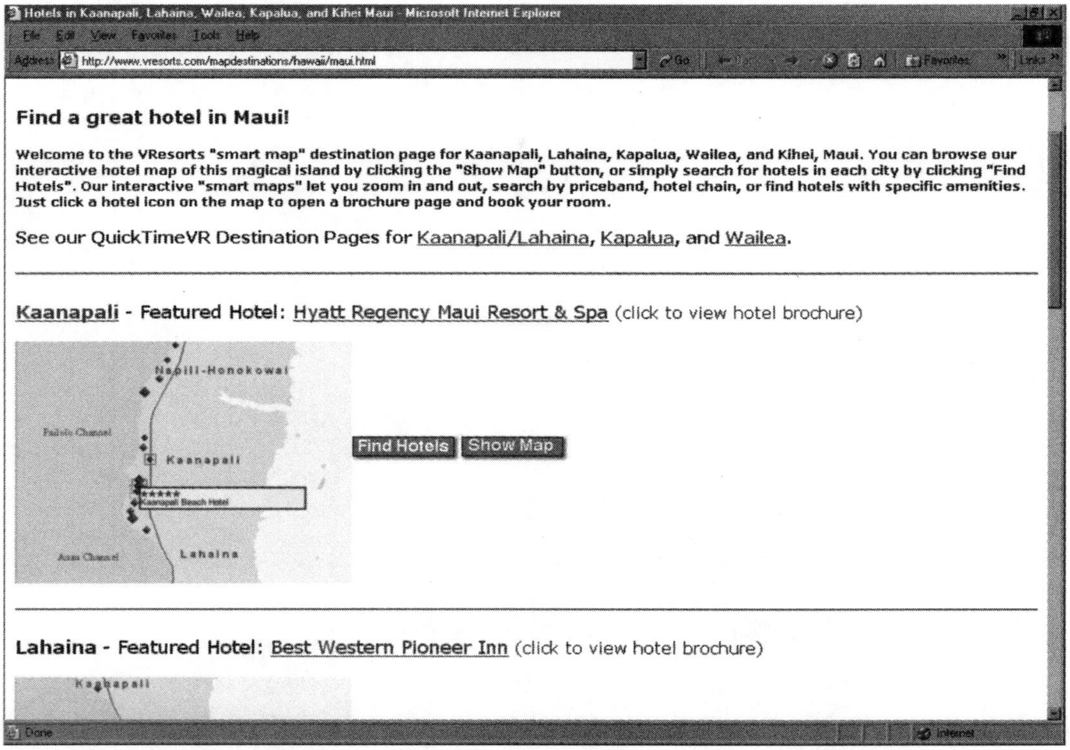

Figure 8-9. *"Smart map" destination page for Maui*

Agile Scorecard for the Mapplet Project

The customer's original concept of the mapplet search form was that it would allow display filtering (i.e., filtering the hotels being displayed by various criteria, such as price band and amenities). However, during one of the design review meetings at ESRI, the team discussed performance ramifications and decided that only the price-band filtering would be done as a *display filter*. The other features (filter by chain, filter by amenity, etc.) would instead be done using a *query filter*.

This decision was driven by performance data on the map server, the estimated amount of traffic, and so on. The idea was that the load on the server could be dramatically reduced by taking the most common display-filter operation (flipping the price-band switch), and caching that operation and its associated data in the user's web browser.

From a design perspective, this still leaves us with a DisplayFilter class on the client side. But there's also a QueryFilter class that is on the server side. And so the sequence diagrams will use both of these classes appropriately.

Note that the performance-driven decisions were made after doing some exploratory coding on the brand-new server software. This is true agility and yet it remains model driven. We're "proving with code" the performance parameters on the Map Server, and then adjusting our modeling based on this information at the same time that we're refining the original models from the JumpStart workshop using the persona analysis.

Summary

In this chapter we began (and concluded) the second release of the mapplet project. We extended the use case diagram that we used for release 1 and produced a plan so that we know what we need to deliver for this release. We also took the use case analysis that we did for release 2 and used it to create a detailed design.

We introduced an extension to ICONIX Process called persona analysis, for designing the product around a core set of target users. The use of persona analysis also means that we can take advantage of additional interaction design techniques. We'll revisit this technique in much more detail in Chapter 10.

Finally, we looked at the source code for release 2, refactored a few minor points here and there, and then basked in the glow of the screenshots from the finished product. Party on!

PART 3

Extensions to ICONIX Process

In this final section of the book, we define some extensions to ICONIX Process that two of this book's authors have tested and found to work well in an agile environment. Specifically, these extensions relate to adaptive planning, persona analysis, and a combined usage of test-driven and use case-driven development.

CHAPTER 9

Agile Planning

Planning an agile, iterative, and incremental project involves many concerns, trade-offs, and judgment calls. In this chapter, we discuss a number of agile planning principles to help you plan (and maintain the plan for) an Agile ICONIX project. These principles are summarized as a top 10 list at the end of the chapter.

Note As you'll learn in this chapter, agile planning is primarily about making a project *planning driven* rather than *plan driven*. In many ways, this is the differentiator between an agile and a nonagile project. Plan-driven projects are predictive, whereas planning-driven projects are adaptive.

Why Agile Planning?

Every software project involves change, to a degree. Even a project with a completely stable and well-understood set of requirements (a mythical beast indeed) would likely involve change at the design level, as coding progresses. So, recognizing the fact that change is almost a certainty and putting some practices in place that help to manage this aspect of software development are pretty important, to say the least.

XP's "planning game" provides some useful pointers on how to plan and track an agile project. In particular, it's useful to divide work into fine-grained, estimable tasks and then track the time spent on these tasks versus the programmer's estimates. Over time, you can use this to measure the project's velocity, which in turn helps to make your planning more accurate.

Balancing Flexibility and Perception

Agile planning in many ways reduces risk, not least of which is the danger that a project gets judged a failure and canceled because upper management felt that it was "running late" (even though it's delivering much more functionality than was originally scheduled). Agile planning instead places the emphasis on the project itself; its success or failure is judged by whether it is delivering business value to the customer and giving good ROI.

However, agile planning isn't without its own risks. The most dangerous of these is that the team may lose sight of how upper management happens to perceive the team's apparent progress. A team delivering good software to its own schedule might be shocked and surprised when upper management, who simply wanted project X to be ready by the 15th, shut the project down because they're still judging it according to the original promised delivery date.

Here's another way to look at it: introducing agility doesn't eliminate real-world constraints. For the most part, a project still needs to be "done" by a specific date.[1]

---

1. For a satirical look at the "software is never done" mind-set, see Chapter 11 of *Extreme Programming Refactored: The Case Against XP.*

How Agile ICONIX Differs from Other Agile Methods

In terms of planning, Agile ICONIX differs from other agile methods because it takes the approach that you design in detail before you begin coding (at least for the current iteration). It might be argued that this makes Agile ICONIX less agile (depending on your definition of agility), but if the goal of agility is to meet the customer's "real" (and probably evolving) requirements in a decent timeframe, then doing the right kind of detailed design (as we describe in Chapter 3, and in the mapplet example) actually helps us to achieve this agile goal.

In addition, with ICONIX Process there is a concept of a project being done. There is a definite milestone when you can refer back to the iteration plan and the design, and say, "Right, that's it—we've finished!" That's not to say that subsequent phases of the project might not be launched, and additional requirements might still be added late in the project, but with Agile ICONIX, the level of completeness of a project is something that can be measured.

Example: Agile Planning in Action

Figure 9-1 shows an example of how a project can be planned out. The list shown in the screenshot is a mixture of functional tasks (feature requests) and defects.

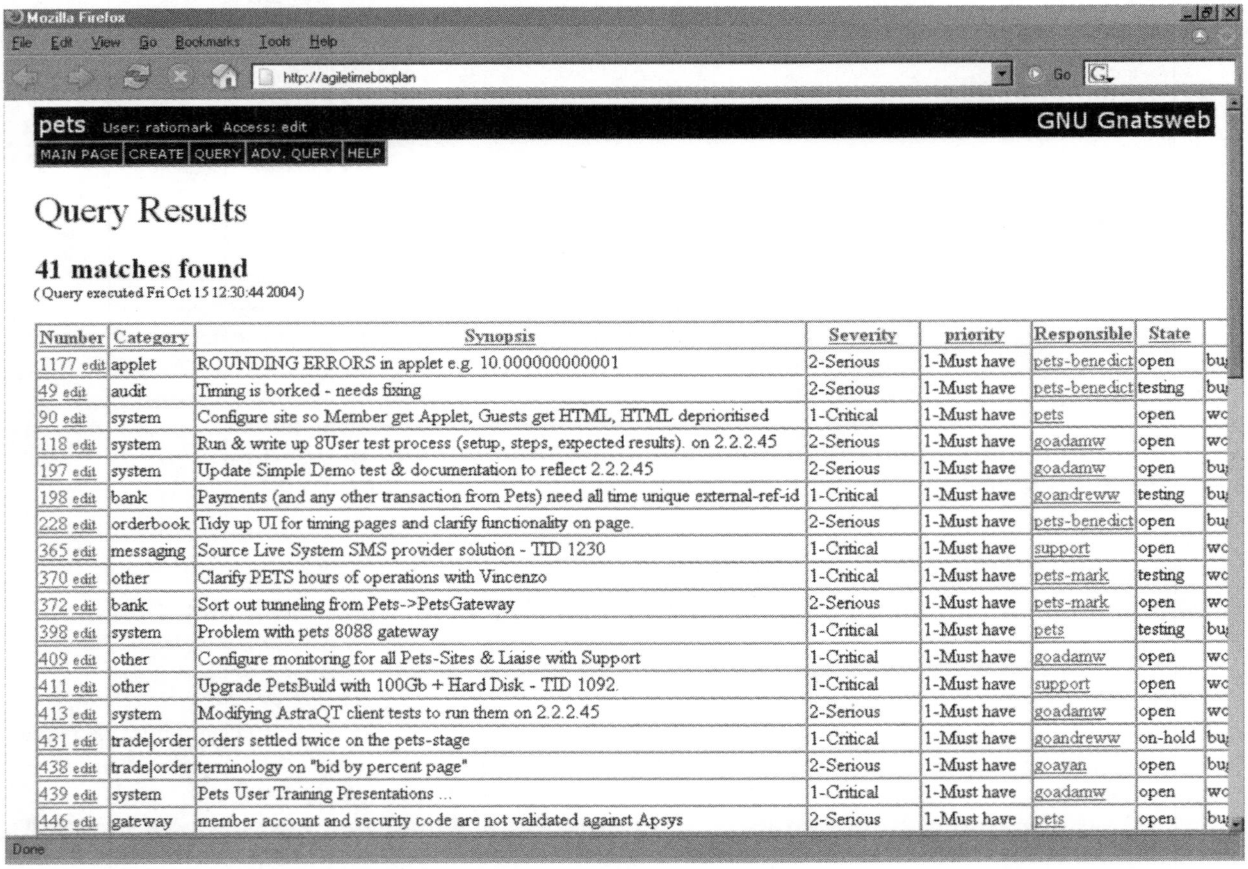

Number	Category	Synopsis	Severity	priority	Responsible	State	
1177 edit	applet	ROUNDING ERRORS in applet e.g. 10.000000000001	2-Serious	1-Must have	pets-benedict	open	bu
49 edit	audit	Timing is borked - needs fixing	2-Serious	1-Must have	pets-benedict	testing	bu
90 edit	system	Configure site so Member get Applet, Guests get HTML, HTML deprioritised	1-Critical	1-Must have	pets	open	wc
118 edit	system	Run & write up 8User test process (setup, steps, expected results). on 2.2.2.45	2-Serious	1-Must have	goadamw	open	wc
197 edit	system	Update Simple Demo test & documentation to reflect 2.2.2.45	2-Serious	1-Must have	goadamw	open	bu
198 edit	bank	Payments (and any other transaction from Pets) need all time unique external-ref-id	1-Critical	1-Must have	goandreww	testing	bu
228 edit	orderbook	Tidy up UI for timing pages and clarify functionality on page.	2-Serious	1-Must have	pets-benedict	open	bu
365 edit	messaging	Source Live System SMS provider solution - TID 1230	1-Critical	1-Must have	support	open	wc
370 edit	other	Clarify PETS hours of operations with Vincenzo	1-Critical	1-Must have	pets-mark	testing	wc
372 edit	bank	Sort out tunneling from Pets->PetsGateway	2-Serious	1-Must have	pets-mark	open	wc
398 edit	system	Problem with pets 8088 gateway	1-Critical	1-Must have	pets	testing	bu
409 edit	other	Configure monitoring for all Pets-Sites & Liaise with Support	1-Critical	1-Must have	goadamw	open	wc
411 edit	other	Upgrade PetsBuild with 100Gb + Hard Disk - TID 1092.	1-Critical	1-Must have	support	open	wc
413 edit	system	Modifying AstraQT client tests to run them on 2.2.2.45	2-Serious	1-Must have	goadamw	open	wc
431 edit	trade|order	orders settled twice on the pets-stage	1-Critical	1-Must have	goandreww	on-hold	bu
438 edit	trade|order	terminology on "bid by percent page"	2-Serious	1-Must have	goayan	open	bu
439 edit	system	Pets User Training Presentations ...	1-Critical	1-Must have	goadamw	open	wc
446 edit	gateway	member account and security code are not validated against Apsys	2-Serious	1-Must have	pets	open	bu

Figure 9-1. *Tracking defects and feature requests*

Each defect and feature request in the list is assigned a Severity and/or a Priority (Must Have, Should Have, Could Have, or Won't Have, using DSDM MoSCoW Rules; see `www.dsdm.org/en/about/moscow.asp`). Each item is also assigned a target Release.

Tip It's important to include defect fixes in a list of deliverables for each release, as defects (or at least the effort put into fixing them) are like features: they can be added to a plan, they take time to fix, they can be prioritized, and (assuming a particular defect isn't an absolute showstopper) they may be pushed out to a future release. As such, tracking and planning defects is a similar activity to tracking and planning new features.

Agile Planning Terminology

Terminology can vary from process to process. For example, where one process might use the term "increment," another process might use "iteration" to mean the same thing. So in this section, we briefly explain the terms we use in this book for planning an ICONIX Process project.

- *Planning iteration*: Mainly for planning and team management, this is a fixed amount of time (ideally about a week) that doesn't result in a customer release.
- *Release increment*: This is a series of iterations resulting in some working software released to the customer (or released to QA, or handed to the customer for early feedback).
- *Release*: This is a milestone on the plan when working software is released to the customer (or at least to QA).

To put it another way, a *release increment* is planned in *weekly planning iterations* and produces a *release* of new functionality (see Figure 9-2).

Figure 9-2. *How iterative and incremental planning fit together*

The weekly planning iteration (which for the rest of the book we'll often shorten to *iteration* or *weekly iteration*) is purely for planning and team management purposes. There isn't a release at the end of each week (except if you want to demo the partially written software [or screenshots] to the project stakeholders to get their early feedback). Instead, the weekly planning iteration works as follows: each Monday morning, you hold a progress update with the team members and sort out what they're going to be working on this week. You then update the plan (which contains the estimates) with the *actuals*—that is, the actual time taken for the tasks as recorded by the team.

This doesn't take very much time, but it means that the plan increasingly reflects reality as the project progresses, as opposed to some project plans, which become more and more steeped in fantasy as deadlines loom nearer. So the weekly iteration is primarily a way of synchronizing the team's efforts with expectations, and also synchronizing each person's work with what the rest of the team is doing (because they're all in one room together talking about what they're working on at the moment).

The iteration doesn't have to be exactly 1 week, although whatever iteration size you choose, you should try to stick with it throughout the whole project. As you'll see later in this chapter, using fixed-length iterations is useful for measuring project speed (or project velocity). We've generally found that iterations of 1 week each work great because they form a natural heartbeat for the project. Each Monday morning, the team members are probably quite unmotivated after their weekend of resting, or going on fishing trips, or whatever they generally get up to, so they could do with a gentle push and some specific direction to get them productive again. The Monday morning meeting works rather well for this.

The release increment ideally should be between 1 and 3 months in length, culminating in a customer release. As we discuss later in this chapter, this may not be a production release as such (i.e., a "live" customer release). In fact, there are three types of release: internal, investigative, and production.

Agile Planning Building Blocks

In this section, we look at various planning techniques that work particularly well on an Agile ICONIX project.

Agile planning is not normally seen as a stand-alone discipline, therefore attempts to define it (like agility itself) can result in a somewhat nebulous description. Indeed, the very name "agile planning" might strike some people as oxymoronic. How can you create a plan for something that by its nature keeps changing?

We see agile planning as something that operates at two levels:

- *Adaptive planning*: Planning ahead, tracking changes, and adapting the plan as the project progresses.
- *Planning for agility*: Preparing for the unknown, so that when changes take place, their impact is kept to a minimum. Agile planning is a way of anticipating and controlling change.

Planning for agility is an essential (and fundamental) aspect of agile development, because it addresses the problem of inexact, inaccurate, and evolving customer requirements. ICONIX Process helps a lot in this matter, as it focuses on identifying gaps in the use cases/requirements and helping to disambiguate them (see Chapter 3; also see the books *Managing Software Requirements: A Use Case Approach*[2] and *Software Requirements*[3]).

For now, let's look at the first item, adaptive planning, which is closer to what people generally mean by the term "agile planning." The techniques described in this section are ways of organizing and maintaining an agile (i.e., flexible) plan. These techniques work well together, but they can also be applied individually as needed. The following are essentially the "core practices" of agile planning:

- Prioritizing requirements
- Estimating
- Release planning
- Tracking project velocity
- Timeboxing

In addition, the following practices should also prove useful:

- Tracing requirements back to goals
- Minimizing the use of Gantt charts (at least for technical planning)

Let's look at each of these practices in more detail. All of them can be used to good effect on an ICONIX project.

Prioritizing Requirements

The following conversation, in various forms, has probably been repeated thousands of times in just as many projects and organizations:

Manager: I need these three items done by next week.

Programmer: I have time to do only one of them. Which one has the highest priority?

Manager: They all do!

(Depending on the type of manager, this might be followed up with, "Achieve wonderful things—make me proud!")

---

2. Dean Leffingwell and Don Widrig, *Managing Software Requirements: A Use Case Approach, Second Edition* (New York: Addison-Wesley, 2003).

3. Karl E. Wiegers, *Software Requirements, Second Edition* (Redmond, WA: Microsoft Press, 2003).

Of course, the problem here is that all three items really do have a high priority. If the available resources just aren't sufficient to cover the work required in the allotted time, then something's got to give. The worst-case scenario is that the programmer "goes for it," attacks all three items, and ends up completing none of them in time. The best-case scenario is that one of the items gets done in time, and the other two, just like the programmer said, don't get done due to lack of time. However, the item that was done ended up being chosen by the programmer (on a technical, personal, or arbitrary basis) rather than by the manager or customer (using more business-oriented criteria).

An extension of this problem is when, at the start of any iteration, the customer is faced with a list of outstanding features, only a few of which can be shoehorned into this iteration. If we consider the manager's inability to decide which of the three features was the highest priority, the same problem is multiplied many times when it comes to prioritization of multiple features over an extended period of time. Then multiply this by the number of actual project stakeholders, bearing in mind that few projects are driven by just a single individual.

Clearly, we need an effective method of eliciting some realistic decisions from the project stakeholders, so that all involved (customers and programmers alike) are happy with what has been planned for the next iteration.

Estimating

Being able to estimate how long something is going to take is, of course, vitally important in software development. Unfortunately, it's also an activity toward which many teams take the least scientific approach. Estimates can range from educated guesses to random numbers. A programmer's "estimation algorithm" frequently involves watching the project manager's face and giving a series of steadily descending numbers until finally the manager stops frowning. Often, a project manager will choose numbers that he likes without even consulting the programmers, the people who will be doing the work.

Note There is also a difference (which often isn't taken into account) between effort and duration. Most estimates are made on effort, and duration is almost always longer than effort.

With a little more method and a little less madness, it's possible to produce some quite accurate estimates. As with many things, the more you practice estimating, the better at it you get. There will always be some intuition involved, but it is also possible to be quite methodical in estimating work.

The main way to make work easier to estimate is to break it down into smaller chunks.[4] Each chunk of work needs to be discrete (i.e., have as few dependencies as possible). This in turn reduces the complexity of having to wait for other parts of the project to be finished.

Programmers beginning a new piece of software are generally embarking on a trip into the unknown. As such, it's understandable that they don't like to be pinned down to a particular deadline. If they don't want to supply a completion date, it's because they genuinely don't know. During the planning and analysis stages, getting the programmers involved helps, because they can do exploratory prototyping work to get a feel for how long the "real thing" will take.

Three-point estimating is particularly useful for extracting estimates from reluctant programmers. Sometimes programmers do have a good idea of how long a piece of work will take but are reluctant to commit, just in case it takes longer. Asking them to specify a range (e.g., 3–6 days) is one possibility, but it's also a bit too fuzzy for planning purposes. Three-point estimating, on the other hand, seems to extract uncannily useful (i.e., accurate) estimates from programmers! The method involves coming up with three effort estimates for each software feature: the *best possible* case, the *worst possible* case, and the *most likely* case. A spreadsheet can be used to combine the three-point estimates in a number of ways.

4. Of course, having a well-defined use case model and detailing the use cases with robustness diagrams is also an enormous help here.

Once the team of programmers has supplied three-point estimates, it's possible to calculate the best estimates for a number of features, using the following formula:

$$E = \sum_i \frac{(w_i + 4m_i + b_i)}{6}$$

where b represents the best possible case estimate, w the worst possible case estimate, and m the most likely case estimate.

For example, say a programmer, Bob, gives this estimate for retrieving and then displaying hotel details on a web page:

Worst possible case = 3 days

Most likely case = 1 day

Best possible case = 0.5 days

This could be shown on a spreadsheet, along with some other estimates, with the worst possible case/most likely case/best possible case estimates shown in brackets:

Show Hotel Information on Web Page	[Bob]	(3/1/0.5)
Create ShapeFile for Map Server	[Bob]	(2.5/1/1)
Generate Hotel Map	[Sally]	(2/0.5/0.5)
Totals		(7.5/2.5/2)

So to calculate the best possible case estimate for Bob's first task ("Show Hotel Information on Web Page"), we would use this:
(3+ 4*1 + 0.5) / 6 = 1.25 days

The best possible case estimate for all three items totaled would be
(7.5 + 4*2.5 + 2) / 6 = 3.25 days

■ Note Three-point estimating is described further in the book *Better Software Faster* by Andy Carmichael and Dan Haywood.[5]

The techniques described in this section are particularly useful for agile planning, because they allow estimates to be produced at a relatively early stage (these estimates are later refined as the project progresses), when the overall design hasn't yet stabilized.

Release Planning

As the name suggests, release planning is all about breaking the project into smaller releases and planning for each release. To achieve this, the project is divided into small, fixed-length iterations of about a month each. We also plan incrementally—that is, we revisit the plan frequently (at a minimum once per iteration), adjusting it as we go.

The advantage of the fixed-length iteration approach is that it introduces a regular heartbeat to the project, a rhythm of design/code/test/release (or design/test/code/release, depending on your methodology). Very quickly, the whole team settles into this rhythm. The iteration size is key: we keep iterations small so that we get the optimum balance of feedback, urgency, planning, focused work, and delivery time for each project deliverable.

5. Andy Carmichael and Dan Haywood, *Better Software Faster* (Upper Saddle River, NJ: Prentice Hall, 2002). See in particular Chapter 5, "The Controlling Step: Feature-Centric Management."

It's preferable to keep the iteration sizes fixed, but if the project release plan is at odds with this approach, it isn't worth having a cow over. The fixed-length iteration approach is either highly recommended or mandated by just about every agile process in existence, but it can also be surprisingly difficult to apply to real-world business constraints, where some functionality must be delivered by a certain date.

To put it another way, *small fixed-length iterations and frequent short releases are often at odds with each other*. If you aim to produce a working piece of software at the end of each month, but you're also producing point releases of the product every couple of months or so, then the effort of releasing the software halfway through a month will be constantly disruptive to the effort of incrementally producing new working software at the end of each month.

Generally, we've found that using fixed 1-month iterations (*timeboxing*, to use DSDM parlance) works extremely well, but we also recommend that you tailor the approach appropriately for your project. If your project is regularly releasing new functionality to the customer (e.g., every 2–3 months), then you may find it sufficient to use this as the project heartbeat. In other words, align the iterations with the releases.[6] An iteration size of 2–3 months is really the maximum, though. Anything longer and you should seriously think about introducing a shorter iteration size within the release schedule.

Tracking Project Velocity

Project velocity is, simply, the speed at which the programmers are completing their programming tasks. It's used in XP to adjust estimates of "ideal development days"[7] required to complete a feature to the actual effort that the team eventually took to complete the feature. This is done repeatedly and ruthlessly throughout the project, so that eventually (we hope) the team gets better and better at estimating its work.

An "ideal day" is a day when everything goes right and there are no interruptions (annoying meetings, lengthy phone calls from depressed-sounding spouses, nasty and unexpected network outages, illnesses, etc.). It also represents the time spent purely working on the feature in question, and it doesn't include other activities such as helping your pair programmer on other tasks.

To effectively track velocity, you need to break down the work into chunks of work of roughly equal size (in terms of the effort taken to complete them). Of course, this won't always be possible, because some atomic items of work are different sizes than other atomic pieces of work; one item might take a day to complete, the other 1.5 days. Generally, this shouldn't be too much of a problem, but if it is, try using an arbitrary unit of measurement (e.g., Gummi Bears) to measure a feature's complexity, or preferably use a smaller base unit (e.g., ideal *hours* instead of ideal *days*).

Work estimates wherever possible should be based on prior experience of writing a feature of a similar size and nature, so if writing a data entry screen last month took a day, a similar screen this month should also take about a day. Using historical data to make new estimates is key to this approach—it means we're not "guesstimating"; rather, we're measuring based on previous experiences.

As with estimates, the historical data needs to be recorded in terms of ideal days. By tracking both the estimated time taken and actual time taken on a weekly basis, we can start to track the project velocity. If fewer of our equal-sized features were delivered this week than last week, then the velocity has dropped.

As we get better at estimating work in terms of ideal work days, if we start to find that the actual time spent on a feature is greater than the estimated time spent, then it could be for one of two reasons:

- The programmers are still underestimating the work.
- There have been too many external interruptions recently (meetings, etc.) distracting the programmers from their work.

If the programmers are underestimating the work (a common industry affliction), perhaps the work units are too large and need to be further broken down, or (equally likely) the estimates weren't based on historical data.

6. Leading Doug to speculate that since this is so simple, why do anything else?
7. Kent Beck and Martin Fowler, *Planning Extreme Programming* (New York: Addison-Wesley, 2000).

> **OR, WE COULD ACTUALLY ESTIMATE BASED ON OUR MODELS INSTEAD OF USING GUMMI BEARS**
>
> A somewhat more scientific alternative to measuring work units in Gummi Bears can be easily accomplished by representing logical software functions as controllers on our robustness diagrams, and by assigning a complexity level and a responsible programmer to each controller. This functionality is built into tools such as EA (see the following image). It's then a simple matter to export this information to a spreadsheet. This doesn't mean we're giving up the adaptive aspects of planning, but it does allow us to do a much better job on the predictive end.

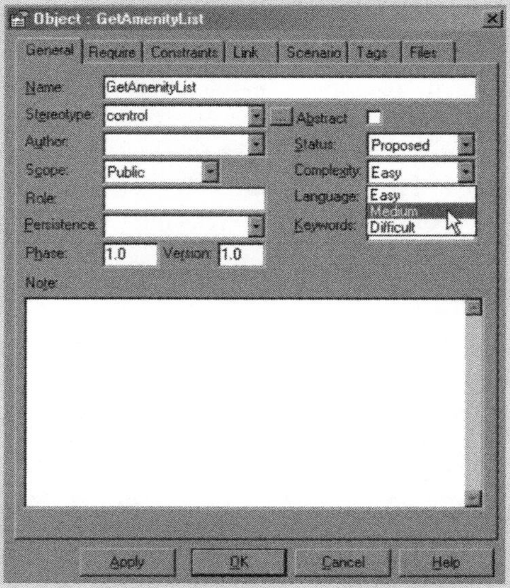

Timeboxing

Timeboxing, like much else in software agility, has sprouted more than one definition. We describe here the two main contexts in which the word "timeboxing" is used. (The first is the more formal definition, whereas the second is the informal way that's commonly used in fast-paced, buzzword-peppered management meetings.)

Planning in Fixed Iterations

The timebox has a set period, usually a few weeks at most. Planning takes place at the start of each timebox. The project stakeholders decide what features to include in the next timebox, and the programmers estimate the features. If there are too many features to fit, one or more features are taken out. (Similarly, it may turn out that more features can be added.)

Timeboxing has its roots in DSDM, but a similar mechanism appears in almost all modern agile processes. Scrum uses fixed monthly iterations known as *sprints*. The list of features that may be included in the next iteration is known as the *sprint backlog*. The project stakeholders decide at the start of each monthly sprint what features from the backlog to work on during the upcoming month.

Similarly, fixed iterations in XP involve the on-site customer deciding at the start of each iteration which features (or *user stories*) to include. A big difference is that the feedback loop in XP is much shorter—the fixed iteration can be as short as a single week.

Whatever the iteration size (we generally recommend a month), timeboxing of this sort is an essential part of pretty much any agile project. The approach helps to reduce risk, because the feedback loop between developers and users is kept short. That is, the customer and end users get to say "This is wrong" or ask "Can this be changed?" sooner rather than later.

Placing a Limit on Indeterminate Work

Outside of DSDM, the word "timebox" is increasingly used to indicate that a certain amount of time (less than a single iteration) has been set aside for a certain activity, and the programmers involved will fit as much "stuff" into the timebox as they can. While this sounds ad-hoc, it can occasionally be useful for activities that by their nature don't have specific criteria for when they're finished. Specifically allocating person-days for the activity helps because it establishes a definite endpoint for the activity.

For example, if a module has been written without very many unit tests, the team members might plan to spend 2 or 3 days simply writing tests and fixing the bugs that they will inevitably uncover as they go. The expression that appears on the project plan might be "Timeboxed unit tests for XYZ module – 2 days."

Although occasionally useful, timeboxing in this sense should be used with care because of its ad-hoc nature. Actual features with specific endpoint criteria should instead be planned for individually.

Timeboxing when used in this context is typically also accompanied by a variety of Buzzword Bingo phrases such as "touching bases," "leveraging the extranet," and "empowering the employees."

Tracing Requirements Back to Goals

Every project should have a set of goals to drive it. These goals are defined at a fairly high level—a higher level than requirements, for example. They're kind of like a project mission statement in bullet-point form. In fact, a typical project probably wouldn't have more than five or ten goals. The purpose of the goals is partly to keep the project focused, but their primary purpose (from an agile planning perspective) is helping us to gauge the impact of any potential change in requirements.

The idea is to keep each requirement traced back to one or more project goals. This is easier than it sounds, mainly because there won't be many goals to trace back to. So, for example, one of the goals might be

[GOAL 3] To put our entire range of services online using a secure Internet connection.

And a couple of the requirements might read

ACC-10. The user must be able to log in at any time and check his/her account balance [GOAL 3]

ACC-20. The user must be able to transfer money to or from his/her account. [GOAL 3]

This helps our agile plan in a number of ways. Midway through the project, it's likely that at least some of the requirements will start to change. If either requirement in the preceding example was to change, we could check with its associated goal to make sure that the change doesn't break its original goal.

Similarly, if the project takes a new strategic direction, then it's likely that one or more of the project goals themselves are going to need to change. For example, GOAL 3 might need to be amended so that this first version of the project will only allow read-only access to the company's range of services—that is, the users can log in and browse, but they can't yet change anything. By checking all of the requirements that are traced back to GOAL 3, it's relatively easy to determine which requirements need to be changed or removed.

Tip This approach is also useful for eliminating redundant requirements. In other words, we might find that certain requirements can be removed altogether without breaking the high-level goals in any way.

Traceability is sometimes seen as nonagile, because it involves additional documentation and extra work to keep the documentation and traceability matrices up to date. We hope we've demonstrated here, though, that a small amount of traceability (without going too wild) can actually help agile projects by indicating which requirements are linked to a common set of goals.

Minimizing the Use of Gantt Charts

Unfortunately, the Gantt chart will always be with us, taunting developers with its quantitative and predictive demands. It's increasingly obvious that Gantt and PERT charts just aren't realistic ways of planning software projects, at least not at the technical level. More appropriate methods of planning tend to be less about predicting X, Y, and Z activities down to the nearest hour, and more about tracking progress and adapting expectations over time. These more appropriate methods reflect the fact that software development is a creative, "fuzzy" activity as much as a precise engineering discipline.

WHAT ABOUT DEPENDENCIES?

Gantt charts do, of course, help with tracking precedence between individual engineering tasks—that is, task A must be completed before task B can begin. While we recognize that these planning dependencies can't be completely eliminated, agile practices (and pure old-fashioned *good design principles*) do help to reduce them, for example:

- Following the design principles of high cohesion and low coupling help to reduce or eliminate dependencies between classes, allowing them to be tested and developed in any order.
- Mock objects can also help to overcome the dependency problem, especially when combining ICONIX modeling with a test-driven approach (see Chapter 12), because it means we can develop classes that use a "mock interface" before the interface has been implemented, as long as we have a set of unit tests to assert that the results are as expected.

Technical development work planning should involve tracking progress on a series of fine-grained engineering tasks and adjusting expectations based on the rate at which these tasks are being completed. These expectations can then be projected onto higher-level (less detailed, less technical) plans which, as you'd expect, become steadily more accurate the further into the project we get.

However, this type of planning isn't going to keep upper management happy. In fact, presenting management with a list of engineering tasks and the level of progress on those tasks is probably only going to annoy them. The problem is, "planning" of this sort is of no use to the big boss, because it doesn't tell him what he needs to know.

Business-level managers love Gantt charts, because Gantt charts represent a model of the world that makes sense at their level. Therefore, in whatever way we approach planning at the technical/project level, at some point our technically precise plan will need to be translated into a nice obtuse Gantt chart to keep upper management happy. Essentially, project plans of this sort are required to keep management apprised of the project's overall progress. If the managers can't see, and plan for, progress at a high level, then they start to become uneasy. So you need to hide the trees so that management can see the forest.

When producing project plans, a common error is to put technical information on them. It's important that with a project plan, just as with any other type of document, you know your audience. Once you acknowledge that the plan is really just for upper management, then you can begin to tailor it according to the information that managers really want to see. It's likely that all they actually want to know about is the following:

- Is the project on track?
- Is the next release (e.g., in 2 months' time) going to be late?
- What will be in the next release?
- Has anything slipped to the next release?

Thus, we can eliminate all the engineering tasks from the project plan (at least from this particular form of plan—obviously, you need to track the engineering tasks somewhere!). So the project plan simply needs to consist of a list of requirements, or high-level deliverables (use case names would be an appropriate level), or even just the project goals (depending how fine-grained they are).

Tip Try to avoid the lure of putting "percentage complete" values on any project plan, because these are—let's face it—valueless and often misleading. You're not fooling anyone with that "90% complete" talk![8] It's probably better just to include the estimated completion date, if there is one, or to include a range (see the three-point estimating discussion earlier in this chapter in the section "Estimating").

---

8. As we all know, the first 90% is the easy part; it's that second 90% that's a killer.

Agile Planning Phases

Agile ICONIX doesn't place any restrictions on how the project is arranged in terms of phases (except that some requirements analysis and design work needs to take place prior to coding). However, the approach outlined in this section works well with ICONIX modeling.

Modeling: Analysis and Design

ICONIX Process at its heart has two phases: analysis and design (see Chapter 3). The analysis phase consists of domain modeling and use cases analysis, and the design phase involves drawing sequence diagrams, filling in the details on the domain model to create a static model, plus coding and testing. The bridge between the two phases is robustness analysis, which involves plugging gaps in the use cases while also identifying the objects (aka classes) that will be used in the design.

The analysis and design phases can be thought of as *inner* phases comprising the core modeling activities. Wrapped around these activities, it's possible to divide the planning process into two *outer* phases: inception and construction. This approach is adapted from FDD's two-phase approach, except it's tailored to suit the ICONIX modeling approach.

During the inception phase, some ICONIX modeling (the analysis part) takes place. During the construction phase, both of the inner ICONIX phases (analysis and design) take place; these in turn are mainly for modeling purposes.

Planning: Inception

The inception phase takes place only once for the entire project. It's a planning and exploration phase, during which the team gets started, explores the requirements, gets familiar with the technology, does some prototyping, and so on. If you can produce a stable customer release from this first phase, then so much the better, but if the result of the inception phase is simply a bunch of prototype code and a set of requirements, then it's still a pretty good start. In our example mapplet project, the first release is a prototyping phase during which the team members familiarize themselves with the beta server that they're working with (see Chapter 6).

Toward the end of this phase, the work should be formalized into a set of use cases (ideally produced with the customer's direct involvement), which the project stakeholders can review and sign off on. Some preliminary design work should also be done in the inception phase.

DOMAIN MODELING: THE FIRST INCEPTION ACTIVITY

Domain modeling (projectwide) and creating use case diagrams within packages (a package per subsystem) across the project should be done during the inception phase. Just the creation of these diagrams (domain, use case, and package) tends to help make sure we haven't left any "holes big enough to drive a truck through" out of the original concept.

Also, a sincere attempt to write down the functional requirements needs to happen at this level. After doing this once, we can choose which use cases to attack during each release of the software. The other projectwide parts of the model can adjust during and after each successive release.

The expectation is neither that we can perfectly model the ideal class structure in the domain model nor that we will perfectly be able to diagram out all the use cases of the system up front. We'll probably miss a few requirements, too, but making a sincere and dedicated effort to do the best we can up front (i.e., trying to get it right the first time) has an enormously beneficial effect. You can usually hit the most important 80% of these things up front, and that makes a huge difference.

The domain model in particular results in a well-defined set of names for the business classes that will participate in the use cases. Almost inevitably, each organization has some name ambiguity in this area, which we can resolve up front.

Planning: Construction

The construction phase takes place for the remainder of the project. This consists of an ongoing series of small frequent releases, each of which may be further divided into smaller iterations for planning purposes.

The core of ICONIX Process is formed of two distinct modeling phases: analysis and design (in which each modeling phase includes specific modeling activities; see Chapter 3). The construction planning phase can be seen as a rapid series of fine-grained analysis and design modeling phases.

Release and maintenance are considered to be part of the construction phase. This is because a product really goes into maintenance from the moment its first release goes to the customer. Similarly, release management is a constant and ongoing activity throughout the construction phase.

Agile Planning Principles

In this section, we cover some basic principles of agile planning and describe how these principles are applied to ICONIX Process. These principles are summed up in a top 10 list at the end of this chapter.

A DRIVING ANALOGY

Imagine you're taking a car journey from London to Budapest. You sit down and write a detailed list of all the roads you're going to take during your trip: A101 (2 hours), B234 (3 hours), B2335 (1 hour), then catch ferry, and so on. With every detail mapped out in advance, you can't go wrong, can you?

Then you find a few hours into your journey that there's a major diversion on the B2335: a bridge is under repair. This, unfortunately, means the next 45 roads on your list are going to be wrong. You'll have to work through all that detail again and replan how to get to the ferry port by the right time. Reality (rather annoyingly) will always intervene to mess things up. The best laid plans of mice and men . . .

The next time you decide to go on a trip, this time from London to Helsinki, you don't bother to plan at all. Well, it was a waste of time the last time, wasn't it? Unfortunately, this time you get lost along the way, miss your ferry by 10 minutes, and have to wait a day for the next one. You finally arrive 2 days later than you thought you would at your destination. Hmm . . .

Try again—London to Barcelona. This time you have it worked out: you need to **plan in appropriate detail,** meaning in depth for the short term and in broad strokes for the long term. So you make a list of the cities you're going to pass through but leave the detailed road planning to coffee breaks along the way, in which you plan a couple of hours' driving at a time. You end up taking quite a different route from the one you thought you might (French truck drivers blockading the motorways again), but you arrive safely in Barcelona only a few hours behind schedule.

Three Types of Plan

When you're planning an Agile ICONIX project, three levels of planning and estimating suggest themselves. The first of these, the *initial scoping plan*, is basically about getting an overall feel of where your project is going (this is easy when undertaking a car journey, but it's somewhat more difficult when developing software). In an ICONIX context, it will involve listing requirements and identifying—but not elaborating on—potential use cases and coming up with some broad estimates for these. Chapter 5 gives examples of starting requirements, which culminate in the use case model also shown in Chapter 5.

The second level of planning, the *release plan*, is about prioritizing and scoping. The customer, following the principle **the customer dictates priority**, is responsible for determining what is going to be implemented and in what order with the project team, and allocates use cases to releases according to business priority and available time and effort. See later in this chapter for the mapplet project release plan.

At this point in the planning process, it's important to realize that many projects are doomed to failure by the imposition of completely unrealistic timescales and deadlines. There is always pressure to get software written quickly—that's life—but many projects are thrown into an immediate state of panic from which they never recover. When the pressure mounts, and the deadline is fixed, apply the planning principle **negotiate with scope**. We'll discuss issues surrounding the ideal duration of a release, and the degree to which we should undertake up-front analysis and design, later in this chapter.

The third and final level of planning is the *detailed release plan*. This is a detailed plan for the next release, and it will contain a list of tasks (based on how to implement the chosen set of use cases) and who is responsible for them. Adopting the principle **the plan follows reality**, later detailed release plans will take into account feedback on estimates, feedback from the customer, potential design improvements, new requirements, and bug fixes. Our colleague Chuck Suscheck, who has been involved in a number of multiple-iteration agile projects, offers some useful guidelines on how to plan releases in detail in the upcoming sidebar titled "Elastic Functionality in Iterations."

ELASTIC FUNCTIONALITY IN ITERATIONS

By Chuck Suscheck

I've been using a technique for keeping iterations on schedule that I call *elastic functionality*. Here's how it works. For each iteration, I divide the functionality into three categories:

- *Category 1 functionality* must be implemented in order for the iteration to be successful. This functionality takes precedence over the iteration due date, which will slip if the items related to this functionality are not completed.
- *Category 2 functionality* will be implemented if the project stays on schedule. The tasks related to this functionality may be omitted from the iteration if the due date starts to slip. While category 2 functionality is expected, it is not critical to the success of the iteration.
- *Category 3 functionality* will be implemented if the iteration is ahead of schedule or if the functionality can be implemented without affecting the schedule. It is likely that category 3 functionality will be omitted from the iteration.

Any iteration must contain functionality of all three categories. By adding category 2 and 3 functionality to an iteration, there is room for dropping functions from an iteration in order to keep the iteration on schedule.

As a typical mix, 80% of the effort should go to category 1 functionality, and 20% of the effort should go to category 2 functionality. Category 3 functionality should be an additional 10% of the effort. (In other words, 100% of the effort goes into categories 1 and 2, and extra effort goes into category 3.)

For example, suppose you have an iteration that is timeboxed at 80 hours. You should have about 64 hours (80%) of category 1 functionality, 16 hours (20%) of category 2 functionality, and 8 additional hours (10%) of category 3 functionality. When planning an iteration, estimate as though category 1 and category 2 functionality will be fully implemented and category 3 will not.

When you plan multiple iterations, you should assume that category 3 functionality won't be completed and, if that functionality will be important as the project progresses, include it in a subsequent iteration. Also, category 3 functionality in one iteration can be listed as category 2 or even category 1 in subsequent iterations.

As the project progresses from iteration to iteration, functionality will be added and dropped. To keep the iterations on track, reevaluate subsequent iterations once an iteration is complete. Certain functionality may have been dropped from an iteration. Reevaluate the following iterations to see if the functionality should be included in a future iteration and if the functionality should change categories. Category 3 functionality may be completed. If that's the case, look at subsequent iterations and see if that functionality is included elsewhere. If so, remove the completed functionality and reevaluate the iterations that follow.

Feedback Is Vital

Feedback is vital in mitigating the many potential risks that software developments face: risks of misunderstandings in functional requirements, risks of an architecture being fundamentally flawed, risks of an unacceptable UI, risks of analysis and design models being wrong, risks that the team doesn't understand the chosen technology, risks that demanding nonfunctional requirements aren't met, risks the system won't integrate properly, and so on.

To reduce risk, we must get feedback—and as early as possible. The way we get feedback is to create a working version of the system at regular intervals—per release in terms of the earlier planning discussion. By doing this, we ensure we know what risks the project is really facing and are able to take appropriate mitigating action. At the same time, incremental development forces the team through the full project life cycle at regular intervals, thus offering the team the opportunity to learn from its mistakes before it's too late.

Three Types of Release

At this point, you may be beginning to wonder about the overheads associated with all these software releases. It's important to understand that all releases are not full production releases. Following the principle of three types of release, a release increment may culminate in

- An internal release, seen only by the development team, which is used to mitigate team- and technology-related risks
- A customer-visible investigative release (a prototype in some circumstances) given to the customer to play with, which is used to mitigate usability- and functionality-related risks
- A customer-visible production release, which is intended to be used "in anger"

While a production release may have higher overheads associated with it (full system and acceptance testing, production of user manuals and user training, etc.), the overheads associated with other types of release can be kept to a minimum. It's not that there isn't some cost involved—as you'll see later—it's just that we consider this cost to be acceptable given the benefits.

Rotting Software

More traditional (nonagile) software development life cycles generally end with a large and somewhat undefined phase called "maintenance" (which developers often strive to avoid like the plague). Maintenance projects tend to focus on two types of work: fixing bugs and generating new requirements. These bear not a passing resemblance to some of the activities that will be identified during detailed release planning.

One of the major problems associated with software maintenance is design decay. Software design is fundamentally an optimization problem based on a defined set of functional and nonfunctional requirements. During design, we try to come up with the software structure that best implements these, making a multitude of trade-offs along the way. The "best" design solution is dependent on the requirements we're trying to implement. If the requirements change, the best solution also changes. During maintenance, slowly but surely, software rot often starts to set in, until eventually the software ends up so brittle that it becomes impossible to change without major additional costs being incurred.

Coming back to Agile ICONIX development, new requirements may have to be dealt with on a per-release basis. These may have been identified in the initial scoping plan, but deferred for later consideration due to their instability or low business priority, or perhaps they've only just been thought of. By adopting an iterative approach, we're running the risk of software rot setting in at a far earlier stage, unless we adopt some practices to stop this from happening.

We stop software rot by following the principle **plan to refactor when necessary**. Refactoring is a development technique involving changing the structure of a software system without changing its functionality.[9] We use refactoring to minimize software rot as new requirements come up.

1. Get a good understanding of the new requirement and the existing design.
2. Analyze the design and work out what changes need to be made to accommodate both the old and the new requirements.
3. Without adding the new functionality, implement the design changes and undertake (hopefully automated) regression testing to make sure the system hasn't been inadvertently broken.
4. Implement and test the new requirement.

Things get a little more hairy when populated databases are involved, and while a detailed discussion of these issues is beyond the scope of this chapter, this web page contains some help on the matter: `www.agiledata.org/essays/databaseRefactoring.html`.

---

9. Martin Fowler, *Refactoring: Improving the Design of Existing Code* (New York: Addison-Wesley, 1999).

No Free Lunches

Although this topic isn't discussed much by the more vociferous proponents of agile software development, it's perhaps apparent from our discussion of the need for refactoring that agile development comes with some costs of its own.

Some years ago, Barry Boehm published a famous paper in which he demonstrated that the cost of software change increased by an order of magnitude during each stage of the development life cycle (requirements, analysis, design, integration, testing, and live implementation). Proponents of methodologies such as XP claim that this "cost curve" has been flattened over the years by improved software development techniques. Although it is true to some degree that good design practices can and should be used to reduce the cost of change, there is very clearly a cost associated with refactoring: if we'd designed in the functionality up front, we wouldn't have to refactor our code at all!

Having said that, some refactoring is almost always necessary. Even if you did all analysis and design up front, you'd still need to refactor as the inevitable change requests appeared, and refactoring as a technique clearly mitigates the risk of accepting change—something we try to do during Agile ICONIX developments. So we're faced with a trade-off expressed in the planning principle **trade-off the costs and benefits of incremental development**.

All Changes Are Not Equal

Following on from this, it's all the more important to understand that some changes will have a high cost associated with them. These changes are most likely related to implementing nonfunctional requirements, such as the need for concurrent multiuser access, security, auditing, and so forth, late in the day.

The costs associated with such changes are high because they cut right across the software, unlike pure functional changes that are likely to be localized. Changing a flat-file, single-user system into a multiuser relational database system is no trivial task, and doing so will affect the majority of components in the system. The more of a system that has been written, the greater the cost of these changes will be, which leads us to our next principle: **consider high-impact design decisions during early iterations**. Note that as **the customer dictates priority**, you will likely need to discuss trade-offs with him. And remember, **try to get it right the first time**. Don't just assume that because you can refactor later you don't have to try to get it right early in the project.

Does Size Matter?

During the earlier discussion, we mentioned that the ideal release size is still the subject of some debate. Agile proponents suggest release durations of a couple of weeks to a couple of months, with a preference for the shorter timescale. Closely related to this are the issues of just how much design we should do up-front and how to balance the cost and benefits of incremental development.

To blur the picture further, we could undertake, say, a month of pure up-front analysis and design while simultaneously doing some architectural investigation, and deliver our working software in two weekly releases thereafter. But the questions still remain: just how much up-front design should we do, and how long should our release increments be?

There are, unfortunately, no simple, formulaic answers to these questions. We have to consider the particular risks a project faces, the stability and business importance of a given set of requirements, external constraints like the ideal time to market, and so on.

However, pulling together some of the issues discussed in this chapter, we recommend the following process:

1. Undertake a project risk analysis, and ensure that early releases are targeted at getting feedback on these risks, noting that these releases are likely to culminate in either internal or investigative releases of the system. Determine which risks you really need to mitigate using incremental delivery and which you're prepared to "take a punt" on.

2. Ensure you have a good understanding of the high-impact decisions your project faces, and try to schedule work on these aspects of the system during the early releases.

3. Consider, with your customer, which requirements are the most stable and business critical, and try to schedule the first production release to accommodate these. Try to avoid dealing with unstable requirements early on.

4. Try, in parallel with the activities in steps 1 and 2, to do enough up-front analysis and design of stable requirements to reduce the cost of refactoring to a minimum. If this starts to look like it's going to take too long (say, over a month), schedule a number of analysis and design activities as the project progresses.

5. Try to keep the time to each production release to a minimum, and if possible undertake a production release at least every 3 months.

6. Try to keep release duration as short as possible (2–6 weeks), but not so short as to deliver nothing of concrete value. (Note that not every release increment has to culminate in a production release.) Where possible, keep consistent release duration to establish a project rhythm.

So on a low-technology-risk, single-user Windows application with about ten use cases, two experienced developers, and a customer who is bright on ideas but bad on detail, we might do a week or so of up-front analysis and design, followed by 2-week releases each delivering, say, two or three use cases' worth of functionality for the customer to review, with a full production release every couple of months.

On a higher-technology-risk, large project, with a dedicated and capable customer, a stable set of requirements, and a team of bright but inexperienced developers, we might undertake two technology verification releases of about 2 weeks. In these releases, we'd also round-trip the whole development process, delivering some functionality at the end of each to make sure the team understands just how its analysis feeds into the design and then into the code. As we became confident that the team members understood this, we could undertake some larger chunks (say 1 month) of analysis and design to reduce the need for refactoring, then deliver the system in functional chunks every month, targeting a production release for every 3 months.

■ **Tip** Always finish a release increment with a formal review to see what was implemented and how the last increment could have been improved. The postmortem aspect of projects is often missed because of time constraints, but without a review (even a short one), it is awfully hard to improve your process.

Summary

In this chapter, we discussed how planning an agile software development involves understanding and mitigating risk, while trading off the benefits of this against the costs it incurs. We suggested a number of agile planning principles to assist in this process, and we outlined a broad approach to adopt when considering how to plan your project.

Here are the top 10 principles for planning an Agile ICONIX project:

10. **Plan in appropriate detail**, meaning in depth for the short term and in broad strokes for the long term.

9. **Negotiate with scope** when faced with an imposed deadline.

8. **The customer dictates priority**. The customer decides what should be implemented and when.

7. **The plan follows reality** using detailed release plans.

6. **Feedback is vital**. Plan to get feedback to mitigate your risks.

5. **Try to get it right the first time**. Don't just assume you can refactor your way out of trouble later.

4. **Use three types of release**: internal, investigative, and production.

3. **Plan to refactor when necessary** to stop design rot from setting in.

2. **Trade-off the costs and benefits of incremental development**.

1. **Consider high-impact design decisions during early iterations**.

CHAPTER 10

Persona Analysis

In this chapter, we show how an important interaction design technique, *persona analysis*, can be used in tandem with ICONIX Process to help create a more focused product.

A *persona* is a description of a fictional person. The person is given a name and a brief description of his or her job, goals and aspirations, level of ability—anything that might be relevant to how that person uses and perceives the product you're designing.

The approach that this chapter proposes makes actors more concrete, more tangible for project stakeholders (the businesspeople—usually nontechnical—who must contribute to and understand the use cases). Many people find actors and use cases too abstract, so this chapter addresses the issue head-on.

Extending ICONIX Process with Persona Analysis

An important part of ICONIX Process involves doing some rapid prototyping of the proposed system. This helps the product at several levels: the technical design level (exploring the system's design and proving it with code early on), the interaction design level (thinking about how the user will interact with the system), and the requirements level (eliciting correct requirements from the customer by showing her what *could* be produced for her).

PERILS OF THE GUI PROTOTYPE

There are also some dangers with GUI prototyping, in particular the following:

- Unless the team (and customer and project manager) is very disciplined, it's tempting to take the prototype, polish it up a bit, and call it the "released system." We show a more controlled and disciplined way of doing this in the mapplet example in Part 2 of this book.
- The customer may see the prototype as a completed project and then get upset that the project is actually going to take months to complete. This issue can be mitigated by setting expectations appropriately, for example, by making sure the prototype looks and feels like a prototype (for an example of this, see Figure 1-2 in Chapter 1, which shows a screenshot using the Napkin Look & Feel).

Interaction design is an important and oft-neglected part of software development. Often, it's applied to a project as an afterthought: "Right. We've created our system; now let's make it look nice." Of course, interaction design is about much more than just the look of a product's UI. It's about how the user will interact with the system to achieve his goals. It's also about analyzing exactly what those goals are.

In this chapter, we look at a specific interaction design artifact, the persona, and examine how it can be applied to ICONIX Process. In so doing, we define an extension to ICONIX Process intended for projects that require a large amount of interaction design. This process would benefit products that are being targeted at multiple customers, because the techniques described in this chapter help to keep the UI focused on a small group of users. Having said that, the process should also benefit custom business software projects.

We'll write some personas for the mapplet example (these personas were used to help drive release 2 of the mapplet; see Chapter 8) and examine how these personas affect some of the use cases. As you saw in Chapter 8, this work formed the basis for the second release of the mapplet.

The Three Pieces of the Jigsaw Puzzle

Use cases have been around for a long time and have pretty much become the de facto method for specifying behavioral requirements. And yet despite this, people still struggle with use cases because they find them too abstract. Use cases have a lot of value to add, but we need to get better at writing them. One way to do this is to make the use case writing process more concrete through the use of personas and scenarios.

The result of combining personas with use case scenarios is a practice that is surprisingly well-geared toward getting the product design right, by identifying the user's goals and designing the product UI around those goals.

Before we launch back into the mapplet example, it's worth briefly defining the three items with which we're extending ICONIX Process: interaction design, personas, and interaction scenarios.

Interaction Design

Interaction design is the art and science of designing a product around the user's needs. The goals of interaction design are pragmatic and incredibly relevant in today's software industry: to design a product that is easy to use, learnable, and eminently suited to the person using it. (If you're interested in interaction design, the book *Interaction Design: Beyond Human-Computer Interaction*[1] is as good a place to start as any other.)

The effect of interaction design is most obvious with the design of physical devices (e.g., a portable MP3 player). If it's designed for, say, Neo (a techno-geek), it will be covered in tiny buttons, LCD displays, and connectors. It will probably also be highly programmable. If it's designed for Arthur (an arthritic late-adopter who listens to Gershwin and not much else), it will consist mostly of a big Start/Stop button.

A key stage of interaction design is to define a small set of target users: personas.

Personas

Personas, as an interaction design tool, were first introduced by Alan Cooper in his book *The Inmates Are Running the Asylum: Why High Tech Products Drive Us Crazy and How to Restore the Sanity*.[2] He also describes them in more detail in *About Face 2.0: The Essentials of Interaction Design*.[3] Also see Karl Wiegers' book *Software Requirements, Second Edition*.[4]

As described earlier, a persona is a description of a fictional person. The persona is a "typical" end user at whom the software is being targeted. In UML terms, a persona can be thought of as an instance of an actor.

Matt describes combining persona analysis with use cases in his article titled "Interaction Design: Persona Power."[5] The approach proposed by Matt involves using personas to drive the UI. The approach described in this chapter, though similar to Matt's, has more to do with using personas to identify specific features.

Interaction Scenarios

In ICONIX Process, use case scenarios are normally written in a very minimal format (which is especially useful when you have 500 use cases to write!). In this chapter, we introduce slightly "fatter" versions of use case scenarios that are intended to explore in more detail the goals that the user is trying to achieve. We call these fatter scenarios *interaction*

---

1. Jennifer Preece, Yvonne Rogers, and Helen Sharp, *Interaction Design: Beyond Human-Computer Interaction* (Hoboken, NJ: John Wiley & Sons, 2002).
2. Alan Cooper, *The Inmates Are Running the Asylum: Why High Tech Products Drive Us Crazy and How to Restore the Sanity* (Indianapolis, IN: Sams Publishing, 1999).
3. Alan Cooper and Robert Reimann, *About Face 2.0: The Essentials of Interaction Design* (Hoboken, NJ: John Wiley & Sons, 2003).
4. Karl E. Wiegers, *Software Requirements, Second Edition* (Redmond, WA: Microsoft Press, 2003).
5. Matt Stephens, "Interaction Design: Persona Power," *Software Development Magazine*, March 2004.

scenarios, because they explore the reasons driving the user's interaction with the system. As such, interaction scenarios are heavily biased toward the user's actions.

A use case typically describes the user interacting with the system and therefore consists of "user action/system response" in roughly equal measure. An interaction scenario, however, consists of much more detail about the user's actions. We'll explore interaction scenarios with some examples later in this chapter.

Interaction scenarios aren't the end product, though. (And you probably wouldn't want to write 500 of them, as they tend to be quite detailed.) They are, instead, a means to an end: transitory artifacts intended to get us to our first goal: the much leaner software use case from which we can derive our sequence diagrams. This process is shown in Figure 10-1.

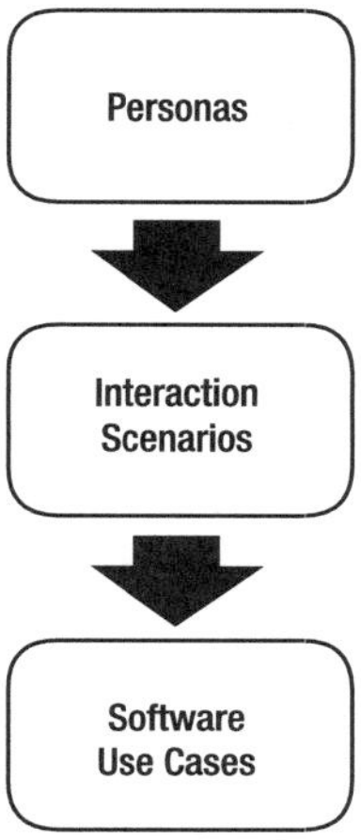

Figure 10-1. *Personas feed into interaction scenarios, which feed into use case scenarios.*

The names of the interaction scenarios are individual instances of the use case. For example, a use case called "Find Nearest Hotel to Specific Location" could include an interaction scenario called "Find Nearest Hilton to My Meeting." However, we wouldn't also go on to write "Find Nearest Hyatt to My Meeting," "Find Nearest Sheraton to My Meeting," and so on (all the instances). We would just write one or two representative interaction scenarios.

Personas are also used to identify the more abstract actors, which we can then put to use in our use cases (see Figure 10-2). Note that in interaction design, sometimes the opposite approach is preached: using abstract actors to identify concrete personas. Either approach works well given the right circumstances. It's generally better to look at your own project and use the approach that's easier for you.

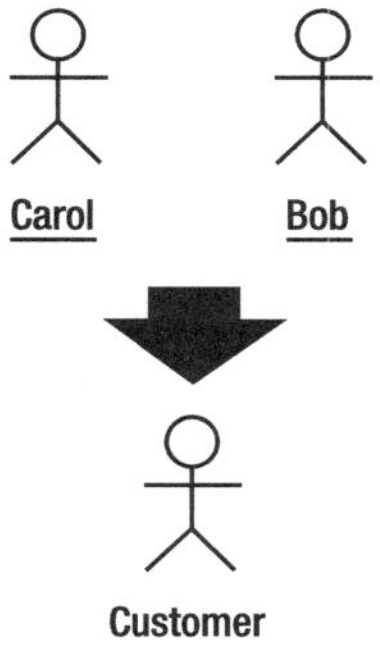

Figure 10-2. *Personas identify actors.*

For the remainder of this chapter, we'll walk through some examples to illustrate how the combined persona analysis/use case process works.

Building the UI Around a Target User

The level of detail that we put in the website, and in particular in the search function, is dependent to a large extent on the types of users at whom the website is being targeted. This is an ideal opportunity to define our first persona!

If we have a marketing department that has readily produced some user demographics, then that information can be used (at a very broad level) to get us started. For example, we might already know that the most common user will be a vacationer in her late twenties to early thirties. Plus, we might have some details about the user's typical occupation, what her likely goals for using the website are, and so on. That isn't the whole story, of course—we don't want to base our persona just on marketing statistics! To get a realistic story of our target user, we also need to interview real-life users and build up a complete picture. We can then boil this mass of real-world information down to a more concise description of our target user. So, here's the persona for Carol:

> *Carol is single and in her late twenties. She's heading over to this year's Mardi Gras in New Orleans. She knows that she's going to be out partying, and she wants a hotel with a spa (where she can get a massage), an indoor pool, and a Jacuzzi. Because she's on a budget, she wants to stay at a hotel in the midrange price band, and she wants it located on Bourbon Street. So she's interested in amenities, price, and location.*

It's vitally important to write the persona before we write the interaction scenarios, because the interaction scenarios will be written in the context of the persona. This is an important point: whereas normally a use case scenario refers to "the user," our interaction scenarios are going to refer to Carol by name. They're also going to be driven by Carol's goals.

This approach helps to keep the use cases focused, because we're writing them with a specific user in mind. You'd be surprised how differently an interaction scenario can turn out when it's based around different people with different backgrounds, motives, and levels of ability.

Writing Interaction Scenarios to Validate the Existing System

With the mapplet, because we're extending what is now an existing system, we'll start with an interaction scenario that covers the basic functionality from release 1. This serves as a sanity check, proving that what the team has created so far is correct for the users' needs. It also forms a jumping-off point, a "base camp" for adding new interaction scenarios that describe the new features we want for release 2.

So without further rambling, here's the basic interaction scenario for probably the most common mapplet activity: finding the nearest hotel to a specific location. As described earlier, interaction scenarios are specific instances of a use case description, so they appear as part of a use case.

Use Case: "Search for a Hotel Using the Mapplet"

Interaction Scenario: Carol goes to New Orleans for Mardi Gras

Persona: Carol

Carol visits `http://smartmaps.vresorts.com`. She moves her mouse over the New Orleans icon, sees the map tip displaying the names of the individual destinations in that region, drills down into the Map Destination page for Louisiana, and clicks the Show Map button next to New Orleans. The system displays a map of the French Quarter along with check boxes for price-band filtering, check boxes for amenity filtering, and a pop-up menu showing a list of hotel chains.

Carol deselects the Luxury price band, since she's on a budget; checks the boxes next to Bar/Lounge, Pool, Fitness Center or Spa, and Room Service; and then clicks the Update Map button. The system queries the hotel database and displays icons for all hotels that match her search criteria, along with a legend below the map, which specifies the active filtering criteria. One of the hotels is on Bourbon Street, which is where Carol wants to stay. She selects the Ramada Plaza Inn on Bourbon Street, and then she clicks the View Hotel Brochure link in the hotel information pop-up window. After viewing the brochure, she clicks the Make Reservation button and books a room.

Alternate Scenario: None of the hotels near Bourbon Street is quite right for Carol's needs (they're too expensive), so she zooms out to find some cheaper hotels in a slightly wider search area.

The screenshot in Figure 10-3 shows release 1 of the mapplet in action. This can be used as a form of validation (a visual acceptance test) by comparing it with the prototype screenshot shown back in Figure 7-1.

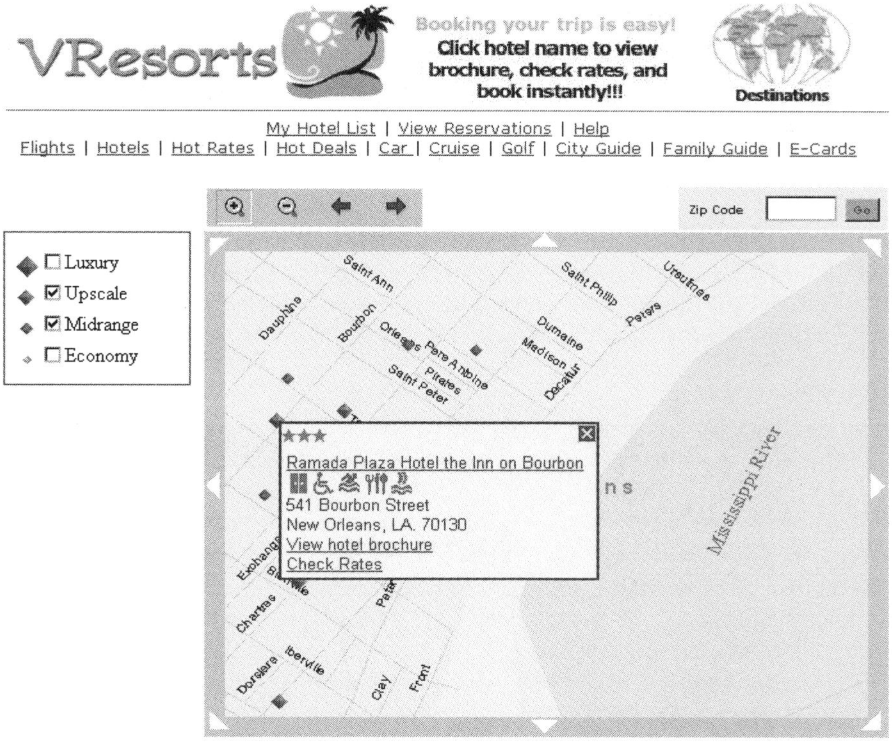

Figure 10-3. *Carol finds a hotel right on Bourbon Street!*

So it looks as if we're in pretty good shape for the second release. No major changes to the existing system are required. However, there are still several new features that we want to add to the mapplet, so we need to write some scenarios that describe these new features.

Using Interaction Scenarios to Describe New Features

Release 1 covered the common or garden-variety vacationer (booking vacations being the most common usage of the VResorts site). For release 2, we add slightly more esoteric (but still useful) functionality that enables the website to cover a broader range of customers.

Let's now introduce our second persona, Bob, who represents this new breed of customer:

> *Bob, who is a frequent traveler, has a Hilton Honors account. He wants to stay at a Hilton hotel whenever possible because he's saving his Hilton points for a trip to Hawaii. So he wants a "Show Me the Nearest Hilton to My Meeting" capability. Unlike Carol, Bob's on an expense account, so he's not concerned about price-band filtering as much as he is about which hotel chain he stays at. He also wants quick access to driving directions to his business-meeting site.*

It looks as if Bob's search requirements are different from Carol's. Bob already knows the location of the hotel at which he wants to stay, and he's looking for a hotel from a specific hotel chain (Hilton) near that location, so he'll go directly to it. Carol, on the other hand, also knows the area in which she wants to stay, but she's more concerned with specific amenities (spa, bar, etc.) than which chain the hotel belongs to.

We can describe Bob's interaction either as alternate scenarios in the same use case as Carol's or as an entirely separate use case. It really depends how different their behavior is. The main thing, however, is to not spend ages deciding which way to go. Pick a method and go with it. As you start to flesh out the scenarios, it will quickly become obvious whether or not they belong in the same use case.

■ **Modeling Tip** In true agile tradition, nothing is ever set in stone. You evolve the model as you go along, iterating back and forth, and moving pieces around until it all makes sense.

For our example, both Bob and Carol are searching for a hotel, so that suggests that they need to share the same use case. In fact, there's another similarity: they're both looking for a hotel near some location or other. Carol is searching for a hotel near Bourbon Street for Mardi Gras, and Bob is searching for a hotel near his San Diego business-meeting location (as we'll see in the following interaction scenario). So for now, let's add Bob's search as another interaction scenario to the same use case that we added Carol's interaction scenario to (the "Search for a Hotel Using the Mapplet" use case).

Use Case: "Search for a Hotel Using the Mapplet"

Interaction Scenario: Bob books a business trip to San Diego

Persona: Bob

Bob travels a lot on business and has a meeting in San Diego. He wants to stay at a Hilton hotel because he's earning frequent traveler points and is close to getting a free weekend in Hawaii. He visits the VResorts San Diego Map Destination page and clicks Show Map. Then he types **San Diego** in the City field, chooses Hilton from the pop-up menu of hotel chains, and clicks the Update Map button. The system searches the hotel database and displays a citywide map showing all Hilton hotels, along with a legend showing the active filter criteria underneath the map. Bob browses over the Hilton hotels, clicks the View Brochure link on the one he wants, and books his reservation.

Alternate Scenario: Bob knows his client's zip code, so after generating the citywide display as just described, he types it into the Zip box and clicks the Zoom To button. The system displays a map showing all Hilton hotels in the target zip code. If no Hilton hotels are found, Bob clicks the Zoom Out icon until the nearest one shows up. After he finds a Hilton hotel, he clicks the View Brochure link on the hotel pop-up and books his reservation.

While adding this scenario for Bob, we also thought of some additional alternate scenarios. Let's add those in (associated with Bob rather than Carol for now, because we're still in a Bob frame of mind):

Alternate Scenario: Incomplete address. Bob knows his client's zip code but doesn't have the complete meeting address.

Alternate Scenario: No Hiltons found within default AOI. The system displays the map with no hotel icons. Bob enlarges the AOI by clicking the Zoom Out button. The system requeries and displays some hotels on the map. Bob also has the option to pan (scroll) the map.

Alternate Scenario: Bob wants driving directions. He clicks the Get Driving Directions link. The system remembers the meeting address that Bob entered on the Query Filter screen and displays the Driving Directions screen, with the hotel address and the meeting address prepopulated, and Get Directions to This Address buttons underneath each address. Bob clicks one of the Get Directions to This Address buttons, and step-by-step directions are displayed in the Driving Directions screen.

This new scenario extends the existing map tip feature from release 1: the ability to display a rollover map tip (pop-up note) with hotel links. The map tip is extended with a new hyperlink to get driving directions. For planning purposes, these features could be listed as follows:

1. Display a rollover map tip (pop-up note) with hotel links.
2. Get driving directions to a hotel.

When the new feature is implemented (check the release plan to find out in which release), the only code that needs to change from release 1 should be the map tip display code, which simply gets another link added to it. Extensive refactoring of the release 1 code should be avoidable.

Although the Get Driving Directions feature is a built-in feature of the ArcGIS Server software and initially looked like low-hanging fruit, this feature was ultimately deferred due to schedule constraints imposed by publishing the mapplet design in the book you're reading.

Normally, we would also include all the possible failure modes in the list of alternate scenarios. The failure scenarios describe how the system should react when things go wrong (e.g., when a search fails because the database connection has been lost).

When do you have enough alternate scenarios? The rule of thumb is simply this: when you and your team can't think of any more. That is to say, wring the towel dry, and brainstorm as many rainy-day scenarios as you can think of (without the scenarios getting too contrived, of course). A more concrete technique is to look at each step in the main scenario and see if it can fail, or make the next steps fail.

Alternate scenarios are quick to write, and yet they're a very effective way of exploring all the different ways that the system might be used. Combining personas with use cases provides an additional means of discovering alternate scenarios. These will prove invaluable later on when we get to the design, because the design is produced with the alternate cases accounted for.

Using Interaction Design to Identify Alternate Scenarios

In his book *Writing Effective Use Cases*, Alistair Cockburn writes

> *Write down what the system detects, not just what happened. Don't write "Customer forgets PIN." The system can't detect that they forgot their PIN. Perhaps they walked away, had a heart attack, or are busy quieting a crying baby. What does the system detect in this case? Inaction, which really means it detects that a time limit was exceeded. Write "Time limit exceeded waiting for PIN to be entered," or "PIN entry time-out."* [6]

This is absolutely correct for when we're writing a "normal" software use case. But how do we identify that there needs to be a PIN entry time-out in the first place? This is a prime example of how interaction design can be used as a means of identifying use case scenarios and failure conditions.

We want to end up with a use case scenario that describes what the system detects ("PIN entry time-out"), not what's happening externally ("user quieting a crying baby"). However, to get there, we can use personas, various UI diagrams, and interaction scenarios. The interaction scenarios absolutely would include things like "user quieting a crying baby," because we're interested in describing the user's world (i.e., what's going on around the user while he's using the system). This gives us a useful perspective on how the user is really going to be interacting with our product. It's also a good way of identifying alternate scenarios and failure modes we might otherwise have missed.

Recall the process shown in Figure 10-1. We start by writing lots of interaction scenarios for our target persona (possibly identifying new personas in the process). Once we have a decent set of scenarios, we can begin to extract the more abstract use cases from these scenarios. The purpose now is to lose all the "external" descriptions that have been so useful up until this moment for driving the UI design but that would only clutter the finished use case text.

This approach is the reverse of what you'd normally expect—that is, we'd usually start by identifying the use cases, and then break these down into more concrete scenarios. Instead, we're starting by identifying the concrete (personas and scenarios) and using them to identify the abstract (actors and use cases).

In practice, it's beneficial to combine these approaches. A brainstorming session in which the team identifies both scenarios and use cases (having first settled on one or two personas) can produce a thorough analysis of the application that we're about to design. Product design at these early stages of development is an organic process, and you don't strictly complete one activity before moving on to the next. Instead, one activity feeds incrementally into the other, and vice versa.

---

6. Alistair Cockburn, *Writing Effective Use Cases* (New York: Addison-Wesley, 2000), (New York: Addison-Wesley, 2000).

Keeping a Tight Rein on Complexity

As we identify more personas, scenarios, actors, and use cases, the product inevitably becomes more complex. It's easy to lose track of our original "clear and simple" product design. We can manage this design entropy, to an extent, by grouping and rearranging the various artifacts, and by expanding individual scenarios into additional use cases where necessary.

But how do we know when to split up personas or roll scenarios into new use cases? From an interaction design standpoint, the process is all about discovering how different the UI needs to be for each target user.

In fact, having identified our first-pass set of personas, there are four possible approaches that we can take depending on how different the personas are. The approaches are as follows (listed here in order, from most similar to most disparate. Not by coincidence, this list is also in order of complexity, from simplest to most complex):

1. Create just a single unified persona—an instance of one or more actors.
2. Create separate personas but define them as instances of the same actor (e.g., we can call the roles "bob : Customer" and "carol : Customer").
3. Create a separate actor for each persona. We'd do this if the personas were different enough to warrant writing separate use cases, not just additional scenarios.
4. Create separate UIs for each persona (essentially, different products).

Approach 1 is the Holy Grail to aspire to. Our goal is always to make the product as focused and simple as possible, and the best way to do this is to design the product around a single target user (i.e., a persona). Of course, this isn't always going to be possible. As the product becomes more complex, we identify more target users. This complexity is managed by moving gradually (or is that grudgingly?) to the next approach in the list, and the next, and so on. As we do this, we end up with a more complex application. By actively controlling these steps as we design the product UI, we always keep the product as focused as possible and just complex enough for what its target users are trying to achieve.

Using Interaction Design to Identify Actors and Use Cases

The techniques described in this chapter can be used to identify concrete examples of the problem domain (represented as personas and interaction scenarios). These can then drive the identification of the more abstract concepts of use cases and actors.

The process is as follows:

1. Identify the personas. Write a short description of each persona.
2. Identify the interaction scenarios.
3. Combine the interaction scenarios into use cases. Give each use case a basic scenario and several alternate scenarios.
4. Flesh out the interaction scenario descriptions.
5. Use the personas to identify the actors. (This sounds counterintuitive, but in practice you start by identifying target users [ideally by interviewing real end-users of the system] and then grouping them into different classifications or roles, thus identifying actors.)
6. Use the interaction scenarios to write the "real" use case scenarios.

The first step is also the most important. The personas drive the entire product design, so it's vital to get this step right. As you work your way through the scenarios and get a better understanding of how the product needs to work (from the user's point of view), you may well need to revisit the personas or even rewrite them altogether.

In many cases, steps 2 and 3 could be reversed. In other words, you might identify the scenarios first and then group them into use cases, or you might identify the use cases first and then identify further alternate scenarios for each use case. The examples we gave earlier used the latter approach. In a large project, it's likely that you would use both approaches combined, identifying the problem domain and filling in the details as you go. Discovery of behavioral requirements is an organic, evolutionary process.

Steps 1 through 3 should take place in parallel—you're identifying the personas as you identify the interaction scenarios. In fact, the whole process is highly iterative. While it's important to get the personas right as early as possible, they're never set in stone.

Step 4 should be left until you have most of the actors and use cases identified. It can be hard work producing the scenario descriptions, so it's better to do this after they've all been identified.

The Finished Use Case

Let's see how our overall finished use case looks. As you can see in Figures 10-4 through 10-7, the finished product follows the steps described in the interaction scenarios to the letter. Not bad!

Use Case: "Search for a Hotel Using the Mapplet"

Interaction Scenario: Carol goes to New Orleans for Mardi Gras

Persona: Carol

Carol visits `http://smartmaps.vresorts.com`. She moves her mouse over the New Orleans icon, sees the map tip displaying the names of the individual destinations in that region, drills down into the Map Destination page for Louisiana, and clicks the Show Map button next to New Orleans. The system displays a map of the French Quarter along with check boxes for price-band filtering, check boxes for amenity filtering, and a pop-up menu showing a list of hotel chains.

Carol deselects the Luxury price band, since she's on a budget; checks the boxes next to Bar/Lounge, Pool, Fitness Center or Spa, and Room Service; and then clicks the Update Map button. The system queries the hotel database and displays icons for all hotels that match her search criteria, along with a legend below the map, which specifies the active filtering criteria. One of the hotels is on Bourbon Street, which is where Carol wants to stay. She selects the Ramada Plaza Inn on Bourbon Street, and then she clicks the View Hotel Brochure link in the hotel information pop-up window. After viewing the brochure, she clicks the Make Reservation button and books a room.

Alternate Scenario: None of the hotels near Bourbon Street is quite right for Carol's needs (they're too expensive), so she zooms out to find some cheaper hotels in a slightly wider search area.

Interaction Scenario: Bob books a business trip to San Diego

Persona: Bob

Bob travels a lot on business and has a meeting in San Diego. He wants to stay at a Hilton hotel because he's earning frequent traveler points and is close to getting a free weekend in Hawaii. He visits the VResorts San Diego Map Destination page and clicks Show Map. Then he types **San Diego** in the City field, chooses Hilton from the pop-up menu of hotel chains, and clicks the Update Map button. The system searches the hotel database and displays a citywide map showing all Hilton hotels, along with a legend showing the active filter criteria underneath the map. Bob browses over the Hilton hotels, clicks the View Brochure link on the one he wants, and books his reservation.

Alternate scenario: Bob knows his client's zip code, so after generating the citywide display as just described, he types it into the Zip box and clicks the Zoom To button. The system displays a map showing all Hilton hotels in the target zip code. If no Hilton hotels are found, Bob clicks the Zoom Out icon until the nearest one shows up. After he finds a Hilton hotel, he clicks the View Brochure link on the hotel pop-up and books his reservation.

Alternate Scenario: Incomplete address. Bob knows his client's zip code but doesn't have the complete meeting address.

Alternate Scenario: No Hiltons found within default AOI. The system automatically zooms out until both the meeting address and the nearest Hilton hotel are visible on the map.

Alternate Scenario: Bob wants driving directions. He clicks the Get Driving Directions link. The system remembers the meeting address that Bob entered on the Query Filter screen and displays the Driving Directions screen, with the hotel address and the meeting address prepopulated, and Get Directions to This Address buttons underneath each address. Bob clicks one of the Get Directions to This Address buttons, and step-by-step directions are displayed in the Driving Directions window.

As you can see, the use case is quite wordy. For a large system, we definitely wouldn't want to write 500 or so of these. It's useful to take this approach for a fairly small cross-section of the use cases. Choose the use cases with care, though—you need to select the ones that will have the most influence on the product design.

Contrast this with the "Generate Hotel Map for AOI" software use case that we wrote in Chapter 6. The software use case was roughly equally balanced in terms of user/system actions. However, our new use case shown here was written as an exercise in interaction design, therefore it focuses more on the user's actions than on the system's responses.

Visual Acceptance Test for Release 2

The following screenshots (from release 2 of the mapplet) form a visual storyboard that matches the interaction scenarios described in the "Search for a Hotel Using the Mapplet" use case. Walking through the UI and comparing it directly with the use case scenarios (whether they're interaction scenarios or "normal" use case scenarios) can be used as validation that the finished UI matches the original spec (let's call this process *visual acceptance testing*). You can see most of the new functionality in release 2 by comparing the following screenshots with release 1 as shown in Figure 10-3.

Starting with Figure 10-4, Carol visits the U.S. map (text from the use case appears in the previous section):

> *Carol visits* `http://smartmaps.vresorts.com`. *She moves her mouse over the New Orleans icon, sees the map tip displaying the names of the individual destinations in that region . . .*

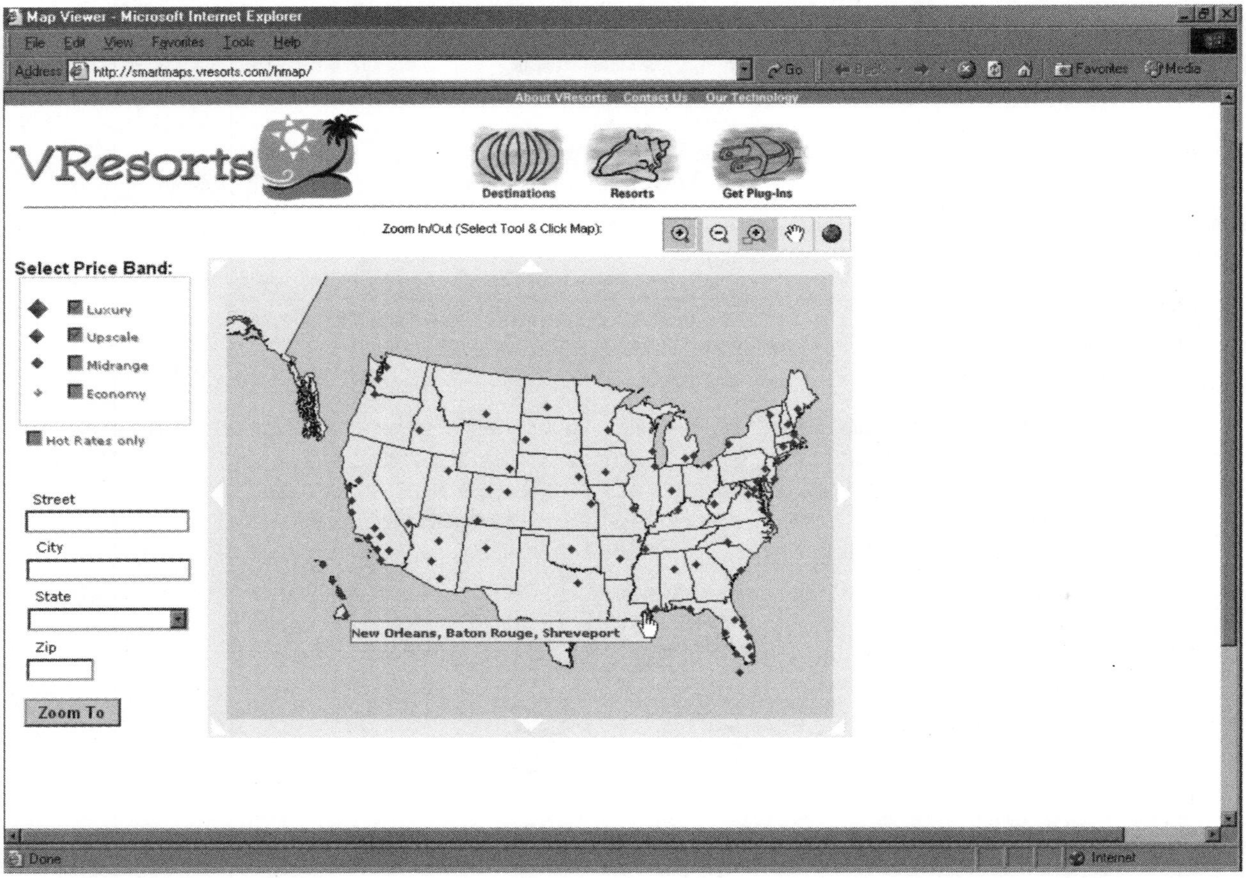

Figure 10-4. *Carol visits the U.S. map page.*

Then in Figure 10-5

The system displays a map of the French Quarter along with check boxes for price-band filtering, check boxes for amenity filtering, and a pop-up menu showing a list of hotel chains.

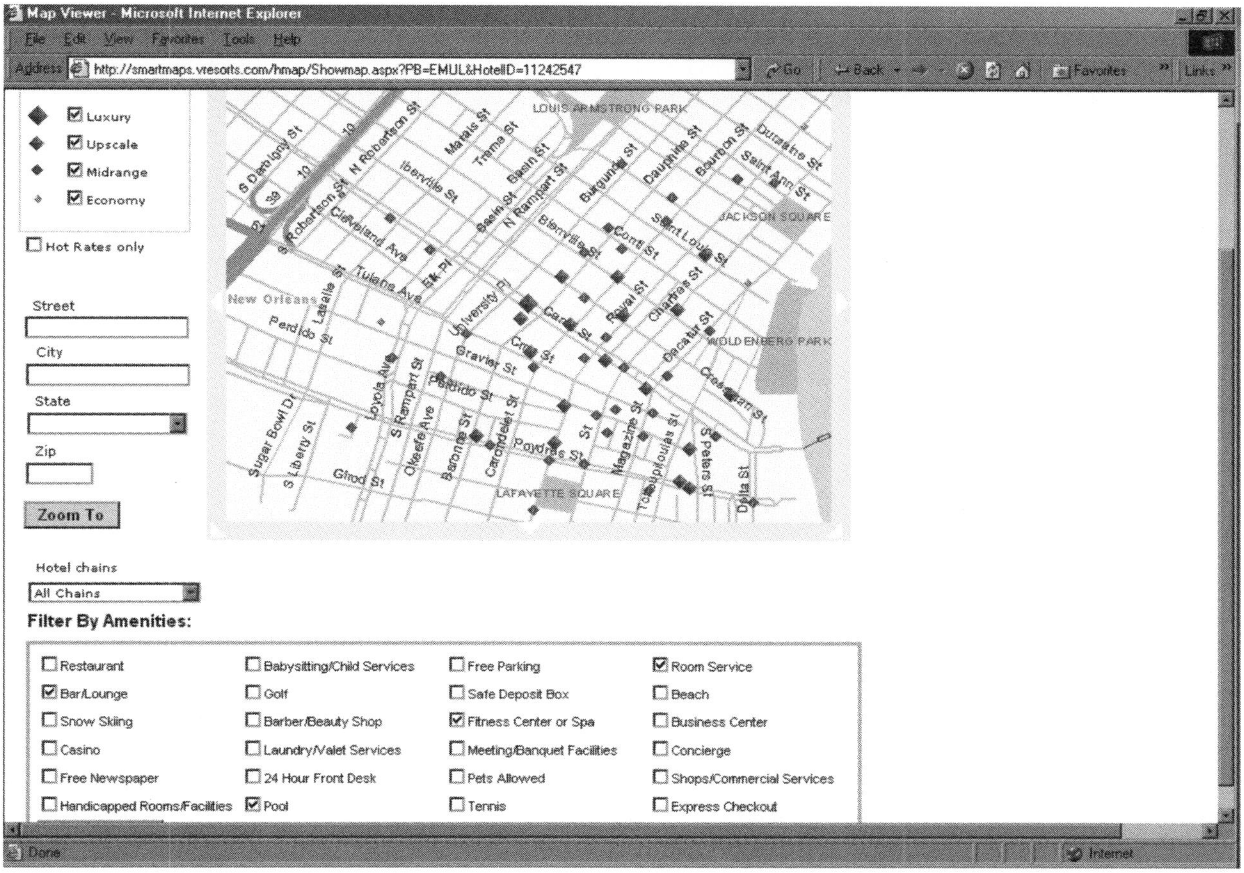

Figure 10-5. *The system displays a map of the French Quarter, and Carol selects the amenities she is looking for.*

And in Figure 10-6

The system queries the hotel database and displays icons for all hotels that match her search criteria, along with a legend below the map, which specifies the active filtering criteria. One of the hotels is on Bourbon Street, which is where Carol wants to stay. She selects the Ramada Plaza Inn on Bourbon Street . . .

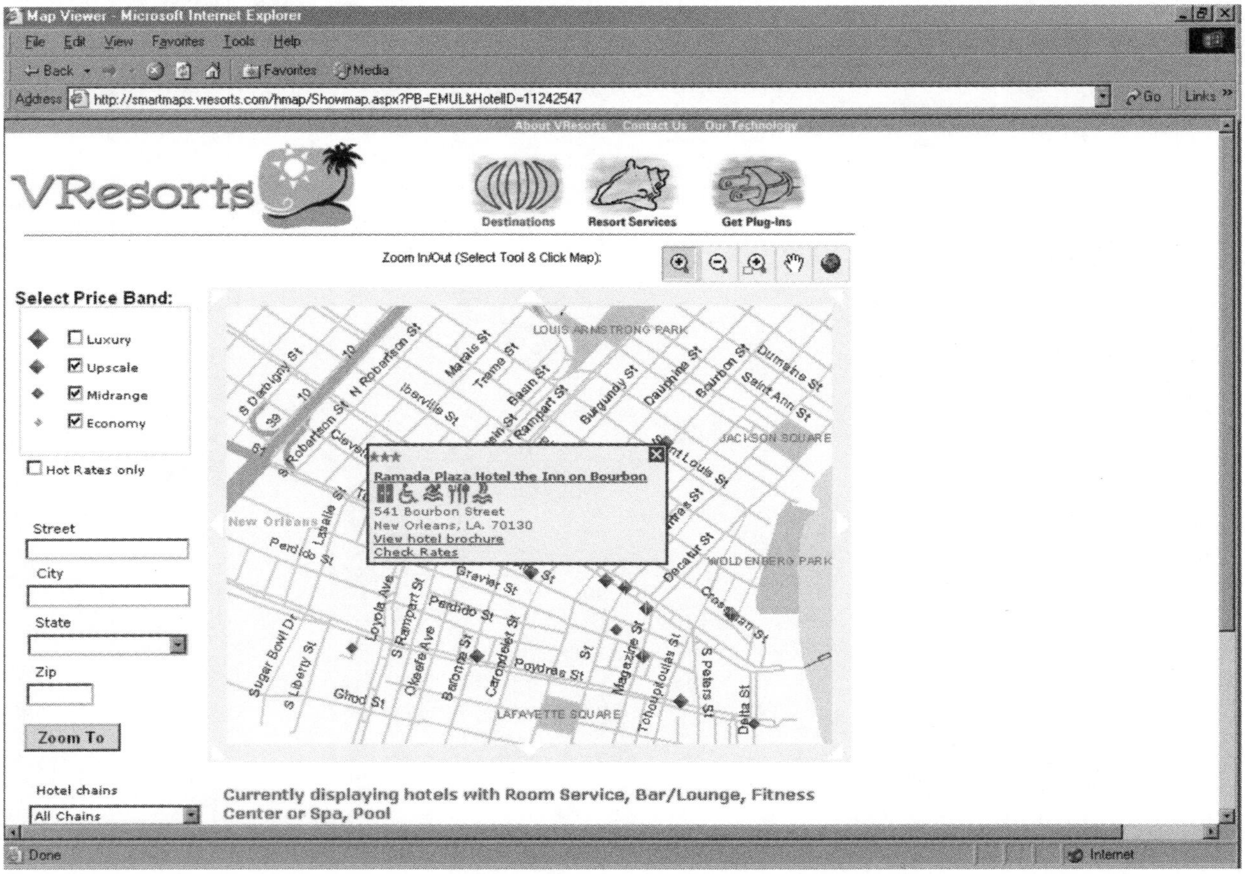

Figure 10-6. *Carol selects the Ramada Plaza Inn on Bourbon Street.*

Let's also take a quick look at the finished result for our alternate target user Bob (see Figure 10-7).

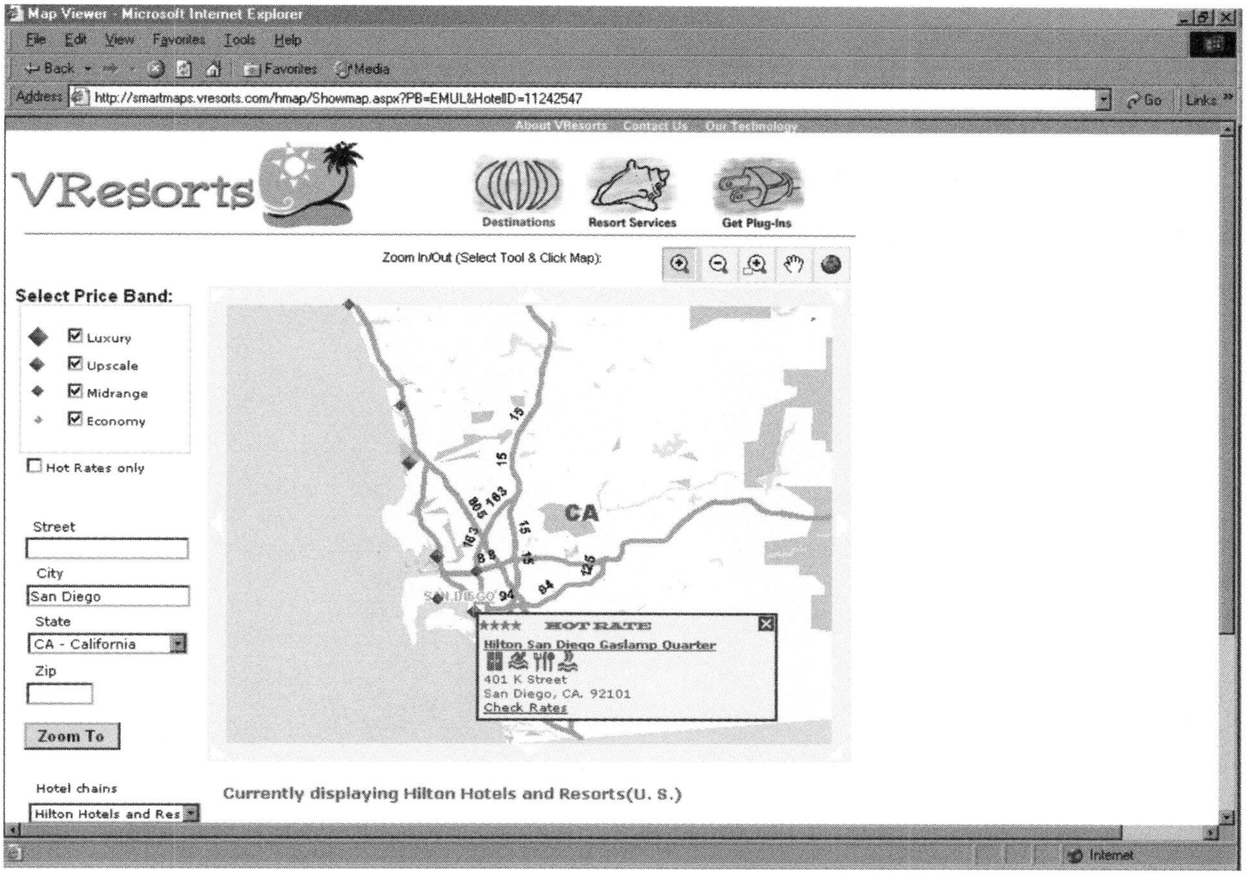

Figure 10-7. *Bob finds a Hilton hotel in San Diego.*

Summary

Persona analysis provides a compelling method of focusing the requirements for any new product. The technique works best when it's applied early in the project life cycle, because it tends to drive the requirements. On the mapplet project, the technique was applied early in release 2 (the first release being a prototype), and the result was that some useful requirements were identified that might otherwise have been missed.

Interaction design isn't just about designing the "look" of a user interface. It's also about designing the behavior—determining how the UI will behave and respond to user inputs. This is why interaction design and use cases work so well together, especially when combined with personas.

CHAPTER 11

A "Vanilla" Test-Driven Development Example

Unit testing has been around for a long time, but it gained in popularity with the advent of Extreme Programming (XP). One of the better ideas to emerge from XP is Test-Driven Development (TDD), an extension of unit testing to cover OO design by writing tests from the client code's perspective.

One of the problems with TDD *used without additional design and requirements testing techniques* is that it focuses on the smaller aspects of design (not a bad thing in itself), without looking more than a few inches ahead at a time (a very bad thing). TDD is most commonly used with XP, and even XP's "thought leaders" recommend that you do a small amount of UML modeling (or other form of up-front design) to complement the TDD design process and also write user acceptance tests which, for each user story, should describe a complete vertical slice of the system.

In fact, it's been widely recognized that TDD needs higher-level design in order to be really effective. Agile Modeling (AM), for example, incorporates this need into a management-oriented process. AM is primarily about promoting "agile teamwork," doing "just enough design," and so forth. But it doesn't go into detail about exactly how to incorporate UML modeling into TDD. So in this chapter and the next, we'll use a practical example to demonstrate how to model up-front using ICONIX Process and then do the detailed, code-level design using TDD.

In terms of design detail, ICONIX Process gets you from roughly 30,000 feet down to 100 feet. TDD is more about designing at 3 feet above sea level, dodging the waves, so this suggests that the two processes should work well together.

In this chapter, we'll provide a brief introduction to TDD and walk through a practical example with a travel theme. Then in the next chapter, we'll hit the Rewind button and show how the same example would have been approached using a combination of TDD and ICONIX Process.[1]

COMPARING APPLES AND TIGERS

As there's some major crossover between TDD and ICONIX Process, you might wonder why we would ever want to combine them on the same project.

Essentially, the processes differ in terms of the philosophy that drives them. TDD is mainly about designing interfaces by writing test code that uses those interfaces: *designing by intent.* On the other hand, ICONIX Process is about designing interfaces by drawing sequence diagrams that implement specific use case scenarios (i.e., designing the software around the user's goals): *use case–driven design.*

In other words, they address different aspects of the thought process that goes into creating a good design. So if we can find a way to combine the two in such a way that duplication of effort is eliminated, then we should end up with a powerful, rigorous design methodology.

1. You might find, as one of our technical reviewers did, that the vanilla TDD example we present in this chapter, without the benefit of any UML diagrams ("Just the code, please"), is a little bit hard to follow. In fact, we find it a bit hard to follow ourselves. That's why we propose using TDD in conjunction with ICONIX Process in the next chapter and explain how to do that. We think it's a lot easier to follow a minimalist set of well-defined modeling steps in advance of TDD.

A Brief Overview of TDD

It's worth stating up-front one of the main principles behind TDD: despite its emphasis on tests, it isn't primarily about testing. TDD is actually about designing.

Using TDD, you design code by writing code. While this sounds circular, it means that you write client test code that serves as both an example and a definition of what you want the object code to do. For example, if you were writing a hotel booking system, you would write tests for placing a booking, adding customer details, retrieving the details, and so on. More specifically, you write unit tests that test for the expected results of doing these things. So a unit test for placing a booking would involve placing the booking and then asserting that the booking was correctly placed in the system.

Knowing which tests to write is driven by the user stories (in XP) or the use cases (in ICONIX Process). As you'll see later in this chapter, the sequence diagrams also play a large part in determining the tests to write.

■ **Micro Testing** TDD is about designing at a very low level using fine-grained tests. In fact, there's a trend away from the term "unit testing" toward "micro testing." "Unit testing" is considered a bit vague, because the test for a large and badly written unit might also be large and badly written. "Micro testing" is more descriptive, in that these tests are meant to be very small.

Using TDD, as mentioned earlier, you're designing at a few feet above ground level. While this is fine for some projects, most of the time you'll need an additional design process that operates at a higher level. ICONIX Process is an ideal candidate for this.

There's some potential crossover in that ICONIX Process takes us to a very low-level design using sequence diagrams (by this stage, the designer/programmer is really thinking in code). We'll discuss how to splice the two processes at this level of crossover in Chapter 12.

TDD uses the YAGNI[2] principle for adding (or, more important, leaving out) features to code at two levels: requirements and design. Requirements-related features are left out on the basis that they're not needed now, so let's add them later. In TDD, this process is taken literally. That is, if there isn't a test to prove that something works, then we don't write the code; we write the test first. Using this process, tests actually drive the design.[3]

To demonstrate this, let's launch straight into an example using "vanilla" TDD. As you'll see, the process as applied here works but can be long-winded. In the next chapter, we'll repeat the example using a more effective mix of up-front design and TDD.

WHY WASN'T TDD USED ON THE MAPPLET PROJECT?

As the mapplet development progressed, one of the issues debated was whether it was necessary or important that the team adopt a test-driven strategy. TDD is a useful technique and a very hot topic these days, and its benefits are enumerated elsewhere in this chapter. Ultimately, it was decided that TDD wasn't a great fit with the mapplet project because it would involve a substantial amount of effort to introduce this practice into the middle of an ongoing release, and because the team felt that many of the potential problem areas might not be best addressed by unit testing (e.g., visual inspection of a large suite of test maps seemed best suited to testing compatibility across different web browsers and operating systems, and for coverage testing across North America).

One issue the team had was that TDD, despite its name, isn't primarily about testing. Of course, tests are a major part of it, but TDD is at its heart a design process, rather like ICONIX Process is a design process. Both processes take the design to the code level and provide techniques and best practices for designing clean, focused interfaces with modular, fine-grained classes and methods.

---

2. YAGNI is an acronym for *You Aren't Gonna Need It*. See `http://c2.com/cgi/wiki?YouArentGonnaNeedIt`.
3. By contrast, in ICONIX Process, use cases drive the design.

A Vanilla TDD Example

We've been using C# until now for the example mapplet code, so to even things out a little we'll switch to Java for this example. For our unit test framework, we'll use the near-ubiquitous JUnit.[4]

Let's say we're creating a web-based system for making hotel bookings that's intended for use by travel agents rather than "Joe Public" users.[5] As such, we'll need a way of managing customers, creating new bookings, and tracking or modifying the bookings afterward.

Written up as user stories, these requirements would be of the following form:

> *As a* <role>, *I would like* <feature> *so that I can* <value>.

For example:

> *As a travel agent, I would like a bookings facility so that I can book my customers into hotels.*

This would then be broken down into tasks as follows:

- Create a new customer.
- Create a hotel booking for a customer.
- Retrieve a customer (so that we can place the booking).
- Place the booking.

We could also have another user story for checking how many bookings have been placed:

> *As a travel agent, I would like to be able to check how many bookings a customer has so that I can bill him accordingly.*

We'll use this small set of requirements as the basis for our first release. (In fact, for this example, we'll just cover the first task, "Create a new customer.")

For this first release, we don't need to retrieve specific bookings or get a list of bookings for a customer. That would be in the next release (which, given that this is very limited functionality, would probably be as early as the next day!).

A nice benefit of TDD is that it encourages you to keep the presentation and model/controller code separate (ICONIX Process also does this by separating your classes into boundaries, controllers, and entities). While this makes the code easier to test (UI code is notoriously difficult to write automated tests for[6]), it also produces a cleaner design with reusable, highly modular code. From a practical point of view, this means that we end up with lots of micro-tested source code containing all the business logic, over which the UI is placed like a thin shell.

Using TDD (even on an XP project), it would be perfectly reasonable to hold a quick design workshop prior to beginning coding for the day. This could include UML diagrams, lines and boxes, and so on—whatever gets the team to start thinking like designers. For this example, we'll show the design emerge purely through the code and tests. This is primarily so that we can illustrate the contrast between vanilla TDD (seeing the design emerge by writing unit tests) and TDD combined with an up-front design process.

---

4. See `www.junit.org`. JUnit is part of a family of testing frameworks for different platforms, including CppUnit for C++ and NUnit for C#/.NET.
5. We'll take it as read that we've done the necessary persona design/role modeling to determine which are the most important user stories for the customer, as that aspect of software development is covered elsewhere in this book.
6. With the advent of GUI fixtures for the FIT framework (see `www.fitnesse.org`) and the Exactor framework from Exoftware (`www.exoftware.com`), both of which are open source, this is becoming a lot easier. Unlike the usual "record and play" type of GUI tester, these can be written up front and used to drive development.

PROPERTIES OF A GOOD STORY

User stories generally need to follow the criteria summarized by the INVEST acronym:

Independent: The user story doesn't rely on any other stories (see below).

Negotiable: There is a range of solutions here that the customer can choose from.

Valuable and **v**ertical: The user story has value for the customer and touches every layer of the system.

Estimable: It is possible (after negotiation) to put a time estimate on how long the user story will take to implement.

Small: The user story shouldn't take more than an iteration to implement.

Testable: We could easily write tests for this user story.

You may be thinking that the "Check how many bookings a customer has" story relies on the previous story, as you can hardly check the customer's bookings count if you haven't done the story to place bookings and create customers yet, but this is where the negotiations start.

The customer decides which story gets done first. Her tests and the functionality required to pass them at that time will determine the estimate for the story. It may be apparent to some that doing the other story first makes the greatest sense, but there are times when it doesn't. For example, it may be that the customer needs to demonstrate this functionality in order to sell the system.

It is possible to implement this story with just enough of the customer and bookings entities for it to be testable and demonstrable.

Our First Test: Testing for Nothingness

Before we can create any bookings, we will, of course, need to be able to create customers. For this purpose we'll use a CustomerManager class. Note this is really a bit of a leap on our part—following TDD to the letter, you might simply start with a class called CreateCustomer or CustomerCreator and its associated test class. But we know that pretty soon we're also going to need to add functions for deleting, retrieving, and counting customers, and that we would later need to refactor all of these into a single "home" or "controller" class, so (to shorten the example a bit) let's do that now.

Checking back to our shortlist of requirements in the previous section, for this first release we only need to be able to create new customers. We don't yet need the ability to retrieve or search for customers. But for the purposes of testing that adding customers works, we'll need to be able to retrieve customers as well (or at least count the number of customers that have been added to the database).

Here's our CustomerManagerTest class with its first test:

```
public class CustomerManagerTest extends TestCase {
    public CustomerManagerTest(String testName) {
        super(testName);
    }

    public static Test suite() {
        TestSuite suite = new TestSuite(CustomerManagerTest.class);
        return suite;
    }

    public void testCustomerCreated() {
        Customer customer = CustomerManager.create("bob");
        Customer found = CustomerManager.findCustomer("bob");
        assertEquals("Should have found Bob", customer, found);
    }
}
```

As you can see, we've straightaway defined two methods for the CustomerManager interface: `create(name)` and `findCustomer(name)`. First, let's try to compile the test class (e.g., using NetBeans, we simply hit F9). Naturally the compilation fails.

Tip Compilation is the first level of testing. It tells us that the classes and methods either do or don't exist. Imagine if you created tests for a class or method you hadn't yet implemented and it compiled without errors. There'd be something wrong there—obviously the class or method already exists, and it's much easier to rename it and fix things at this stage than it is to later try to figure out why the wrong method or class is being called.

Let's implement the two methods on CustomerManager in the simplest way possible (at this stage, we just want to get the test class compiling):

```
public class CustomerManager {
    public static Customer create(String name) {
        return null;
    }

    public static Customer findCustomer(String name) {
        return null;
    }
}
```

We also need a "skeleton" Customer class so that the code compiles:

```
public class Customer {
}
```

Let's run this test through JUnit's TestRunner. Note that what we're hoping for initially is a failure, because that verifies the test itself (it's a two-way process). We can then write the code to make the test pass, confident that the test works.

However, the output that we get from JUnit is as follows:

```
.
Time: 0

OK (1 test)
```

Rather surprisingly, our test passed, even though there isn't any code in there to create or retrieve a customer! So what's going on? Each method in CustomerManager is currently just returning null, but our unit test is checking for equality. In the eyes of JUnit, null equals null. But adding a Customer and then trying to retrieve it—and getting null for our efforts—really should cause a test failure. So let's add a test that makes this condition fail:

```
    public void testCustomerNotNull() {
        Customer customer = CustomerManager.create("bob");
        Customer found = CustomerManager.findCustomer("bob");
        assertNotNull("Retrieved Customer should not be null.", found);
    }
```

This still doesn't seem quite right. Our micro-test is actually testing two things here: the `create` method and the `findCustomer` method. However, it should be testing only the `create` method. So let's get rid of our new `testCustomerNotNull()` method—it just doesn't feel right—and redo our original `testCustomerCreated()` method. The test here should simply be to determine whether the returned customer value is null. Let's rewrite the test to do just that:

```
public void testCustomerCreated() {
    Customer customer = CustomerManager.create("bob");
    assertNotNull("New Customer should not be null.", customer);
}
```

Running CustomerManagerTest through JUnit's TestRunner now, we get a nice satisfying failure:

```
.F.
Time: 0
There was 1 failure:
1) testCustomerCreated(CustomerManagerTest)junit.framework.AssertionFailedError:
        New Customer should not be null.
        at CustomerManagerTest.testCustomerCreated(CustomerManagerTest.java:14)

FAILURES!!!
Tests run: 1,  Failures: 1,  Errors: 0
```

Now we have something to test against. When this test passes, it's a safe bet that the creating customers part of the system works. Later when we want to be able to retrieve customers, we can add in some methods to test for that (including the `testCustomerNotNull()` method).

At the moment, our `testCustomerCreated()` test method is still failing, so we need to do something about that straightaway. We'll add some code into CustomerManager:

```
public class CustomerManager {
    public static Customer create(String name) {
        return new Customer(name);
    }
}
```

Attempting to compile this fails because Customer needs a new constructor to take the name, so let's add that:

```
public class Customer {
    public Customer(String name) {
    }
}
```

Running this, our test passes.

So that's just about that, at least for the first task ("Create a new customer") on the list. Let's pick another task from the list: "Retrieve a customer." Ah, yes. We guess we'll need our `testCustomerNotNull()` method back now . . .

So we add that back into CustomerManagerTest and add the following method to CustomerManager:

```
public static Customer findCustomer(String name) {
    return new Customer("bob");
}
```

Okay, but that's cheating, right? Well, in theory at least, for a system that creates and deals with only one customer (who happens to be called "bob"), this is entirely sufficient. And at the moment, our unit tests are specifying a system that does exactly that. What we actually need is a test that tries adding a second customer. Remember, our goal here, as always, is to write a test that initially fails (to validate the test), so that we then write code to make it pass.

```
public class CreateTwoCustomersTest extends TestCase {
    private Customer bob;
    private Customer alice;

    public CreateTwoCustomersTest(java.lang.String testName) {
        super(testName);
    }

    public static Test suite() {
        TestSuite suite = new TestSuite(CreateTwoCustomersTest.class);
        return suite;
    }

    public void setUp() {
        bob = CustomerManager.create("bob");
        alice = CustomerManager.create("alice");
    }

    public void testBobNotNull() {
        Customer foundBob = CustomerManager.findCustomer("bob");
        assertNotNull("Bob should have been found.", foundBob);
    }

    public void testAliceNotNull() {
        Customer foundAlice = CustomerManager.findCustomer("alice");
        assertNotNull("Alice should have been found.", foundAlice);
    }
}
```

It's worth stressing again that the test methods are very fine-grained. As a general rule, each test method should contain only one "assert" statement (two at most), and it should test only one method on the class under test.

Tip If you find yourself adding more assert statements into one test method, you should think about splitting them into different methods (using `setUp()` and private member variables to create and track the test data). If you then find that `setUp()` is having to do different things for different tests, then immediately break the test class into two or more classes.

But that's all well and good. This test class actually passes when run:

```
..
Time: 0.01

OK (2 tests)
```

Evidently, just checking for null isn't enough to make the tests prove that Bob or Alice was created. We need to prove that the Customer object returned from `findCustomer` is either Bob or Alice, as expected. So let's replace the `testBob/AliceNotNull` tests as follows:

```
    public void testBobFound() {
        Customer foundBob = CustomerManager.findCustomer("bob");
        assertEquals("Bob should have been found.", foundBob, bob);
    }

    public void testAliceFound() {
        Customer foundAlice = CustomerManager.findCustomer("alice");
        assertEquals("Alice should have been found.", foundAlice, alice);
    }
```

Running this now, we get a failure, though not quite as expected:

```
.F.F
Time: 0.01
There were 2 failures:
1) testBobNotNull(CreateTwoCustomersTest)junit.framework.AssertionFailedError:
        Bob should have been found. expected:<Customer@6eb38a> but
            was:<Customer@1cd2e5f>
        at CreateTwoCustomersTest.testBobNotNull(CreateTwoCustomersTest.java:17)
2) testAliceNotNull(CreateTwoCustomersTest)junit.framework.AssertionFailedError:
        Alice should have been found. expected:< Customer@1fee6fc> but
            was:<Customer@1eed786>
        at CreateTwoCustomersTest.testAliceNotNull(CreateTwoCustomersTest.java:22)

FAILURES!!!
Tests run: 2,  Failures: 2,  Errors: 0
```

That `Customer@6eb38a` in the test output doesn't look too helpful. It's the default output from Java's `toString()` method, so let's override that in Customer to get something a bit more pleasant:

```
public class Customer {
    private String name;

    public Customer(String name) {
        this.name = name;
    }

    public String toString() {
        return name;
    }
}
```

and rerun the test:

```
.F.F
Time: 0.01
There were 2 failures:
1) testBobFound(CreateTwoCustomersTest)junit.framework.AssertionFailedError:
        Bob should have been found. expected:<bob> but was:<bob>
        at CreateTwoCustomersTest.testBobFound(CreateTwoCustomersTest.java:17)
2) testAliceFound(CreateTwoCustomersTest)junit.framework.AssertionFailedError:
        Alice should have been found. expected:<bob> but was:<alice>
        at CreateTwoCustomersTest.testAliceFound(CreateTwoCustomersTest.java:22)

FAILURES!!!
Tests run: 2,  Failures: 2,  Errors: 0
```

The interesting thing here is that `testAliceFound()` is failing (which we'd expect, because `CustomerManager.findCustomer(..)` is "cheating" and always returning a new Bob), and `testBobFound()` is also failing (which we wouldn't expect). `testBobFound()` is failing because the `equals()` method isn't doing the right thing—currently it's still using Java's default `Object.equals()` implementation—so at this time, one Bob instance doesn't equal another Bob instance.

Evidently, equality is a subjective thing in Bob-land. So we need to override the `equals()` method in Customer as follows:

```
    public boolean equals(Object obj) {
        if (obj == null ||
            !(obj instanceof Customer)) {
            return false;
        }
        Customer customer = (Customer) obj;
        return name.equals(customer.getName());
    }

    public String getName() {
        return name;
    }
```

Notice also the new `getName()` method. This is the first time we've needed to retrieve the customer's name, and we don't add the method until we need it.

Our new `equals()` method first tests to see if the object being passed in is null or isn't a Customer object. If either case is true, it's a fair bet that the object isn't equal. Our real equality test (the one we're really interested in), though, is comparing the customer names.

If we compile and run the tests again now, we hope that the `testAliceFound()` method still fails, but at least the `testBobFound()` method passes:

```
..F
Time: 0.01
There was 1 failure:
1) testAliceFound(CreateTwoCustomersTest)junit.framework.AssertionFailedError:
        Alice should have been found. expected:<bob> but was:<alice>
        at CreateTwoCustomersTest.testAliceFound(CreateTwoCustomersTest.java:22)

FAILURES!!!
Tests run: 2,  Failures: 1,  Errors: 0
```

Getting there—adding the `Customer.equals()` method passed the "should be the real Bob" test. But, as we expected, the "real Alice" test is still failing. We'd be kind of worried if it passed, in fact, because there's currently no source code in CustomerManager that actually does anything.

Let's do something about that next.

Making CustomerManager Do Something

We need to add some code to CustomerManager, so that it really does manage customers, which should make our failing "real Alice" test pass:

```
public class CustomerManager {
    private static HashMap customersByName = new HashMap();

    public static Customer create(String name) {
        Customer customer = new Customer(name);
        customersByName.put(name, customer);
        return customer;
    }

    public static Customer findCustomer(String name) {
        return (Customer) customersByName.get(name);
    }
}
```

Running JUnit again now, we find that all the tests pass. Hurrah!

We also need to test the negative path: what happens if we try to find a customer that hasn't been added to the system? Let's add a test to find out:

```
public void testCustomerNotFound() {
    Customer jake = CustomerManager.findCustomer("jake");
    assertNull("Jake isn't in the system so should be null.", jake);
}
```

We'll put this in a test class called CustomerNotFoundTest. With our new implementation of CustomerManager, this test passes straightaway.

Another useful test would be to try adding the same customer twice and ensure that we get a suitable error—but you get the general idea.

Now that we have the customer management side of things more or less wrapped up, we'll now move onto managing the customer's bookings.

Our First BookingManager Test: Testing for Nothingness

We need a component that returns the number of hotel bookings a customer has made. As we don't yet have a way of placing bookings, our first test should be pretty straightforward: we can test that no bookings have yet been placed. We would, of course, expect this test to pass with flying colors!

DRIVING THE DESIGN FROM THE REQUIREMENTS

But how do we *know* that we need a component that returns the number of hotel bookings a customer has made? Using XP, there would need to be a user story that states simply

> *As a travel agent, I would like to be able to check the number of bookings a customer has made so I can bill him accordingly.*

Using ICONIX Process, there would be a use case, either for specifically getting the number of bookings or for a larger task such as viewing a Customer Details screen (which would include the number of bookings made by that customer).

Let's start by creating a JUnit test class called BookingManagerTest. Initially, this contains just our single test method:

```
public void testInitialState() {
    BookingManager.clearAll();
    Customer bob = CustomerManager.create("Bob");
    assertEquals("Bob hasn't booked any rooms yet.",
                 0, BookingManager.getNumBookings(bob));
}
```

To make this code pass its test, we'd write the minimum amount of code needed:

```
public class BookingManager {
    public static void clearAll() {
    }

    public static int getNumBookings(Customer customer) {
        return 1;
    }
}
```

■ Note As with CustomerManager, we're making BookingManager a very simple class consisting purely of static methods, to keep the example short. In reality, you'd probably make it a Singleton[7] or instantiate it based on some context or other (e.g., a session or transaction ID).

Notice that `getNumBookings()` currently returns 1. This is deliberate because we initially want to see our unit test fail, to prove that it works. Running BookingManagerTest, then, we get this:

```
.F
Time: 0
There was 1 failure:
1) testInitialState(BookingManagerTest)junit.framework.AssertionFailedError:
        Bob hasn't booked any rooms yet. expected:<0> but was:<1>
        at BookingManagerTest.testInitialState(BookingManagerTest.java:13)

FAILURES!!!
Tests run: 1,  Failures: 1,  Errors: 0
```

Thus reassured, we can change `getNumBookings()` to return 0 (a more valid number at this stage), and the test passes:

```
.
Time: 0.01

OK (1 test)
```

RUN ALL YOUR TESTS REGULARLY, BY HOOK OR BY CROOK

Running through the example in this chapter, you'll notice that we're mostly running the test classes individually. In a production environment, it's better (essential even) to run your entire test suite every time, instead of running individual test classes. This is actually a fundamental part of TDD: knowing that with each change you make, you haven't broken the functionality that's been written so far.

Of course, as the number of tests grows, it becomes more difficult to run an entire test suite, because the tests take longer and longer. When this happens, there are a few things you can do:

- Look at ways of speeding up the tests (e.g., is the code that's in each `setUp()` and `teardown()` method strictly necessary?).
- Use mock objects to avoid having to connect to remote databases or application servers, which can slow tests down by several orders of magnitude.
- Look for (and eliminate) duplicated tests.
- Break code into separate modules that can be developed and tested independently (while avoiding the dreaded "big-bang integration" syndrome, where modules that have never been run together are jammed together near the end of a project and expected to somehow interoperate perfectly).
- Run a separate build PC that regularly gets all the latest code, builds it, and runs the tests. This is an increasingly commonplace practice, and it is nowadays regarded as essential (not only by teams that follow TDD).

Of course, these practices also apply if you're using TDD combined with ICONIX Process (see Chapter 12).

7. In fact, Singletons these days are widely considered to be an antipattern. See Matt's article titled "Perils of the Singleton" at `www.softwarereality.com/design/singleton.jsp`.

Adding a Vector: Testing for Something

All well and good so far. Our first BookingManager test passes. But of course that isn't the whole story—we now need to add an additional test, a vector, to ensure that the correct number of bookings is returned:

```
public void testOneBookingPlaced() {
    BookingManager.clearAll();
    Customer bob = CustomerManager.create("Bob");
    Booking booking = new Booking (bob, Booking.WALDORF_ASTORIA);
    BookingManager.placeBooking(bob, booking);
    assertEquals("Bob has made one booking.", 1,
                 BookingManager.getNumBookings(bob));
}
```

To get the code to compile, we also need to add the `placeBooking(..)` method to BookingManager. For now, let's add it as an empty method:

```
public static void placeBooking(Customer customer, Booking booking) {
}
```

This is also the first time we've needed a Booking class, so let's create that now:

```
public class Booking {
    public static final String WALDORF_ASTORIA = "Waldorf Astoria";

    public Booking(Customer customer, Object hotel) {
    }
}
```

Notice that we've included a `WALDORF_ASTORIA` constant. Of course, in a real-life system we'd want to be able to look up hotels by various search criteria. We'd also want a proper Hotel class (probably with attributes for rooms, amenities, and so on).

But, you know, something doesn't seem quite right here. Our BookingManager class is being used for creating (placing) a Booking, but it seems like it would make sense for it to operate in a consistent way with the CustomerManager class that we created earlier—that is, there should be a `create(..)` method (instead of `placeBooking()`) that returns the new Booking instance. We should then have a test method that creates a booking and asserts that the returned Booking object wasn't null. Once we have this, we can add further tests to test for the alternative paths (i.e., to test that one booking was placed, two bookings, and so on). So, instead of writing this:

```
Customer bob = CustomerManager.create("Bob");
Booking booking = new Booking(bob, Booking.WALDORF_ASTORIA);
BookingManager.placeBooking(bob, booking);
```

we would write this:

```
Customer bob = CustomerManager.create("Bob");
Booking booking = BookingManager.create(bob, Booking.WALDORF_ASTORIA);
```

The `testOneBookingPlaced()` test method creates a new Customer (Bob) and a Booking at the Waldorf, and then places the Booking with the BookingManager. Finally, the test asserts that Bob has exactly one booking (the one we just placed). Of course, running this test will fail at this stage, because `getNumBookings()` always returns 0. We could change it to return 1 instead, but then the `testNoBookingsMade()` test would fail because it's expecting 0. So it looks as if we're going to need to write some additional code to keep track of the bookings that have been placed. (D'oh! And we thought this was going to be an easy ride!)

A Quick Bout of Refactoring

But before we do that, there's some common code in the previous two tests, so let's quickly refactor what we have so far to root out the commonality. Both test methods start by calling `BookingManager.clearAll()` to set up the test, and then both test methods create a Customer called Bob. So it makes sense to move this code into a separate method. Once again, we can use JUnit's `setUp()` method:

```
public void setUp() {
    BookingManager.clearAll();
    Customer bob = CustomerManager.create("Bob");
}

public void testInitialState() {
    assertEquals("Bob hasn't booked any rooms yet.", 0,
                 BookingManager.getNumBookings(bob));
}

public void testOneBookingMade() {
    Booking booking =
                  BookingManager.create(bob, Booking.WALDORF_ASTORIA);
    assertEquals("Bob has made one booking.", 1,
                  BookingManager.getNumBookings(bob));
}
```

Note If BookingManager wasn't a Singleton, then we wouldn't need to clear it out in this way in the `setUp()` method. Instead, we'd probably create a local instance of it to be used by the test methods in this test class.

Another Note Strictly following TDD, we also shouldn't add the call to `clearAll()` at all, until the tests start failing. At this point, we'd identify the need to clear out the data prior to each test method, and add `clearAll()` so that the tests pass.

Now let's modify the BookingManager class to make both tests pass:

```
public class BookingManager {
    protected static int numBookings = 0;

    public static void clearAll() {
        numBookings = 0;
    }

    public static Booking create(Customer customer, Object hotel) {
        numBookings++;
        return new Booking(customer, hotel);
    }

    public static int getNumBookings(Customer customer) {
        return numBookings;
    }
}
```

Running this, both tests now pass. However, at this point you'd do well to bury your face in your hands and groan loudly. It's painfully obvious that the preceding code isn't particularly useful. True, it passes the tests, but we also know (from peeking at the requirements) that we'll need to track and find bookings that have previously been placed. So let's add the code now for retrieving a Booking.

Retrieving a Booking

In TDD, you never write code without first writing a test, so we'll add a test that retrieves a Booking:

```
public void testRetrieveBooking() {
    Booking booking = BookingManager.create(bob, Booking.WALDORF_ASTORIA);
    Object bookingID = booking.getID();
    Booking retrievedBooking = BookingManager.findBooking(bookingID);
    assertEquals("Booking ID should find the same booking.", booking, retrievedBooking);
}
```

Remember, we don't need to create Bob here as he's already created in the `setUp()` method.

This test reveals the need for a booking ID, so that bookings can be uniquely looked up. Notice how writing the test itself is driving the design. TDD is useful for designing interfaces, as the tests are written from a client object's perspective.

Note that as we're using `assertEquals()`, we'd also need a `booking.equals()` method that tests that two bookings are the same (alternatively, we could test `booking.getID()`). If we had a technical requirement that each Booking object must be a Singleton (not recommended!), then we could use `assertSame()` instead of `assertEquals()` to test that the retrieved Booking object is the same instance.

We now update both the Booking and BookingManager classes so that our test compiles:

```
public class Booking {
    public static final String WALDORF_ASTORIA = "Waldorf Astoria";

    private Object id;
    private Customer customer;
    private Object hotel;

    public Booking(Object id, Customer customer, Object hotel) {
        this.id = id;
        this.customer = customer;
        this.hotel = hotel;
    }

    public Object getID() {
        return id;
    }

    public String toString() {
        return "Booking " + id + " for Customer " + customer + " in hotel " + hotel;
    }
}
```

The main change to Booking is that we've added an ID to its constructor and a `getID()` method, which the test needs. We've also given Booking a `toString()` method so that we get some useful contextual information when the tests fail. And we've added fields for customer and hotel (at the moment, they're needed only by `toString()`).

We also need to modify BookingManager (which creates Bookings) so that it allocates a new ID and passes this into new Bookings:

```
public class BookingManager {
    protected static int numBookings = 0;

    public static void clearAll() {
        numBookings = 0;
    }

    public static Booking create(Customer customer, Object hotel) {
        numBookings++;
        Object bookingID = new Integer(numBookings);
        return new Booking(bookingID, customer, hotel);
    }

    public static Booking findBooking(Object bookingID) {
        return null;
    }

    public static int getNumBookings(Customer customer) {
        return numBookings;
    }
}
```

If we rerun BookingManagerTest now, we'd expect a failure because `BookingManager.findBooking()` is returning null:

```
...F
Time: 0.02
There was 1 failure:
1) testRetrieveBooking(BookingManagerTest)junit.framework.AssertionFailedError:
        Booking ID should find the same booking. expected:<Booking 1 for
            Customer Bob in hotel Waldorf Astoria> but was:<null>
        at BookingManagerTest.testRetrieveBooking(BookingManagerTest.java:29)

FAILURES!!!
Tests run: 3,  Failures: 1,  Errors: 0
```

Exactly right! Okay, let's do something to make this test pass.

```
public class BookingManager {
    private static int numBookings = 0;
    private static Map bookingsByID = new HashMap();

    public static void clearAll() {
        numBookings = 0;
        bookingsByID.clear();
    }

    public static Booking create(Customer customer, Object hotel) {
        numBookings++;
        Object bookingID = new Integer(numBookings);
        Booking booking = new Booking(bookingID, customer, hotel);
        bookingsByID.put(bookingID, booking);
        return booking;
    }
```

```
    public static Booking findBooking(Object bookingID) {
        return (Booking) bookingsByID.get(bookingID);
    }

    public static int getNumBookings(Customer customer) {
        return numBookings;
    }
}
```

To keep the code as simple as possible, we're using a HashMap to store the Bookings and retrieve them by their ID. Let's give this a quick test now to see if it passes:

```
...
Time: 0.01

OK (3 tests)
```

Looking at the new version of BookingManager, we could also refactor it slightly, as `numBookings` is now superfluous—we can get the same information from our new `bookingsByID` HashMap. Now that we have the confidence of a passing suite of tests, we can take a moment to tidy up the code. If the tests still pass, it's a fairly safe bet that our refactoring didn't break anything.

```
public class BookingManager {
    private static Map bookingsByID = new HashMap();

    public static void clearAll() {
        bookingsByID.clear();
    }

    public static Booking create(Customer customer, Object hotel) {
        Object bookingID = newBookingID();
        Booking booking = new Booking(bookingID, customer, hotel);
        bookingsByID.put(bookingID, booking);
        return booking;
    }

    public static Object newBookingID() {
        return new Integer(++newBookingID);
    }
    private static int newBookingID = 0;

    public static Booking findBooking(Object bookingID) {
        return (Booking) bookingsByID.get(bookingID);
    }

    public static int getNumBookings(Customer customer) {
        return bookingsByID.size();
    }
}
```

We've also separated out the part that allocates new booking IDs into a separate method, which makes more sense and keeps each method focused on doing one thing.

Our tests still pass, so let's move on.

Testing for Bookings by More Than One Customer

It's been said that programmers only really care about three numbers: 0, 1, and infinity.[8] Any number greater than 1 might as well be infinity, because the code that we write to deal with quantities of 2 to *n* tends to be basically the same.[9]

For our hotel booking system, we're obviously going to need a system that works for more than one customer. Let's add a test method to BookingManagerTest to verify this:

```
public void testBookingsPlacedByTwoCustomers() {
    Customer bob = CustomerManager.create("Bob");
    Booking bobsBooking = BookingManager.create(bob, Booking.WALDORF_ASTORIA);

    Customer alice = CustomerManager.create("Alice");
    Booking alicesBooking =
                    BookingManager.create(alice, Booking.PENNSYLVANIA);
    Booking alicesSecondBooking =
                    BookingManager.create(alice, Booking. WALDORF_ASTORIA);

    assertEquals("Bob has placed one booking.", 1,
                    BookingManager.getNumBookings(bob));
    assertEquals("Alice has placed two bookings.", 2,
                 BookingManager.getNumBookings(alice));
}
```

This test fails, of course, because `getNumBookings()` always returns the total number of bookings placed, regardless of which customer is being passed in:

```
....F
Time: 0.01
There was 1 failure:
1) testBookingsPlacedByTwoCustomers(BookingManagerTest)
        junit.framework.AssertionFailedError:
        Bob has placed one booking. expected:<1> but was:<3>
        at BookingManagerTest.testBookingsPlacedByTwoCustomers(
        BookingManagerTest.java:39)

FAILURES!!!
Tests run: 4,  Failures: 1,  Errors: 0
```

Clearly we need a way of isolating Bookings that belong to a single Customer. We could replace the `bookingsByID` HashMap with, say, `bookingListsByCustomer` (which stores Lists of Bookings keyed by Customer). But this would cause our `testRetrieveBooking()` test to fail (in fact, the code probably wouldn't compile). We definitely don't want to break or remove existing functionality by adding new stuff.

8. Alan Cooper, *The Inmates Are Running the Asylum: Why High Tech Products Drive Us Crazy and How to Restore the Sanity* (Indianapolis, IN: Sams Publishing, 1999), p. 100.

9. Obviously that's a bit of a generalization—we're not taking into account really big values or quantities, and what to do if your computer runs out of heap space, bandwidth, processing time, hard disk space, and so on. But as a general rule . . .

So instead, let's add bookingListsByCustomer as an additional HashMap. The BookingManager class would then look something like this:

```
public class BookingManager {

    private static Map bookingsByID = new HashMap();
    protected static HashMap bookingListsByCustomer = new HashMap();

    public static void clearAll() {
        bookingsByID.clear();
        bookingListsByCustomer.clear();
    }

    public static Booking create(Customer customer, Object hotel) {
        Object bookingID = newBookingID();
        Booking booking = new Booking(bookingID, customer, hotel);
        bookingsByID.put(bookingID, booking);

        List customerBookings = findBookings(customer);
        customerBookings.add(booking);

        return booking;
    }

    public static Object newBookingID() {
        return new Integer(++newBookingID);
    }
    private static int newBookingID = 0;

    public static Booking findBooking(Object bookingID) {
        return (Booking) bookingsByID.get(bookingID);
    }

    public static int getNumBookings(Customer customer) {
        return findBookings(customer).size();
    }

    private static synchronized List findBookings(Customer customer) {
        List customerBookings = (List) bookingListsByCustomer.get(customer);
        if (customerBookings == null) {
            customerBookings = new ArrayList();
            bookingListsByCustomer.put(customer, customerBookings);
        }
        return customerBookings;
    }
}
```

We've added a worker method, findBookings(Customer), which gets called by both create() and getNumBookings(). The findBookings() method handles the case where a List of Bookings hasn't been added yet for a Customer. Currently it's also the way that new Booking Lists are instantiated.

This code compiles and passes the tests, so we can move on, but just before we do, here's a word from our conscience. . .

Note Of course, this code is adding quite a bit of responsibility to BookingManager. When you start having Lists of Lists, or Maps of Lists, it's a sign that you probably need another class in there to handle the complex relationship between Customers and their Bookings. This is the sort of situation that we would identify early on in an up-front design approach (see the next chapter). As it is, we could now refactor BookingManager so that it has a separate BookingList class, which contains the Bookings for a single Customer.

We won't cover that here because the pub closes soon (and we're guessing that you can see what TDD is about by now), so let's move on.

TESTING PRIVATE METHODS (OR NOT)

If we were particularly diligent, we'd add a test or two for the `findBookings()` method. This would involve making it public, though, which we don't want to do, because currently no client code needs to call it directly. The answer, then, is to make sure that all its possible failure cases are covered by the tests that invoke it indirectly (e.g., via `BookingManager.create()`).

If a private method has a failure mode that is never caused by the public methods that use it, then it shouldn't actually be a problem because that failure mode is never going to occur. Of course, if there was an entire subsystem behind that method (i.e., the method was delegating to some other class or group of methods to do some complex processing), then we would want to make sure that code was adequately unit-tested.

This tends to be more of a problem with legacy code. Using TDD, it's less likely that the failure mode would appear: the code is only written to pass tests, so where did the failure mode come from? If every public method is micro-tested in every way that it can be used, and the application is exercised in every way that it is used by the acceptance tests, any problems would be discovered very early on.

Similarly, if we did make the `findBookings()` method public, then we would first have to write some additional tests for it. In that sense, TDD is about testing functionality that has been exposed via a public interface. How the classes go about implementing the code "behind the scenes" is largely immaterial (from the tests' perspective). If there are failure modes that never occur because the program never enters that state, then it probably doesn't matter—as long as the tests cover all states that the program could enter when it goes live.

One Last User Story and We're Done (So We're 90% Complete, Then!)

At this stage, the programming team members hope they're finished. There's only one more user story to go, the customer is expecting a live demo that afternoon, and the team prepares to party like there's no tomorrow. However, to remind us that software is never done, the final user story reads

All the Customer and Booking data must be persisted.[10]

Dang! After the project manager is picked up off the floor and given some smelling salts, the team settles down and works out what must be done to make the data persistent. Because our basic framework for adding and retrieving Customer and Booking data is in place, and we have a set of unit tests that tell us if these classes stop working, then it shouldn't be too difficult to gradually replace the back-end code with some code that stores/retrieves the data from a database management system (DBMS). At each stage, with each microscopic change that we make, we can run the tests again to make sure we haven't broken the basic functionality.

Although the process is long-winded, a nice side effect of TDD is that the code interfaces usually do end up being very clean and shouldn't impose a particular database persistence solution on the client code. That is, the client code doesn't have to know whether we're using Enterprise JavaBeans (EJB), or CORBA, or web services, or

---

10. Of course, we're being quite tongue-in-cheek with this example. Realistically, this requirement would have been discussed in the planning game. It is possible, though, that the customer might have given one answer—for example, deciding to go with "in-memory" state first (i.e., no persistence)—to get an initial prototype working, or he may have decided to go with flat-file persistence first and decided upon database persistence later.

punched card, or whatever behind the scenes. In fact, the client code doesn't have to know any details at all about our data access layer. (In the next chapter, we'll revisit the example to show how a similarly clean design can be achieved using ICONIX Process.)

In the Java universe, we have many surprisingly diverse choices for adding a persistence layer, including the following:

- Using a persistence framework like JDO or Hibernate[11]
- Using a code generator such as JGenerator[12] to create the persistence layer for us
- Using EJB
- Adding SQL directly into our BookingManager class (or adding a data access object that BookingManager delegates to)
- Persisting to local text files (really not a recommended solution for the majority of cases, as we'd very quickly run into limitations)

Persistence Option: Hibernate

For our travel example, Hibernate would actually be a good choice, because it's well suited to persisting plain old Java objects (POJOs). In our example, we've created Java classes such as Customer and Booking. Using Hibernate, it would be very easy to create a database schema and middle tier directly from these objects.

Hibernate includes a tool for generating database schemas from POJOs (actually from an intermediate XML mapping file, which can be created manually or via a generator such as XDoclet[13]).

The steps involved in creating a persistence framework from our Java classes are as follows:

1. Write the JavaBeans (Customer, Booking, etc.).
2. Add XDoclet tags to the classes to generate the Hibernate XML mapping (or create the mapping by hand).
3. Generate our database schema using a Hibernate utility called hbm2ddl.
4. Export the schema to a database.

Using Hibernate would be a good option. But for this example, we want to show how we would use the tests to help us safely modify the code after making a slightly sharp right-hand turn in the design. So to demonstrate this, let's take the road less traveled . . .

Persistence Option: Raw SQL via Handwoven DAOs

So we've decided to add a BookingManagerDAO (data access object) class, which BookingManager delegates to. BookingManagerDAO in turn contains simple SQL statements to persist and read back the data from a database. We would change the methods in BookingManager one at a time, rerunning the complete suite of unit tests at each stage to make sure we haven't broken anything.

Here's the initial, rather empty version of BookingManagerDAO:

```
public class BookingManagerDAO {
    public BookingManagerDAO() {
    }

    public void save (Booking booking) {
    }
```

---

11. See www.hibernate.org.
12. See www.javelinsoft.com/jgenerator
13. See http://xdoclet.sourceforge.net.

```
public Booking find (Object bookingID) {
        return null;
    }

    public int getNumBookings(Customer customer) {
        return 0;
    }
}
```

Unlike its counterpart, BookingManager, we're giving BookingManagerDAO a constructor, and BookingManager will create and destroy it as needed. This is primarily so that we can control the object's life cycle—that is, the point at which it connects to the database, closes its connections, and so on.

The BookingManagerDAO class compiles, but as you can see, it doesn't do very much. It also doesn't have any unit tests of its own. We could add some, but for our purposes the tests that we've already written for BookingManager will confirm whether the DAO is writing and returning Booking objects correctly.

Note This approach is borderline "testing by side-effect," which isn't particularly desirable. You really want tests that assert specifically that something passes or fails. But in this case, we're testing persistence code behind the scenes (aka *black-box testing*) and are mainly interested in making sure our existing functionality isn't broken. In a production environment, however, we probably would add additional tests to cover the new persistence model.

To put this to the test, let's make our first modification to BookingManager to make it use the new DAO:

```
public static synchronized BookingManagerDAO getBookingManagerDAO() {
    if (dao == null) {
        dao = new BookingManagerDAO();
    }
    return dao;
}
private static BookingManagerDAO dao = null;

public static Booking create(Customer customer, Object hotel) {
    Object bookingID = newBookingID();
    Booking booking = new Booking(bookingID, customer, hotel);
    getBookingManagerDAO().save(booking);
    return booking;
}
```

BookingManager creates a Booking instance as before, but now instead of using Lists and Maps to keep track of Bookings, it's going to rely on the new data-access class to save and retrieve the Bookings in the database.

If we compile this and run the tests, of course we get failures all over the place. Our data is no longer being stored anywhere (not even in memory!). Changing the underlying persistence model can safely be called a "big refactoring," with far-reaching consequences. We still want to try and take this in baby steps if we can, but we need to get back to having a passing suite of tests again as soon as possible, so that we can validate our steps as we go along.

Let's add the code to BookingManagerDAO to save the booking:

```
public void save(Booking booking) {
    try {
        String url = " jdbc:microsoft:sqlserver://localhost:1433";
        String sql = "INSERT INTO Bookings " +
                                "(BookingID, CustomerName, HotelID) " +
                     "VALUES (" +
                                booking.getID() + ", " +
                                booking.getCustomer().getName() + ", " +
                                booking.getHotel() + ")";

        Class.forName(
                 "com.microsoft.jdbc.sqlserver.SQLServerDriver");
        Connection con =
                 DriverManager.getConnection(url, "MyLoginName", "MyPassword");
        Statement stmt = con.createStatement();
        stmt.execute(sql);

        stmt.close();
        con.close();
    }
    catch (Exception e) {
        // do some error handling...
    }
}
```

We'd then add similar code to find Bookings and count the number of Bookings saved for a Customer.

Although this "solution" leaves quite a bit to be desired, it's sufficient for our purposes: to illustrate how we add a persistence layer and use our existing tests to assert that nothing has changed semantically or been broken. At a stretch, this code might also just scrape past the "just good enough to fit the requirements" criterion, if the requirements are for a single-user, nonscalable system!

Leave It for the Next Release

The functionality that we've created thus far is obviously limited, and some of the implementation details (e.g., the use of "raw" SQL instead of a decent persistence framework, the lack of a connection pool, etc.) very much limit the system to precisely what was in the user stories. Therein lies the value (and danger) of TDD: we write only what we need, at the time, to make the customer's tests pass,[14] and no more. The tests, in turn, are driven by the requirements that have been scheduled for this release.

The danger is that we may store up an unnecessary amount of rework for ourselves later. For example, in the next release, a user story that the customer had prioritized as low on the list might be "Must be able to scale to 1,000 users, at least 100 concurrently." So we would then have to rewrite the entire persistence layer. The work that we did on separating responsibilities and the unit tests that we wrote should allow us to do this without too many problems. But even so . . .

You probably noticed that we didn't write any front-end code (mainly in the interest of keeping the example short). This could be, for example, a Swing or SWT front-end using our code as a middle tier to connect to a database, or a JSP front-end if we're creating a web application. When you're implementing the UI, it's prudent to use a customer acceptance testing framework such as FitNesse or Exactor.

---

14. More specifically, using TDD we only write code to make the *customer's* tests pass (i.e., the acceptance tests). We haven't shown these here, as they're outside this chapter's scope. See `http://c2.com/cgi/wiki?AcceptanceTest` for more information about acceptance testing.

You'll find that customer acceptance testing frameworks drive the requirements from the UI (though not quite to the extent that a use case–driven approach does, as you'll see in the next chapter). The requirements define the UI behavior, and the UI in turn defines what tests we need to write. Then the tests define the source code.

Summary of Vanilla TDD

So you get the basic idea of how vanilla TDD works. As you can see, only a small part of TDD is actually about testing. Its main drive has to do with design: proving code as you go along, and only writing code that you strictly need. As you can see, TDD also promotes fine-grained methods and encapsulation of "dirty" implementation details. The fact that you also end up with a complete set of unit tests at the end is a nice bonus.

The main drawback is that the process can be long-winded, to say the least. If you wrote all your code like this, you'd be there all night. At the risk of generalizing, "test-infected" programmers inevitably start to take shortcuts, writing small batches of tests and then writing the code to implement those tests. In our previous example, if we'd written the `testTwoBookingsPlaced()` and `testTwoCustomers()` unit tests in one go, and then written the code to make them pass, we wouldn't have gone through the intermediate solution of using a `numBookings` int field—we'd have gone straight to the HashMap solution.

However, when using TDD without in-depth design modeling up front, you'll often want to go through these intermediate steps, because then you're much more likely to avoid overlooking design issues or failure modes. It sure can take a long time, though.

In the next chapter, we'll discuss how to apply some of the TDD principles to design modeling (where change and refactoring are much less expensive). In particular, we'll show how to use the "vector" principle (two tests at different extremes) to model expected class and UI behavior. We'll also show how to cut down the number of "intermediate" design steps needed in TDD, by creating a design model up front. To demonstrate these principles, we'll repeat the preceding example using a suitable mixture of up-front design and TDD.

Summary

In this chapter, we walked through a practical example of TDD in action. Although TDD is often accompanied with a small amount of up-front UML diagramming, we deliberately avoided that in the example. This was to contrast the techniques used to create a design using vanilla TDD with the techniques used to create a design using up-front UML diagramming.

In the next chapter, we hit the Rewind button and repeat the example using TDD plus some up-front analysis and design (A&D). Naturally, we use ICONIX Process as the A&D methodology.

CHAPTER 12

Test-Driven Development with ICONIX Process

In the previous chapter, we put together an example system using "vanilla" test-driven development (TDD). In this chapter, we repeat the example using a mixture of TDD and ICONIX modeling.

How Agile ICONIX Modeling and TDD Fit Together

There's a prevailing opinion in the agile world that "formal" up-front design modeling and TDD are mutually exclusive. This is summed up in the book *Test-Driven Development: A Practical Guide* by David Astels, in which he refers to the concept of *Big Design Up Front*:

> *I feel very strongly that, while it is a cornerstone of XP, TDD can be used in many development processes. The caveat is that Big Design Up Front (BDUF) conflicts with TDD, so you do need to be using a fairly agile process that lets you evolve the design organically. In particular, you need to be practicing an agile approach to modeling and design.*[1]

In this chapter, we're going to demonstrate that TDD can in fact be *particularly* effective with an up-front design method like ICONIX Process.

ICONIX Process takes the design to a low level of detail via sequence diagrams—one sequence diagram for each use case. These diagrams are used to allocate behaviors to the class diagrams. The code can then be written quickly without much need for refactoring. However, the coding stage is still not exactly a brainless activity. The programmer (who, incidentally, should also be actively involved in the design modeling stage) still needs to give careful thought to the low-level design of the code. This is an area to which TDD is perfectly suited.

The "Vanilla" Example Repeated Using ICONIX Modeling and TDD

Let's pause and rewind, then, back to the start of the example that we began in the previous chapter. To match the example, we're going to need a system for travel agent operatives to place hotel bookings on behalf of customers.

To recap, the following serves as our list of requirements for this initial release:

- Create a new customer.
- Create a hotel booking for a customer.
- Retrieve a customer (so that we can place the booking).
- Place the booking.

1. David Astels, *Test-Driven Development: A Practical Guide* (Upper Saddle River, NJ: Prentice-Hall, 2003), p. 203.

As luck would have it, we can derive exactly one use case from each of these requirements (making a total of four use cases). Because we explain the process in a lot more detail here than in Chapter 11, we'll only actually cover the first use case. This will allow us to describe the motivations behind each step in more depth.

You would normally do the high-level analysis and preliminary design work up front (or as much of it as possible) before delving into the more detailed design work for each use case. In many cases, this ends up as a system overview diagram. There's a lot to be said for putting this diagram on a big chart someplace where everyone can see it, so that everyone can also see when it changes.

Following ICONIX Process, the high-level analysis and preliminary design work means drawing all the robustness diagrams first; we can then design and implement one use case at a time. Let's start by creating a domain model that contains the various elements we need to work with, as shown in Figure 12-1. As you can see, it's pretty minimal at this stage. As we go through analysis, we discover new objects to add to the domain model, and we possibly also refine the objects currently there. Then, as the design process kicks in, the domain model swiftly evolves into one or more detailed class diagrams.

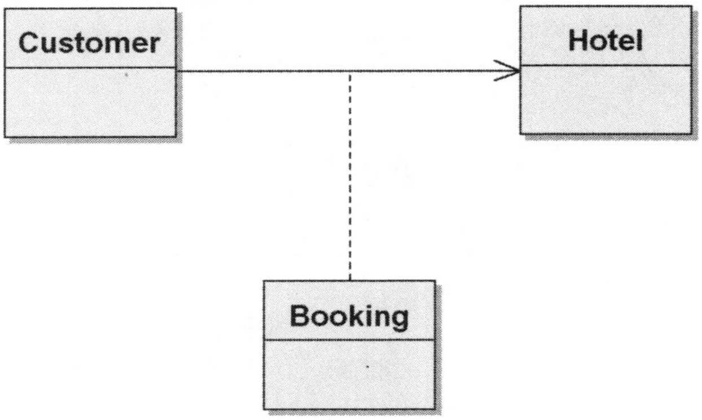

Figure 12-1. *Domain model for the hotel booking example*

The objects shown in Figure 12-1 are derived simply by reading through our four requirements and extracting all the nouns. The relationships are similarly derived from the requirements. "Create a hotel booking for a customer," for example, strongly suggests that there needs to be a Customer object that contains Booking objects. (In a real project, it might not be that simple—defining the domain model can be a highly iterative process involving discovery of objects through various means, including in-depth conversations with the customer, users, and other domain experts. Defining and refining the domain model is also a continuous process throughout the project's life cycle.)

If some aspect of the domain model turns out to be wrong, we change it as soon as we find out, but for now, it gives us a solid enough foundation upon which to write our use cases.

Use Case: "Create a New Customer"

Basic Course: The user (travel agent) clicks the Create New Customer button and the system responds with the Customer Details page, with a few default parameters filled in. The user enters the details and clicks the Create button, and the system adds the new customer to the database and then returns the user to the Customer List page.

Alternative Course: The customer already exists in the system (i.e., someone with the same name and address).

Alternative Course: A different customer with the same name already exists in the system. The user asks the customer for something extra to help identify them (e.g., a middle initial) and then tries again with the modified name.

Use Case: "Search for a Customer"

Basic Course: The user clicks the Search for a Customer link, and the system responds with a search form. The user enters some search parameters (e.g., "Crane", "41 Sleepy Hollow"). The system locates the customer details and displays the Customer Details page. Among other things, this page shows the number of bookings the customer has placed using this system.

Alternative Course: The customer exists in the system but couldn't be found using these search parameters. The user tries again with a different search.

Alternative Course: The customer doesn't exist in the system. The user creates a new customer record (see the "Create a New Customer" use case).

Use Case: "Create a Hotel Booking for a Customer"

Basic Course: The user finds the customer details (see the "Search for a Customer" use case), and then clicks the Create Booking link. On the Create a Booking page, the user chooses a hotel, enters the start and end dates, plus options such as nonsmoking, double occupancy, and so on, and then clicks Confirm Booking. The system books the room for the customer and responds with a confirmation page (with an option to print the confirmation details).

Alternative Course: The selected dates aren't available. The user may either enter some different dates or try a different hotel.

Notice that already this process is forcing us to think in terms of how the user will be interacting with the system. For example, when creating a hotel booking, the user first finds the customer details, then goes to the Create a Booking page, and then finds the hotel details. The order of events could be changed (e.g., the user finds the hotel details first, and then goes to the Create a Booking page). This is where interaction design comes in handy, as we can optimize the UI flow around what the user is trying to achieve.

Notice also that our use case descriptions show a certain bias toward a web front-end with words such as "page" and "link." However, such terms can be safely treated as an abstraction. In other words, if the customer suddenly decided that he actually wanted the entire UI to be written using Macromedia Flash, Spring Rich Client, or even a 20-year-old green-screen terminal, the fact that we used words like "button" and "page" shouldn't cause a problem.

While it's not absolutely necessary, we've created a use case diagram to show these use cases grouped together (see Figure 12-2). Modeling the use cases visually, while not essential, can sometimes help because it eases the brain gently into "conceptual pattern" mode, ready for creating the robustness diagrams.

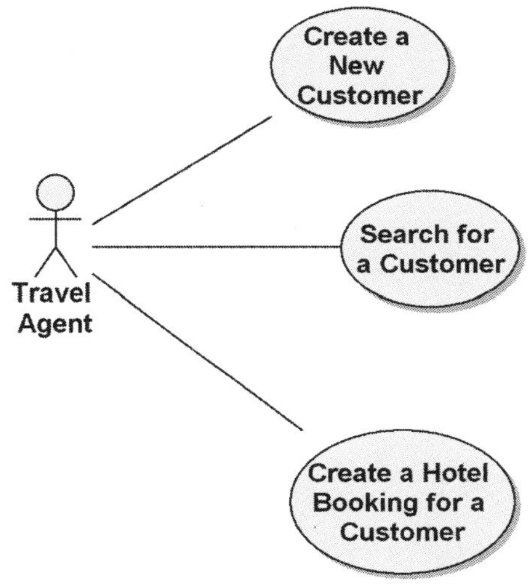

Figure 12-2. *Use case diagram for the hotel booking example*

Ideally, the modeling should take place on a whiteboard in front of the team, rather than on a PC screen with the finished diagram being filed away in the bowels of a server somewhere where nobody ever sees it. Or, here's a slightly different concept: how about doing the model in a visual modeling tool that's hooked up to a projector if it's a whole-team brainstorming exercise? Also, if the diagram is on public display ("public" in the sense that it's displayed in the office), it's more likely to be updated if the use case ever changes, and it can be deleted (i.e., taken down) when it's no longer needed.

Implementing the "Create a New Customer" Use Case

In this section, we'll walk through the implementation of the "Create a New Customer" use case using a combination of ICONIX and TDD (hereafter referred to as ICONIX+TDD), all the way from the use case itself to the source code.

Robustness Diagram for "Create a New Customer"

Let's start by creating the robustness diagram for "Create a New Customer" (see Figure 12-3).

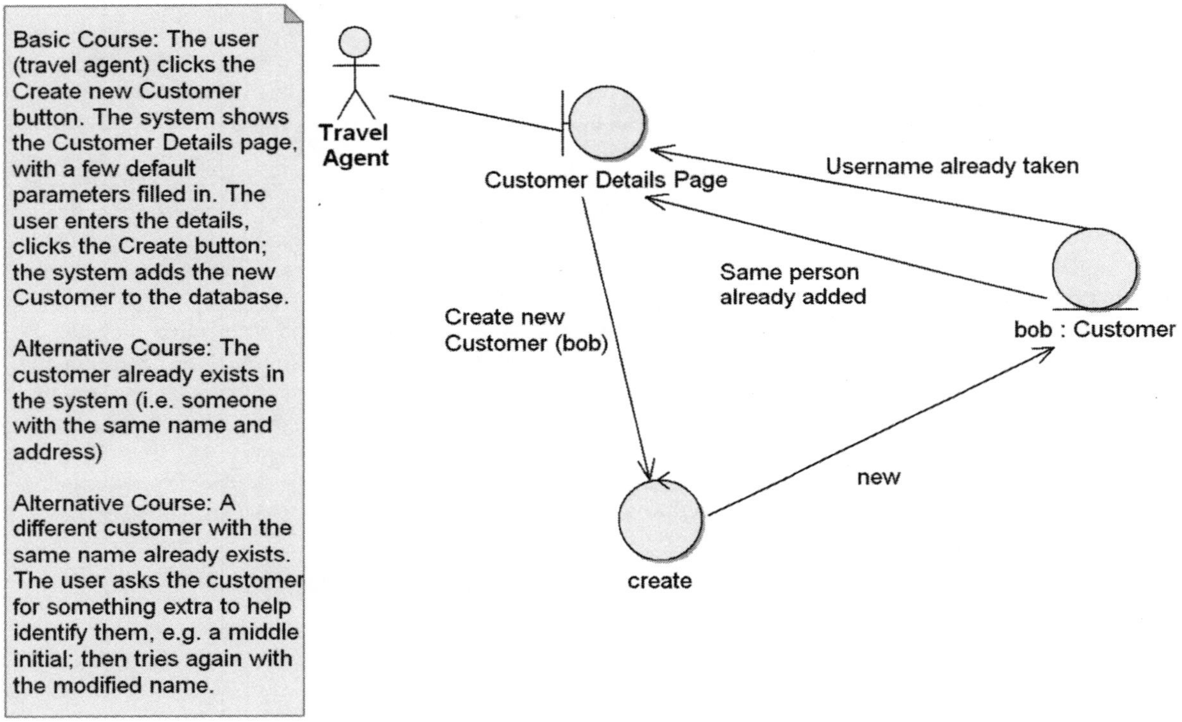

Figure 12-3. *First attempt at a robustness diagram for the "Create a New Customer" use case*

In the early stages of modeling, the first few diagrams are bound to need work, and this first robustness diagram is no exception. Let's dissect it for modeling errors, and then we'll show the new cleaned-up version. Picture a collaborative modeling session with you and your colleagues using a whiteboard to compare the first version of this diagram with the use case text, and then erasing parts of it, and drawing new lines and controllers as, between you, you identify the following issues in the diagram:

- The first part of the use case, "The user (travel agent) clicks the Create New Customer button," isn't shown in the diagram. This is probably because this part of the use case is actually outside the use case's "natural" scope, so modeling it in the robustness diagram proved difficult. This is a good indication that the use case itself needs to be revisited.

- The line from the Customer Details page to the first controller should be labeled "Click Create".
- The two controllers that check the customer against the database also need to be connected to Customer and an object called Database.
- Who is "bob"?
- The diagram shows a Boundary object talking to an Entity. However, noun-noun communication is a no-no, and it's a useful warning sign that something on the diagram isn't hanging together quite right. You can find more detail on why this is a no-no in *Use Case Driven Object Modeling with UML: A Practical Approach* (specifically Figure 4-3, "Robustness Diagram Rules"):

> *Boundary and entity objects on robustness diagrams are nouns, controllers are verbs. When two nouns are connected on a robustness diagram, it means there's a verb (controller) missing. Since the controllers are the "logical functions," that means there's a software function that we haven't accounted for on our diagram (and probably in our use case text), which means that our use case and our robustness diagram are ambiguous. So we make a more explicit statement of the behavior by adding in the missing controller(s).*[2]

- The diagram is very light on controllers. For example, the diagram doesn't show controllers for any of the UI behavior.
- Probably the reason the diagram is missing the controllers is that the use case text doesn't discuss any validations (e.g., "the system validates that the username is unique"). However, the use case magically assumes that these validations happen. This part of the use case needs to be disambiguated.
- The two alternative courses are very similar; we can see from the robustness diagram that trying to separate them out doesn't really work, as they're essentially the result of the same or similar validation. It makes sense to combine these in the use case text.

As you can see, most of the issues we've identified in the robustness diagram actually are the result of errors in the use case, because the robustness diagram is an "object picture" of the use case. *The way to improve the robustness diagram is to correct the use case text* and then redraw the diagram based on the new version.

Here's the new version of the "Create a New Customer" use case.

Use Case: "Create a New Customer"

Basic Course: The system shows the Customer Details page, with a few default parameters filled in. The user enters the details and clicks the Create button; the system validates that all the required fields have been filled in; and the system validates that the customer name is unique and then adds the new Customer to the database. The system then returns the user to the Customer List page.

Alternative Course: Not all the required fields were filled in. The system informs the user of this and redisplays the Customer Details form with the missing fields highlighted in red, so that the user can fill them in.

Alternative Course: A customer with the same name already exists. The system informs the user and gives them the option to edit their customer details or cancel.

2. Doug Rosenberg and Kendall Scott, *Use Case Driven Object Modeling with UML: A Practical Approach* (New York: Addison-Wesley, 1999), p. 69.

We can now use this revised use case to redraw the robustness diagram (see Figure 12-4).

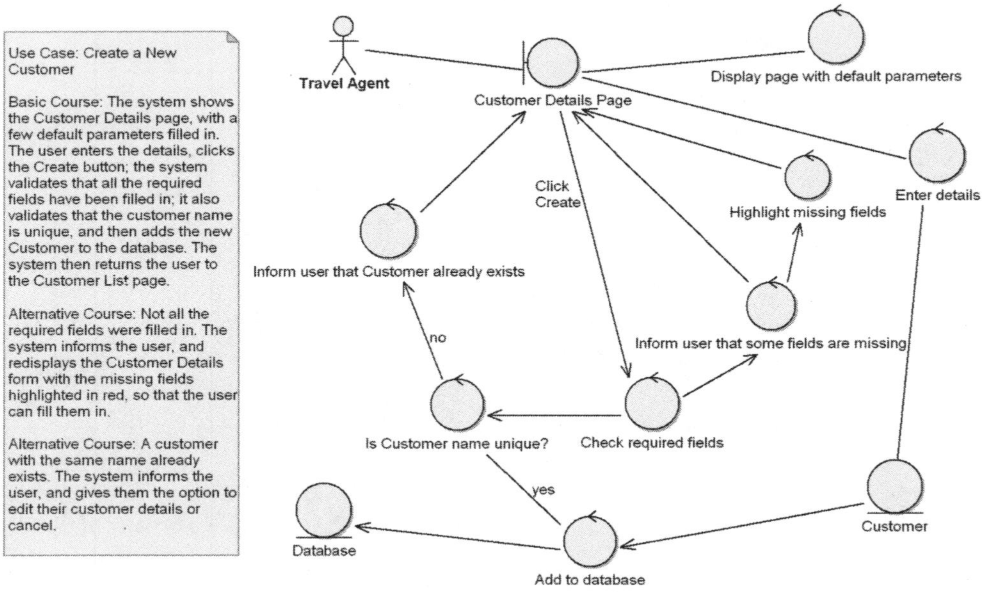

Figure 12-4. *Corrected robustness diagram for the "Create a New Customer" use case*

If we had identified any new entities at this point, we would revisit the domain model to update it; however, all the new elements appear to be controllers (this means we hadn't described the system behavior in enough detail in the use case), so it should be safe to move on.

MODELING TIP: SYNCHRONIZING USE CASE TEXT ACROSS DIAGRAMS

Because A&D modeling (particularly ICONIX modeling) is such a dynamic process, you need to be able to update and correct diagrams at a rapid pace, without being held back by concerns over other diagrams becoming out of sync.

If your diagrams are all on a whiteboard or were hand-scribbled on some sticky notes, then it shouldn't take long to manually update them. If you're using a CASE tool, then (depending on the tool's abilities, of course) the situation is even better (e.g., EA allows you to link use case text to notes on other diagrams). For example, Figure 12-4 shows the "Create a New Customer" use case text pasted directly into a note in the diagram. If we change the text, then the note will also need to be updated—unless there's a "live" link between the two.

Setting this up in EA is straightforward, if a little convoluted to explain. First, drag the use case "bubble" onto the robustness or sequence diagram. Then create an empty Note, add a Note Link (the dotted-line icon on the toolbar) between the two elements, right-click the new Note Link dotted line, and choose Link This Note to an Element Feature. The linkup is now "live," and you can delete the use case bubble from the diagram. Now anytime the use case text is updated, the note on the diagram will also be updated.

MODELING TIP: CREATING TEST CASES IN EA

While we're on the subject of EA (see the previous sidebar), in EA a test case is a use case with a stereotype of <<test case>>. Test cases show up with an "X" in the use case bubble.

You can find them on the "custom" toolbar. You can drop one of these onto a robustness diagram and connect it to a controller (for example) with a <<realize>> arrow. You can find more information on this in the section "Stop the Presses: Model-Driven Testing" near the end of this chapter.

Sequence Diagram for "Create a New Customer"

Now that we've disambiguated our robustness diagram (and therefore also our use case text), let's move on to the sequence diagram (see Figure 12-5).

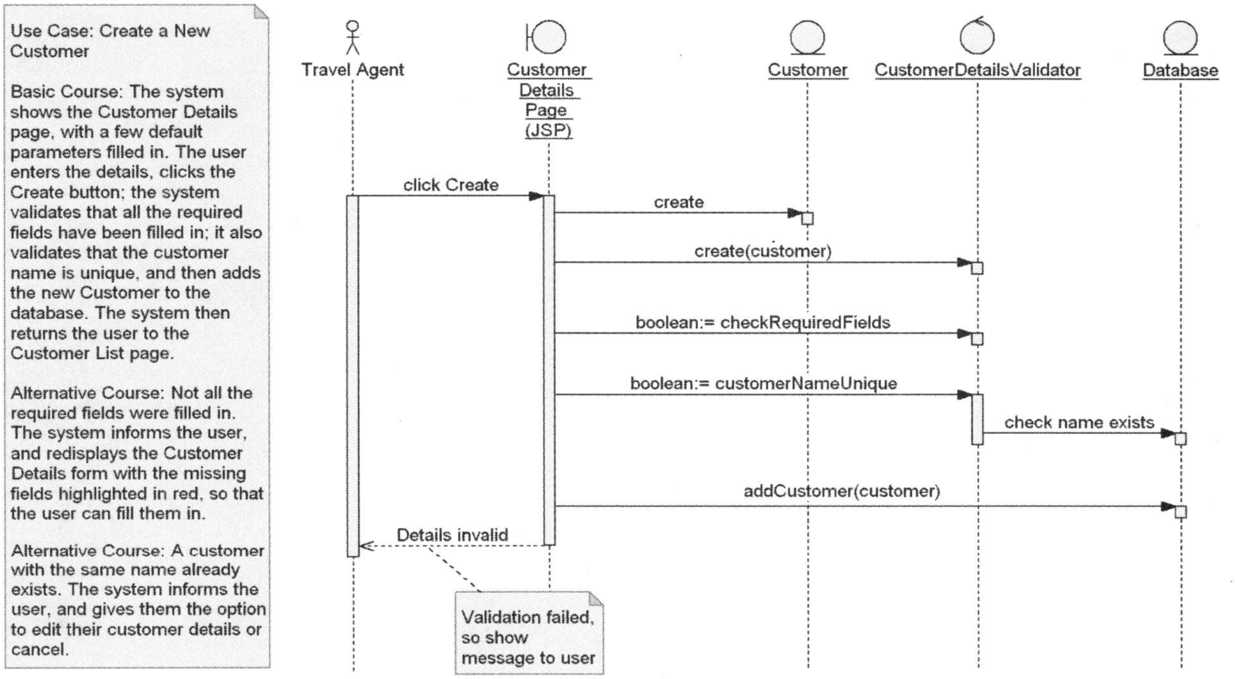

Figure 12-5. *Sequence diagram for the "Create a New Customer" use case*

Notice how the sequence diagram shows both the basic course and alternative courses. (Currently, both alternative courses are handled by the "Details invalid" message to be displayed to the user. As we show later on, more detail was needed in this area, so we'll need to revisit the sequence diagram.)

We've added a controller class, CustomerDetailsValidator, to handle the specifics of checking the user's input form and providing feedback to the user if any of the fields are invalid or missing. It's questionable whether this validation code should be a part of the Customer class itself (although that might be mixing responsibilities, as the Customer is an entity and validating an input form is more of a controller thing). However, as you'll see later, CustomerDetailsValidator disappears altogether and is replaced with something else.

More Design Feedback: Mixing It with TDD

The next stage is where the ICONIX+TDD process differs slightly from vanilla ICONIX Process. Normally, we would now move on to the class diagram, and add in the newly discovered classes and operations. We could probably get a tool to do this part for us, but sometimes the act of manually drawing the class diagram from the sequence diagrams helps to identify further design errors or ways to improve the design; it's implicitly yet another form of review.

We don't want to lose the benefits of this part of the process, so to incorporate TDD into the mix, we'll write the test skeletons as we're drawing the class diagram. In effect, TDD becomes another design review stage, validating the design that we've modeled so far. We can think of it as the last checkpoint before writing the code (with the added benefit that we end up with an automated test suite).

Tip If you're lucky enough to be using a twin display (i.e., two monitors attached to one PC), this is one of those times when this type of setup really comes into its own. There's something sublime about copying classes and methods from UML diagrams on one screen straight into source code on the other screen!

So, if you're using a CASE tool, start by creating a new class diagram (by far the best way to do this is to copy the existing domain model into a new diagram). Then, as you flesh out the diagram with attributes and operations, simultaneously write test skeletons for the same operations.

Here's the important part: *the tests are driven by the controllers and written from the perspective of the Boundary objects.*

If there's one thing that you should walk away from this chapter with, then that's definitely it! The controllers are doing the processing—the grunt work—so they're the parts that most need to be tested (i.e., validated that they are processing correctly). Restated: *the controllers represent the software behavior that takes place within the use case*, so they need to be tested.

However, the unit tests we're writing are *black-box tests* (aka *closed-box tests*)—that is, each test passes an input into a controller and asserts that the output from the controller is what was expected. We also want to be able to keep a lid on the number of tests that get written; there's little point in writing hundreds of undirected, aimless tests, hoping that we're covering all of the failure modes that the software will enter when it goes live. The Boundary objects give a very good indication of the various states that the software will enter, because the controllers are only ever accessed by the Boundary objects. Therefore, writing tests from the perspective of the Boundary objects is a very good way of testing for all *reasonable* permutations that the software may enter (including all the alternative courses). Additionally, a good source of individual test cases is the alternative courses in the use cases. (In fact, we regard testing the alternative courses as an essential way of making sure all the "rainy-day" code is implemented.)

Okay, with that out of the way, let's write a unit test. To drive the tests from the Control objects and write them from the perspective of the Boundary objects, simply walk through each sequence diagram step by step, and systematically write a test for each controller. Create a test class for each controller and one or more test methods for each operation being passed into the controller from the Boundary object.

■ Note If you want to make your unit tests really fine-grained (a good thing), create a test class for each operation and several test methods to test various permutations on the operation.

Looking at the sequence diagram in Figure 12-5, we should start by creating a test class called CustomerDetailsValidatorTest, with two test methods, `testCheckRequiredFields()` and `testCustomerNameUnique()`:

```
package iconix;

import junit.framework.*;

public class CustomerDetailsValidatorTest extends TestCase {

    public CustomerDetailsValidatorTest(String testName) {
        super(testName);
    }

    public static Test suite() {
        TestSuite suite = new TestSuite(CustomerDetailsValidatorTest.class);
        return suite;
    }

    public void testCheckRequiredFields() throws Exception {
    }

    public void testCustomerNameUnique() throws Exception {
    }
}
```

At this stage, we can also draw our new class diagram (starting with the domain model as a base) and begin to add in the details from the sequence diagram/unit test (see Figure 12-6).

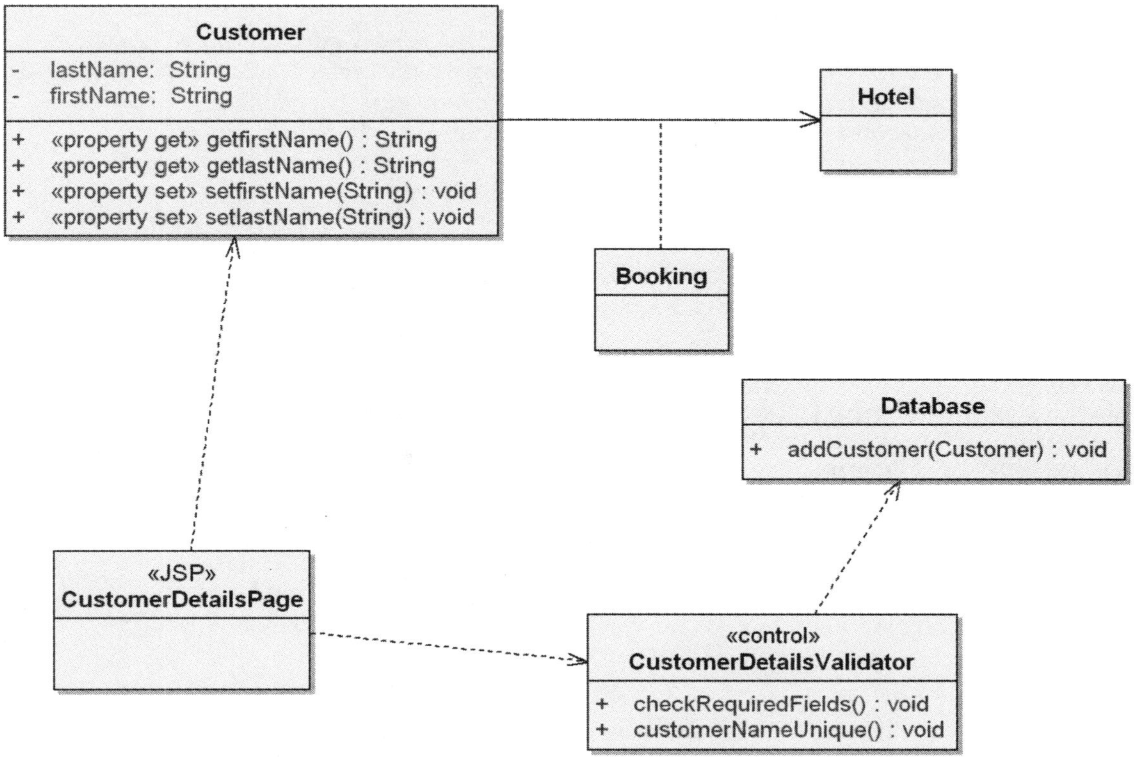

Figure 12-6. *Beginnings of the detailed class diagram*

As you can see in Figure 12-6, we've filled in *only the details that we've identified so far using the diagrams and unit tests.* We'll add more details as we identify them, but we need to make sure that we don't guess at any details or make intuitive leaps and add details just because it seems like a good idea to do so at the time.

Tip Be ruthlessly systematic about the details you add (and don't add) to the design.

In the class diagram in Figure 12-6, we've indicated that CustomerDetailsValidator is a <<control>> stereotype. This isn't essential for a class diagram, but it does help to tag the control classes so that we can tell at a glance which ones have (or require) unit tests.

In the Customer class, we've added `lastName` and `firstName` properties; these are the beginnings of the details the user will fill in when creating a new customer. The individual fields will probably already have been identified for you by various project stakeholders.

Note Our CASE tool has automatically put in the property accessor methods (the get and set methods in Figure 12-6), though this feature can be switched off if preferred. It's a matter of personal taste whether to show this level of detail; our feeling is that showing the properties in this way uses a lot of text to show a small amount of information. So a more efficient way (as long as it's followed consistently) is to show just the private fields (`lastName`, `firstName`) as public attributes. As long as we follow "proper" Java naming conventions, it should be obvious that these are really private fields accessed via public accessor methods. We'll show this when we return to the class diagram later on.

Next, we want to write the actual test methods. Remember, these are being driven by the controllers, but they are written from the perspective of the Boundary objects and in a sense are directly validating the design we've created using the sequence diagram, before we get to the "real" coding stage. In the course of writing the test methods, we may identify further operations that might have been missed during sequence diagramming.

Our first stab at the `testCheckRequiredFields()` method looks like this:

```
public void testCheckRequiredFields() throws Exception {
    List fields = new ArrayList();
    Customer customer = new Customer (fields);
    boolean allFieldsPresent = customer.checkRequiredFields();
    assertTrue("All required fields should be present", allFieldsPresent);
}
```

Naturally enough, trying to compile this initially fails, because we don't yet have a CustomerDetailsValidator class (let alone a `checkRequiredFields()` method). These are easy enough to add, though:

```
public class CustomerDetailsValidator {
    public CustomerDetailsValidator (List fields) {
    }

    public boolean checkRequiredFields() {
        return false;    // make the test fail initially.
    }
}
```

Let's now compile and run the test. Understandably, we get a failure, because `checkRequiredFields()` is returning false (indicating that the fields didn't contain all the required fields):

```
CustomerDetailsValidatorTest
.F.
Time: 0.016
There was 1 failure:
1) testCheckRequiredFields(CustomerDetailsValidatorTest)
     junit.framework.AssertionFailedError:
        All required fields should be present
        at CustomerDetailsValidatorTest.testCheckRequiredFields(
                                   CustomerDetailsValidatorTest.java:21)

FAILURES!!!
Tests run: 2,  Failures: 1,  Errors: 0
```

However, where did this `ArrayList` of fields come from, and what should it contain? In the `testCheckRequiredFields()` method, we've created it as a blank `ArrayList`, but it has spontaneously sprung into existence—an instant warning sign that we must have skipped a design step. Checking back, this happened because we didn't properly address the question of what the Customer fields are (and how they're created) in the sequence diagram (see Figure 12-5). Let's hit the brakes and sort that out right now (see Figure 12-7).

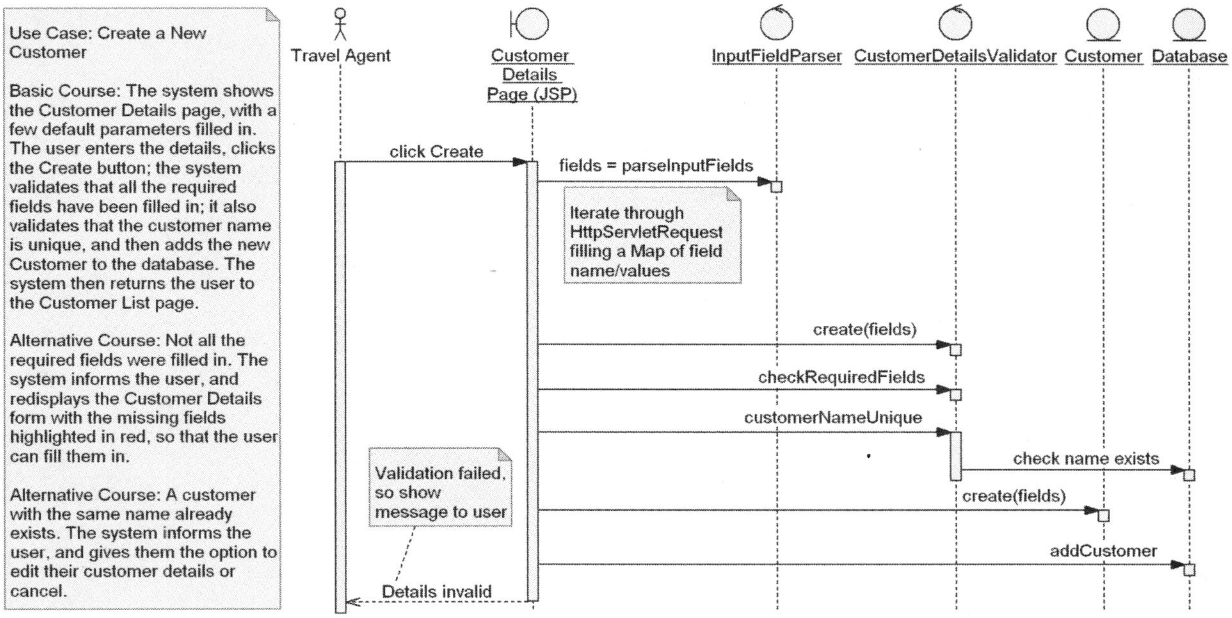

Figure 12-7. *Revisiting the sequence diagram to add more detail*

Revisiting the sequence diagram identified that we really need a `Map` (a list of name/value pairs that can be looked up individually by name) and not a sequential List.

As you can see, we've added a new controller, InputFieldParser (it does exactly what it says on the tin; as with class design in general, it's good practice to call things by literally what they do and then there's no room for confusion). Rather than trying to model the iterative process in some horribly convoluted advanced UML fashion, we've simply added a short note describing what the `parseInputFields` operation does: it iterates through the HTML form that was submitted to CustomerDetailsPage and returns a `Map` of field name/value pairs.

At this stage, we're thinking in terms of HTML forms, `POST` requests, and so forth, and in particular we're thinking about HttpServletRequests (part of the Java Servlet API) because we've decided to use JSP for the front-end. Making this decision during sequence diagramming is absolutely fine, because sequence diagrams (and unit tests, for that matter) are about the nitty-gritty aspects of design. If we weren't thinking at this level of detail at this stage, then we'd be storing up problems (and potential guesswork) for later—which we very nearly did by missing the InputFieldParser controller on the original sequence diagram.

Because our sequence diagram now has a new controller on it, we also need a new unit test class (InputFieldParserTest). However, this is starting to take us outside the scope of the example (the vanilla TDD example in Chapter 11 didn't cover UI or web framework details, so we'll do the same here). For the purposes of the example, we'll take it as read that InputFieldParser gets us a `HashMap` crammed full of name/value pairs containing the user's form fields for creating a new Customer.

Now that we've averted that potential design mishap, let's get back to the CustomerDetailsValidator test. As you may recall, the test was failing, so let's add some code to test for our required fields:

```
public void testCheckRequiredFields() throws Exception {
    Map fields = new HashMap();
    fields.put("userName", "bob");
    fields.put("firstName", "Robert");
    fields.put("lastName", "Smith");
    Customer customer = new Customer(fields);
    boolean allFieldsPresent = customer.checkRequiredFields();
    assertTrue("All required fields should be present", allFieldsPresent);
}
```

A quick run-through of this test shows that it's still failing (as we'd expect). So now let's add something to CustomerDetailsValidator to make the test pass:

```
public class CustomerDetailsValidator {
    private Map fields;

    public CustomerDetailsValidator (Map fields) {
        this.fields = fields;
    }

    public boolean checkRequiredFields() {
        return fields.containsKey("userName") &&
                 fields.containsKey("firstName") &&
                 fields.containsKey("lastName");
    }
}
```

Let's now feed this through our voracious unit tester:

```
CustomerDetailsValidatorTest
..
Time: 0.016

OK (2 tests)
```

Warm glow all around. But wait, there's trouble brewing . . .

In writing this test, something that sprang to mind was that `checkRequiredFields()` probably shouldn't be indicating a validation failure by returning a boolean. In this OO day and age, we like to use exceptions for doing that sort of thing (specifically, a `ValidationException`), not forgetting that our use case stated that the web page should indicate to the user which fields are missing. We can't get that sort of information from a single Boolean, so let's do something about that now (really, this should have been identified earlier; if you're modeling in a group, it's precisely the sort of design detail that tends to be caught early on and dealt with before too much code gets written).

In fact, in this particular case a Java Exception might not be the best way to handle a validation error, because we don't want to drip-feed the user one small error at a time. It would be preferable to run the user's input form through some validation code that accumulates a list of all the input field errors, so that we can tell the user about them all at once. This prevents the annoying kind of UI behavior where the user has to correct one small error, resubmit the form, wait a few seconds, correct another small error, resubmit the form, and so on.

Looking back at the sequence diagram in Figure 12-7, we're asking quite a lot of the CustomerDetailsPage JSP page: it's having to do much of the processing itself, which is generally considered bad form. We need to move some of this processing out of the page and into a delegate class. While we're at it, we want to add more detail to the sequence diagram concerning how to populate the page with feedback on the validation errors. This is quite a lot to do directly in the code, so let's revisit the sequence diagram and give it another going over with the new insight we gained from having delved tentatively into the unit test code. The updated sequence diagram is shown in Figure 12-8.

Although the "flavor" of the design is basically the same, some of the details have changed considerably. We've gotten rid of the CustomerDetailsValidator class entirely, and we've moved the validation responsibility into Customer itself. However, to bind all of this form processing together, we've also added a new controller class, CreateCustomerDetails. This has the responsibility of controlling the process to create a new Customer object, validating it, and (assuming validation was okay) creating it in the Database.

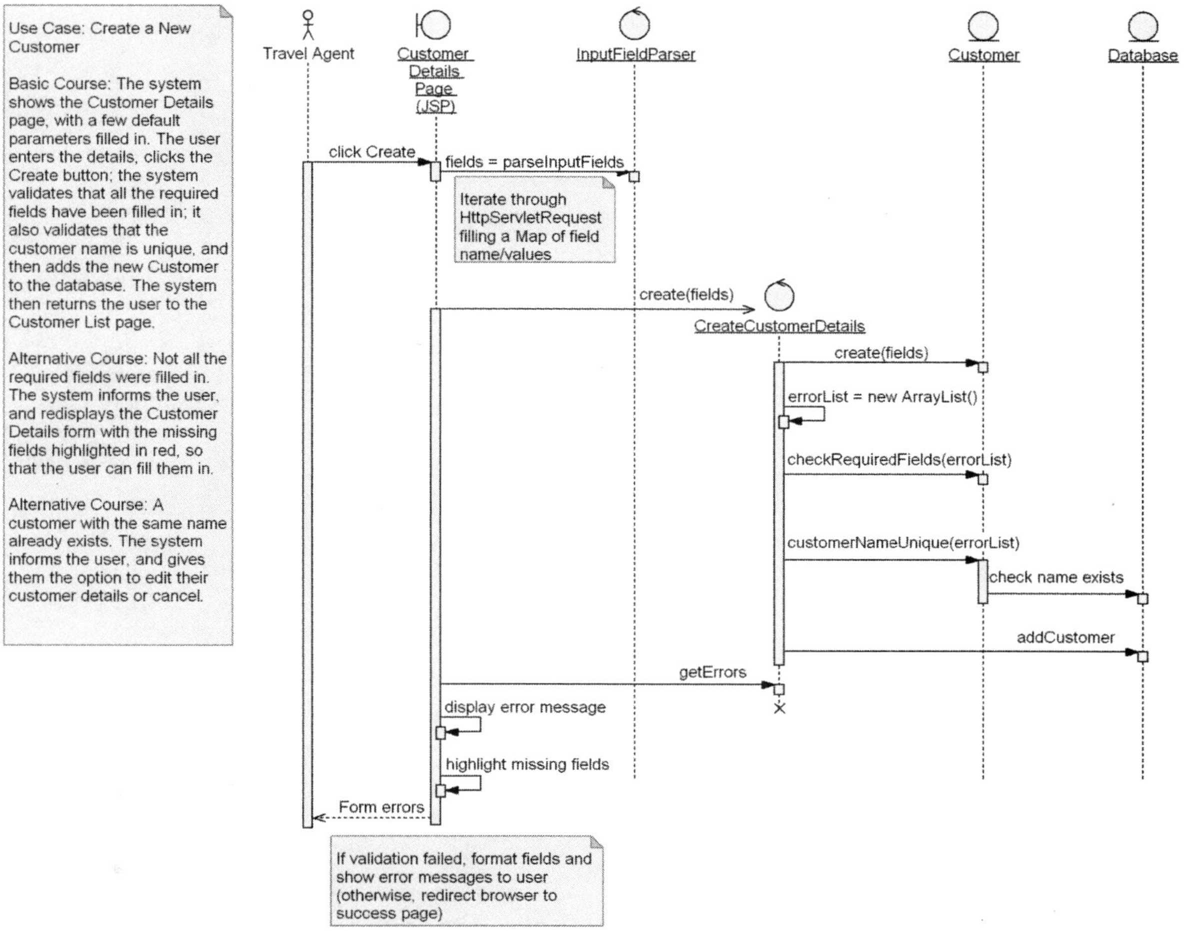

Figure 12-8. *Revisiting the sequence diagram form processing*

■Note The decision was 50:50 on whether to create a dedicated class for CreateCustomerDetails or simply add it as a method on the Customer class. Normally, controllers do tend to end up as methods on other classes; however, in this case our primary concern was to move the controller logic out of the JSP page and into a "real" Java class. In addition, Customer was already starting to look a little crowded. As design decisions go, it probably could have gone either way, though.

As we now have a new controller (CreateCustomerDetails), we need to create a unit test for it. Let's do that now:

```
public class CreateCustomerDetailsTest extends TestCase {

    public CreateCustomerDetailsTest(java.lang.String testName) {
        super(testName);
    }

    public static Test suite() {
        TestSuite suite = new TestSuite(CreateCustomerDetailsTest.class);
        return suite;
    }
```

```
    public void testNoErrors() throws Exception {
        Map fields = new HashMap();
        fields.put("userName", "bob");
        fields.put("firstName", "Robert");
        fields.put("lastName", "Smith");

        CreateCustomerDetails createCustomerDetails =
                                                  new CreateCustomerDetails(fields);
        List errors = createCustomerDetails.getErrors();
        assertEquals("There should be no validation errors", 0, errors.size());
    }
}
```

As you can see, this code replicates what used to be in CustomerDetailsValidatorTest. In fact, CustomerDetails-ValidatorTest and CustomerDetailsValidator are no longer needed, so can both be deleted.

Initially, our new code doesn't compile because we don't yet have a CreateCustomerDetails class to process the user's form and create the customer. Let's add that now:

```
public class CreateCustomerDetails {

    private Map fields;

    public CreateCustomerDetails(Map fields) {
        this.fields = fields;
    }

    public List getErrors() {
        return new ArrayList(0);
    }
}
```

Our first test is checking that if we create a "perfect" set of user input fields, there are no validation errors. Sure enough, this passes the test, but mainly because we don't yet have any code to create the validation errors! A passing test of this sort is a bad thing, so it would really be better if we begin with a test that fails if there aren't any validation errors. This will give us our initial test failure, which we can then build upon.

```
    public void testRequiredFieldMissing() throws Exception {
        Map fields = new HashMap();
        fields.put("firstName", "Robert");
        fields.put("lastName", "Smith");

        CreateCustomerDetails createCustomerDetails =
                                                  new CreateCustomerDetails(fields);
        List errors = createCustomerDetails.getErrors();
        assertEquals("There should be one validation error", 1, errors.size());
    }
```

This test creates a field map with one required field missing (the user name). Notice how these unit tests correspond exactly with the alternative courses for the "Create a New Customer" use case. The `testRequiredFieldMissing()` test is testing for the "Not all the required fields were filled in" alternative course.

If we run the test case now, we get our failure:

```
CreateCustomerDetailsTest
..F
Time: 0.015
There was 1 failure:
1) testRequiredFieldMissing(CreateCustomerDetailsTest)
     junit.framework.AssertionFailedError:
        There should be one validation error expected:<1> but was:<0>
        at CreateCustomerDetailsTest.testRequiredFieldMissing(
                    CreateCustomerDetailsTest.java:39)

FAILURES!!!
Tests run: 2,  Failures: 1,  Errors: 0
```

Now we can add some code into CreateCustomerDetails to make the tests pass:

```
public class CreateCustomerDetails {

    private Map fields;
    private List errorList;
    private Customer customer;

    public CreateCustomerDetails(Map fields) {
        this.fields = fields;
        this.errorList = new ArrayList();
        this.customer = new Customer(fields);
        customer.checkRequiredFields(errorList);
        customer.customerNameUnique(errorList);
    }

    public List getErrors() {
        return errorList;
    }
}
```

This class currently doesn't compile because we haven't yet updated Customer to accept `errorList`. So we do that now:

```
    public void checkRequiredFields(List errorList) {
    }

    public void checkCustomerNameUnique(List errorList) {
    }
```

This gets the code compiling, and running the tests returns the same error as before, which validates that the tests are working. Now we write some code to make the failing test pass:

```
public void checkRequiredFields(List errorList) {
    if (!fields.containsKey("userName")) {
        errorList.add("The user name field is missing.");
    }
    if (!fields.containsKey("firstName")) {
        errorList.add("The first name field is missing.");
    }
    if (!fields.containsKey("lastName")) {
        errorList.add("The last name field is missing.");
    }
}
```

and do a quick run-through of the unit tests:

```
CreateCustomerDetailsTest
..
Time: 0.016

OK (2 tests)
```

Now we're talking!

The code in `checkRequiredFields()` seems a bit "scrufty," though—there's some repetition there. Now that we have a passing test, we can do a quick bit of refactoring (this is the sort of internal-to-a-method refactoring that occasionally goes beneath the sequence diagram's radar; it's one of the reasons that sequence diagrams and unit tests work well together):

```
public void checkRequiredFields(List errorList) {
    checkFieldExists("userName", "The user name field is missing.", errorList);
    checkFieldExists("firstName", "The first name field is missing.", errorList);
    checkFieldExists("lastName", "The last name field is missing.", errorList);
}

private void checkFieldExists(String fieldName,
                              String errorMsg,
                              List errorList) {
    if (!fields.containsKey(fieldName)) {
        errorList.add(errorMsg);
    }
}
```

If we compile this and rerun the tests, it all still passes, so we can be reasonably confident that our refactoring hasn't broken anything.

So, what's next? Checking back to the use case text (visible in the sequence diagram in Figure 12-8), we still have an alternative course that's neither tested nor implemented. Now seems like a good time to do that. Once we've tested and implemented the alternative course, we'll pause to update the class diagram (a useful design review process).

To refresh your memory, here's the alternative course:

Alternative Course: A customer with the same name already exists. The system informs the user and gives them the option to edit their customer details or cancel.

We can see this particular scenario mapped out in the sequence diagram in Figure 12-8, so the next step, as usual, is to create the skeleton test cases, followed by the skeleton classes, followed by an updated class diagram, followed by the unit test code, followed by the "real" implementation code (punctuating each step with the appropriate design validation/compilation/testing feedback).

CreateCustomerDetailsTest already has an empty test method called `testCustomerAlreadyExists()`, so let's fill in the detail now:

```
public void testCustomerAlreadyExists() throws Exception {
    Map fields = new HashMap();
    fields.put("userName", "bob");
    fields.put("firstName", "Robert");
    fields.put("lastName", "Smith");

    CreateCustomerDetails createCustomerDetails1 =
                                        new CreateCustomerDetails(fields);
    CreateCustomerDetails createCustomerDetails2 =
                                        new CreateCustomerDetails(fields);
    List errors = createCustomerDetails2.getErrors();
    assertEquals("There should be one validation error", 1, errors.size());
}
```

This simply creates two identical Customers (by creating two CreateCustomerDetails controllers) and checks the second one for validation errors. Running this, we get our expected test failure:

```
CreateCustomerDetailsTest
...F
Time: 0.015
There was 1 failure:
1) testCustomerAlreadyExists(CreateCustomerDetailsTest)
     junit.framework.AssertionFailedError:
There should be one validation error expected:<1> but was:<0>
       at CreateCustomerDetailsTest.testCustomerAlreadyExists(
                                        CreateCustomerDetailsTest.java:51)

FAILURES!!!
Tests run: 3,  Failures: 1,  Errors: 0
```

Obviously, we now need to add some database code to actually create the customer, and then test whether the customer already exists.

Before we do that, though, we've been neglecting the class diagram for a while, so let's update it now. We'll use the latest version of the sequence diagram (see Figure 12-8) to allocate the operations to each class. The result is shown in Figure 12-9.

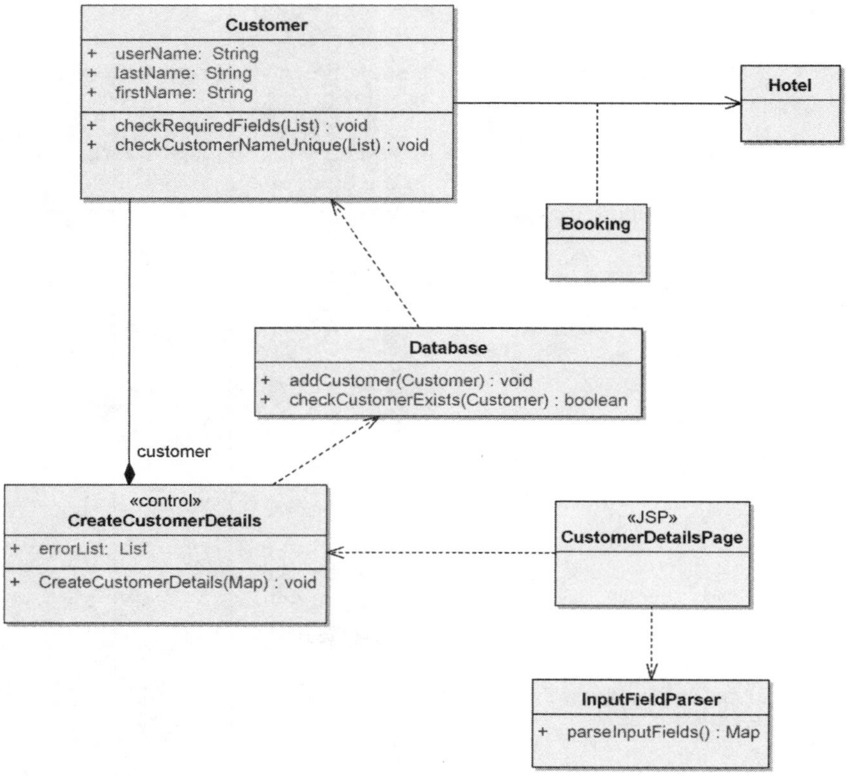

Figure 12-9. *Class diagram updated with new classes, attributes, and operations*

As you can see, we still haven't even touched on the detail in Hotel or Booking yet, because we haven't visited these use cases; so they remain empty, untested, and unimplemented, as they should be at this stage.

To finish off, we'll add the database access code to make the latest unit test pass. Checking the sequence diagram, we see that we need to modify CreateCustomerDetails to add a new customer if all the validation tests passed (the new code is shown in bold):

```
public CreateCustomerDetails(Map fields) {
    this.fields = fields;
    this.errorList = new ArrayList();
    this.customer = new Customer(fields);
    customer.checkRequiredFields(errorList);
    customer.checkCustomerNameUnique(errorList);
    if (errorList.size() == 0) {
        new Database().addCustomer(customer);
    }
}
```

We also need to implement the `checkCustomerNameUnique()` method on Customer to check the Database:

```
public void checkCustomerNameUnique(List errorList) {
    if (new Database().checkCustomerExists(this)) {
        errorList.add("That user name has already been taken.");
    }
}
```

And finally, we need the Database class itself (or at least the beginnings of it):

```
public class Database {

    public Database() {
    }

    public void addCustomer(Customer customer) {
    }

    public boolean checkCustomerExists(Customer customer) {
        return true;
    }
}
```

Running the tests at this stage caused a couple of test failures:

```
CreateCustomerDetailsTest
.F.F.
Time: 0.015
There were 2 failures:
1) testNoErrors(CreateCustomerDetailsTest)junit.framework.AssertionFailedError:
        There should be no validation errors expected:<0> but was:<1>
        at CreateCustomerDetailsTest.testNoErrors(CreateCustomerDetailsTest.java:29)
2) testRequiredFieldMissing(CreateCustomerDetailsTest)
     junit.framework.AssertionFailedError:
        There should be one validation error expected:<1> but was:<2>
        at CreateCustomerDetailsTest.testRequiredFieldMissing(
                                        CreateCustomerDetailsTest.java:39)

FAILURES!!!
Tests run: 3,  Failures: 2,  Errors: 0
```

Though it should have been obvious, it took a moment to work out that it was the new check (`Database.checkCustomerExists()` returning true) that was causing both of the existing validation checks to fail. Clearly, we need a better way of isolating validation errors, as currently any validation error will cause any test to fail, regardless of which validation error it's meant to be checking for.

To do this, we could add some constants into the Customer class where the validation is taking place, where each constant represents one type of validation error. We could also add a method for querying a list of errors; our assert statements can then use this to assert that the list contains the particular kind of error it's checking for. In fact, it would make a lot of sense to create a CustomerValidationError class that gets put into the `errorList` instead of simply putting in the error message. (We'll leave this as an exercise for the reader, though, as we're sure you get the general idea by now!)

So, to finish off, here's the Database class all implemented and done:

```
public class Database {

    public Database() {
    }

    public void addCustomer(Customer customer) throws DatabaseException {
        try {
            runStatement("INSERT INTO Customers VALUES ('" +
                         customer.getUserName() + ", " +
                         customer.getLastName() + ", " +
```

```
                        customer.getFirstName() +
                        "')");
        }
        catch (Exception e) {
            throw new DatabaseException("Error saving Customer " +
                                        customer.getUserName(), e);
        }
    }

    public boolean checkCustomerExists(Customer customer) throws DatabaseException {
        ResultSet customerSet = null;
        try {
            customerSet = runQuery(
                    "SELECT CustomerName " +
                    "FROM Customers " +
                    "WHERE UserName='" + customer.getUserName() + "'");

            return customerSet.next();
        }
        catch (Exception e) {
            throw new DatabaseException(
                    "Error checking to see if Customer username '" +
                    customer.getUserName() + "' exists.", e);
        }
        finally {
            if (customerSet != null) {
                try {
                    customerSet.close();
                }
                catch (SQLException e) {}
            }
        }
    }

    private static void runStatement(String sql)
    throws ClassNotFoundException, SQLException {
        java.sql.Connection conn;
        Class.forName(
               "com.microsoft.jdbc.sqlserver.SQLServerDriver");
                conn = DriverManager.getConnection(
                      "jdbc:microsoft:sqlserver://localhost:1433",
                      "database_username",
                      "database_password");
        Statement statement = conn.createStatement();
        statement.executeUpdate(sql);
    }

    private static ResultSet runQuery(String sql)
            throws ClassNotFoundException,
                   SQLException {

        java.sql.Connection conn;
        Class.forName(
                "com.microsoft.jdbc.sqlserver.SQLServerDriver");
```

```
        conn = DriverManager.getConnection(
                    "jdbc:microsoft:sqlserver://localhost:1433",
                    "matt",   // username
                    "pass");  // password

        Statement statement = conn.createStatement();
        return statement.executeQuery(sql);
    }

}
```

Note Obviously, in a production environment you'd use an appropriate data object framework, not least to enable connection pooling (Spring Framework, EJB, JDO, Hibernate, etc.), but this code should give you a good idea of what's needed to implement the last parts of the "Create a New Customer" use case.

Running this through JUnit gives us some nice test passes. However, running it a second time, the tests fail. How can this be so? Put simply, the code is creating new Customers in the database each time the tests are run, but it's also testing for uniqueness of each Customer. So we also need to add a `clearCustomers()` method to Database:

```
public void clearCustomers() throws DatabaseException {
    try {
        runStatement("DELETE * FROM Customers");
    }
    catch (Exception e) {
        throw new DatabaseException("Error clearing Customer Database.", e);
    }
}
```

and then call this in the `setUp()` method in CreateCustomerDetailsTest:

```
public void setUp() throws Exception {
    new Database().clearCustomers();
}
```

This does raise the question of database testing in a multideveloper project. If everyone on the team is reading and writing to the same test database, then running all these automated tests that create and delete swaths of Customer data will soon land the team in quite a pickle. One answer is to make heavy use of mock objects (see the upcoming sidebar titled "Mock Objects"), but this isn't always desirable. Of course, the real answer is to give each person on the team his own database schema to work with. Not so long ago this notion would have been snorted at, but these days it's considered essential for each developer to have his own database sandbox to play in.

As we implement further use cases, we would almost certainly want to rename the Database class to something less generic (e.g., CustomerDatabase). This code has also identified for the first time the need to add the `username`, `lastName`, and `firstName` properties to Customer. We suspected we might need these earlier, but we didn't add them until we knew for sure that we were going to need them.

And that about wraps it up. Running this through JUnit gives us some nice test passes. For every controller class on the sequence diagram, we've gone through each operation and created a test for it. We've also ensured that each alternative course gets at least one automated test.

As mentioned earlier, we won't repeat the example for the other two use cases, as that would belabor the point somewhat, but hopefully this chapter has given you some good insight into how to mix an up-front A&D modeling process with a test-driven development process.

MOCK OBJECTS

We haven't covered *mock objects*[3] in this or the previous chapter, but the ICONIX+TDD process is, broadly speaking, the same if you incorporate mock objects into the mix. A mock object is simply a class that stands in for "real" functionality but doesn't perform any significant processing itself.

Mock objects are often used to speed up unit tests (e.g., to avoid accessing the database). A mock object will simply create and return the same data object each time it's invoked. This can even reduce the overall time spent running a suite of tests from minutes down to seconds. However, it should be noted that when you use mock objects in this way, you're not testing your application's database code at all; you're simply testing the application logic.

In our combined ICONIX+TDD process, you'd use mock objects to avoid having to implement classes too early. This reduces the issue where you need to implement code before the iteration when it's due for release just to get some of the tests working.

For example, if we're implementing a "Create Customer" use case, we'd want a test that proves the customer was indeed created. To do this, we would need to retrieve the customer we just created and assert that it's the same customer (and not null, for example). But this functionality would really be covered by the "Retrieve Customer" use case, which might not be due until a later iteration. Using mock objects to provide stand-in functionality in the meantime (e.g., always returning the same Customer object without accessing the database at all) gets around this problem.

Again, however, it should be stressed that you're not testing the database code at all using this technique, so you'd still want to at least manually check the database every now and again to make sure the customer record is in there (at least until the real Customer-retrieval functionality has been written).

Summarizing ICONIX+TDD

Following the combined ICONIX+TDD process, we wrote fewer unit tests than we would have using TDD on its own, because we systematically wrote the tests following the controllers on the sequence diagrams. We also were able to write specific tests for each alternative course.

We also thrashed out most of the design details simply using robustness, sequence, and class diagrams. The unit tests then acted as an additional design-review safety net to catch any design issues we may have missed. The result was that we ended up with a realistic, well-factored design before the "guts" of the implementation code had been written, saving time that would have been spent refactoring code later.

What's interesting is how each method (ICONIX+TDD versus vanilla TDD) leads us to implement different parts of the system first and to take a different approach:

- With ICONIX+TDD, we tend to implement more of the system up front, but we get the overall system finished in less time because we're writing the code in larger chunks (as defined by the design model).
- With vanilla TDD, we implement less of the system in each sitting, and we do it in small baby-steps, but the overall system takes longer to write because there's much reworking of existing code.

Because ICONIX+TDD is driven directly from the use cases (the behavioral requirements), and the tests themselves are driven directly from the objects on the sequence diagrams, we know precisely when we've finished. The alternative courses also provide an important source of additional unit tests, as we saw.

In addition, the design process forced us to think more about certain implementation details earlier (in particular, how the code was going to fit into the JSP web framework). However, we still produced code that would be easily transferable to some other framework, because the business logic (e.g., the validation code) was kept separate from the presentation and persistence layers.

3. See `www.mockobjects.com`.

Stop the Presses: Model-Driven Testing

As we were finishing up this ICONIX+TDD chapter, a couple of new ideas occurred to us, which we decided to publish here at the eleventh hour as an extension to ICONIX Process (and a core part of Agile ICONIX), to link our models more closely to testing, and in fact to drive a testing effort from our use case–driven models. We've always thought that testing was a good thing, and that there was great potential to drive tests from use cases. For a different approach to the testing problem, see Jeff Kantor's November 2001 article titled "Use Case Driven Testing," which is available from `www.iconixsw.com/Articles/Articles.html`.

The approach we present here drives the identification of test cases directly from the robustness diagram, in a parallel manner to the way we drive the creation of a skeleton sequence diagram from a robustness diagram. In short, the nouns (Entity and Boundary objects) from the robustness diagram become object instances on the sequence diagram, and the verbs (controllers) get test cases created for them. Figure 12-10 shows the overall concept.

```
Create a new Sequence Diagram
Create a new Test Case Diagram
Repeat for all symbols on the robustness diagram

        if (stereotype=ENTITY) or (stereotype=BOUNDARY) then
                add it to the sequence diagram
        if (stereotype=CONTROL) then
                add it to the testcase diagram
                create a testcase for it, and link them

End Repeat
```

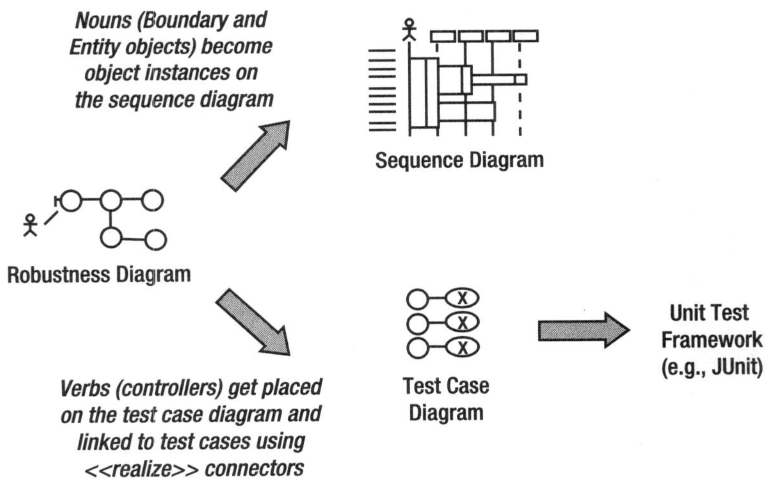

Figure 12-10. *Overview of model-driven testing*

As Figure 12-10 shows, we can automatically transform a robustness diagram into both a skeleton sequence diagram and a test case diagram using a simple script. Tests can subsequently be exported to unit testing frameworks like JUnit or NUnit.

Now we'll provide a more detailed explanation, which we'll illustrate step by step with an example. Since we've already identified the logical functions within a use case as controllers, it seemed natural that all of these functions would need to be tested. Figure 12-4 shows our robustness diagram. Working from this robustness diagram, we can create a test case diagram showing a test case for each controller.

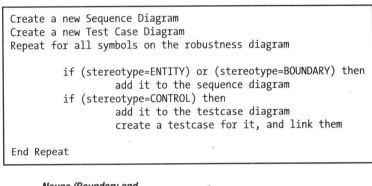

How do we do this? Easy. We copy all of the controllers from the robustness diagram onto a new diagram, and then we link a test case to each one using <<realize>> connectors. Note that the EA tool has a test case element that is a stereotyped use case. Figure 12-11 shows our test case diagram.

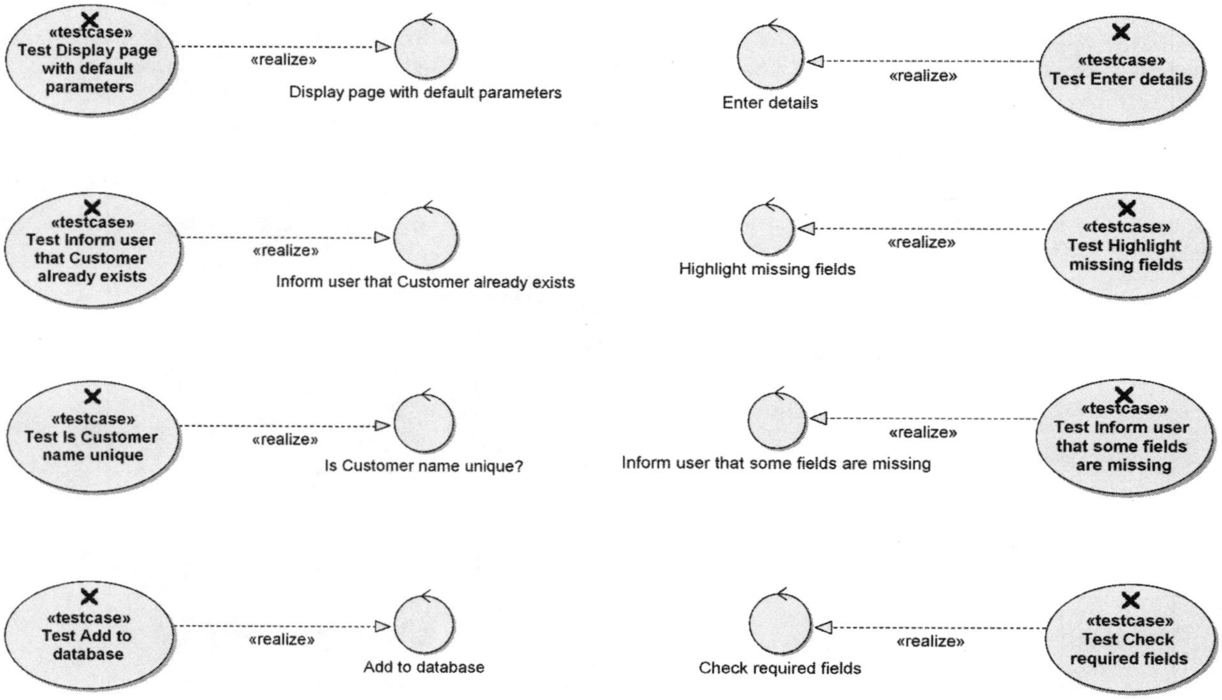

Figure 12-11. *Test case diagram for the example shown earlier in this chapter*

Note that each test case can contain multiple test scenarios, as illustrated in Figure 12-12.

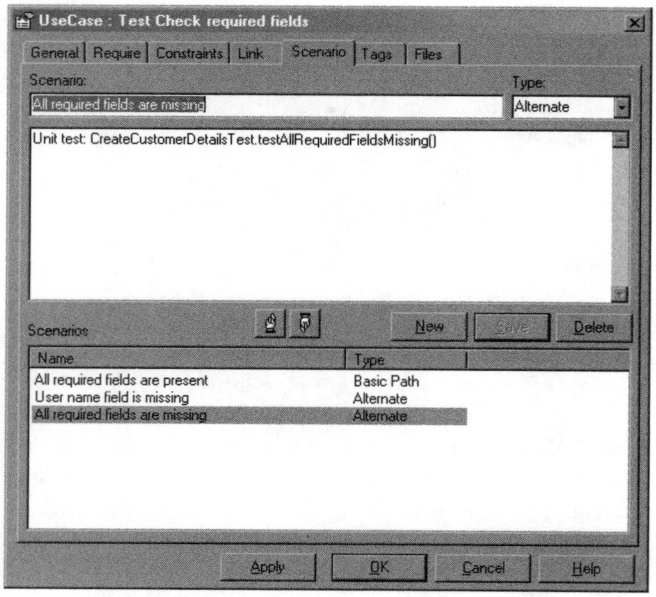

Figure 12-12. *EA test case spec dialog set to the Scenario tab, with a short test description visible*

So, not only can we drive design (sequence diagrams) from the robustness diagram—we can drive the testing effort as well. At the time of this writing, we're exploring the possibilities of generating unit test code directly from the test case specifications.

As we were formalizing this approach, it further dawned on us that this whole process is scriptable in a visual modeling tool like EA. So, we went ahead and built the script. You can see a fragment of the Visual Basic code in Figure 12-13.

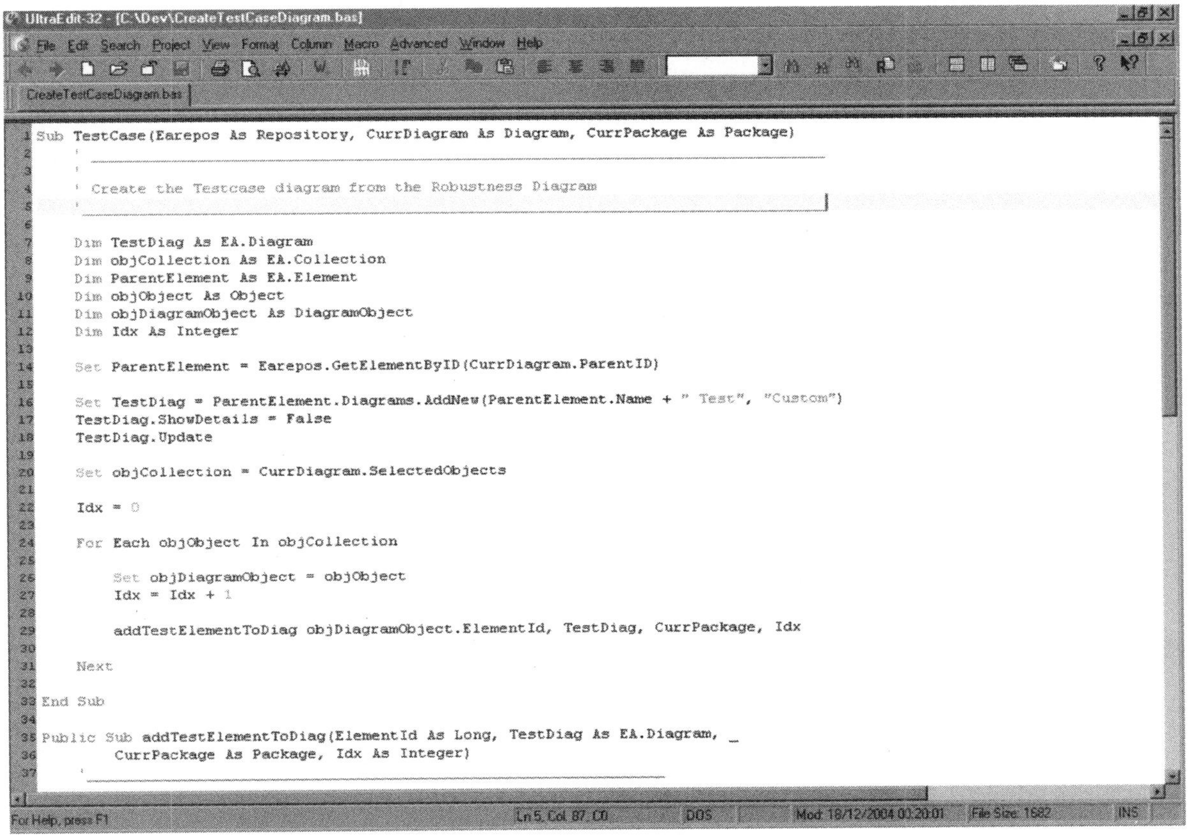

Figure 12-13. *Script fragment screenshot*

This script is available in Doug's multimedia tutorial, "Enterprise Architect for Power Users" (more information is available at `www.iconixsw.com`).

Summary

In this chapter, we examined how ICONIX Process and TDD can be combined to great effect. To combine these two disciplines, we have had to rewrite the rules slightly for TDD, but the basics are pretty much the same.

Using TDD on its own without any up-front design modeling is actually very rare. Even in XP a certain amount of up-front design modeling is generally used—this is normally a collaborative design workshop held just before the coding session, also known as Just-in Time (JIT) Design.[4] In such environments, consider using ICONIX Process as described here to improve the collaborative design process.

Finally, at the end of the chapter, we described an automated, model-driven testing process that you can use to drive a testing effort from your use case–driven models.

---

4. Named after "Just-in-Time" compilers used in runtime environments such as Java HotSpot, and also used in quality management.

Index

S